THE

I CHING HANDBOOK

A Practical Guide to

Personal and Logical Perspectives

from the Ancient Chinese Book of Changes

by

Edward A. Hacker

Paradigm Publications — Brookline, Massachusetts

1993

THE I CHING HANDBOOK
by
Edward A. Hacker

The Concordance, Appendix N, is used with permission from *The I Ching or Book of Changes,* Richard Wilhelm, tr. Cary F. Baynes, Bollingen Series XIX, Princeton University Press, Copyright 1950 and 1977 by the Bollingen Foundation.

Library of Congress cataloging-in-publication data

```
Hacker, Edward A., 1930-
      The I ching handbook / Edward A. Hacker.
        p.   426    cm.
      Includes bibliographical references and index.
      ISBN 0-912111-36-4 :  $ 49.95
      1.  I Ching
      PL2464.Z7H3 1993
      299'.51282-dc20                    92-28290
                                            CIP
```

Copyright © 1993 Paradigm Publications

Paradigm Publications
44 Linden Street
Brookline, Massachusetts 02146 U.S.A.

Published by: **Paradigm Publications**
Publisher: Robert L. Felt
Editor: Jack Lincoln
Distribution: Redwing Book Company, Brookline, MA
Trade Distribution: Talman Company, New York

TABLE OF CONTENTS

APPENDICES

PREFACE

I first encountered the *I Ching* (Book of Changes) in 1955 when I saw a copy of the Wilhelm/Baynes translation on a bookstore shelf. At that time I was in college, a philosophy major, so I had heard of the *I Ching*. I knew that it was an ancient Chinese book which was used for prophecy. But that was all I knew. The Sixties had not yet arrived; there was little public or academic interest in oriental philosophy. Yet, browsing through the book, I was intrigued by the curious six line symbols and the cryptic messages. I bought the book and, except for the Forward by Karl Jung and the Introduction by Richard Wilhelm, found nothing intelligible in it. The Forward and Introduction made it clear that the hexagrams—the six line symbols—represented states of changes and that all of these states were interrelated. But just how the interrelations were obtained was not explained although copious cryptic hints were provided.

The Sixties brought with them not only the student revolution but the sexual revolution, not only alternative life styles but alternative ways of thought. NASA explored outer space and landed on the moon, youths explored inner space and experimented with drugs. Existentialism and Zen Buddhism flourished. Radical politics and radical philosophies abounded on college campuses, while the streets of our major cities teemed with hippies, flower children, and would-be revolutionists. It was a time of rejection, expectation, and introspection.

The generation of the Sixties discovered the *I Ching*. The second edition of the Wilhelm/Baynes translation came out in 1961, and the third edition was published in 1967. By 1985 it had gone through twenty-one printings. The Legge translation was brought out by Dover Publications in 1963, and by University Books in 1964. Both went through multiple printings. In 1966 the Blofeld translation was published by E. P. Dutton & Company.

In the late Sixties I taught my first course on Chinese Philosophy. I found ample material for my lectures on Confucianism, Taoism, and Legalism, but there was a dearth of material on the *I Ching*. The Blofeld translation was helpful as were Needham's *Science and Civilization in China* (most especially volume 2), and Fung Yu-Lan's *History of Chinese Philosophy*. These works contained valuable information but I could find no single book which contained all the information I wanted.

I was looking for a book that would cover at least the following topics:

A) The origin of the *I Ching*. I wanted to know what scholarly opinion was concerning the history of the *I Ching*. The traditional account of the origin of the *I Ching* is well known, but I was interested in knowing what evidence, if any, there was to support this tradition.

B) The interrelationships of the hexagrams. I wanted to know how the hexagrams were interrelated and how to determine these relations.

C) The *I Ching* as oracle. I wanted to know the various ways in which the *I Ching* could be consulted for advice. Also, I wanted to know if there were any essential differences between these modes of consultation.

D) An annotated bibliography of the *I Ching* literature. In 1975 a short partially annotated bibliography by Hellmut Wilhelm was published. It was a start, but hardly satisfactory.

I taught Chinese Philosophy once a year for the next twenty-two years. As time passed I accumulated a substantial library and a goodly number of journal articles on the *I Ching*. The time I devoted to the *I Ching* in my course increased from two lectures to ten. The Sixties had passed, but the public's interest in the *I Ching* did not. One translation after another came off the presses; specific topics such as the DNA molecule and the *I Ching* were discussed at length. Still I found no single book that brought together the scholarly information which was scattered throughout the extensive *I Ching* literature.

In 1988 I decided to write an annotated bibliography on the *I Ching*. I had already collected some eighty books on the subject as well as three dozen articles. I began my projected bibliography by adding to my collection all the unpublished doctor's and master's dissertations that University Microfilms International could locate in their computer database. The Interlibrary Loan Department at Northeastern University Library worked diligently for me, obtaining copies of hundreds of journal articles. From this material the annotated bibliography of this book was constructed.

Reading the various books and articles I had collected made it clear to me that I had the information I needed to write the book I had always wanted. The thought became father to the deed and this book was born.

There is nothing original in this book except the classification of the hexagrams, the hexagram stories, the hexagram flowers, and a new way of classifying nuclear hexagrams. All other information can be found in the books and articles listed in the bibliography. What makes this book unique is that a great deal of diverse information on the *I Ching* is gathered together in one place. It is the book I wished I had had when I began my study of the *I Ching*.

I would like to thank the publisher, Robert Felt, and the editor, Jack Lincoln, for their technical assistance, their enduring encouragement, and their whole hearted support in publishing this book. May the *I Ching* always give them favorable lines.

I would also like to thank the scholars of the *I Ching* whose articles and books made this one possible.

INTRODUCTION:
THE MANY VIEWS OF
THE I CHING

2. Sprouting

Introductory Remarks: The *I Ching* may be studied from many different viewpoints. One may take a historical viewpoint and be interested in what the *I Ching* can tell us about the social, political, and religious institutions of ancient China and the cosmological views held by its makers. One may take a linguistic viewpoint and be concerned with problems of translation and the etymology of the Chinese characters that compose its text. There is also the moral viewpoint: that is, consulting the *I Ching* for moral advice and guidance.

The *I Ching* may also be studied from a formal viewpoint. Hexagrams can be classified by their component primary trigrams and nuclear trigrams, by the number of yang or yin lines they contain, or by algorithms based on these lines. The names and text of these hexagrams then may be consulted to see if any textually meaningful patterns emerge.

The formal viewpoint may be mathematical. The hexagrams and trigrams may be turned into numbers and one may seek a textual coherence in the groups of hexagrams or trigrams generated by mathematical algorithms.

There is also the literary viewpoint. Each hexagram may be regarded as a sign standing for a complex of metaphors. For example, Hexagram 1, *Heaven,* represents Creativity, Strength, Strong Action, and so forth. All sixty-four hexagrams may be regarded as a set of interrelated multi-metaphors. The hexagram text and its line text may also be viewed as a poem and read for the richness of its allusions and metaphorical implications.

One may also take a philosophical viewpoint. Many see in the *I Ching* an expression of a holistic philosophy, that is, a philosophy which views the world in terms of interacting opposites; these opposites do not war with one another, but instead complement one another to form a dynamic whole. Also found in the *I Ching* is a cyclical view of process which opposes the linear view so rampant in our modern civilization. As there are cycles in nature, so are there personal, social, and political cycles.

Finally there is the divinatory viewpoint, which views the *I Ching* as a magical or supernatural means of acquiring knowledge. Undoubtedly, one of the earliest uses of the book was divinatory. Since those early times the *I Ching* has developed into a moral system with a philosophical foundation.

It is my opinion that all of these viewpoints are valid ways of studying and using the *I Ching,* except the one which views the *I Ching* as magical or supernatural. A book may provide useful advice on a variety of issues without invoking claims of magical powers. The *I Ching* can give sound moral advice that is relevant to a person's particular problem in the same way that one can find relevant moral guidelines in the Bible, the Buddhist Sutras, and the Upanishads. The fruitfulness of this approach depends upon the ability of the inquirer to interpret the text associated with a particular hexagram (hexagram text) so that the advice obtained is appropriate and helpful.

Generally, when the *I Ching* is consulted for moral advice, a hexagram is selected by some chance device, e.g., the three-coin or the yarrow-stalk method, and the text of this hexagram is then read for counsel. Undoubtedly, there are many scholars who would regard such procedures as unmitigated nonsense, not worthy of comment. However, there have been scholars of stature, such as Carl Jung, who did not regard the use of such chance devices (i.e., the yarrow-stalk method of divination) as rank superstition, but on the contrary, regarded the advice obtained by such devices worthy of serious consideration.

In my opinion the use of such chance devices in consulting the *I Ching* for advice does have value. And I am not basing this claim upon the assumption that the *I Ching* has magical or mystical powers. The advice offered by the *I Ching* may be helpful when a problem arises for which one's usual habits and guidelines do not provide a ready solution. In trying to relate the advice given by the *I Ching* to one's problem, one is forced to view his problem from a different perspective. The advice given by the *I Ching* may or may not provide the answer sought, but even if it does not, the new perspective might render an insight which may broaden one's understanding of the issues involved and thus help one to formulate an answer to his problem.

If any hexagram selected at random leads us to fresh insights concerning a moral problem, then why should we bother with the tedious yarrow-stalk method of determining a hexagram or even with the coin method? Why not simply open a translation of the *I Ching* at random and select the hexagram on that page? The answer is that if one approaches the *I Ching* without a serious commitment to invest some time in studying the selected hexagram, the results will be inconclusive. If one spends fifteen or twenty minutes using the traditional yarrow-stalk method of selecting a hexagram, one is apt to spend an equal amount of time—or longer—studying the text of this hexagram. In short, there is a tendency to devalue advice that comes too easily. If the problem which leads one to consult the *I Ching* is not serious enough to warrant the time needed to use the traditional yarrow-stalk method, then it is a trivial problem and there is little need to consult the *I Ching* for its solution. For this reason, I recommend the traditional yarrow-stalk method described in the Wilhelm/Baynes or Blofeld translations or the more ancient yarrow-stalk method described in Whincup's translation. Both of these methods are also described in this book.

Purpose of Book: The purpose of this book is to provide students of the *I Ching* with information to facilitate their studies. Primarily, this volume deals with the combinatory aspects of the trigrams and hexagrams and related formal considerations (nuclear hexagrams, hexagram flowers, hexagram cycles, etc.), but some chapters also deal with textual subjects such as the names of the hexagrams and attempts to classify the hexagrams by common themes. This book does not contain a translation of the *I Ching*.

In this work there are two annotated bibliographies to English works on the *I Ching* and related topics. Bibliography A lists books and Bibliography B lists journal articles. Hereafter these bibliographies shall be designated [A] and [B]. An attempt was made to make both bibliographies as extensive as possible—

unpublished dissertations are listed—but no bibliography on a book as ancient and popular as the *I Ching* can ever be complete.

Also given in this book is a glossary of terms, topics, and people related to the *I Ching* which should prove useful to the intermediate as well as the beginning student. Care was taken not to change terminology or definitions in common usage. New terms and their stipulated definitions were introduced only when necessary, that is, when names were needed for new concepts.

Since the author of this book is not a sinologist, all translations from Chinese into English are based on the works of reputable sinologists, such as James Legge, Wilhelm/Baynes, John Blofeld, Greg Whincup, and others. Extensive footnotes are given documenting the sources of information given in this book.

The sixty-four hexagrams and their names are listed in the following table. For further information on the English names of the hexagrams see Chapter 4. By "binary number" is meant the decimal number equivalent to the hexagram expressed as a binary number. For further explanation on binary numbers, see Appendix A.

THE HEXAGRAMS GIVEN IN TEXTUAL SEQUENCE

Hexagram (Lines)	Hexagram (Digits)	Textual Number	Binary Number	English Name
	111-111	1	(63)	Heaven
	000-000	2	(0)	Earth
	100-010	3	(34)	Sprouting
	010-001	4	(17)	The Young Shoot
	111-010	5	(58)	Getting Wet
	010-111	6	(23)	Grievance
	010-000	7	(16)	An Army
	000-010	8	(2)	Alliance
	111-011	9	(59)	Small Restraint/Small Accumulation
	110-111	10	(55)	Treading
	111-000	11	(56)	Peace/Flowing
	000-111	12	(7)	Standstill
	101-111	13	(47)	Companions
	111-101	14	(61)	Great Possessions
	001-000	15	(8)	Modesty
	000-100	16	(4)	Contentment
	100-110	17	(38)	The Chase
	011-001	18	(25)	Illness/Decay
	110-000	19	(48)	Authority Approaches
	000-011	20	(3)	Observing

THE HEXAGRAMS GIVEN IN TEXTUAL SEQUENCE

Hexagram (Lines)	Hexagram (Digits)	Textual Number	Binary Number	English Name
☲	100-101	21	(37)	Biting Through
☲	101-001	22	(41)	Adornment
☶	000-001	23	(1)	Falling
☷	100-000	24	(32)	Return
☰	100-111	25	(39)	No Error/No Expectations
☰	111-001	26	(57)	Big Restraint/ Big Accumulation
☶	100-001	27	(33)	Bulging Cheeks
☱	011-110	28	(30)	Big in Excess
☵	010-010	29	(18)	Water
☲	101-101	30	(45)	Fire
☱	001-110	31	(14)	Mutual Influence
☳	011-100	32	(28)	Constancy
☶	001-111	33	(15)	The Piglet
☳	111-100	34	(60)	Big Uses Force
☲	000-101	35	(5)	Advance
☷	101-000	36	(40)	The Bright (Calling) Pheasant
☴	101-011	37	(43)	The Family
☲	110-101	38	(53)	Estrangement
☵	001-010	39	(10)	Obstruction
☳	010-100	40	(20)	Obstruction Removed

THE HEXAGRAMS GIVEN IN TEXTUAL SEQUENCE

Hexagram (Lines)	Hexagram (Digits)	Textual Number	Binary Number	English Name
	110-001	41	(49)	Decrease
	100-011	42	(35)	Increase
	111-110	43	(62)	Decisive
	011-111	44	(31)	Meeting/Subjugated
	000-110	45	(6)	Gathering Together
	011-000	46	(24)	Pushing Upwards
	010-110	47	(22)	Burdened/Exhausted
	011-010	48	(26)	A Well
	101-110	49	(46)	Revolution
	011-101	50	(29)	The Ritual Caldron
	100-100	51	(36)	Thunder
	001-001	52	(9)	Mountain
	001-011	53	(11)	Gradual Advance
	110-100	54	(52)	A Maiden Marries
	101-100	55	(44)	Abundance
	001-101	56	(13)	The Traveler
	011-011	57	(27)	Wind
	110-110	58	(54)	Lake
	010-011	59	(19)	Flood/Dispersion
	110-010	60	(50)	Restraint (Regulations)
	110-011	61	(51)	Inmost Sincerity (Allegiance)
	001-100	62	(12)	Small in Excess
	101-010	63	(42)	Already Across the River
	010-101	64	(21)	Not Yet Across the River

Symbols Used In This Text:

Boldface Terms. When a term in the text is boldface (except as the boldface title of a chapter, section, table or diagram), this means that the term is explained in the Glossary. The Glossary may contain additional terms which are not boldface in the text.

Footnotes. If the author has only one work listed in Bibliography A or Bibliography B, then only the author's name will be given in the footnote. If the author has two or more works listed in the bibliography, then the author's name and the title of the work cited will be given. The symbols [A] or [B] preceding the author's name indicate the bibliography in which the full reference will be found.

Symbolizing Trigrams and Hexagrams. In this text a **yang line** will be represented by either the numeral **1** or ▬ or both. A **yin line** will be represented by the numeral **0** or ▬▬. Thus Hexagram 3, *Sprouting,* is represented as 100-010 or ䷂. The digit on the extreme left is the bottom line of the hexagram (line 1) and the digit on the extreme right is the top line of the hexagram (line 6). The hyphen which separates the lower primary trigram from the upper primary trigram makes the six-digit group easier to read. It has no other significance.

The advantage of using the numerals "1" and "0" to represent the lines of trigrams and hexagrams is that they facilitate interpreting the trigrams and hexagrams as binary numbers. In general, the line form will be used unless there is a specific need for the binary form. See Appendix A.

The abbreviation "Hex." means "Hexagram."

Recommended Translations. Although the following translations are not above criticism, they are standard works and recommended for the beginner.

[A] Wilhelm/Baynes, *The I Ching or Book of Changes.*
[A] James Legge, *The I Ching.*

The Legge translation is in common domain and has been published by different presses. The Bantam Book edition, edited by Ch'u Chai and Winberg Chai, has an introduction and study guide. The Dover Press edition has larger type and is a more durable book. Both of these works contain a translation of the *Ten Wings,* the traditional commentaries of the *I Ching.*

Also recommended are:

[A] Blofeld, *The Book of Change,* and
[A] Whincup, *Rediscovering the I Ching.*

The Blofeld translation is very readable and contains a clear explanation of the yarrow-stalk method of divination as well as the coin method. This translation, Blofeld states, was written to be used for divinatory purposes. The book does not contain a translation of the *Ten Wings.*

Whincup's book, published in 1986, is a newer translation than the other three and makes use of recent scholarship in translating some of the names of the hexagrams. The book also contains a brief, but relevant history of ancient China—the time when the *I Ching* was written. Useful information is also contained in the appendices. A translation of the *Ten Wings* is not included. The annotations of these books should be consulted in Bibliography [A] for further information.

Thomas Cleary published three translations of the *I Ching* (1986, 1987, 1988): the first with Taoist commentaries, the second with Buddhist commentaries, and the third with the commentaries of Cheng Yi (an 11th century scholar). They are not without merit. The *Ten Wings* is not included.

The more advanced student will find Kunst's unpublished Ph.D. dissertation "The Original 'Yijing' " very useful. It contains the Chinese text of the *I Ching*, a phonetic transcription, a word-for-word translation and a free translation of the *I Ching*. See annotation in Bibliography [A] for a fuller description of this excellent work.[1]

Recommended Books on Chinese Philosophy and History. The following books are highly recommended:

[A] Fung Yu-Lan, *History of Chinese Philosophy,* vol. 2, and
[A] Joseph Needham, *Science and Civilization in China,* vol. 2.

Both of these works treat the *I Ching* and relevant historical information, especially Needham's. The books were published in 1953 and 1956 respectively, so they do not contain the latest findings and theories on the history of the *I Ching.* More recent works on these topics are found in Kunst's dissertation, mentioned above, and in Shaughnessy's dissertation:

[A] Edward Lewis Shaughnessy, "The Composition of the 'Zhouyi.' "

The Chinese Calendars. The Chinese use both a solar and a lunar calendar. The Chinese lunar calendar from 1910 to 1990 is given in Appendix B in:

[A] W. A. Sherrill and W. K. Chu, *An Anthology of the I Ching.*

A full explanation of the Chinese lunar calendar and a brief treatment of the solar calendar is given in Chapter 3, "The Chinese Calendar" in:

[A] Derek Walters, *Chinese Astrology.*

---

[1] Unpublished dissertations may be ordered from University Microfilms International, 300 N. Zeeb Road, Ann Arbor, Michigan 48106.

Study Guide. It is not expected that the reader will work his way through the following exercises before continuing to Chapter 2. The exercises are presented as a means of deepening one's understanding of the *I Ching*.

A. The Trigrams. The family relationships and the main attributes (metaphorical associations) of the trigrams should be known. The attributes are given in the *Eighth Wing* of the *I Ching* and should be read very carefully. A translation of the *Eighth Wing* may be found in [A] Wilhelm/Baynes, pp. 262–79 and [A] Legge, pp. 422–32. Some of the attributes of the trigrams (based on Legge's translation) are given in Appendix B.

The natural attributes of the trigrams (e.g., 111, ☰, *Heaven;* 000, ☷, *Earth;* 100, ☳, *Thunder;* 011, ☴, *Wind;* 010, ☵, *Water;* 101, ☲, *Fire;* 001, ☶, *Mountain;* 110, ☱, *Lake*) are important metaphors since they are used in this work as the names of their respective trigrams. Some time should be devoted to finding and studying the associations of these metaphors. For example, some of the associations of the metaphor Mountain are: stillness, stubbornness, immovability. Some of the associations of the metaphor Wind are: unseen force, pervading force, that which penetrates.

Each trigram is a multi-metaphor and the serious student of the *I Ching* will learn them all. Another set of metaphors of the Trigram 001, ☶, *Mountain,* is doors, gates, and openings. The symbol 001 when written as two yin lines under a yang line looks like a door. The space between the two yin lines is the door, the yang line the lintel. Another metaphor for Trigram 001 is fruits of trees. The single yang line on top represents fruit on a tree. The direction of movement in a trigram (or hexagram) is upwards, so the yang line cannot move upwards; it must—like ripe fruit—fall.

B. The Binary System. For those who are interested in studying the formal aspects of the trigrams and hexagrams, a knowledge of the **binary system** of counting is extremely useful. The method of translating numbers from the decimal system into the binary system and vice-versa is explained in Appendix A.

C. The Sixty-Four Hexagrams. There are sixty-four hexagrams. Each is composed of six lines, each line is either yin or yang, and—when obtained by the traditional yarrow-stalk method—each line is either **static** or **moving**. Each hexagram has a name, a hexagram text and a line text. Each hexagram— as with the trigrams—is a multi-metaphor and represents a dynamic moment in a system of interconnected stages.

C1. Learning the Names and the Textual Order of the Hexagrams. It is not suggested that the first step in studying the *I Ching* is to memorize all sixty-four names and textual numbers of the hexagrams. This will come about automatically through the analysis of the individual hexagrams and the study of their formal relationships. However, the following techniques are useful for facilitating learning the names and textual numbers of some of the hexagrams.

Every even-numbered hexagram in the **textual sequence** is either the **inverse** or **opposite** of its succeeding hexagram. Thus every odd-numbered hexagram and its even-numbered successor are a pair of inverses or opposites. For example, Hexagram 1, ☰ 111-111 and Hexagram 2, ☷ 000-000 are a pair of opposites. Hexagram 51, ䷲ 100-100 and Hexagram 52, ䷳ 001-001 are a pair of inverses. Thus, if one learns how to write the lines of the odd-numbered hexagrams, one will also be able to write the lines of the even-numbered hexagram.

There are eight hexagrams which may be formed by doubling each of the eight trigrams. Thus for each of these hexagrams the upper **primary trigram** is the same as the lower primary trigram. These are called the **Double Hexagrams** (also House Hexagrams). In this work these hexagrams are named after their component primary trigrams. Hence:

Hexagram 1	☰	111-111	is *Heaven*
Hexagram 2	☷	000-000	is *Earth*
Hexagram 29	䷜	010-010	is *Water*
Hexagram 30	䷝	101-101	is *Fire*
Hexagram 51	䷲	100-100	is *Thunder*
Hexagram 52	䷳	001-001	is *Mountain*
Hexagram 57	䷸	011-011	is *Wind*
Hexagram 58	䷹	110-110	is *Lake*

If you know the names of the trigrams, then you know the names of hexagrams 1, 2, 29, 30, 51, 52, 57, 58, since these hexagrams are named after the trigrams which constitute them.

Hexagrams 63, ䷾ 101-010, *Already Across the River,* and Hexagram 64, ䷿ 010-101, *Not Yet Across the River,* are unique, since they are not only the last two hexagrams in the textual sequence, but they are the only hexagrams composed entirely of alternating opposite lines (i.e., yin followed by yang or vice-versa).

Many times the name of a hexagram is suggested by its lines and their arrangement. For example, Hexagram 7, ䷆ 010-000, *An Army,* has only one yang (strong) line in line position 2, the position of an Official who is not in proximity to the Ruler. All the other lines are yin (weak). This is a suitable symbol for an army—one who is not the Ruler (Emperor), rules many who are weak.

There are also partial patterns of recurring primary trigrams in the textual sequence. For example, hexagrams 3, 5 and 7 all have 010, ☵ *Water,* as a primary trigram. And hexagrams 9, 11, and 13 all have 111, ☰ *Heaven,* as a primary trigram.

C2. The Primary Trigrams of the Hexagrams: The Image. Every hexagram may be viewed as a combination of two trigrams: the lower primary trigram (lines 1, 2, and 3) and the upper primary trigram (lines 4, 5, and 6). The names or attributes of the primary trigrams in a hexagram is its image. Hence, Hexagram 23, ☶☷ 000-001, *Falling,* is Mountain over Earth, which is the Image of Hexagram 23. The Images are given in the appendix to the *I Ching* called *The Commentary on the Images* (3rd and 4th Wings), which is an attempt to explain the meaning of the hexagrams. Taking Hexagram 23 as an example, we have the Fruit of Trees, *Mountain* (upper trigram) over *Earth* (lower trigram). The one yang line on top (the ripe fruit) being pushed upwards by the yin lines (direction in a hexagram is always upwards), has no place to go and will fall to Earth. Hence, the name of the Hexagram is *Falling.*

Not all of the hexagrams can be analyzed so neatly, but it is excellent practice for students to select at random various hexagrams and attempt to analyze their meanings by their Images. It must always be kept in mind that the metaphorical system of the *I Ching* was constructed in a society far removed from Western culture both in distance and in time, with the consequence that a Chinese student of the *I Ching* may have quite different associations from those of the late 20th century American student. For example, the Trigram 010 ☵, *Water,* seems to be associated with danger, trouble, or incompleteness, when it appears as a lower primary trigram in Hexagrams 4, 6, 7, 29, 40, 47, 59, and 64. The names of these hexagrams are, respectively, *The Young Shoot, Grievance, An Army, Water (The Pit), Obstruction Removed, Burdened/Exhausted, The Flood/Dispersion,* and *Not Yet Across the River.* One can only guess at the reasons for this. Perhaps the ancient Chinese, not being a seafaring people, regarded large bodies of water as dangerous; perhaps it was because of seasonal floods, or perhaps it was because the Yellow River separated the Chou—where the *I Ching* developed—from their enemy, the Shang. The Trigram 010 ☵, *Water* appears as an upper primary trigram in Hexagrams 3, 5, 8, 29, 39, 48, 60, and 63. Their names are, respectively, *Sprouting, Getting Wet, Alliance, Water (The Pit), Obstruction, A Well, Restraint/Regulations, Already Across the River.* As can be seen, not all of these names have negative connotations, but then the Trigram 010 ☵, *Water,* has other attributes (other metaphorical meanings) besides water. One should also keep in mind that what is dangerous in one context may not be dangerous in another. It is good to have a full well; it is not good to need to ford a deep river.

C3. The Line Positions and their Meanings. The **line positions** are numbered from 1 to 6, from the bottom of a hexagram to the top.

C3 a. Earth, Man, and Heaven. The top two line positions (lines 5 and 6) represent Heaven, the middle two positions (lines 3 and 4) represent Man, and the bottom two positions (lines 1 and 2) represent Earth. In reading the line text of a hexagram one may interpret the lines in positions 1 and 2 to represent earthly forces, natural and material influences; the lines in positions 3 and 4 to represent human or social influences; and lines in positions 5 and 6 to represent moral or spiritual influences. Sometimes this interpretation proves fruitful.

C3 b. The Ruler, the Great Official and Others. Each line position also represents a certain station in life. Line position 6 is the position of the Sage, one who does not participate in human affairs and lives in harmony with nature. Line position 5 is the position of the Ruler. Normally, but not always, this is the ruling line of a hexagram. Line position 4 is the position of a person close to the Ruler, a Minister or Advisor. It is a position that requires caution, recognized so even in Western society as witnessed by the saying "Close to the King, close to the Gallows." Position 3 is an insecure position, since it is one of transition from a lower rank to a higher one. Advancement to a position of power is fraught with danger. The Great Official is represented by the line in position 2. This line is usually favorable as it is far enough from the Ruler to escape his immediate influence. The line at the bottom—line position 1—is like the line in the 6th position; it represents a person who does not affect the situation described by the hexagram name and text. The line in position 6 is leaving or has left the situation; the line in position 1 is entering or has not yet entered the situation. Thus a line in this position represents a person who as yet has little or no power over the circumstances. This may be the position of the common-man.

Just as the trigrams and hexagrams are multi-metaphors so are the line positions. The different line positions may represent different family members. Thus line position 6 may represent an elderly man who no longer participates in family life. Line position 5 then is the husband, line position 4 the eldest son and/or daughter, line position 3 the middle children, line position 2 the mother, and line position 1, young or unborn children. When a hexagram is interpreted to apply to a social or political situation then the above social and/or family interpretations apply, but when applied to a situation that does not involve people, then a shift of interpretation is required. For example, the line in position 5 would then represent the dominant influencing factor of the situation, and so forth.

As an exercise, read the text of line position 3 for all sixty-four hexagrams. Note the ones that warn of danger and the ones that do not. Do the hexagrams in which the text for line 3 warns of danger have any theme in common? Do the hexagrams in which the text for line 3 does **not** warn of danger, have a theme in common? Also note if there is any difference between the line texts for yin lines and yang lines in this position.

This exercise can be done for each of the line positions. One would, of course, read each line position in accordance with its station as described for the six positions above.

C4. The Lines and their Relationships. As the relation between the primary trigrams in a hexagram may assist one to analyze the meaning of that hexagram, so can the relation between its individual lines or between a line and its line position, aid in determining its meaning. There are three such relationships: the relationship of a line to its line position (**Correctness of a Line**), the relationship of a line to a line immediately above or below it (**Holding Together**), and the relationship between pairs of lines occupying positions 1 and 4, 2 and 5, or 3 and 6, respectively, when the members of the pair are opposite (**Correspondence**). A full description of these relationships and examples is given in [A] Wilhelm/Baynes, pp. 360–64. Also see Glossary.

C4 a. Correctness of a Line. A line in a hexagram is correct if and only if it is a yang line in position 1, 3 or 5 or if and only if it is a yin line in position 2, 4, or 6. All of the lines in Hexagram 63, ䷾ 101-010, *Already Across the River,* are correct. None of the lines in Hexagram 64, ䷿ 010-101, *Not Yet Across the River,* is correct.

As an exercise, find the six hexagrams which contain exactly five correct lines and the six hexagrams which contain exactly five incorrect lines. Read the Judgments (hexagram texts) of both groups. Are there any general differences?

C4 b. Holding Together. Two lines in successive line positions in a hexagram hold together if they are opposites (one yin, the other yang). Holding together is most important between lines in positions 4 and 5, and positions 5 and 6.

As an exercise, note the sixteen hexagrams wherein there is a yin line in position 4 and a yang line in position 5 (holding together of lines 4 and 5). Are the Judgments (hexagram texts) of the hexagrams in this group similar to one another in any way?

Also examine the two groups where lines 4 and 5 do not hold together: the sixteen hexagrams with a yang line in positions 4 and 5 and the sixteen with a yin line in positions 4 and 5. In general, are the hexagrams where lines 4 and 5 hold together more favorable than those where they do not? And is one kind of holding together (yin in position 4, yang in position 5) more favorable than the other (yang in position 4, yin in position 5)?

The above exercise should be repeated for the holding together of lines 5 and 6.

C4 c. Correspondence. Opposite lines in positions 1 and 4, 2 and 5, and 3 and 6 correspond to each other. Correspondence is most important between opposite lines in positions 3 and 5 (the positions of the Great Official and the Ruler).

Compare the hexagram texts of the sixteen hexagrams that have a yang line in position 3 and a yin line in position 5 (Strong Official and Weak Ruler). Are these sixteen hexagrams generally favorable or unfavorable?

Find the sixteen hexagrams that have a yin line in position 3 and a yang line in position 5. In general, are these hexagrams more or less favorable than the above group?

C5. Hexagrams and their Inverses. The **inverse** of a hexagram can be derived by writing its lines in reverse order. For example, the inverse of Hexagram 3, ䷂ 100-010, *Sprouting,* is Hexagram 4, ䷃ 010-001, *The Young Shoot.* The inverse of Hexagram 33, ䷠ 001-111, *The Piglet,* is Hexagram 34, ䷡ 111-100, *Big Uses Force.* Sometimes the inverse of a hexagram is itself; the inverse of Hexagram 27, ䷚ 100-001, *Bulging Cheeks,* if written in reverse order, is the same.

Find the eight hexagrams that have themselves as inverse. Note how they all have either a yin or a yang line in both positions 1 and 6, 2 and 4, and 3 and 5.

C5 a. There are twenty-eight pairs of inverses where the hexagrams in each pair are not identical. Many of these pairs seem to express opposite meanings. For example, Hexagram 39, ䷦ 001-010, *Obstruction* and its inverse Hexagram 40, ䷧ 010-100, *Obstruction Removed,* and Hexagram 41, ䷨ 110-001, *Decrease* and its inverse Hexagram 42, ䷩ 100-011, *Increase,* express opposite concepts. Examine each of these twenty-eight pairs and by reading the hexagram texts and studying the images try to interpret each hexagram and its inverse as expressing opposite meanings.

C6. Hexagrams and their Opposites. The **opposite** of a hexagram is derived by changing every line in the hexagram to its **opposite** (yin to yang, yang to yin). The opposite of Hexagram 1, ䷀ 111-111, *Heaven* is Hexagram 2, ䷁ 000-000, *Earth* and the opposite of Hexagram 3, ䷂ 100-010, *Sprouting,* is Hexagram 50, ䷱ 011-101, *Ritual Caldron.*

C6 a. Test the hypothesis that opposite hexagrams, like inverses, might express polar opposites.[2] There are thirty-two pairs of opposites to test. For example, the opposites Hexagrams 1 and 2, *Heaven* and *Earth,* clearly express polar meanings. However, the polar meanings expressed by Hexagram 3, *Sprouting,* and its opposite Hexagram 50, *The Ritual Caldron,* are not obvious. A little thought, however, might yield the following: Hexagram 3 is talking about the beginnings of situations and relationships, and the difficulties that are inherent in these early stages. Hexagram 50 is talking about ritual and how knowing the required ritual for a situation is to know how to behave in that situation. Hence, when one is entering into a new relationship or into a new situation, as described in Hexagram 3, the danger is from not knowing how to behave. Once one learns what constitutes proper (moral) behavior for this situation, the danger of inappropriate behavior is past.

C6 b. Assuming that a hexagram and its inverse express polar meanings, then a hexagram that has itself as inverse has no polar meaning, except for its opposite hexagram. For example, Hexagram 1, ☰ 111-111, *Heaven,* which represents the *Creative Force,* is its own inverse. It has an **opposite** (see C6.) which is Hexagram 2, ☷ 000-000, *Earth, the Great Receptive.* In section C5 a. there are eight hexagrams that have themselves as inverses. What do these eight hexagrams have, if anything, in common?

C6 c. Sometimes the opposite of a Hexagram is the **same** as its inverse. For example, the opposite **and** inverse of Hexagram 11, ䷊ 111-000, *Peace/Flowing,* is Hexagram 12, ䷋ 000-111, *Standstill.* There are exactly six pairs of opposites which are also pairs of inverses. Find these six pairs. Do you note anything special about the meanings expressed by the hexagrams in each of these pairs?

C7.   Opposites and Inverses. It has been hypothesized that the inverse and opposite of a hexagram is a hexagram that expresses a polar meaning. Since many hexagrams have inverses and opposites that are not identical, it follows from the hypothesis that there is more than one kind of polar meaning. Assume as a hypothesis that there are two kinds of polar meanings: one kind we can call **complementary**, the second **contrary**.

Complementary opposites are qualities or things that complement or support each other. In a sense, each member of a pair of complementary opposites needs the other. Complementary opposites do not, by definition, exclude one another. They both may exist side by side, and often one cannot exist

---

2 I use the term "polar opposite" to cover a wide range of occurrences. All of the following I call examples of pairs of opposites: Cause/Effect, Man/Woman, Hot/Cold, Light/Dark, Creative/Receptive, Increase/Decrease, Big/Small, Inside/Outside, Front/Back, and Mountain/Valley.

without the other. Examples of complementary opposites are: Male/Female, Cause/Effect, Concave/Convex, and Inside/Outside.

Contrary opposites are pairs of qualities of which each precludes the existence of the other. Contrary opposites cannot co-exist, but it is possible for an entity to have neither quality. A pair of contrary opposites is Hot/Cold. If something is hot then it is not cold and vice-versa, but it is possible for an object to be neither hot nor cold. Other examples of contrary opposites are: Big/Small, Increase/Decrease, Friend/Enemy.

C7 a. Examine all pairs of inverses and opposites and see how many you can classify as examples of complementary or contrary opposites. If any of them do not fit either category then define another category to describe the relation between hexagrams in these pairs.

Are there more complementary opposites exemplified by pairs of inverses or pairs of opposites?

C8. Hexagram Stories. (See Chapter 7.) For each **story**, study the names and the text of the hexagrams in the story. Search for some sequential development of meaning from the first hexagram in the story to the last.

C9. Hexagram Flowers. (See Chapter 7.) Analyze each hexagram **flower**. Try to determine how the petals clarify the meaning of the flower center. In doing so distinguish between petals that are **antecedent** and **consequent hexagrams**.

C10. Hexagram Cycles. (See Chapter 7.) Determine what line arrangements of a hexagram yield **cycles** that have no pairs of inverses and what line arrangements yield cycles that have one or more pairs of inverses. Determine the differences between hexagrams that have a cycle of three and those that have a cycle of six.

2

I CHING:
STRUCTURE, ORIGIN,
AND INTERPRETATIONS

19. Authority Approaches

Introduction. The *I Ching* (*I* means "change," *Ching* means "Classic,") is translated as "Classic of Change," "Book of Changes," "Book of Change," or "Classic Book of Changes."[1]

The *I Ching* is one of the **Five Classics** of Chinese Literature and perhaps the most influential of all Chinese books.[2] It dates back to at least 800 B.C. and could be several centuries older. Schulz writes:

> The bulk of commentary material on the *Classic of Change* produced over the course of Chinese history is impressive. The table of contents to the *Ching i k'ao* ..., a comprehensive survey of material from the Han Dynasty through the seventeenth century, lists some two thousand and fifty titles on the *Change,* fully a fourth of all works included.[3]

Undoubtedly one of the earliest functions of the *I Ching* was divination. Kunst states:

> The text of the *Yijing* grew organically over a period of many centuries, perhaps a millennia, as it was transmitted orally among the professional diviners who used the yarrow plant to obtain oracles. It served as a manual of ready reference of the consequences of relevant past divinatory determinations.[4]

Under the influence of the Confucianists, the *I Ching* became a handbook of moral wisdom. And in the Han dynasty the *I Ching,* combined with the **Five Agents** system and numerology, also became a cosmology.

The Structure of the I Ching. The original *I Ching* is an ancient Chinese book containing approximately 4,100 Chinese characters.[5] The book is divided into 64 chapters (units); each chapter comments on a hexagram, a symbol composed of six horizontal lines arranged one over the other. Each line may be either yang (a solid line, e.g., ▬) or yin (a broken line; broken lines have a gap in the middle, e.g., ▬▬). Since there are six lines and either may be yang or yin the total number of combinations is: $2^6 = 64$.

Each hexagram has a name given in one or two Chinese characters. The name of the hexagram always precedes the hexagram text, which is called the **Decision** or **Judgment**, and which describes a situation of which the hexagram is a symbol. The Judgment is more than a descriptive passage; it is also interpreted as giving moral advice, that is, a recommendation—given the specific

---

[1] It should be noted that most nouns in Chinese have neither a singular nor plural form; hence, *I* could translate as either "Change" or "Changes."

[2] The *I Ching* became a Confucian Classic in 136 B.C. [A] Smith, p. 22.

[3] [A] Schulz, p. 3.

[4] [A] Kunst, p. 4.

[5] [A] Kunst, pp. 3 and 449.

context—for action or non-action.[6]

For example, the Judgment for Hexagram 10, *Treading,* is "Stepping on the Tiger's Tail. It does not bite. No error." The Judgment for Hexagram 21, *Biting Through,* is "Favorable for bringing legal action." The Judgment for Hexagram 23, *Falling,* is "Not favorable to go in any direction." Sometimes the Judgment is longer. For example, the Judgment for Hexagram 24, *Return,* is "In going and coming there is no error. Friends come without blame. They go back the way they came. Coming and going in seven days. Favorable to have somewhere to go."[7]

Following the hexagram text is the line text, which is composed of short descriptions associated with each line of the hexagram. There are six such descriptions, one for each line. (Hexagrams 1 and 2 each have an additional description that pertains to a special case.) The line texts are regarded as describing various stages (e.g., early, middle, or later stages) of the situation described by the hexagram text. The line text, like the hexagram text, is interpreted as giving moral advice.

The line text for Hexagram 24, *Return,* is:

Line 1. Returning from not far. No need to repent. Very favorable.
Line 2. Good return. Favorable.
Line 3. Repeated returns. Danger, but no misfortune.
Line 4. Returning alone on the road, although in the midst of others.
Line 5. A noble return. No misfortune.
Line 6. Going astray. Not returning. Danger. If armies are set marching there will be a great defeat to ruler of state and for ten years there will be trouble.[8]

The Ten Wings. The *Ten Wings* is a collection of the earliest commentaries or appendices to the original *I Ching.*

The First and Second Wings are called "Commentary on the Judgment" (*T'uan Chuan*). The Third and Fourth Wings are called "Commentary on the Images" (*Hsiang Chuan*). The Fifth and Sixth Wings are called "The Great Treatise" (*Hsi Tz'u Chuan* or *Ta Chuan*). The Seventh Wing is called "Commentary on Words of the Text" (*Wen Yen*). The Eighth Wing is called "Discussion of the Trigrams" (*Shuo Kua*). The Ninth Wing is called "Sequence of the Hexagrams (*Hsu Kua*). And the Tenth Wing is called "Miscellaneous Notes on the Hexagrams" (*Tsa Kua*).[9]

---

[6] For a discussion of the meaning of the Judgment, see [A] Lee, *Understanding the I Ching,* pp. 154–59.

[7] Translations are based on those of [A] Kunst, [A] Legge, and [A] Wilhelm/Baynes.

[8] Translations based on those of [A] Kunst, [A] Legge, and [A] Wilhelm/Baynes.

[9] A discussion of the Ten Wings is given in [A] Wilhelm/Baynes, pp. 225–61; also in

Commentary on the Judgment (*T'uan Chuan*). This commentary is in two parts, comprising the First and Second Wings of the *Ten Wings*. The first part covers hexagrams 1 to 30; the second, hexagrams 31 to 64. This corresponds to the division of the hexagrams in the *I Ching* itself.[10] By tradition authorship of the *T'uan Chuan* is attributed to Confucius.

The commentary sometimes talks about the lines in the hexagram, how they relate to one another and whether they are in the correct position[11] or not, and it discusses other considerations concerning the formal structure of the hexagram. Sometimes the commentary relates the hexagram situation to cosmic and natural phenomena and sometimes the commentary gives moral advice. For example, the *Commentary on the Judgment* says the following about Hexagram 10, *Treading:*

> In Hexagram 10, *Treading,* we have the symbol of weakness treading on strength. The lower trigram indicates pleasure and satisfaction and responds to the upper indicating strength. Hence it is said, "He treads on the tail of a tiger, which does not bite him; there will be progress and success." The fifth line is strong, in the center, and in its correct place. Its subject occupies the God position, and falls into no distress or failure;—His action will be brilliant.[12]

This commentary is looked upon as foreshadowing the two main schools of interpreting the *I Ching:* the **Hsiang Shu** and **I Li** schools. The Hsiang Shu school emphasizes the formal aspects of the hexagram—how the lines relate to one another and how one hexagram can be transformed into another, and so forth. The I Li school emphasizes the hexagram text and its moral message. More will be said about these two schools later in this chapter.

Commentary on the Images (*Hsiang Chuan*). This commentary is in two parts and like the *First Wing,* the first part covers hexagrams 1 to 30 and the second part covers hexagrams 31 to 64. The first part of this commentary is the *Third Wing;* the second part, the *Fourth Wing.* Swanson states that, "The commentary parts, taken as a whole, form a long three hundred and eighty-four line poem."[13]

This commentary has a section for each hexagram called the Great Images and a section called the Small Images. The Great Images gives an image for each of the **primary trigrams** in each hexagram and for a majority of the

---

[A] Goodman, pp. 158–68 and in [A] Smith, pp. 7–17.

[10] The text of the *I Ching* is divided into two parts: hexagrams 1 to 30 and hexagrams 31 to 64. I have not been able to find a justification for this unequal division of the hexagrams.

[11] See Glossary, Correctness of a Line.

[12] Based on Legge's translation ([A] Legge, pp. 222-23).

[13] [A] Swanson, p. 6.

hexagrams tells what the superior man or ancient kings would do in such a situation. For example, the Great Images says, concerning Hexagram 10, *Treading,* ☰ 110-111:

> The upper trigram represents the sky and the lower trigram represents the waters of a marsh. The superior man, in accordance with this, discriminates between high and low, and gives settlement to the aims of the people.[14]

The Small Images section does not deal with images at all. It repeats the line text and gives a brief commentary on it. Richard Wilhelm says:

> It must have been owing to some misapprehension, or perhaps to chance, that this commentary on the text of the individual lines found its way into the Commentary on the Images...It may be that the Small Images are mnemonic phrases taken from a more detailed commentary. It is certain that they are very old and originated with the Confucian school, but I should not like to say definitely how close the connection with Confucius himself may be.[15]

The Small Images[16] for Hexagram 24, *Return,* are:

> Line 1. Return from not far is the start of self-cultivation.
> Line 2. The good fortune that comes from a good return is due to being dependent on virtue.
> Line 3. Even though there is danger from repeated returns, there is no error.
> Line 4. Returning alone on the road although in the midst of others. His object is to pursue the proper path.
> Line 5. A noble return. No misfortune. In this central position one perfects oneself.
> Line 6. The evil of going astray and not returning results from not pursuing the proper course for a ruler.[17]

Great Treatise (*Hsi T'zu Chuan* or *Ta Chuan*). This commentary is also known as the *Commentary on the Appended Judgments.*[18] It is the largest

---

[14] Based on Legge's translation, [A] Legge, p. 280.

[15] [A] Wilhelm/Baynes, pp. 257–58.

[16] I shall continue to use the title "Small Images," although this title is obviously incorrect. See [A] Wilhelm/Baynes, pp. 258–59.

[17] Based on Legge's translation, see [A] Legge, p. 297–98.

[18] Richard Wilhelm points out that the *Great Treatise* does not discuss the appended Judgments. [A] Wilhelm/Baynes, pp. 258–59. Swanson notes that the name *Commentary on the Appended Judgments* "is found only in texts of the latter Han"([A] Swanson, p. 6).

and, according to some scholars, the most significant commentary of the *Ten Wings*. It contains approximately 4,400 Chinese characters, making it longer than the *I Ching* itself.[19] The *Great Treatise*, which is in two parts, comprises the 5th and 6th Wings of the *Ten Wings*. The two part division of this commentary **does not** correspond to the two part division of the *I Ching*. Tradition attributes the authorship of the *Great Treatise* to Confucius (551–479 B.C.). Although some scholars dispute this tradition, it is generally agreed that the *Great Treatise* was written not later than 90 B.C.[20]

The *Great Treatise* is a collection of essays on the *I Ching* which, according to Swanson, were written to solve three problems: (1) To develop a cultural history based on semi-divine mythical kings; (2) To synthesize the information on the trigram and hexagram into one coherent whole; and (3) To integrate the *I Ching* with Yin-Yang and **Five Agents** schools.[21]

Commentary on the Words of the Text (*Wen Yen*). This commentary makes up the *Seventh Wing* of the *Ten Wings*. Probably it is the remains of a much longer commentary.[22] It comments only on Hexagram 1, *Heaven,* and Hexagram 2, *Earth* with most of the comments being on Hexagram 1. Authorship is attributed to Confucius or his school.[23]

Discussion of the Trigrams (*Shuo Kua*). This commentary is the *Eighth Wing* of the *Ten Wings*. It contains information on the trigrams. Richard Wilhelm believes that this commentary contains "many fragments antedating Confucius."[24] It is in this commentary that the associations of the trigrams are given, the **King Wen** and **Fu Hsi Arrangements** of trigrams, and the order in which Trigram 1, *Father,* and Trigram 2, *Mother,* produce the rest of the family of trigrams.

Sequence of the Hexagrams (*Hsu Kua*). This commentary is the *Ninth Wing* of the *Ten Wings*. According to Richard Wilhelm it was not authored by Confucius.[25] It attempts to explain the **textual sequence** of the hexagrams. A paragraph of this commentary, translated by Legge, reads:

Hexagram 3, Sprouting, is descriptive of things on their first

---

[19] [A] Swanson, p. 8.

[20] The *Great Treatise* is mentioned in the *Shih Chi* (*Historical Record*), written about 90 B.C., so it cannot have been written later than this. [A] Swanson, p. 9. Swanson believes that the *Great Treatise* was written in late Chou. [A] Swanson, p. 10.

[21] [A] Swanson, pp. 11-12.

[22] [A] Wilhelm/Baynes, p. 259.

[23] [A] Wilhelm/Baynes, p. 259. Swanson states that "Parts of it are quoted in the *Tso chuan* (the enlargement of the *Spring and Autumn Annals* compiled between 430–250 B.C.) and so is probably older than the *Great Treatise*" ([A] Swanson, p. 6).

[24] [A] Wilhelm/Baynes, p. 260.

[25] [A] Wilhelm/Baynes, p. 260.

production. When so produced they are sure to be in an undeveloped condition. Hence, Hexagram 3 is followed by Hexagram
4, The Young Shoot. The Young Shoot is descriptive of what
is undeveloped—the young of creatures and things. These in
that state require to be nourished. Hence The Young Shoot
is followed by Hexagram 5, Waiting.[26] Hexagram 5, Waiting
is descriptive of the way in which meat and drink (come to
be supplied). Over meat and drink there are sure to be con-
tentions. Hence Hexagram 5, Waiting, is followed by Hexagram
6, Grievance.[27]

Wilhelm/Baynes state that it "offers a rather unconvincing explanation of the
present sequence of the hexagrams."[28]

Miscellaneous Notes on the Hexagrams (*Tsa Kua*). This commentary is the *Tenth Wing* of the *Ten Wings*. This commentary, which rhymes, is
a series of comments on the names of the hexagrams. Legge's translation of the
first few lines of this commentary is:

> Strength in *Heaven*, weakness in *Earth*. We find *Alliance* shows
> us joy, and *An Army* the anxious mind. The *Authority Ap-
> proaches* gives, *Observing* seeks;—such are the several themes.
> Their different figures were to teach designed. *Sprouting* mani-
> fests itself, yet keeps its place; 'Mid darkness still, to light *The
> Young Shoot* sets its face.'[29]

The Traditional Account of the Origin of the I Ching. Four
names are associated with the traditional account of the creation of the *I Ching:*
Fu Hsi, King Wen, the Duke of Chou, and Confucius.

Fu Hsi is one of the Five Emperors (all legendary, semi-divine beings)
who ruled China before the Hsia dynasty (which was also considered legendary
until archaeological finds in 1978).[30] Fu Hsi (3322 B.C.)[31] is given the credit for

---

[26] In this text we translate the name of Hexagram 5 to mean "Getting Wet." Legge
translated it as "Waiting."

[27] This is a quotation from Legge, [A] Legge (Dover), p. 433, in which I have replaced
Legge's untranslated names for the hexagrams with their hexagram number and an
English translation. Legge has a footnote to this passage where he states that it is
difficult to see how Hexagram, 5, Waiting, represents nourishment. Note that in this
work the name of Hexagram 5 is *Getting Wet.*

[28] [A] Wilhelm/Baynes, p. 260.

[29] This is a quotation from Legge in which I have replaced Legge's untranslated names
for the hexagrams with an English translation (Legge (Dover), p. 441).

[30] Archaeological sites dating from this period were discovered in 1978. The source is
"Chronology of Chinese History" published by The Center for Teaching about China.
Chicago, Ill: 1979.

[31] Date given by Legge, attributing it to Chinese scholars. No source given. ([A] Legge

formulating the laws of humanity, inventing the net, the snare, marriage (uniting husband and wife), and discovering the eight trigrams.[32]

Table 1. The First Three Chinese Dynasties

DYNASTIES	YEARS
Hsia Dynasty	2000–1750 B.C.[33]
Shang Dynasty	1750–1000 B.C.[34]
Chou Dynasty	1000–256 B.C.
(Warring States)	403–221 B.C.
Chin Dynasty	221–206 B.C.
Han Dynasty	206 B.C.–220 A.D.

King Wen, in the last days of the Shang dynasty, ruled Chou, a small state in western China. King Wen was imprisoned by the tyrant of Shang. A year later the King's friends secured his release. While in prison legend has it that King Wen increased the eight trigrams to sixty-four hexagrams and for each one wrote a brief paragraph explaining its significance.[35]

Smith writes:

> Chinese tradition holds that the culture-hero Fu Xi ...(trad. 34th century B.C.) devised the Eight Trigrams ...Beyond that there is some disagreement. It is said that Fu Xi or King Wen ...(trad. rg. 1171–1122 B.C.) created the hexagrams...([A] Smith, pp. 1–2).

King Wen's son, King Wu, defeated the Shang forces and became the

---

(Dover), p. 5.)

[32] The source for this information is the *Third Wing* of the *I Ching, The Great Treatise,* Part II, Chapter II, paragraphs 1–2. For translation see Wilhelm/Baynes, pp. 328–29. *The Great Treatise,* according to Swanson, was written in the late Chou period (Swanson, pp. 8–10).

[33] Dates are approximations. By tradition the dates for the Hsia dynasty are 2205-1766 B.C. Source is Wilhelm/Baynes, f.n., p. lviii.

[34] Dates are approximations. By tradition the dates for the Shang Dynasty are 1766-1150 B.C. Source is Wilhelm/Baynes, f.n., p. lviii.

[35] Legge in a footnote, [A] Legge, p. 6, gives the following source, "Sze-ma Khien (*History of the Kau Dynasty,* p. 3) relates that 'when he was confined in Yu-li, Wan [King Wen] increased the 8 trigrams to 64 hexagrams.' " Wei Tat writes as though the 64 hexagrams existed long before the time of King Wen, although Tat does allow that King Wen explained each hexagram with a short paragraph. Tat says, "During this period of imprisonment, he [King Wen] devoted himself to contemplating the meanings of the sixty-four symbols. He knew full well that in previous dynasties those symbols, though arranged in different orders, had been regarded as images of metaphysical significance...([A] Tat, p. 3).

first ruler of the Chou dynasty. When King Wu died his young son ascended the throne, but the real ruler was his appointed guardian, the Duke of Chou, King Wu's brother. The Duke of Chou is alleged to have written the text for the individual lines of the hexagrams.[36] According to tradition Confucius wrote *The Great Treatise,* which is the largest and perhaps the most important commentary of the *I Ching.*

Scholarly Opinion for the Date of the I Ching. One of the earliest mentions of the *I Ching* is in the *Lun Yu (The Analects of Confucius),* the Ku version, Book VII, 16. It reads: "If some years were added to my life, I would give fifty to the study of the *Yi (I Ching),* and might then escape falling into great errors."[37]

Needham points out that there is good reason to suspect that this passage was corrupted at a later date.[38] The *I Ching* is also mentioned in the *Chou Li (Record of Rites of the Chou),* which was compiled in the Western Han dynasty (202 B.C.– 9 A.D.)[39] The *Chou Li* mentions three books of changes: the *Lien Shan (Manifestation of Change in the Mountains), Kuei Tsang (Flow and Return to Womb and Tomb),* and the *Chou I (Book of Changes of the Chou Dynasty).*[40] Only fragments of the first two works remain. The *I Ching* as we know it today is the *Chou I.*

The *I Ching* is mentioned in the *Commentary on the Spring and Autumn Annals* (the *Tso Chuan*), which was compiled between 430 B.C. and 250 B.C. It lists sixteen instances of the use of the *I Ching* for divination.[41] But Needham writes, "If the views here outlined about the dates of this book (referring I believe to the *I Ching*) are accepted, it follows that all the *kua*-consultations in the *Tso Chuan* must be regarded as interpolations."[42]

The traditional view is that Confucius (and/or his immediate students) wrote *The Great Treatise,* which means that the *I Ching* existed in the 6th century B.C. However, Swanson summarizes evidence that points to the late

---

[36] Wilhelm/Baynes, p. lix.

[37] [A] Legge (Dover), p. 1.

[38] [A] Needham, vol. 2, p. 307.

[39] Legge writes, "The earliest mention of the classic is found in the Official Book of the Kau dynasty..." ([A] Legge, p. 3). The book referred to by Legge is the *Chou Li (Record of Rites of the Chou).* Needham agrees with Legge and writes "The crucial fact is that there is no other mention (besides the corrupted passage in the *Analects*) of the *I Ching* in any reliable contemporary text before the -3rd century..." ([A] Needham vol. 2, p. 307). The dates given for the Western Han dynasty are those of Needham ([A] Needham vol. 2, p. 697).

[40] Translations of titles are from Needham, vol. 2, p. 307.

[41] These sixteen instances are listed and translated in Shchutskii, pp. 191–92. Shchutskii states, "Throughout the course of the seventh century B.C., the feudal lords used the *Book of Changes* exclusively as a divinatory text" (p. 192).

[42] [A] Needham, vol. 2, p. 307.

Chou period as the date of *The Great Treatise.*[43]

Contemporary views held by scholars concerning the date of the *I Ching* range between the following dates:

1. It was written before 1000 B.C.
2. It was written as late as the 3rd century B.C.

Whincup, avoiding extremes, writes:

> My own hypothesis is that the text of the *I Ching* was compiled by diviners, beginning around 1000 B.C., and that it was more or less as it is now by at least 500 B.C., and probably as early as around 700 B.C. The hexagrams and the divinatory tradition probably antedate the text.[44]

and Swanson, in basic agreement with Whincup, states:

> I think it can be demonstrated that the line texts of the *I Ching* partake of the same function words and grammatical patterns as certain parts of the *Shih Ching* (*Book of Odes*). This would place the line texts at about the eighth century B.C.[45]

Thus the hexagrams and hexagram texts could be several centuries older. Shaughnessy devotes the first chapter of his dissertation to establishing the date of the *I Ching*. He puts the date of the *I Ching* at about 800 B.C.

> In conclusion then, its literary development and linguistic usage show the *Zhouyi* (The *I Ching* of the Chou Dynasty) to be a product of the latter stage of the Western Zhou dynasty, and the historical context of this period suggests a composition date in the early years of King Xuan's reign: most probably, during the last two decades of the ninth century, B.C.[46]

And Kunst also fixes upon 800 B.C. when he writes:

> As far as historical truth is concerned, the text is now universally recognized to have had its origin in the rich divinatory tradition of early China. It was not a political or moral treatise but a diviner's manual. It did not have a single identifiable author or even authors, but was the result of gradual accretion over centuries. The most that could be claimed is that a single editor, working the waning years of the Western Zhou dynasty, that is,

---

[43] Swanson, pp. 9-10.

[44] [A] Whincup, p. 15.

[45] [A] Swanson, f.n. 3, p. 245.

[46] [A] Shaughnessy, p. 49.

roughly 800 B.C.E., wrote down the text and subjected it to extensive polishing.[47]

Since there is no hard evidence for the century in which the *I Ching* originated, it cannot be claimed to be the oldest Chinese classic. Parts of the *Shu Ching* (*Book of History*) go back to the 10th century B.C. and parts of the *Shih Ching* (*Book of Odes*) go back to the 9th century.[48]

Major Schools of Interpretation of the I Ching: Hsiang Shu and I Li.[49]

In essence, the *hsiang shu* (Image and Number[50]) approach emphasizes the form of the lines, trigrams and hexagrams, and their relationship to each other, to numbers, and to natural objects, events, and categories.[51] It relates the trigrams and hexagrams to the Five Agents, to the eight directions, to the seasons, to the days and months of the year, to the parts of the body, and so forth.

The *i li* (Moral Principle or Meaning and Principle) approach emphasizes the hexagram names, the hexagram texts, and line texts. The purpose of this textual analysis is to derive moral principles and moral instructions.

Both the *hsiang shu* and the *i li* approaches can be found in the first two commentaries of the *Ten Wings*. Seeds of these two schools also are found in some of the other Wings.[52]

Adler states: "*I-li*, then, is basically textual analysis, while *hsiang shu* is symbolic analysis."[53]

Proponents of the Hsiang Shu School. The *hsiang shu* started in the Han dynasty with Cheng Shi, Chiao Kan, and Ching Fang (1st century B.C.). In the later Han, the most important member of this school was Yu Fan (164–233 A.D.). According to Schulz:

> evidence of interest among Confucian scholars in the non-verbal aspects of the *Classic of Change* does not reappear until the Northern Sung, when Chou-Tun-i (1017–1073), Chang Tsai

---

[47] [A] Kunst, pp. 3–4.

[48] [A] Legge, pp. 6–7 and [A] Needham, vol. 2, p. 603.

[49] Schulz further divides the schools: "Both schools featured three sub-schools, or 'lines,' the former's including pre-Han mantic practice, Han Dynasty omenology, and Sung Dynasty mathematical speculation, while the latter's included the so-called Neo-Taoism of Wang Pi, the Neo-Confucianism of Northern Sung, and the historicism of Li Kuang and Yang Wan-li" ([A] Schulz, p. 11).

[50] Members of the *Hsiang Shu* school are called "mutationists" by Needham ([A] Needham vol. 2, p. 343). Also see entry "Wang Pi" in Needham's Index, p. 694.

[51] [A] Adler, p. 42.

[52] For further details concerning elements of the *hsiang shu* and *i li* approaches in the *Ten Wings*, see [A] Smith, pp. 7–17.

[53] [A] Adler, p. 45.

(1020–1077), and Shao Yung (1011–1077) initiated a second influx of non-Confucian material into the exegetical tradition.[54]

Shao Yung was the most influential member of the *hsiang shu* tradition in the Sung dynasty. He acquired considerable fame as a numerologist, but his emphasis on numerology was for the purpose of formulating a cosmology, not solely for divination.[55]

Proponents of the I Li School. Wang Pi (226–249 A.D.) emphasized the view that the symbols (the hexagrams and the trigrams) were only a means of arriving at an underlying idea, and were no longer necessary once the idea was determined. Wang Pi advocated concentrating on the meaning of the symbol and the text, not upon the symbol itself.

Ch'eng I (1033–1107 A.D.) and his brother Ch'eng Hao (1032–1085 A.D.) were among the founders of Neo-Confucianism of the Sung dynasty. Ch'eng I wrote a commentary on the *I Ching* interpreting it in terms of the Confucian virtues of the Mean and Correctness.[56]

The Great Synthesizer: Chu Hsi.[57] Chu Hsi (1130–1200 A.D.) was a Neo-Confucianist who tried to synthesize a variety of cosmologies within a Neo-Confucian context.[58] He also tried to synthesize the *hsiang shu* and *i li* schools. Adler states:

> What Chu Hsi attempted to do with *hsian shu* was to apply its technique and its subject matter to the actual problems and difficulties of moral cultivation as he understood them.[59]

In addition, Douglas White writes:

> He (Chu Hsi)...felt very strongly that the *I-ching* originally was compiled as a handbook for practical divination, and he encouraged its use for this purpose by writing an essay in which he attempted to reconstruct in detail the method of manipulating the yarrow stalks to obtain the oracle. As mentioned earlier, he also promoted the numerological speculations and diagrams of Shao Yung.[60]

---

[54] [A] Schulz, p. 27. Chinese symbols omitted from quote and Shao Yung's dates added.

[55] [A] White, p. 75.

[56] See [A] White, Douglas. p. 89. Adler stated that the most prominent *i li* commentator of the Northern Sung was Ch'eng I. [A] Adler, p. 164.

[57] Called by Fung Yu-Lan "the greatest synthesizer in the history of Chinese thought." [A] Fung Yu-Lan, vol. 2, p. xxiii.

[58] [A] Fung Yu-Lan vol. 2, Chapter XIII, "Chu Hsi," pp. 533-71. See also [A] Adler, Chapter III B. "Chu Hsi and *Hsiang-Shu I*" pp. 161–209, and [A] White, Douglas. Chapter V. "Chu Hsi: the Great Synthesizer," pp. 96–104.

[59] A] Adler, p.162.

[60] [A] White, Douglas, pp. 96–97.

3

YIN AND YANG LINES, FOUR EMBLEMS, AND TRIGRAMS

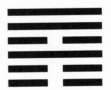

53. Gradual Advance

Yin and Yang Lines. In the *I Ching* a yang line is represented by an undivided horizontal line ▬ ; a yin line is represented by a divided horizontal line ▬▬. The terms "yin" and "yang," however, do not go back beyond the Chou dynasty and do not appear in the main text of the *I Ching*.[1] Legge writes:

> It is in this Appendix [Legge's Appendix III, The Great Treatise: 5th and 6th Wings of the *I Ching*] that we first meet with the names yin and yang... Up to this point, instead of them, the names for the two elementary forms of the lines have been kang (Kang) and *zâu* (Jou), which I have translated by 'strong and weak,'[2] and which also occur here ten times ([A] Legge (Dover), p. 43).[3]

The attributes of Yin and Yang, which are associated with the lines that they name, are presented in Table 1:

Table 1. Yin and Yang Attributes

YANG	YIN
Sunny	Shady[4]
Light	Dark[5]
Warmth	Cold[6]
Dryness	Moisture[7]
Male	Female[8]
Day	Night[9]
Fire	Water[10]
Strong	Weak[11]
Hard	Soft[12]
Active	Passive[13]
Odd Numbers	Even Numbers[14]
Heaven	Earth[15]

---

[1] See [B] Leopold De Saussure, "On the Antiquity of the Yin-Yang Theory." [A] Wilhelm/Baynes write, "In the Commentary on the Decison the terms used for the opposites are 'the firm' and 'the yielding,' not yang and yin" (p. lvi).

[2] Wilhelm/Baynes translate these terms as "firm"/"yielding."

[3] The passage where the terms yin and yang first occur is in Part I, Chapter V of the *Great Treatise*. It is translated by Legge as "The successive movement of the inactive and active operations constitutes what is called the course (of things)" ([A] Legge (Dover), p. 355). Needham does not think that this translation is satisfactory ([A] Needham, vol. 2, fn c., p. 274). It is translated by Swanson as "Now *yin,* now *yang,* that we call the *tao*" ([A] Swanson, p. 113).

Moving and Static Lines. A moving line is one that is changing into its opposite. The opposite of a yin line is a yang line and vice-versa. A static line is one that is not in the process of change.

The numbers 9 and 7 designate, respectively, a moving and static yang line, and the numbers 6 and 8 designate, respectively, a moving and static yin line. The assignment of these numbers to the lines probably came from the yarrow-stalk method of divination.[16]

Table 2. The Numbers of the Lines

	Moving	Static
Yang Line	9	7
Yin Line	6	8

[4] See [A] Needham, vol. 2, p. 274. Needham also mentions that Yang refers to heat and to the summer months.

[5] This association mentioned by [A] Wilhelm/Baynes, p. lvi. See also [A] Needham, vol. 2, p. 274.

[6] Given by [A] Fung Yu-Lan, vol. 2, p. 7. See also [A] Needham, vol. 2, p. 274.

[7] Given by [A] Fung Yu-Lan, vol. 2, p. 7.

[8] Given by [A] Fung Yu-Lan as "masculinity," "femininity," vol. 2, p. 7. See also [A] Needham, vol. 2, p. 274.

[9] Needham translates part of a Han Confucianist text (ca. 135 B.C.) in which day is referred to as Yang time and night as Yin time ([A] Needham, vol. 2, p. 275).

[10] Needham translates a part of a Han Confucianist text (ca. 137 B.C.) wherein water is associated with Yin. "At night (the Yin) time the waters (a Yin element) flood more, by several inches" ([A] Needham, vol. 2. p. 275). I assume that since yang is opposite of yin, and fire is opposite of water, that fire is an association of yang.

[11] Legge translated Yang and Yin as "strong and weak," respectively. See note above.

[12] Legge states that "Yang lines are strong (or hard), and Yin lines are weak (or soft)" ([A] Legge (Dover) p. 16).

[13] Given as "activity/passivity" by [A] Fung Yu-Lan, vol. 2, p. 7.

[14] In the *Great Treatise,* Book I, Chapter IX the odd numbers from one to nine are associated with Heaven and the even numbers from two to ten are associated with Earth. See translation by [A] Wilhelm/Baynes, p. 308 or [A] Legge (Dover), p. 365. It may be safe to assume that odd numbers have all the associations of yang and the even numbers the associations of yin.

[15] This association I have not been able to find in Wilhelm/Baynes, Legge, Needham, or Fung Yu-Lan, but the association seems obvious since Trigram 1, *Heaven* contains all yang lines and Trigram 2, *Earth* contains all yin lines. This also holds, respectively, for Hexagram 1, *Heaven,* and Hexagram 2, *Earth.*

[16] Legge claims that these numbers come from the river scheme [The Yellow River Map, *Ho T'u*], and this map by legend is supposed to antedate the *I Ching* ([A] Legge (Dover), p. 42). However, Fung Yu-Lan implies that this diagram goes back to the Taoist Ch'en T'uan (ca. 906–989 A.D.) ([A] Fung Yu-Lan, vol. 2, p. 453). Fung Yu-Lan also mentions (p. 8) that Confucius said "The phoenix comes not, the river gives forth no chart" (*Analects*, IX, 5). The chart Confucius is referring to is supposed to be the Yellow River Map that appeared to the legendary Fu Hsi. See [A] Fung Yu-Lan, p. 8, n. 3.

A **kinetic line** is a line designated as moving or static.

The Four Emblems. The four emblems, also known as the four images and the four emblematic symbols,[17] are as follows:

Table 3. The Four Emblems

Name	Symbol	Number	Binary #	Element[18]	Season[19]
Great Yang (Old Yang)	═	9	11	Fire	Summer
Little Yang (Young Yang)	⚍	7	10	Wood	Spring
Great Yin (Old Yin)	⚏	6	00	Water	Winter
Little Yin (Young Yin)	⚎	8	01	Steel	Autumn

Not all authorities agree with the linear symbolism of the Lesser Yang and Yin,[20] but the symbols given above are in agreement with Wilhelm/Baynes[21] and Swanson. Swanson writes:

> The bottom line in each case of mixed lines is that which deter-
> mines its name, i.e., ⚎ young *yin*, rather than young *yang* ([A]
> pp. 151–52).

There is also some confusion regarding the numbers assigned to the young yin and young yang, but, since the *Great Treatise* calls 7 a Heavenly number, and 8 an Earthly number, the above assignment seems reasonable. Additional evidence is that the number 7 signifies a static yang line and the number 8 signifies a static yin line.

It is important to note that in the Chinese calendar the equinoxes and solstices occur in the middle of a season. If this was also true in the Chou

---

[17] [A] Wilhelm/Baynes use the expression "the four images" (p. 319). Legge (Dover) uses "the four emblematic Symbols" (p. 12). The former is too wide a term, since 'image' has another meaning in reference to the hexagrams. The latter expression is unnecessarily long.

[18] These associations are given in the Writing from the Lo River Maps (*Lo Shu*) ([A] Wilhelm/Baynes, p. 308).

[19] [A] Wilhelm/Baynes mention that the four emblems are associated with the four seasons, but unfortunately do not list them. However, since wood is associated with spring, fire with summer, steel with autumn, and water with winter, these following seasonal associations seem correct.

[20] See [B] Hacker, "The Linear Representations of the Four Images."

[21] [A] Wilhelm/Baynes, p. 319.

dynasty, then their seasons started about a month and half earlier than ours.[22]

The Trigrams. A **trigram** is a symbol composed of three horizontal lines. Each line is either **yin** or **yang**. Therefore there are 8 trigrams ($2^3 = 8$). The trigrams, their arrangements, and attributes are discussed in the *Eighth Wing, Discussion of the Trigrams (Shuo Kua)* of the *I Ching*. A table of the trigrams follows:

Table 4. Trigrams

Trigram	Text Number	Binary Number	Name
☰	1	111	Heaven
☷	2	000	Earth
☳	3	100	Thunder
☴	4	011	Wind
☵	5	010	Water
☲	6	101	Fire
☶	7	001	Mountain
☱	8	110	Lake

The sequence above is that given in Chapter 10 of the *Eighth Wing*.[23] Henceforth, the binary or line symbolism will be used as deemed appropriate. A yang line is 1, a yin line is 0. The digit on the extreme left is the bottom line (first line) of the trigram. The digit on the extreme right is the top line (third line) of the trigram.

Each trigram can symbolize a number of **attributes** or **associations**. Each of these in turn can represent a host of additional objects and situations. For example, Trigram 1 is taken to symbolize the Head, Heaven, Father, Ruler, Horse, Jade, Metal, etc. The Head in turn can be a metaphor for a ruler, intelligence, a governing body, and so on. Therefore Hexagram 1 can by analogy also symbolize these meanings as well.

One of the most important attributes of the trigrams is its family relation. Four of the trigrams are male and four are female. Two different assignments of family relationships exist: one from the Earlier Heaven Sequence of the Trigrams, the other from the Later Heaven Sequence of the Trigrams. Both are given below.

Family Relationships. The following table gives the family relationships for the trigrams in the **Earlier** and **Later Heaven Sequence**. Note that only the last four trigrams differ.

---

[22] See [A] Walters, *Chinese Astrology,* Chapter 3, "The Chinese Calendar"; [A] Martin Palmer and others, *T'ung Shu,* p. 64; and [A] Fung Yu-Lan, vol. 2, pp. 115–17.

[23] [A] Wilhelm/Baynes, p. 274. [A] Legge (Dover), pp. 429–30.

Table 5. Family Relationships

Trigram #	Trigram	Symbol	Earlier Heaven	Later Heaven
1	☰	111	Father	Father
2	☷	000	Mother	Mother
3	☳	100	Eldest Son	Eldest Son
4	☴	011	Eldest Daughter	Eldest Daughter
5	☲	101	Middle Son	Middle Daughter
6	☵	010	Middle Daughter	Middle Son
7	☱	110	Youngest Son	Youngest Daughter
8	☶	001	Youngest Daughter	Youngest Son

In the Earlier Heaven Sequence the bottom line of the **trigram** is the sex determinant. In the Later Heaven Sequence **sex** is determined by the kind of line which occurs an odd number of times. Hereafter, unless otherwise specified, we shall use the Later Heaven Sequence of family relationships.

The following attributes, except for the two noted, are found in the *Discussion of the Trigrams*.[24]

Table 6. Trigram Attributes

Trigram Number	Main Property	Natural Object	Type of Person	Part of Body	Animal
1	Strength	Heaven	King	Head	Horse
2	Receiving	Earth	People	Belly	Ox
3	Initiating	Thunder	Gate Keepers[25]	Feet	Dragon
4	Penetrating	Wind, Wood	Merchants	Thighs	Fowl
5	Dangerous	Water	Thieves	Ear	Pig
6	Depending	Fire	Amazons[26]	Eye	Pheasant
7	Halting	Mountain	Porter	Hand	Dog
8	Pleasure	Lake	Sorceress	Mouth	Sheep

A very complete list of attributes is given by Diana ffarington Hook in *I Ching and You*, Appendix 3. Unfortunately, no reference is given. A table of attributes more complete than the one above is given by Needham in *Science and Civilization in China*, vol. 2, pp. 312–13.

---

[24] For a translation of the *Discussion of the Trigrams* see [A] Legge (Dover), Appendix V or [A] Wilhelm/Baynes, pp. 262–279.

[25] Listed by [A] Needham, vol. 2, p. 313, but not given in *Discussion of the Trigrams* (*Eighth Wing*).

[26] See f.n. 2.

The Earlier Heaven Sequence. This sequence, also known as **Fu Hsi's Arrangement** of the Trigrams, World of Thought Arrangement, Primal Arrangement, and Before the World Sequence, is a circular arrangement of the trigrams, such that **opposites**[27] are diametrically opposite each other:[28]

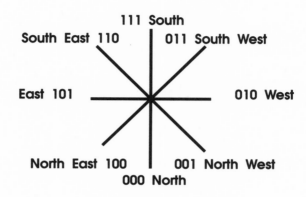

Figure 1.
Earlier Heaven Sequence of the Trigrams

This diagram, minus the compass directions, is described in the *Discussion of the Trigrams* (*The Eighth Wing*). Legge translates one passage that indirectly describes this sequence as follows:

> Chapter III. 5. (The symbols of) heaven and earth received their determinate positions; (those for) mountains and collections of water interchanged their influences; (those for) thunder and wind excited each other the more; and (those for) water and fire did each other no harm. (Then) among these eight symbols there was a mutual communication.
>
> 6. The numbering of the past is a natural process; the knowledge of the coming is anticipation. Therefore in the Yi we have (both) anticipation (and the natural process) ([A] Legge (Dover), p. 424).[29]

---

[27] The opposite of a trigram is another trigram which has a yin line where the first trigram has a yang line and a yang line where the first has a yin line. In short, a pair of opposite are two trigrams (emblems or hexagrams) having different lines in each line position.

[28] It is customary for the Chinese to orient their maps so that south is at the top and north at the bottom.

[29] For Wilhelm/Baynes translation see [A] Wilhelm/Baynes, p. 265.

Wilhelm/Baynes state that this passage is probably a very ancient saying and believe that the arrangement depicted in Figure 1 was in existence at the time the *Book of Changes* was compiled in the Chou dynasty.[30] Legge says these paragraphs are "understood, though not very clearly"[31] to refer to the **Fu Hsi Arrangement** of the trigrams (Figure 1 above). Both Legge and Wilhelm/Baynes give a diagram of the Earlier Heaven Sequence, with the compass directions assigned to the trigrams as shown in Figure 1, but neither state the source for these directions. [32] The same compass directions are also given by Needham,[33] but his source for this is also not made clear.

Binary Order and the Earlier Heaven Sequence. It has been noted by contemporary scholars that the trigrams in the Earlier Heaven Sequence can be connected so that they follow a binary order: 000, 001, 010, 011, 100, 101, 110, and 111. This order starts with Trigram 2, 000, at the bottom and ascends counter clockwise to Trigram 4, 011. Diagonally opposite Trigram 4 is Trigram 3, 100 (the next highest number in binary count) and the binary order continues clockwise to Trigram 1, 111, at the top. See Figure 2.

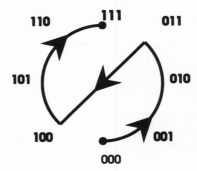

Figure 2.
Binary Order and the Earlier Heaven Sequence

The similarity of this diagram to the Yin-Yang symbol (also known as Tai Chi), when a line is drawn connecting the numbers in numerical order, has been observed by contemporary scholars; but there is no evidence that the ancient Chinese were aware of the binary order or binary arithmetic. Needham writes:

---

[30] [A] Wilhelm/Baynes, pp. 265–66.

[31] [A] Legge (Dover), p. 424.

[32] The Earlier Heaven Arrangement is given in [A] Wilhelm/Baynes, p. 266 and in [A] Legge (Dover), Plate III, Fig. 2.

[33] [A] Needham, Vol. 2, pp. 312-13.

In so far as the diviners worked with 'mutations' of the hexagrams, substituting broken for unbroken lines and vice versa, they might be considered to have been executing simple binary arithmetical operations, but they certainly did so without realising it (Vol. 2, pp. 342–43).

The Four Emblems and the Earlier Heaven Sequence. The method used by the ancient Chinese for deriving the Earlier Heaven Sequence is not known, but Chappell Brown[34] has devised an ingenious way in which the Sequence can be derived from the Four Emblems. He arranges the four emblems in the following traditional order:

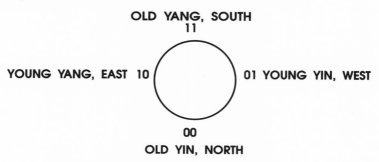

Figure 3.
The Four Emblems

The four emblems are turned into the eight trigrams by application of the following rule: An emblem is placed on top of an emblem such that the resulting tetragram has the same 2nd and 3rd lines, which are then reduced to one line. Thus when Old Yang is placed on top of itself, the result is the tetragram 1111. Lines 2 and 3 are the same and are reduced to 1 line. The result is Trigram 1, ☰ 111, Heaven. Old Yin is placed on top of itself and the result, when lines 2 and 3 are reduced to one, is Trigram 2, ☷ 000, Earth. When Young Yin is placed on top of Young Yang the result is 1001. When lines 2 and 3 are reduced to one, Trigram 6, ☲ 101, Fire, is formed. In similar fashion when Young Yang is placed on top of Young Yin, the result is tetragram 0110, which reduces to Trigram 5, ☵ 010, Water. The other four trigrams are formed in like manner. Young Yang over Old Yang yields Trigram 8, ☱ 110, Lake; Old Yang over Young Yin yields Trigram 4, ☴ 011, Wind; Young Yin over Old Yin yields Trigram 7, ☶ 001, Mountain; and Old Yin over Young Yang yields Trigram 3, ☳ 100, Thunder.

The Later Heaven Sequence. This sequence, also known as **King Wen's Arrangement,** World of Senses Arrangement, Inner World Arrangement, is a circular arrangement of the eight trigrams which shows "the temporal

---

[34] [B] Brown, Chappell. "The Tetrahedron as an Archetype for the Concept of Change in the *I Ching*."

progression in which they manifest themselves in the phenomenal world in the cycle of the year" ([A] Wilhelm/Baynes, p. 268).

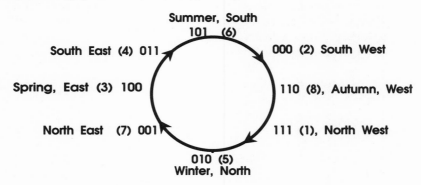

Figure 4.
Later Heaven Sequence of the Trigrams

The Later Heaven Sequence starts with Trigram 3, ☳ 100 *Spring* and proceeding clockwise ends with Trigram 7, ☶ 001 *Late Winter, Early Spring*. Thus, as Wilhelm/Baynes state, this arrangement of the trigrams may represent the year, but it may also represent a day: Trigram 3, ☳ 100, being early morning; Trigram 4, ☴ 011, being late morning; Trigram 6, ☲ 101, being noon, and so forth. The temporal direction for the Later Heaven sequence is always clockwise.

The Later Heaven Sequence is given, as was the previous sequence, in *The Discussion of the Trigrams* (*The Eighth Wing*). One passage of the *Eighth Wing* which describes this sequence is translated by Legge (the trigram binary symbolism has been substituted for the name of the trigram) as follows:

> God comes forth in 100 (to His producing work); He brings (His processes) into full and equal action in 011; they are manifested to one another in 101; the greatest service is done for Him in 000; He rejoices in 110; He struggles in 111; He is comforted and enters into rest in 010; and He completes (the work of the year) in 001 ([A] Legge (Dover), p. 425).

Concerning the Later Heaven Sequence, John Blofeld states:

> It is difficult to see the logic of this arrangement; but, since it is found in all Chinese editions of the *I Ching,* I have included it here. It is said in China that beings above the level of humans are able to discover the meaning of this order, whereas humans are no longer able to do so ([A] John Blofeld, p. 218).

The Seasonal Order of the Later Heaven Sequence. One can make some sense of the order of the trigrams in the Later Heaven Sequence since the meanings of the trigrams do coincide fairly well with their assigned seasons. Trigram 3, *Thunder* represents spring. This is the time that plants and trees start to become active; the bottom yang line pushing upward is akin to a seed beginning to grow. Trigram 4, *Wind,* represents late spring and early summer, the dispersing agent; the seeds are scattered. This Trigram also represents *Wood,* the symbol of growing things. Trigram 6, *Fire,* appropriately symbolizes summer, the time of greatest heat. Trigram 2, *Earth,* represents late summer and early autumn. It is a time of fruitfulness. Trigram 8, *Lake,* represents autumn, a time of harvest, a time of joy. Trigram 1, *Heaven,* represents late autumn and early winter. It is the Trigram that symbolizes elderly men and the aging part of the year. At this time of the year the yang fights a losing battle with the yin; heat gives way to cold. Trigram 5, *Water,* which generally stands for toil and trouble, symbolizes winter. It is at this time of the year that all creatures must make a special effort to survive. Trigram 7, *Mountain,* represents late winter and early spring, which is a time of stillness. It should be remembered that it is probable that the seasons in ancient China were regarded as occurring about a month and a half earlier than we do ours.

Formal Order in the Later Heaven Sequence. There is no reason why there should be a formal order to the Later Heaven Sequence, as the seasonal order represented might well have been sufficient to the ancient Chinese. But since the trigrams lend themselves so readily to formal manipulations and since there are formal orders to the Earlier Heaven Sequence, it might well be that there is a formal order to the Later Heaven Sequence.

The Later Heaven Sequence contains the following formal properties:

1. The trigrams are grouped by sex. Going in a clockwise direction, the group of four female trigrams in the sequence starts with Trigram 4, ☴ 011 *Wind.* The male group starts with Trigram 1, ☰ 111, *Heaven.*[35]

2. From the four male trigrams (clockwise 1, *Heaven;* 5, *Water;* 7, *Mountain;* and 3, *Thunder*), there is an algorithm which will generate the rest of the sequence, which are the female trigrams 4, *Wind;* 6, *Fire;* 2, *Earth;* and 8, *Lake.* This algorithm is:

> a. Divide the four male trigrams into three pairs, which are (clockwise): Trigrams 1 and 5, 5 and 7, 7 and 3.
>
> b. From each pair construct a trigram such that its bottom line is the top line of the first trigram in the pair and its second and third line are the first and second lines of the second trigram in the pair. The first pair will yield Trigram 6, *Fire;* the second will

---

[35] The sex of a trigram is a formal property, since its sex is determined by the kind of line and the number of its occurrences in the trigram. A trigram is male if it contains an odd number (1 or 3) of yang lines; it is female if it contains an odd number (1 or 3) of yin lines.

yield Trigram 2, *Earth,* and the third, Trigram 8, *Lake.* It should be noted that the constructed trigram is always diametrically opposed to the second trigram of each pair. See Figure 4 above.

c. Consider Trigram 8 and 1 to be a pair. Using the procedure described in b., construct a trigram. It will be Trigram 4, *Wind.*

3. The Later Heaven Sequence can be constructed from the *Lo Shu* (Lo River Map) Square. Write the trigrams as binary numbers in a square of 3, from left to right, leaving the center cell blank. Zero is written first (000), followed by the four odd binary numbers—001, 011, 101, 111—in ascending order. Next the even binary numbers—010, 100, 110—are written from the left to right in ascending order. The square now looks like this:

000	001	011
101		111
010	100	110

Figure 5.

Now if the trigrams in Figure 5 above are selected according to the sequence of numbers in the *Lo Shu* Square, see below:

4	9	2
3	5	7
8	1	6

Figure 6.

then 100 would be selected first, 011 selected second, and so forth. The result is the Later Heaven Sequence, which starts with Trigram 3, ☳, 100, *Thunder* first and is followed by Trigram 4, ☴, 011, *Wind,* and so forth.

There is no evidence that the ancient Chinese constructed the Later Heaven Sequence by using any of the formal orders mentioned above, or even that they were aware of these orders. But the fact that these orders can be found in the Later Heaven Sequence may suggest that some formal considerations were given to its construction.

4

ENGLISH NAMES
OF THE HEXAGRAMS

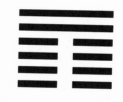

20. Observing

Many times the translators of the *I Ching* disagree as to what the English name of a hexagram should be. Sometimes this disagreement is slight; for example, when Hexagram 8 is called *Holding Together* by one translator and *Alliance* by another. In such cases both translators agree as to the basic meaning of its Chinese name and differ only in their choice of the English word which they think best expresses this meaning. At other times there is disagreement as to what the Chinese name itself means; for example, the Chinese name of Hexagram 5 means *Waiting* to most translators, but Whincup translates it as *Getting Wet.* In such cases the entire interpretation of the Hexagram is generally changed.

In Table 1 are listed the names of the hexagrams as given by six translators of the *I Ching.* The initials of these translators and the titles of their works are:[1]

W/B	[A]	Richard Wilhelm, *The I Ching or Book of Changes.*
JB	[A]	John Blofeld, *The Book of Change.*
GW	[A]	Greg Whincup, *Rediscovering the I Ching.*
TC	[A]	Thomas Cleary, *The Buddhist I Ching.*
KH	[A]	Kerson Huang, *I Ching: The Oracle.*
TY	[A]	Titus Yu, "The I Ching: An Etymological Perspective."

An asterisk after a name in the following list indicates the name recommended and used hereafter in this text. Generally, the recommended name is selected from those given by the translators; however, in a few cases a new name is offered which is either a composite of several of the names given or a name based on translations not listed. Table 2 lists the names of the hexagrams recommended and is followed by an explanation of the guidelines used in their selection.

A slash between names indicates that there is a close connection between them, causal or semantic. For example, the recommended name for Hexagram 26 is Big Restraint/Big Accumulation. The connection here is one of causality. A big restraint leads to a big accumulation of energy. A large dam accumulates a lot of water behind it. The recommended name for Hexagram 11 is *Peace/Flowing.* The relation here is semantic. The meaning of each name helps to clarify what is meant by the other. It is not the peace of stillness, but the peace of harmonious movement (flow). The word "flow" alone is insufficient to convey the full meaning, since a flow may be turbulent, or smooth and harmonious.

Where the connection between the first and second meaning seems less obvious, the second meaning is enclosed in parentheses, as for example in Hexagram 25, *No Error (No Expectations).* The relation (if any) between no error and

---

[1] My rationale for the order in which the translators are listed is as follows: printed works are listed before unprinted works and the most widely known translations are listed first.

no expectations is not apparent. Hence, the second meaning is put in parentheses. The second meaning—given a particular context—may be more appropriate than the first and should not be judged to be less reliable simply because of its parenthetical status.

Legge's translation is not listed because Legge did not translate the names of the hexagrams in a clear and consistent manner. For example, concerning the name of Hexagram 44, Legge writes "The name tells us that the successful accomplishment of whatever the writer had in his mind had not yet been realized" ([A] Legge (Dover), p. 208). For other hexagrams he is more specific, the name of Hexagram 48 "is the symbol of a well" ([A] Legge (Dover), p. 166).

Also consulted was Richard Kunst's unpublished dissertation, "The Original *I Ching*," which contains a word-for-word translation and free translation of the *I Ching*. Unfortunately, Kunst gives no translations of the names of the hexagrams.

Table 1. English Names of the Hexagrams

HEXAGRAM #	HEXAGRAM	SYMBOL	NAME OF HEXAGRAM	SOURCE
Hexagram 1.	☰	111-111	The Creative	W/B
			The Creative Principle	JB
			Strong Action	GW
			Heaven*	TC
			Heaven	KH
			Enflaming Inspiration	TY
Hexagram 2.	☷	000-000	The Receptive	W/B
			The Passive Principle	JB
			Acquiescence	GW
			Earth*	TC
			Earth	KH
			Earth's Fecundity	TY

Table 1. English Names of the Hexagrams

HEXAGRAM #	HEXAGRAM	SYMBOL	NAME OF HEXAGRAM	SOURCE
Hexagram 3.	䷂	100-010	Difficulty at the Beginning	W/B
			Difficulty	JB
			Gathering Support	GW
			Difficulty	TC
			Retrenchment	KH
			Sprouting*	TY
Hexagram 4.	䷃	010-001	Youthful Folly	W/B
			Immaturity	JB
			The Young Shoot*	GW
			Darkness	TC
			Blindness	KH
			The Neophyte	TY
Hexagram 5.	䷄	111-010	Waiting (Nourishment)	W/B
			Calculated Inaction	JB
			Getting Wet*[2]	GW
			Waiting	TC
			Waiting	KH
			Impending Relief	TY
Hexagram 6.	䷅	010-111	Conflict	W/B
			Conflict	JB
			Grievance*	GW
			Contention	TC
			The Court	KH
			Arbitration	TY

---

[2] Kunst does not translate the names of the hexagrams, but in the line text he uses the expression "It gets wet" indicating that he is in agreement with Whincup's translation. See [A] Kunst, pp. 248–49.

Table 1. English Names of the Hexagrams

HEXAGRAM #	HEXAGRAM	SYMBOL	NAME OF HEXAGRAM	SOURCE
Hexagram 7.	䷆	010-000	The Army	W/B
			The Army	JB
			An Army*	GW
			The Army	TC
			The Army	KH
			A Troop of Warriors	TY
Hexagram 8.	䷇	000-010	Holding Together (Union)	W/B
			Unity, Co-ordination	JB
			Alliance*	GW
			Accord	TC
			Support	KH
			Emulating	TY
Hexagram 9.	䷈	111-011	The Taming Power of the Small	W/B
			The Lesser Nourisher	JB
			Small is Tamed	GW
			Small Obstruction (Nurturance of the Small)	TC
			Small Cattle	KH
			Small Cultivation of Ch'i	TY
			Small Restraint/ Small Accumulation*[3]	
Hexagram 10.	䷉	110-111	Treading (Conduct)	W/B
			Treading (Conduct)	JB
			Treading*	GW
			Treading	TC
			Treading	KH
			Treading	TY

---

[3] I follow Legge in using "Small Restraint" as the name of Hexagram 9. See [A] Legge (Dover), p. 77. I added the second meaning of "Small Accumulation" to parallel Legge's translation of Hexagram 26. He states that Hexagram 26 has two meanings. "It is the symbol of restraint, and of accumulation." He then goes on to say that its name is "The Great Accumulation." [A] Legge (Dover), p. 113.

Table 1. English Names of the Hexagrams

HEXAGRAM #	HEXAGRAM	SYMBOL	NAME OF HEXAGRAM	SOURCE
Hexagram 11.	䷊	111-000	Peace	W/B
			Peace	JB
			Flowing	GW
			Tranquillity	TC
			Peace	KH
			Intermingling	TY
			Peace/Flowing*	
Hexagram 12.	䷋	000-111	Standstill* (Stagnation)	W/B
			Stagnation, Obstruction	JB
			Blocked	GW
			Obstruction	TC
			Stagnation	KH
			Alienation	TY
Hexagram 13.	䷌	101-111	Fellowship with Men	W/B
			Lovers, etc.[4]	JB
			With Others	GW
			Sameness	TC
			Gathering	KH
			Companions*	TY
Hexagram 14.	䷍	111-101	Possession in Great Measure	W/B
			Great Possessions*	JB
			Great Wealth	GW
			Great Possession	TC
			Great Harvest	KH
			Great Possession	TY
Hexagram 15.	䷎	001-000	Modesty*	W/B
			Modesty	JB
			Modesty	GW
			Humility	TC
			Modesty	KH
			The Emptied	TY

---

[4] Beloved, Friends, Like-Minded Persons, Universal Brotherhood.

Table 1. English Names of the Hexagrams

HEXAGRAM #	HEXAGRAM	SYMBOL	NAME OF HEXAGRAM	SOURCE
Hexagram 16.	䷏	000-100	Enthusiasm	W/B
			Repose	JB
			Contentment*	GW
			Joy	TC
			Weariness	KH
			Elephant Dance[5]	TY
Hexagram 17.	䷐	100-110	Following	W/B
			Following, According with	JB
			The Hunt	GW
			Following	TC
			The Chase*[6]	KH
			Following	TY
Hexagram 18.	䷑	011-001	Work on What Has Been Spoiled (Decay)	W/B
			Decay	JB
			Illness	GW
			Degeneration	TC
			Work	KH
			A Can of Worms	TY
			Illness/Decay *[7]	
Hexagram 19.	䷒	110-000	Approach	W/B
			Approach	JB
			Leadership	GW
			Overseeing	TC
			Prevailing	KH
			On the Threshold	TY
			Authority Approaches*[8]	

---

[5] Yu gives no explanation for this translation. Kunst, who does not translate the names of the hexagrams, does mention elephants three times in the line text. He mentions "trumpeting elephants," "staring elephants," and "an elephant in the darkness," but no "dancing elephants" ([A] Kunst, p. 271). No other English translators that I know of mention elephants in their translation of the text of this Hexagram.

[6] Kunst, who does not translate the names, uses the word "pursuit" in the line text. "The Pursuit" or "Pursuing" are also acceptable names (Kunst, p. 273).

[7] Both illness and decay are given as meanings of the name of this hexagram. It has also been translated as work or business. See [A] Whincup, p. 75 and [A] Huang, *I Ching: The Oracle*, p. 75.

[8] I follow Legge, who says that this Hexagram "denotes the approach of authority—to inspect, to comfort, or to rule" ([A] Legge (Dover), p. 98).

Table 1. English Names of the Hexagrams

HEXAGRAM #	HEXAGRAM	SYMBOL	NAME OF HEXAGRAM	SOURCE
Hexagram 20.	☷☴	000-011	Contemplation (View)	W/B
			Looking Down	JB
			Watching	GW
			Observing*	TC
			View	KH
			Bird's Eye View	TY
Hexagram 21.	☲☳	100-101	Biting Through*	W/B
			Gnawing	JB
			Biting Through	GW
			Biting Through	TC
			Biting	KH
			Teeth Close	TY
Hexagram 22.	☶☲	101-001	Grace	W/B
			Elegance	JB
			Adorned	GW
			Adornment*	TC
			Decoration	KH
			Iridescently Composed	TY
Hexagram 23.	☶☷	000-001	Splitting Apart	W/B
			Peeling Off	JB
			Destruction	GW
			Stripping Away	TC
			Loss	KH
			Fracturing	TY
			Falling*[9]	

---

[9] I follow Legge, who translates the name of this hexagram as "falling or causing to fall" ([A] Legge (Dover), p. 106).

Table 1. English Names of the Hexagrams

HEXAGRAM #	HEXAGRAM	SYMBOL	NAME OF HEXAGRAM	SOURCE
Hexagram 24.	䷗	100-000	Return* (The Turning Point)	W/B
			Return	JB
			Return	GW
			Return	TC
			Return	KH
			Turning Back	TY
Hexagram 25.	䷘	100-111	Innocence (The Unexpected)	W/B
			Integrity, The Unexpected	JB
			No Expectations	GW
			No Error	TC
			Propriety	KH
			Without Expectations	TY
			No Error (No Expectations)*	
Hexagram 26.	䷙	111-001	The Taming Power of the Great	W/B
			The Great Nourisher	JB
			Big is Tamed	GW
			Great Buildup	TC
			Big Cattle[10]	KH
			Great Cultivation of Ch'i	TY
			Big Restraint/ Big Accumulation*[11]	
Hexagram 27.	䷚	100-001	The Corners of the Mouth (Providing Nourishment)	W/B
			Nourishment (literally "Jaws")	JB
			Bulging Cheeks*	GW
			Nourishment	TC
			The Cheeks	KH
			The Jaw	TY

---

[10] Huang gives no explanation for this translation.

[11] Legge points out that the name of this hexagram has two meanings: restraint and accumulation (of virtue). [A] Legge (Dover), p. 113.

Table 1. English Names of the Hexagrams

HEXAGRAM #	HEXAGRAM	SYMBOL	NAME OF HEXAGRAM	SOURCE
Hexagram 28.	䷛	011-110	Preponderance of the Great	W/B
			Excess	JB
			Big Gets By	GW
			The Passing of Greatness	TC
			Great Excess	KH
			Flying Way Above	TY
			Big in Excess*[12]	
Hexagram 29.	䷜	010-010	The Abysmal (Water)	W/B
			The Abyss	JB
			Pits	GW
			Multiple Danger	TC
			Water*	KH
			Testing Wings Over the Chasm	TY
Hexagram 30.	䷝	101-101	The Clinging Fire	W/B
			Flaming Beauty	JB
			Shining Light	GW
			Fire*	TC
			Fire	KH
			The Sun Beast	TY
Hexagram 31.	䷞	001-110	Influence (Wooing)	W/B
			Attraction, Sensation	JB
			Movement	GW
			Sensing[13]	TC
			Cutting	KH
			Stimulation	TY
			Mutual Influence*[14]	

---

[12] See note to recommended name for Hexagram 62.

[13] Concerning the upper and lower trigrams, Cleary writes: "These two are subject and object to one another, sensitively responding to one another; hence the name *sensing*...When there is sensitive response, there must be communication getting through." [A] Cleary, *The Buddhist I Ching*, pp. 128–29. This is close to the recommended name "mutual influence."

[14] Legge states that the meaning of this hexagram is "mutual influence" ([A] Legge (Dover), p. 124).

Table 1. English Names of the Hexagrams

HEXAGRAM #	HEXAGRAM	SYMBOL	NAME OF HEXAGRAM	SOURCE
Hexagram 32.	䷟	011-100	Duration	W/B
			The Long	JB
			Enduring	
			Constancy*	GW
			Constancy	TC
			Steadfastness	KH
			Inner Light	TY
Hexagram 33.	䷠	001-111	Retreat	W/B
			Yielding,	JB
			Withdrawal	
			The Piglet*	GW
			Withdrawal	TC
			The Little Pig	KH
			The Pig	TY
Hexagram 34.	䷡	111-100	The Power of	W/B
			the Great	
			The Power of	JB
			the Great	
			Big Uses Force*	GW
			The Power of	TC
			the Great	
			Great Injury	KH
			Great Force	TY
Hexagram 35.	䷢	000-101	Progress	W/B
			Progress	JB
			Advancement	GW
			Advance*	TC
			Advance	KH
			Rising	TY

Table 1. English Names of the Hexagrams

HEXAGRAM #	HEXAGRAM	SYMBOL	NAME OF HEXAGRAM	SOURCE
Hexagram 36.	䷣	101-000	Darkening of the Light	W/B
			Darkening of the Light, Injury	JB
			The Bright Pheasant	GW
			Damage of Illumination (Concealment of Illumination)	TC
			The Crying Pheasant	KH
			Feigning Bird[15]	TY
			Bright (Calling) Pheasant*[16]	
Hexagram 37.	䷤	101-011	The Family*	W/B
			The Family .	JB
			The Household	GW
			People in the Home	TC
			The Family	KH
			Family Members	TY
Hexagram 38.	䷥	110-101	Opposition	W/B
			The Estranged, Opposition	JB
			Estrangement*	GW
			Opposition	TC
			Abandoned	KH
			Not Eye To Eye	TY
Hexagram 39.	䷦	001-010	Obstruction*	W/B
			Trouble	JB
			Stumbling	GW
			Trouble	TC
			Admonishment	KH
			Stumbling Blocks	TY

---

[15] Yu gives no explanation of what is meant by "feigning bird."

[16] Kunst, who does not translate the names of the hexagrams, uses the expression "calling pheasant" four times in the line text ([A] Kunst, p. 311).

Table 1. English Names of the Hexagrams

HEXAGRAM #	HEXAGRAM	SYMBOL	NAME OF HEXAGRAM	SOURCE
Hexagram 40.	䷧	010-100	Deliverance	W/B
			Release	JB
			Getting Free	GW
			Solution	TC
			Letting Loose	KH
			Cutting Through	TY
			Obstruction Removed*[17]	
Hexagram 41.	䷨	110-001	Decrease*	W/B
			Loss, Reduction	JB
			Reduction	GW
			Reduction	TC
			Decrease	KH
			Taking Away	TY
Hexagram 42.	䷩	100-011	Increase*	W/B
			Gain	JB
			Increase	GW
			Increase	TC
			Increase	KH
			Giving To	TY
Hexagram 43.	䷪	111-110	Break-through (Resoluteness)	W/B
			Resolution	JB
			Flight	GW
			Decision (Parting)	TC
			Stride	KH
			Incisive	TY
			Decisive*[18]	

---

[17] This name indicates with a clearer sense than the others that it is the obstruction in Hexagram 39 that is being removed.

[18] Concerning this Hexagram Cleary states that "action must be decisive" ([A] Cleary, *The Buddhist I Ching*, p. 167). Yu, although he translates the name of this Hexagram as "Incisive," uses the word "decisive" three times in his translation of its commentary ([A] Yu, See commentary on Hexagram 43, no page numbers to the dissertation).

Table 1. English Names of the Hexagrams

HEXAGRAM #	HEXAGRAM	SYMBOL	NAME OF HEXAGRAM	SOURCE
Hexagram 44.	䷫	011-111	Coming to Meet	W/B
			Contact (Sexual Inter-course, Meeting, etc.)	JB
			Subjugated	GW
			Meeting	TC
			Rendezvous	KH
			The Matriarch	TY
			Meeting/Subjugated*	
Hexagram 45.	䷬	000-110	Gathering Together* (Massing)	W/B
			Gathering Together, Assembling	JB
			Gathering Around	GW
			Gathering	TC
			Illness[19]	KH
			Congregating for the Harvest	TY
Hexagram 46.	䷭	011-000	Pushing Upward*	W/B
			Ascending	JB
			Rising	GW
			Rising	TC
			Ascendance	KH
			Ascending	TY
Hexagram 47.	䷮	010-110	Oppression (Exhaustion)	W/B
			Adversity, Weariness	JB
			Burdened[20]	GW
			Exhaustion	TC
			Trapped	KH
			Circumscribed	TY
			Burdened/Exhausted*	

---

[19] Huang offers no explanation for this translation.

[20] Wilhelm/Baynes gives "exhaustion" as the secondary meaning of the hexagram ([A] p. 181, f.n. 1).

Table 1. English Names of the Hexagrams

HEXAGRAM #	HEXAGRAM	SYMBOL	NAME OF HEXAGRAM	SOURCE
Hexagram 48.	䷯	011-010	The Well	W/B
			A Well*	JB
			The Well	GW
			The Well	TC
			The Well	KH
			The Well	TY
Hexagram 49.	䷰	101-110	Revolution* (Molting)	W/B
			Revolution, Leather, Skin	JB
			Revolution	GW
			Change	TC
			Revolution	KH
			Skinning the Hide	TY
Hexagram 50.	䷱	011-101	The Caldron	W/B
			Sacrificial Vessel	JB
			The Ritual Caldron*	GW
			The Cauldron	TC
			The Caldron	KH
			The Cauldron	TY
Hexagram 51.	䷲	100-100	The Arousing (Shock, Thunder)	W/B
			Thunder*	JB
			Thunderbolts	GW
			Thunder	TC
			Thunder	KH
			Shock	TY
Hexagram 52.	䷳	001-001	Keeping Still, Mountain	W/B
			Desisting, Stilling	JB
			Keep Still	GW
			Mountain*	TC
			Mountain	KH
			Concentrating	TY

Table 1. English Names of the Hexagrams

HEXAGRAM #	HEXAGRAM	SYMBOL	NAME OF HEXAGRAM	SOURCE
Hexagram 53.	䷴	001-011	Development (Gradual Progress)	W/B
			Gradual Progress	JB
			Gradual Advance*	GW
			Gradual Progress	TC
			Progress	KH
			Navigating	TY
Hexagram 54.	䷵	110-100	The Marrying Maiden	W/B
			The Marriageable Maiden	JB
			A Maiden Marries*	GW
			Marrying a Young Girl	TC
			The Marrying Maiden	KH
			Young Woman Marries	TY
Hexagram 55.	䷶	101-100	Abundance* (Fullness)	W/B
			Abundance	JB
			Abundance	GW
			Richness	TC
			Abundance	KH
			Bountiful	TY
Hexagram 56.	䷷	001-101	The Wanderer	W/B
			The Traveler*	JB
			The Wanderer	GW
			Travel	TC
			The Traveler	KH
			Travelling	TY
Hexagram 57.	䷸	011-011	The Gentle (The Penetrating, Wind)	W/B
			Willing Submission, Gentleness, Penetration	JB
			Kneeling in Submission	GW
			Wind*	TC
			Wind	KH
			A Waft of Air	TY

Table 1. English Names of the Hexagrams

HEXAGRAM #	HEXAGRAM	SYMBOL	NAME OF HEXAGRAM	SOURCE
Hexagram 58.	☱	110-110	The Joyous, Lake	W/B
			Joy	JB
			Stand Straight	GW
			Delight	TC
			Lake*	KH
			Opens Up	TY
Hexagram 59.	☴	010-011	Dispersion (Dissolution)	W/B
			Scattering	JB
			The Flood[21]	GW
			Dispersal	TC
			Flowing	KH
			Diffusing	TY
			Flood/Dispersion*	
Hexagram 60.	☵	110-010	Limitation	W/B
			Restraint	JB
			Restraint	GW
			Regulation	TC
			Frugality	KH
			Balance	TY
			Restraint (Regulations)*[22]	
Hexagram 61.	☴	110-011	Inner Truth	W/B
			Inward Confidence and Sincerity	JB
			Wholehearted Allegiance	GW
			Sincerity of the Center	TC
			Sincerity*	KH
			Centering Nurtured Integrity	TY
			Inmost Sincerity (Allegiance)*	

---

[21] Whincup also gives "disperse" as another meaning of this hexagram ([A] Whincup, p. 193).

[22] Legge points out that the name of this hexagram contains the ideas of "regulating and restraining" ([A] Legge (Dover), p. 198).

Table 1. English Names of the Hexagrams

HEXAGRAM #	HEXAGRAM	SYMBOL	NAME OF HEXAGRAM	SOURCE
Hexagram 62.	䷽	001-100	Preponderance of the Small	W/B
			The Small Get By	JB
			Small Gets By	GW
			Small Excess	TC
			Small Excess	KH
			Flying Just Above	TY
			Small in Excess*[23]	
Hexagram 63.	䷾	101-010	After Completion[24]	W/B
			After Completion	JB
			Already Across	GW
			Settled	TC
			Fulfillment	KH
			Having Crossed the River	TY
			Already Across the River*[25]	
Hexagram 64.	䷿	010-101	Before Completion*	W/B
			Before Completion	JB
			Not Yet Across	GW
			Unsettled	TC
			Unfulfillment	KH
			Having Not Crossed the River	TY
			Not Yet Across the River*[26]	

[23] Legge states that the name means "small excesses" or "exceeding in what is small" ([A] Legge (Dover), p. 203). The name recommended "Small in Excess" is very close to Cleary's "Small Excess." The name recommended for Hexagram 28, "Big in Excess" parallels the recommended name of Hexagram 62.

[24] Legge interprets this hexagram to mean that a **successful** completion has taken place ([A] Legge (Dover), p. 206). The expression "After Fulfillment" seems to convey this idea better than "After Completion," since what is complete is not always what is successful. The recommended name "Already Across the River" conveys the idea of a *successful* completion.

[25] More complete than Whincup's name, in that the recommended name indicates that a *dangerous* undertaking is completed.

[26] More complete than Whincup's name.

Table 2. Recommended English Names for the Hexagrams

1. Heaven	33. The Piglet
2. Earth	34. Big Uses Force
3. Sprouting	35. Advance
4. The Young Shoot	36. The Bright (Calling) Pheasant
5. Getting Wet	37. The Family
6. Grievance	38. Estrangement
7. An Army	39. Obstruction
8. Alliance	40. Obstruction Removed
9. Small Restraint/Small Accumulation	41. Decrease
10. Treading	42. Increase
11. Peace/Flowing	43. Decisive
12. Standstill	44. Meeting/Subjugated
13. Companions	45. Gathering Together
14. Great Possessions	46. Pushing Upward
15. Modesty	47. Burdened/Exhausted
16. Contentment	48. A Well
17. The Chase	49. Revolution
18. Illness/Decay	50. The Ritual Caldron
19. Authority Approaches	51. Thunder
20. Observing	52. Mountain
21. Biting Through	53. Gradual Advance
22. Adornment	54. A Maiden Marries
23. Falling	55. Abundance
24. Return	56. The Traveler
25. No Error (No Expectations)	57. Wind
26. Big Restraint/Big Accumulation	58. Lake
27. Bulging Cheeks	59. Flood/Dispersion
28. Big in Excess	60. Restraint (Regulations)
29. Water	61. Inmost Sincerity (Allegiance)
30. Fire	62. Small in Excess
31. Mutual Influence	63. Already Across the River
32. Constancy	64. Not Yet Across the River

The guidelines used in selecting the recommended names of the hexagrams were:

Guideline 1: Natural image names were used whenever possible. For example, Hexagram 52 has for both its primary trigrams, Trigram 7, *Mountain.* Associated with the image of mountain are the properties of stubbornness, immovability, keeping still, and so forth. No associative property of the image was used as the Hexagram's name. It was simply called *Mountain.* To select one associative property of *Mountain* as the name of Hexagram 52 is to limit the metaphor unnecessarily and arbitrarily.

Thus Hexagrams 1, 2, 29, 30, 51, 52, 57, and 58, which are formed by doubling the eight trigrams, are named after these trigrams: *Heaven, Earth, Water, Fire, Thunder, Mountain, Wind,* and *Lake.*[27]

Also *Sprouting* and *The Young Shoot* were preferred for Hexagrams 3 and 4 over such names as *Difficulty at the Beginning* and *Youthful Folly* because they are natural images and less abstract than the latter.

Guideline 2: Names were selected to reflect the polarity relationships that exist between odd-numbered hexagrams and their even-numbered successors. The hypothesis was made that there is polarity between these hexagrams. In some cases this polarity is obvious, as in Hexagram 1 and 2, *Heaven* and *Earth,* and in Hexagrams 41 and 42, *Decrease* and *Increase.* In other cases this polarity is not obvious. Therefore, whenever possible, names were picked which indicated a polarity. For example, in Hexagrams 11 and 12 no polarity would be revealed by naming Hexagram 11, *Peace,* and Hexagram 12, *Standstill.* But by naming Hexagram 11, *Peace/Flowing,* the contrast with Hexagram 12 was made clear. Hexagram 11 symbolizes a smooth harmonious motion in a certain direction while Hexagram 12 symbolizes no motion.

Guideline 3: If possible parallelism between names should be as complete as possible. For example, Legge states that Hexagram 26 is the symbol of restraint and accumulation. He also states, "What is repressed and restrained accumulates its strength and increases its volume."[28] Legge translates the name of Hexagram 25 as *The Great Accumulation.*[29] Since other translators emphasize the meaning of restraint, the name recommended for Hexagram 26 was *Big Restraint/Big Accumulation.* Legge also states that the name of Hexagram 9 means *Small Restraint.*[30] However, if a big restraint leads to a big accumulation then a small restraint leads to a small accumulation and by analogy the name of Hexagram 9 should be *Small Restraint/Small Accumulation.*

Guideline 4: The name should convey as much information as possible while being neither too broad nor too narrow in denotation. For example, I

---

[27] Here I follow [A] Kerson Huang, *I Ching: The Oracle.*

[28] [A] Legge (Dover), p. 113.

[29] [A] Legge (Dover), p. 113.

[30] [A] Legge (Dover), p. 77.

find Cleary's name *Sensing* for Hexagram 31, *Mutual Influence,* much too broad as I do Whincup's name *Movement.* Cleary does explain the meaning of the Hexagram in a way that is compatible with the Wilhelm/Baynes and Blofeld translations (see note to Cleary's name for Hexagram 31 above.). But one has no hint of this meaning from the name *Sensing.* Whincup's name *Movement* also gives no clue as to the specific meaning of the Hexagram.

Guideline 5: A name was not recommended if it deviated from majority opinion and no argument was given for the deviation. For example, Yu gives *Elephant Dance* as the name of Hexagram 16 but gives no evidence or explanation for his translation. Hence, his name was not considered. Another example is Huang's *Small Cattle* and *Big Cattle* for Hexagrams 9 and 26. Huang gave no justification for these translations, which deviate from the standard translations.

Guideline 6: Names that deviate from the Legge, Blofeld or Wilhelm/Baynes translations were accepted if justification was given for the deviation. For example, Wilhelm/Baynes translates the name of Hexagram 33 as *Retreat.* Blofeld translates it as *Yielding.* But more recently (1983) Yu translates it as *Pig.* Huang in 1984 translates it as *The Little Pig.*[31] Whincup, in 1986, called it *The Piglet.* Whincup attributed his translation to the Chinese scholar Heng Gao.[32] The recommended name for Hexagram 33, following Whincup, is *The Piglet.*

For Hexagram 5, Wilhelm/Baynes translates its name as *Waiting,* Blofeld as *Calculated Inaction.* However, Whincup translates it as *Getting Wet* and Kunst, in his impressive dissertation (1985), uses the expression *It gets wet* five times in the line text for this Hexagram.[33] Whincup gives a note justifying his translation,[34] so I recommended Whincup's translation *Getting Wet.*

Hexagram 36, translated as the *Darkening of the Light* by Wilhelm/Baynes and *Intelligence Wounded* by Legge, has been translated as *Feigning Bird* by Yu, *Crying Pheasant* by Huang, and *The Bright Pheasant* by Whincup.[35] In the line text Kunst uses the expression *Calling Pheasant.* Yu's *Feigning Bird* is not at all clear and he gives no explanation for his translation. That a bird is being referred to makes sense in the context of the hexagram, as the text for the

---

[31] In private correspondence with the author, Professor Huang stated that Gao was one of his sources for his translations. As far as I know Professor Huang's book *I Ching, The Oracle* was the first popular text to make use of recent Chinese scholarship in this area.

[32] The source referred to by Whincup—Chinese symbols omitted—is Gao Heng, *Zhou Yi gujing jinzhu.* Shanghai: Kaiming Shudian (1947) ([A] Whincup, p. 236).

[33] [A] Kunst, p. 249.

[34] Whincup states that in ancient times the word for "wait" and "get wet" were written in the same way. His translation is based on the hexagram's context and structure ([A] Whincup, p. 38).

[35] Whincup, following Gao Heng, a contemporary scholar, gives a brief explanation of how the Chinese character for "wounded" could have been confused with the similar character for "pheasant" ([A] Whincup, p. 127).

first line mentions lowering of a wing during flight, and the text for the other lines mention wounds. Therefore, *Bright (Calling) Pheasant* was recommended.

5

CLASSIFYING
THE HEXAGRAMS

45. Gathering Together

Few western writers on the *I Ching* attempt to classify the hexagrams. A notable exception is Needham, who groups all but thirteen of the hexagrams under the categories of space, time, and motion.[1]

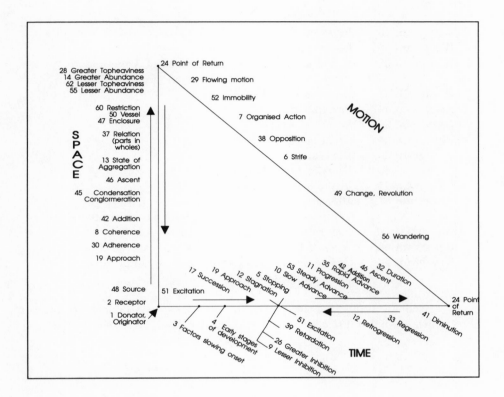

Figure 1.
Needham's Classification of the Hexagrams

---

[1] [A] Needham, vol. 2, p. 324.

The thirteen hexagrams not categorized in the above diagram are (the names and comments given are those of Needham):

Table 1

Hexagram 15.	*Highness in Lowness.*
Hexagram 16.	*Inspiration.*
Hexagram 30.	*Deflagration* (with the undertone of Adhesion, which might justify it for insertion on the diagram).
Hexagram 31.	*Reaction, interweaving.*
Hexagram 44.	*Reaction, fusion.*
Hexagram 54.	*Reaction, union.*
Hexagram 34.	*Great power.*
Hexagram 36.	*Darkening.*
Hexagram 43.	*Decisive breakthrough.*
Hexagram 21.	*Biting or burning through.*
Hexagram 57.	*Mild penetration* (as of airs and winds). Compare number 53, which may have a similar sense with reference to aqueous penetration.
Hexagram 58.	*Serenity* (with the undertone of a calm sea).
Hexagram 22.	*Ornament, pattern* (which could be applied to animal and plant pattern).

Needham states that these thirteen hexagrams "may be said to represent ideas which are naturalistic but not spatio-temporal." [2]

---

[2] [A] Needham, vol. 2, p. 323.

Needham also gives the following table classifying the hexagrams by categories:[3]

Table 2

			Number of *kua* in each category
Donator			1
Receptor and origin			2
Temporal	Duration	1	
	Forward motion	10	
	Stationary	2	
	Backward motion	3	
		16	16
Inhibition and retardation			4
Point of return			1
Spatial	Aggregating	6	
	Stationary	9	
	Disaggregating	6	
		21	21
Concepts involving motion		6	
Concept of immobility		1	
		7	
Naturalistic but not spatio-temporal			13
Truth and Order			3
Irreducibly human			3
			71

Needham's classification is interesting, but is, as he admits, incomplete, since thirteen hexagrams are left unclassified. It is also a classification scheme that seems to be borrowed from physics, as the categories of space, time, and motion are basic concepts of Western mechanistic science.

The following classification scheme captures all sixty-four of the hexagrams in eight categories, eight hexagrams in each category, with a minimum of procrustean interpretation of the hexagrams.

---

[3] [A] Needham, vol. 2, p. 325.

Table 3. An Eightfold Classification of the Hexagrams

I. GROUPS	II. RELATIONSHIPS
7. An Army	3. Sprouting
8. Alliance	4. The Young Shoot
13. Companions	6. Grievance
31. Mutual Influence	21. Biting Through
32. Constancy	38. Estrangement
37. The Family	49. Revolution
45. Gathering Together	54. A Maiden Marries
48. A Well	56. The Traveler
III. SMALL ADVANCING	**IV. BIG ADVANCING**
10. Treading	24. Return
18. Illness/Decay	35. Advance
23. Falling	40. Obstruction Removed
33. The Piglet	42. Increase
36. The Bright (Calling) Pheasant	43. Decisive
44. Meeting/Subjugated	46. Pushing Upwards
47. Burdened/Exhausted	51. Thunder
62. Small in Excess	53. Gradual Advance
V. OBSTACLES & LIMITATIONS	**VI. BIG IN POWER**
5. Getting Wet	14. Great Possessions
9. Small Restraint/Small Accumulation	16. Contentment
26. Big Restraint/Big Accumulation	17. The Chase
27. Bulging Cheeks	19. Authority Approaches
29. Water	20. Observing
39. Obstruction	28. Big in Excess
41. Decrease	34. Big Uses Force
60. Restraint (Regulations)	55. Abundance
VII. PROPER CONDUCT	**VIII. COSMIC & SOCIAL**
15. Modesty	1. Heaven
25. No Error (No Expectations)	2. Earth
30. Fire	11. Peace/Flowing
52. Mountain	12. Standstill
57. Wind	22. Adornment
58. Lake	50. The Ritual Caldron
59. Flood/Dispersion	63. Already Across the River
61. Inmost Sincerity (Allegiance)	64. Not Yet Across the River

I. GROUPS. All of the hexagrams in this group refer to social, political and/or physical factors that result in the formation of a group (i.e. a body of people, such as an Army, a Family, an Alliance, etc.). Hexagram 48, *A Well,* refers to a group in the sense that a well is located in the center of a town and the well, which is necessary for the town's people, is the joint property of all of its inhabitants. The well provides water, which is necessary for all the people in the town. The well makes the existence of the town possible.

II. RELATIONSHIP PROBLEMS. In this category the hexagrams refer to specific types of relationship problems. These problems may occur between individuals, individuals and groups, or between groups. The names of the hexagrams in this group are indicative of the type of problem involved, except for Hexagram 54, *A Maiden Marries,* and Hexagram 56, *The Traveler.* One of the interpretations of Hexagram 54, *A Maiden Marries,* is that a young girl initiates the marriage, a violation of propriety. She is too forceful in seeking the marriage. Also there is too great a discrepancy in the ages of the bride and bridegroom. More generally speaking, the lowly should not boldly and forcefully seek an alliance with the high. To do so results in difficulties. Hexagram 56, *The Traveler,* may be interpreted to mean the problems that a stranger may have in relating to groups. Hexagram 56 advises such travelers (strangers) to have humility and integrity.

III. SMALL ADVANCING. All of the hexagrams in this category refer to the small (the weak, the inferior man) coming into power. In Hexagram 10, *Treading,* the small treads upon "the tail of the tiger." In Hexagram 44, *Meeting/Subjugated,* the Small is starting to intrude upon the Big, and unless checked the Small will grow in power. The judgment and/or the line text of the other hexagrams in this group clearly refer to the advance of the Small and the retreat of the Big.

IV. BIG ADVANCING. The names of the hexagrams in this category refer to the increasing power of the Big, except for Hexagram 40, *Obstruction Removed,* and Hexagram 43, *Decisive.* Hexagram 40, *Obstruction Removed,* can be interpreted to mean that a return to normalcy is now possible since the difficulty has now been removed. Hexagram 43, *Decisive,* gives the advice that the Small in power are not to be removed by force of arms but by force of character. In this way the Big (the superior) may overcome the Small (the inferior).

V. OBSTACLES AND LIMITATIONS. All the names in this group, except Hexagrams 5, *Getting Wet,* 27, *Bulging Cheeks,* and 41, *Decrease,* explicitly denote an obstacle or limitation. Hexagram 5, *Getting Wet,* may be interpreted to mean a person who is facing a danger so great that he cannot advance. Now is the time to wait even though it may be uncomfortable to do so. Hexagram 27, *Bulging Cheeks,* may indicate limitation in that all beings need nourishment and are all constrained by this need. Whincup interprets this hexagram as giving the advice that by staying where one is one will be safe and gain nourishment.[4] Hexagram 41, *Decrease,* may refer to decrease in wealth, power, or rank;[5] hence, a limitation.

VI. BIG IN POWER. An alternative name for this category might well be "Advice to the Big in Power." The names of Hexagrams 16, *Contentment,* 17, *The Chase,* and 20, *Observing,* do not identify them as obvious members of this category. However Hexagram 16, *Contentment,* may be interpreted as meaning a time of contentment (or enthusiasm) when it is favorable to make progress (to set armies marching). Hexagram 17, *The Chase,* according to Wilhelm/Baynes[6] gives advice to both leaders and followers regarding the proper relations between these two groups and the timing for forming such relationships. Whincup translates the name of Hexagram 17 as *The Hunt.* He comments on the Judgment by saying "He goes out after what he wants and gets it."[7] This interpretation also justifies the hexagram's inclusion in this category. Hexagram 20, *Observing* means, according to Legge, "the sovereign and his subjects, how he manifests himself to them, and how they contemplate him."[8] The sovereign should appear to be sincere and dignified. He should be a good example to his subjects.

VII. PROPER CONDUCT. Under this category are listed the hexagrams that deal with virtues and conduct. By "conduct" is meant not overt behavior, but proper inner attitude. Hexagram 15, *Modesty,* clearly belongs to this category. The following hexagrams need some explanation to justify their membership in this category. Hexagram 25, *No Error (No Expectations),* according to Legge, has as its subject "one who is entirely simple and sincere."[9] Wilhelm/Baynes gives "Innocence" as the name of this Hexagram. Whincup gives as part of his meaning of this Hexagram "To have no expectations is supremely blessed."[10] Hexagram 30, *Fire,* according to Legge, means "adhering closely to what is correct, he must be able to act in obedience to it, as docile as a cow, and then there will be good fortune."[11] Regarding Hexagram 59, *Flood/Dispersion,* Wilhelm/Baynes states, "Here the subject is the dispersing and dissolving of divisive egotism. DISPERSION shows the way, so to speak, that leads to gath-

---

[4] [A] Whincup, p. 99.

[5] [A] Legge/Dover, p. 148 and [A] Wilhelm/Baynes, p. 158, interpret decrease to mean a decrease in the wealth or prosperity of the people. Whincup interprets this Hexagram to mean a self-reduction in rank ([A] Whincup, p. 140). Both interpretations may be regarded as a limitation.

[6] [A] Wilhelm/Baynes, p. 72.

[7] [A] Whincup, p. 70.

[8] [A] Legge/Dover, p. 100.

[9] [A] Legge/Dover, p. 111.

[10] [A] Whincup, p. 93.

[11] [A] Legge/Dover, p. 121-22.

ering together." [12] Legge writes, "It [Hexagram 59] is descriptive primarily of men's minds alienated from what is right and good. This alienation is sure to go on to disorder in the commonwealth; and an attempt is made to show how it should be dealt with and remedied." [13] Hua Ching Ni says, "If one is guided by clarity and calm, one can successfully avert or correct problems and handle the aftermath of dispersion." [14]

VIII. COSMIC AND SOCIAL CONCEPTS. Of the eight hexagrams in this category, six of them signify basic cosmic forces and transitions. Hexagram 1, *Heaven,* and Hexagram 2, *Earth,* are the two primary forces (states) of the cosmos. The extremes of the relations between Hexagram 1 and 2 are captured by the meanings of Hexagrams 11 and 12. Hexagram 11, *Peace/Flowing,* is described in part by Wilhelm/Baynes, who state, "This Hexagram denotes a time in nature when heaven seems to be on earth...their powers unite in deep harmony." [15] Hexagram 12, *Standstill,* called "Stagnation" by Wilhelm/Baynes, is the opposite of Hexagram 11. Hexagram 12, *Standstill,* is a time when "The creative powers are not in relation. It is a time of standstill and decline." [16] Hexagrams 63 and 64 represent transitions between Hexagrams 11 and 12. Hexagram 63, *Already Across the River,* "is the evolution of T'ai, PEACE (11)." [17] This evolution ends with Hexagram 12. The Hexagram 64, *Not Yet Across the River,* "depicts the transition from P'i, STANDSTILL (12) to T'ai, PEACE (11)." [18]

Hence, in this eighth classification the two primary forces of creation are given (Hexagrams 1 and 2). The two states depicting their extremes in relationships are shown by Hexagrams 11 and 12. In Hexagram 11 these two forces are in harmony; in Hexagram 12, they are in disharmony. The two major transitions between these states are shown by Hexagrams 63 and 64. Hexagram 63 signifies the transition from harmony to disharmony; Hexagram 64, disharmony to harmony.

Hexagram 50, *The Ritual Caldron,* refers, so Whincup says, to "the establishment of a new ruling regime." [19] Wilhelm/Baynes say that "Ting (the name of the Hexagram) shows the correct way of going about social reorganization." [20] Hexagram 50 may be looked upon as the Hexagram which signifies how cosmic forces are to be correctly expressed in culture and society. It is through the proper rituals that man receives cosmic guidance.

---

[12] [A] Wilhelm/Baynes, p. 227.

[13] [A] Legge (Dover), p. 196.

[14] [A] Ni, p. 611.

[15] [A] Wilhelm/Baynes, p. 48.

[16] [A] Wilhelm/Baynes, p. 52.

[17] [A] Wilhelm/Baynes, p. 244.

[18] [A] Wilhelm/Baynes, p. 714.

[19] [A] Whincup, p. 165.

[20] [A] Wilhelm/Baynes, p. 641.

Regarding Hexagram 22, *Adornment,* Wilhelm/Baynes say, "Grace—beauty of form—is necessary in any union if it is to be well ordered and pleasing rather than disordered and chaotic";[21] whereas, Hexagram 50, *The Ritual Caldron,* refers to the spiritual component of the rituals that is necessary for a cohesive, harmonious culture, and Hexagram 22, *Adornment,* refers to the aesthetic component that accompanies such rituals. This aesthetic component is not as important as the spiritual one. It is form rather than substance, but nevertheless it serves the function of making substance attractive. Traditions and rituals that are both beautiful and spiritually meaningful, as well as long lasting, are the very structure and substance of culture.

Hexagram 22, *Adornment,* does have cosmic meaning. Wilhelm/Baynes say that Hexagram 22 represents the "form of heaven" by its primary and nuclear trigrams. Its lower primary trigram represents the sun, its lower nuclear trigram the moon, its upper nuclear trigram the Great Bear, a constellation of stars, and its upper primary trigram the other constellations.[22]

---

21 [A] Wilhelm/Baynes, p. 90.
22 [A] Wilhelm/Baynes, p. 496.

6

NUCLEAR TRIGRAMS
AND HEXAGRAMS

61. Inmost Sincerity

Primary Trigrams. Any three successive lines of a hexagram form a trigram. A trigram may be formed from the lines in positions 1, 2 and 3, by the lines in positions 2, 3 and 4, by the lines in positions 3, 4 and 5, and finally by the lines in positions 4, 5 and 6.

The trigram formed by the first three lines of a hexagram (lines 1, 2 and 3) is called its **lower primary trigram** and the trigram formed by the last three lines (lines 4, 5, and 6) is called its **upper primary trigram**. For example, Hexagram 25, ☰ 100-111, *No Error (No Expectations)*, has Trigram 3, ☳ 100, *Thunder,* as its lower primary trigram and Trigram 1, ☰ 111, *Heaven,* as its upper primary trigram:

Hexagram 25,	1	0	0	1	1	1	*No Error*
Line Positions:	1	2	3	4	5	6	*(No Expectations)*
Lower Primary Trigram							
of Hexagram 25,	1	0	0				*Thunder*
Line Positions:	1	2	3				
Upper Primary Trigram							
of Hexagram 25,				1	1	1	*Heaven*
Line Positions:				4	5	6	

Nuclear Trigrams.[1] The trigram formed by the lines in line positions 2, 3 and 4 of a hexagram is called its **lower nuclear trigram** and the trigram formed by the lines in positions 3, 4, and 5 of a hexagram is called its **upper nuclear trigram**. Lines 1 and 6 are not used to derive nuclear trigrams. For example:

Hexagram 25,	1	0	0	1	1	1	*No Error*
Line Positions:	1	2	3	4	5	6	*(No Expectations)*
Lower Nuclear Trigram		0	0	1			*Mountain*
Line Positions in Hexagram 25:		2	3	4			
Upper Nuclear Trigram			0	1	1		*Wind*
Line Positions in Hexagram 25:			3	4	5		

---

[1] The first person known to have discovered nuclear trigrams is Ching Fang (77–37 B.C.). See [A] White, pp. 16–17.

In the Wilhelm/Baynes *I Ching* the importance and definition of the nuclear trigrams is stated:

> ... it is decidedly necessary (for an understanding of the hexagrams) to make use of the so-called nuclear trigrams, *hu kua*... These form the four middle lines of each hexagram, and overlap each other so that the middle line of the one falls within the other (p. 358).

The Wilhelm/Baynes edition does not give any instructions on how to use the nuclear trigrams to understand the hexagrams. However, in the *Commentaries* the nuclear trigrams for each hexagram are given and Wilhelm, in most cases, mentions the nuclear trigrams in his analysis of the *Commentary on the Decisions*.

Nuclear Hexagrams. The **primary nuclear hexagram** (or simply **nuclear hexagram**) is formed from a hexagram by placing its **upper nuclear trigram** over its **lower nuclear trigram**. In other words, the lines in positions 2, 3, 4, 3, 4, 5 of a hexagram form the lines of its nuclear hexagram.

For example, the nuclear hexagram of Hexagram 25, 100-111, *No Error* (*No Expectations*), is Hexagram 53, 001-011, *Gradual Advance*.

Hexagram 25,	1	0	0	1	1	1	*No Error*
Line Positions:	1	2	3	4	5	6	(*No Expectations*)
Nuclear Hexagram of 25							
is Hexagram 53	0	0	1	0	1	1	*Gradual Advance*
Line Positions from 25:	2	3	4	3	4	5	

It should be noted that the lines in the first and sixth line positions of a hexagram are not used to form its primary nuclear hexagram.

Nuclear hexagrams are not mentioned by name in Wilhelm/Baynes, but one is referred to in Book III, *Commentaries*. With regard to Hexagram 13, 101-111, *Fellowship with Men*,[2] Wilhelm/Baynes writes:

> The movement of both primary trigrams is upward, hence parallel. In the same way the two nuclear trigrams, Ch'ien and Sun, which together form the hexagram of COMING TO MEET (44), indicate fellowship.[3]

No mention of nuclear hexagrams appears in Blofeld, Whincup, Ni, Cleary, Z. D. Sung, or Legge. Nuclear hexagrams are discussed by Sherrill and Chu, Charles Poncé, and Diana ffarington Hook. Sherrill and Chu, and Poncé give no source

---

[2] [A] Wilhelm/Baynes' name.

[3] [A] Wilhelm/Baynes, p. 451. [A] Hook refers to this passage in her book, *The I Ching and You*, p. 75.

for their concept of nuclear hexagrams. Hook gives a reference to the Wilhelm/Baynes source, quoted above.

Sherrill and Chu state:

> We must remember that ancient symbolism was used and still exists in the basic text of the *I Ching*. This next step... illustrates this quite clearly. We now come to the inner hexagram, that is, the hexagram within the hexagram under consideration. The inner hexagram is that hexagram made up of the two nuclear trigrams (lines 2, 3 and 4; and lines 3, 4 and 5)... The inner hexagram plays a part in the overall view of a given situation.[4]

Charles Poncé states that each hexagram has five nuclear hexagrams. According to Poncé, the five other nuclear hexagrams of Hexagram 26, 111-001, *Big Restraint/Big Accumulation,* would be:

First (Primary) Nuclear Hexagram 54	1	1	0	1	0	0	*A Maiden Marries*
Line Positions from 26:	2	3	4	3	4	5	
Second (Lower) Nuclear Hexagram 43	1	1	1	1	1	0	*Decisive*
Line Positions from 26:	1	2	3	2	3	4	
Third (Upper) Nuclear Hexagram 27	1	0	0	0	0	1	*Bulging Cheeks*
Line Positions from 26:	3	4	5	4	5	6	
Fourth Nuclear Hexagram 34	1	1	1	1	0	0	*Big Uses Force*
Line Positions from 26:	1	2	3	3	4	5	
Fifth Nuclear Hexagram 41	1	1	0	0	0	1	*Decrease*
Line Positions from 26:	2	3	4	4	5	6	

The five varieties of nuclear hexagrams of Hexagram 26 are:

First Nuclear Hexagram 54	110-100		*A Maiden Marries*
Second Nuclear Hexagram 43	111-110		*Decisive*
Third Nuclear Hexagram 27	100-001		*Bulging Cheeks*
Fourth Nuclear Hexagram 34	111-100		*Big Uses Force*
Fifth Nuclear Hexagram 41	110-001		*Decrease*

A hexagram's lower nuclear trigram over its lower primary trigram forms its **second (lower) nuclear hexagram**. A hexagram's upper primary trigram over its upper nuclear trigram forms its **third (upper) nuclear hexagram**. A hexagram's upper nuclear trigram over its lower primary trigram forms its

---

[4] [A] Sherrill and Chu, *An Anthology of I Ching,* pp. 33–34.

fourth nuclear hexagram. A hexagram's upper primary trigram over its lower nuclear trigram forms its **fifth nuclear hexagram**.

Poncé claims that the first, second, and third nuclear hexagrams are the most important of five nuclear hexagrams. He writes:

> The reason these three nuclear hexagrams are of greater importance than the two yet to be discussed [the fourth and fifth nuclear hexagrams] is that in each of the three either the first or last line occupies the second or fifth place of the primary hexagram... The other two nuclear hexagrams, it will be found, rarely shed as much light as the first three.[5]

This paragraph causes some confusion as neither the second nor third nuclear hexagram has a first or last line that is the second or fifth line of the primary hexagram. The fourth and fifth nuclear hexagrams do have such lines.

Poncé uses these five nuclear hexagrams to analyze a hexagram's meaning. The five nuclear hexagrams yield information concerning the primary hexagram. Poncé states:

> The nuclear hexagrams often reveal either the cause of the "time" of the hexagrams, or the factors actively influencing that time. The safest rule of thumb is to view the nuclear hexagram as one of the "causes" of the primary hexagram's condition.[6]

But Poncé warns:

> On one day the information of a nuclear hexagram might be of particular significance, while on another the same nuclear hexagram, contained in the same primary hexagram, might be absolutely empty of meaning. All this depends on the question asked at the particular time.[7]

Diana ffarington Hook also believes that a nuclear hexagram is of value in interpreting its primary hexagram.[8] She develops the interesting and fruitful idea of repeatedly taking the nuclear hexagram of a nuclear hexagram. When this is done for each of the sixty-four hexagrams, Hook found that "each one finally merges into either hexagram 1, 2, 63 or 64, which explains why these four hexagrams are placed at the beginning and ending of the (textual) series." [9]Hook writes:

---

[5] [A] Poncé, pp. 37–38.

[6] [A] Poncé, p. 35.

[7] [A] Poncé, p. 39.

[8] [A] Hook, *The I Ching and You*, p. 75.

[9] [A] Hook, *The I Ching and You*, p. 77.

Thus we have every hexagram linked either with creation (Hexagram 1), reception (Hexagram 2), perfection (Hexagram 63) or transition (Hexagram 64)... The reasons for this are, first, that mathematically these four hexagrams are the only combinations which will appear at the end of such re-arrangements of the nuclear trigrams; and, second, that in heaven (Hexagram 1) and on the earth (Hexagram 2), the change of phenomena is always from transition (Hexagram 64) to climax (Hexagram 63) and from climax to transition.[10]

For example, the nuclear hexagram of Hexagram 56, 001-101, *The Traveler,* is Hexagram 28, 011-110, *Big in Excess,* and the nuclear hexagram of Hexagram 28, 011-110, *Big in Excess,* is Hexagram 1, 111-111. Another example, the nuclear hexagram of Hexagram 18, 011-001, *Illness/Decay,* is Hexagram 54, 110-100, *A Maiden Marries,* and the nuclear hexagram of Hexagram 54, *A Maiden Marries,* is Hexagram 63, 101-010, *Already Across the River.* Hook is correct; by successively taking the nuclear hexagram of a hexagram the result is always Hexagram 1, 2, 63, or 64. Hook points out that those hexagrams that result in Hexagram 63 or Hexagram 64 "oscillate back and forth between these two forever." [11] This is because the nuclear hexagram of Hexagram 63 is Hexagram 64 and the nuclear hexagram of Hexagram 64 is Hexagram 63.

Although Hook, Poncé, Sherrill and Chu mention the concept of a nuclear hexagram, none of them uses the concept to classify the hexagrams by the nuclear hexagrams they have in common. The rest of this chapter will present such a classification.[12]

Non-Nuclear Hexagrams. A **non-nuclear** hexagram is a hexagram that cannot be the (primary) nuclear hexagram of any hexagram. A (primary) nuclear hexagram is formed from the lines in line positions 2, 3, 4, 3, 4, 5 of the parent hexagram. Hence a nuclear hexagram must have the same kind of line in line positions 2 and 4 and the same kind of line in line positions 3 and 5.

Line Positions of Hexagram:	1	2	3	4	5	6
Rearrangement of Lines in Nuclear Hexagram:	2	3	4	3	4	5

If a hexagram does not meet this condition, that is, if it has different lines in positions 2 and 4 or in positions 3 and 5, then it cannot be the nuclear hexagram of any hexagram and it is a non-nuclear hexagram. An example of a non-nuclear hexagram is Hexagram 14, 111-101, *Great Possessions.* Hexagram 14 is non-nuclear because it has different lines in positions 3 and 5. A non-nuclear hexagram, like any other hexagram, has a nuclear hexagram, but it cannot be

---

[10] [A] Hook, *The I Ching and You,* p. 77.

[11] [A] Hook, *The I Ching and You,* p. 77.

[12] The following classification of hexagrams and accompanying terminology originates— as far as is known—with the author.

a nuclear hexagram. There are forty-eight non-nuclear hexagrams. See Figures 1–4.[13]

Intermediate and Basic Nuclear Hexagrams.[14] An **intermediate** nuclear hexagram is a hexagram of a non-nuclear hexagram. There are twelve different intermediate nuclear hexagrams. Each intermediate hexagram is the nuclear hexagram of four non-nuclear hexagrams. See Figures 1–4.

A **basic** nuclear hexagram is a nuclear hexagram of an intermediate nuclear hexagram. There are only four basic nuclear hexagrams: Hexagram 1, 111-111, *Heaven;* Hexagram 2, 000-000, *Earth;* Hexagram 63, 101-010, *Already Across the River;* and Hexagram 64, 010-101, *Not Yet Across the River.* The nuclear hexagrams of Hexagrams 1 and 2 are themselves. The nuclear Hexagrams of 63 and 64 are each other.

Each basic nuclear hexagram is the nuclear hexagram of three intermediate nuclear hexagrams. Hence there are four groups of intermediate nuclear hexagrams. See Figures 1–4. It can be expected that the three intermediate hexagrams in each group, because they have a nuclear hexagram in common, might also have some meaning in common. These four groups of intermediate nuclear hexagrams and some of the possible meanings that the hexagrams in each group have in common will be explored below.

Hexagram 1, Heavenly Action Group.[15] (See Figure 1.) This group is composed of Hexagrams 28, 43, and 44. These three hexagrams have Hexagram 1 as their nuclear hexagram.

Hexagram 28	☰	011-110	*Big in Excess*
Hexagram 43	☰	111-110	*Decisive*
Hexagram 44	☰	011-111	*Meeting/Subjugated*

The meaning that these hexagrams have in common is that peaceful action is necessary for the Big (or Great) to maintain its purity (i.e., its freedom from corruption). Hexagram 28 warns of an unstable situation and advises that non-forceful action be taken as quickly as possible. Hexagram 43 advises that decisive action must be taken against an inferior man who is in power, but that this action must arise not out of hatred or be conducted by force; our motives must be pure. Hexagram 44 warns the Big (or the Great) not to tolerate the encroachment of inferiors; otherwise inferiors will gain power.

On the cosmic level Hexagram 43 represents the state just before the last yin line is expelled; the next state is Hexagram 1, all yang lines. In Hexagram 44, which represents the state just after Hexagram 1, the yin returns. The return of the yin in Hexagram 44 also signifies the time when earth and heaven meet. This

---

[13] I have not found the concept of non-nuclear hexagrams elsewhere in English.

[14] I have not found the concept of intermediate nuclear hexagrams in any other English-language source.

[15] The concept, name, and analysis of this group of hexagrams, and the following three groups, I have not found elsewhere in English.

is a time of prosperity if one's motives are pure. Hexagram 28 may be viewed as representing the highly unstable state that exists between the two conditions symbolized by Hexagrams 43 and 44.

Hexagram 2, Earthly Cycle Group. (See Figure 2.) This group is composed of Hexagrams 23, 24, and 27. These three hexagrams have Hexagram 2 as their nuclear hexagram.

Hexagram 23	䷖	000-001	*Falling*
Hexagram 24	䷗	100-000	*Return*
Hexagram 27	䷚	100-001	*Bulging Cheeks*

These three hexagrams represent the earthly cycle of death, birth, and nourishment. The yang line in the sixth position in Hexagram 23, *Falling,* represents a large, mature fruit ready to fall. Hexagram 27, *Return,* represents a seed starting to grow. The process of growth starts again. Wilhelm/Baynes write, "The thought here (Hexagram 23), taken with that in the next hexagram [Hexagram 24], shows the connection between decay and resurrection. Fruit must decay before new seed can develop."[16] Hexagram 27 signifies that which is required to sustain the cycle of decay and resurrection, namely nourishment.

Hexagram 63, Marriage of Heaven and Earth Group. (See Figure 3.) This group is composed of Hexagrams 38, 40, and 54. These three hexagrams have Hexagram 63 as their nuclear hexagram.

Hexagram 38	䷥	110-101	*Estrangement*
Hexagram 40	䷧	010-100	*Obstruction Removed*
Hexagram 54	䷵	110-100	*A Maiden Marries*

Hexagram 38, *Estrangement,* represents the opposition that naturally occurs in a family when the younger daughter (the lower primary trigram) and the middle daughter (the upper primary trigram) marry and leave home. The daughters form different opinions and opposition occurs. In a more general sense this Hexagram represents, as Legge says, "a social state in which division and mutual alienation prevail, and the hexagram teaches how in small matters this condition may be healed, and the way prepared for the cure of the whole system."[17] And in a cosmic sense this hexagram denotes the dynamic opposition between Heaven and Earth. This opposition is the force that moves the situation to the next stage. Wilhelm/Baynes state that Confucius "shows that opposition is actually the natural prerequisite for union."[18]

Hexagram 40, *Obstruction Removed,* "refers to a time in which tensions and complications begin to be eased."[19] It represents a movement away from an

---

[16] [A] Wilhelm/Baynes, p. 500.

[17] [A] Legge, p. 140.

[18] [A] Wilhelm/Baynes, p. 575.

[19] [A] Wilhelm/Baynes, p. 155.

obstacle or a dangerous situation. The opposition referred to by Hexagram 38 is being left behind.

In the *Commentary on the Decisions* on Hexagram 54, *A Maiden Marries,* it is written:

> The MARRYING MAIDEN describes the great meaning of heaven and earth. If heaven and earth do not unite, all creatures fail to prosper.
> The MARRYING MAIDEN means the end and beginning of humanity.[20]

In summary, the group composed of the three hexagrams 38, 40 and 54 symbolizes the tension that exists between Heaven and Earth. This tension is the source of movement which alters the situation and finally results in the union of Heaven and Earth. The group has Hexagram 63, *Already Across the River,* as its nuclear hexagram, which is appropriate, since Hexagram 63 is the symbol "that the transition from confusion to order is completed."[21] Of course, once perfect order has been achieved only disorder can follow, but that is the eternal cycle.

Hexagram 64, Conduct of Heaven and Earth Group. (See Figure 4.) This group contains Hexagrams 37, 39 and 53.

Hexagram 37	䷤	101-011	*The Family*
Hexagram 39	䷦	110-101	*Obstruction*
Hexagram 53	䷴	001-011	*Gradual Advance*

What these hexagrams have in common is that they symbolize different kinds of relationships between people. Hexagram 37, *The Family,* represents "the laws obtaining within the family."[22] Hexagram 39, *Obstruction,* warns that there is a danger ahead of us and that one should retreat and "join forces with friends of like mind..."[23] Hexagram 53, *Gradual Advance,* represents the gradual development of events leading up to the marriage of a young woman. The theme is "correct relationships of co-operation."[24]

On the cosmic level these three hexagrams represent the proper integration of Heaven and Earth (the yin and yang principles). Hexagram 37, *The Family,* represents the successful marriage of Heaven and Earth. The yin (woman) and yang (man) are united in marriage and have children (they give birth to the ten thousand things); they constitute a family. Hexagram 39, *Obstruction,* can be interpreted to mean that the encountering of obstacles indicates that one is

---

[20] [A] Wilhelm/Baynes, p. 664.
[21] [A] Wilhelm/Baynes, p. 244.
[22] [A] Wilhelm/Baynes, p. 143.
[23] [A] Wilhelm/Baynes, p. 151.
[24] [A] Wilhelm/Baynes, p. 205.

not in tune with the cosmic forces of yin and yang. If one is in the right place (with friends) at the right time, then there is harmony and order. Hexagram 53, *Gradual Advance,* which is concerned with the proper conduct between a man and a woman leading to marriage, means on the cosmic level that there is a correct way for the yin and yang forces to merge. The proper outcome of a marriage of yin and yang is a harmonious, creative relationship. This can only be accomplished when the yin and yang observe the proper rules of conduct preliminary to their uniting. These proper rules of conduct on the cosmic level are expressed in the first two groups: Heavenly Action and Earthly Cycle. It is fitting and proper for Heaven (the yang principle) to act to maintain its power and purity of yangness and it is fitting and proper—when it is timely—for Earth (the yin principle) to be receptive to the yang principle (for the female is impregnated by the male, Hexagram 24). When the time is suitable it is also proper for Earth to nourish the relationship (Hexagram 27) and eventually for Earth to overthrow Heaven (Hexagram 23).

HEXAGRAM 1, HEAVENLY ACTION

BASIC NUCLEAR HEXAGRAMS   **INTERMEDIATE NUCLEAR HEXAGRAMS**   **NON-NUCLEAR HEXAGRAMS**

Hexagram 1. 111-111
☰ *Heaven*

Hexagram 28. 011-110
☱ *Big in Excess*

Hexagram 43. 111-110
☱ *Decisive*

Hexagram 44. 011-111
☰ *Meeting/Subjugated*

Hexagram 30. 101-101
☲ *Fire*

Hexagram 55. 101-100
☳ *Abundance*

Hexagram 56. 001-101
☲ *The Traveler*

Hexagram 62. 001-100
☳ *Small in Excess*

Hexagram 14. 111-101
☲ *Great Possessions*

Hexagram 32. 011-100
☳ *Constancy*

Hexagram 34. 111-100
☳ *Big Uses Force*

Hexagram 50. 011-101
☲ *The Ritual Caldron*

Hexagram 13. 101-111
☰ *Companions*

Hexagram 31. 001-110
☱ *Mutual Influence*

Hexagram 33. 001-111
☰ *The Piglet*

Hexagram 49. 101-110
☱ *Revolution*

Figure 1

HEXAGRAM 2, EARTHLY CYCLE

BASIC NUCLEAR HEXAGRAMS	INTERMEDIATE NUCLEAR HEXAGRAMS	NON-NUCLEAR HEXAGRAMS

Hexagram 2. 000-000
☷☷ *Earth*

Hexagram 23. 000-001
☶☷ *Falling*

> Hexagram 3. 100-010
> ☵☳ *Sprouting*
>
> Hexagram 8. 000-010
> ☵☷ *Alliance*
>
> Hexagram 20. 000-011
> ☴☷ *Observing*
>
> Hexagram 42. 100-011
> ☴☳ *Increase*

Hexagram 24. 100-000
☷☳ *Return*

> Hexagram 4. 010-001
> ☶☵ *The Young Shoot*
>
> Hexagram 7. 010-000
> ☷☵ *An Army*
>
> Hexagram 19. 110-000
> ☷☱ *Authority Approaches*
>
> Hexagram 41. 110-001
> ☶☱ *Decrease*

Hexagram 27. 100-001
☶☳ *Bulging Cheeks*

> Hexagram 29. 010-010
> ☵☵ *Water*
>
> Hexagram 59. 010-011
> ☴☵ *Flood/Dispersion*
>
> Hexagram 60. 110-010
> ☵☱ *Restraint (Regulations)*
>
> Hexagram 61. 110-011
> ☴☱ *Inmost Sincerity*

Figure 2

HEXAGRAM 63, MARRIAGE OF HEAVEN AND EARTH

| BASIC NUCLEAR HEXAGRAMS | INTERMEDIATE NUCLEAR HEXAGRAMS | NON-NUCLEAR HEXAGRAMS |

Hexagram 38. 110-101 *Estrangement*
- Hexagram 5. 111-010 *Getting Wet*
- Hexagram 9. 111-011 *Sm. Restr./Sm. Acc.**
- Hexagram 48. 011-010 *A Well*
- Hexagram 57. 011-011 *Wind*

Hexagram 63. 101-010 *Already Across The River*

Hexagram 40. 010-100 *Obstr. Removed†*
- Hexagram 15. 001-000 *Modesty*
- Hexagram 22. 101-001 *Adornment*
- Hexagram 36. 101-000 *The Brt. (Clg.) Pheas.***
- Hexagram 52. 001-001 *Mountain*

Hexagram 54. 110-100 *A Maiden Marries*
- Hexagram 11. 111-000 *Peace/Flowing*
- Hexagram 18. 011-001 *Illness/Decay*
- Hexagram 26. 111-001 *Big Restr./Big Acc.‡*
- Hexagram 46. 011-000 *Pushing Upwards*

Figure 3
* Small Restraint/Small Accumulation. ** The Bright (Calling) Pheasant. † Obstruction Removed. ‡ Big Restraint/Big Accumulation.

HEXAGRAM 64, CONDUCT OF HEAVEN AND EARTH

BASIC NUCLEAR HEXAGRAMS	INTERMEDIATE NUCLEAR HEXAGRAMS	NON-NUCLEAR HEXAGRAMS

Hexagram 6. 010-111
☲ *Grievance*

Hexagram 10. 110-111
☱ *Treading*

Hexagram 37. 101-011
☲ *The Family*

Hexagram 47. 010-110
☵ *Burdened/Exhausted*

Hexagram 58. 110-110
☱ *Lake*

Hexagram 16. 000-100
☷ *Contentment*

Hexagram 21. 100-101
☲ *Biting Through*

Hexagram 39. 001-010
☵ *Obstruction*

Hexagram 35. 000-101
☲ *Advance*

Hexagram 51. 100-100
☳ *Thunder*

Hexagram 64. 010-101 ☲
Not Yet Across The Water

Hexagram 12. 000-111
☰ *Standstill*

Hexagram 17. 100-110
☱ *The Chase*

Hexagram 53. 001-011
☴ *Gradual Advance*

Hexagram 25. 100-111
☰ *No Error (No Expect.)* *

Hexagram 45. 000-110
☱ *Gathering Together*

Figure 4

* No Error (No Expectations)

The Position of the Nuclear Hexagrams (Basic and Interme-diate) in the Textual and Binary Sequence. Two of the basic nuclear hexagrams (Hexagrams 1 and 2) head the textual sequence and two of the basic nuclear hexagrams (Hexagrams 63 and 64) end the sequence. Also, if the textual sequence is presented in an 8 by 8 square (see Table 1 below), then the intermediate nuclear hexagrams 27 and 28 are symmetrically positioned in the square with respect to the intermediate nuclear hexagrams 37 and 38. The eight intermediate nuclear hexagrams 23, 24, 39, 40, 43, 44, 53, and 54, are not symmetrically distributed in Table 1.

Table 1. Position of Nuclear Hexagrams in the Textual Sequence

01	**02**	03	04	05	06	07	08
09	10	11	12	13	14	15	16
17	18	19	20	21	22	**23**	**24**
25	26	**27**	**28**	29	30	31	32
33	34	35	36	**37**	**38**	**39**	**40**
41	42	**43**	**44**	45	46	47	48
49	50	51	52	**53**	**54**	55	56
57	58	59	60	61	62	**63**	**64**

(Nuclear hexagrams are **boldface**.)

The arrangement of the nuclear hexagrams in the binary sequence and presented as an 8 by 8 square (see Table 2 below) shows a pattern: two nuclear hexagrams head the sequence and two end it, four occur in succession in the middle of the sequence (30, 31, 32, 33), and the rest are separated by eight non-nuclear hexagrams. See Table 2 below. (Note: The numbers in the square below are not the textual numbers of the hexagrams, but the decimal equivalent of the hexagram expressed as a binary number. Thus, the number '01' represents Hexagram 23, ䷖, 000-001, *Falling,* and so forth. See Appendix A, The Binary System.)

**Table 2. Position of Nuclear Hexagrams
in the Binary (Fu Hsi's) Sequence**

00	**01**	02	03	04	05	06	07
08	09	**10**	**11**	12	13	14	15
16	17	18	19	**20**	**21**	22	23
24	25	26	27	28	29	**30**	**31**
32	**33**	34	35	36	37	38	39
40	41	**42**	**43**	44	45	46	47
48	49	50	51	**52**	**53**	54	55
56	57	58	59	60	61	**62**	**63**

(Nuclear hexagrams are **boldface**.)

Analyzing the Non-Nuclear Hexagrams by their Nuclear Hexagrams. There are twelve groups (four to a group) of non-nuclear hexagrams. Each group has one intermediate nuclear hexagram in common which reveals a common meaning of the four hexagrams in the group.

For example, the intermediate nuclear Hexagram 38, ☲, 110-101, *Estrangement,* is the primary nuclear hexagram of the following (and only the following) non-nuclear hexagrams:

Hexagram 5	☲	111-010	*Getting Wet*
Hexagram 9	☲	111-011	*Small Restraint/Small Accumulation*
Hexagram 48	☲	011-010	*A Well*
Hexagram 57	☲	011-011	*Wind*

Consequently, some aspect of the meanings of these four hexagrams should deal with estrangement. The following analysis is given to support this hypothesis.

All four of the hexagrams 5, 9, 48, and 57 have in common the theme, among other things, that humans are dependent creatures. Concerning Hexagram 5, *Waiting (Nourishment)* Wilhelm/Baynes say, "All beings have need of nourishment from above. But the gift of food comes in its own time, and for this one must wait."[25] Rain, of course, comes from Heaven. The Judgment of Hexagram 9, *Small Restraint,* talks about dense clouds, but no rain from the western regions. Advice is given that it is not the time for large scale action and that the weak can restrain the strong only by peaceful means. Hexagram 48, *A Well,* points out that a well is the center of a village. The people can move, but the well cannot be moved. Two evils can occur: the rope can be too short to reach the water in the bottom of the well, or the jug (the bucket) can break. This hexagram like Hexagram 5 points out that humans are dependent

[25] [A] Wilhelm/Baynes, p. 24.

upon water (i.e., Heaven). Hexagram 57, *Wind,* advises that it is beneficial for the weak to join the strong.

Another meaning that these four hexagrams have in common is estrangement: estrangement of humanity from Heaven (Hexagram 5), estrangement of the weak from power (Hexagrams 9 and 57), and estrangement of the weak from the strong. In each case, estrangement leads to dependence. In a cosmic sense we are dependent upon Heaven (reality) for our very being. In a natural sense we are dependent upon Heaven (the sky) for rain for our crops. In a social sense we are dependent upon our skills and technology (the rope and bucket necessary to draw the water out of the well) in order to supply us with nourishment. And in a political sense we are dependent upon our diplomatic skills to negotiate with those who are more powerful than we are.

HEXAGRAM CYCLES, FLOWERS, AND STORIES

30. Fire

Hexagram Cycles: Each hexagram has traditionally been pictured as a form in unending motion, in which each line is always ascending to the position above it; upon reaching the top position, the line takes its place at the lowest position once again. One complete sequence of motion is a **hexagram cycle,** each phase of which is formed simply by moving the top line of a hexagram to its bottom, and the other lines up by one position. The process is repeated, deriving new hexagrams for as long as a unique hexagram in the cycle can be formed. (The cycles of the Sixty-Four Hexagrams are given in Appendix I.)

The cycle of Hexagram 24, *Return,* contains six hexagrams.

Hexagram #	Hexagram	Text #	Binary #	Name
100-000		24	(32)	*Return*
010-000		7	(16)	*An Army*
001-000		15	(8)	*Modesty*
000-100		16	(4)	*Contentment*
000-010		8	(2)	*Alliance*
000-001		23	(1)	*Falling*

A cycle can contain only three hexagrams, as for example the cycle of Hexagram 51, *Thunder.*

Hexagram #	Hexagram	Text #	Binary #	Name
100-100		51	(36)	*Thunder*
010-010		29	(18)	*Water*
001-001		52	(9)	*Mountain*

A cycle can contain only two hexagrams, as for example the cycle of Hexagram 63, *Already Across the River.*

Hexagram #	Hexagram	Text #	Binary #	Name
101-010		63	(42)	*Already Across the River*
010-101		64	(21)	*Not Yet Across the River*

And of the two hexagrams, Hexagram 1, 111-111 ☰, *Heaven,* and Hexagram 2, 000-000 ☷, *Earth,* each contains only one hexagram in its cycle—itself, since moving its sixth line to position 1 yields an identical hexagram.

Hexagram cycles may be explored to see if there are semantic or causal connections between successive hexagrams in a given cycle. Such an exploration will not be given in this work.

Hexagram Flowers:[1] We may take any hexagram and by changing one of its lines—yin to yang or yang to yin—form another hexagram. By such a method a total of six other hexagrams may be formed. The original hexagram is called the **flower center**. The six hexagrams, each of which differs in only one line from the original, are called **flower petals**. See Appendix H.

For example, from Hexagram 7, 010-000 ☷, *An Army*, we derive the following six petals:

Hexagram 19	䷒	110-000	*Authority Approaches*
Hexagram 2	䷁	000-000	*Earth*
Hexagram 46	䷭	011-000	*Pushing Upwards*
Hexagram 40	䷧	010-100	*Obstruction Removed*
Hexagram 29	䷜	010-010	*Water*
Hexagram 4	䷃	010-001	*The Young Shoot*

Structurally, each petal differs from its flower center only by having a yang line where the flower center has a yin line, or vice-versa. Consider the following two Hexagrams 19 and 7 (a petal and its center):

Petal Hexagram 19	䷒	110-000	*Authority Approaches*
Center Hexagram 7	䷆	010-000	*An Army*

They differ only in that Hexagram 19 has a yang line in position 1, where Hexagram 7 has a yin line. It is three times more probable that a yang line will change into a yin line than that a yin line will change to a yang one.[2] Therefore, it may be concluded that Hexagram 19 is more likely to be the cause of Hexagram 7 than its consequent. In fact, of all the other hexagrams, none has a greater probability than Hexagram 19 of turning into Hexagram 7.[3]

Petal 2 (Hexagram 2) has a yin line in the position where its center (Hexagram 7) has a yang line.

Petal 2, Hexagram 2	䷁	000-000	*Earth*
Center, Hexagram 7	䷆	010-000	*An Army*

In this case it is more likely that Hexagram 2 is the outcome of Hexagram 7 than the other way around, since—as has been said—it is three times more likely for

---

[1] As far as the author knows, the concept of Hexagram Flowers does not occur elsewhere in English literature.

[2] The probability of obtaining a moving yang line—in casting a hexagram by the traditional yarrow-stalk method—is $\frac{3}{16}$, while the probability of obtaining a moving yin line is $\frac{1}{16}$. See Chapter 9.

[3] Of course, there are four other hexagrams that have a probability equal to that of Hexagram 19 of turning into Hexagram 7. These four hexagrams are petals of Hexagram 7; namely, Hexagrams 46, 40, 29, and 4. These petals also have a yang line where Hexagram 7 has a yin line.

a yang line to turn into a yin line than vice-versa. In fact, of all the other hexagrams, none has a greater probability of turning into Hexagram 2 than does Hexagram 7.[4]

If one hexagram differs from a second only by having a yang line in a position where the other has a yin line, the first is said to be formally **antecedent** to the second, and the second to be formally **consequent** to the first. Each petal is either antecedent or consequent to its center hexagram.

For example, consider the following:

Flower Center Hexagram 7			010-000	*An Army*
Hexagram 19		A	110-000	*Authority Approaches*
Hexagram 2		C	000-000	*Earth*
Hexagram 46		A	011-000	*Pushing Upwards*
Hexagram 40		A	010-100	*Obstruction Removed*
Hexagram 29		A	010-010	*Water*
Hexagram 4		A	010-001	*The Young Shoot*

An "A" prefix means that the petal hexagram is antecedent to its center; a "C" prefix means that the petal hexagram is consequent to its center.

Formal causality also provides insight into semantic connections between a center and its petals. The meanings of the petals are **not** offshoots of the meaning of the center hexagram. Each petal is either the most probable antecedent state of the condition indicated by the center, or else the most probable consequent state of the center.

In the example above, all the petals are antecedent to its center hexagram, except Hexagram 2. Hence, these are the five hexagrams (situations) that can most readily lead to a military organization. The first is Hexagram 19, *Authority Approaches,* which Legge says "denotes the approach of an authority,— to inspect, to comfort, or to rule."[5]

Hexagram 46, *Pushing Upwards,* gives the psychological reason for the existence of the military, namely, the desire to obtain power.

Hexagram 40, *Obstruction Removed,* symbolizes a time when a problem has been solved, a time of deliverance from an obstruction and from inferior people.

But in transition from Hexagram 40 to Hexagram 7, the yang line in position 4 changes into a yin line. This symbolizes that the superior man (the yang line in position 4 in Hexagram 40), who is the advisor to a weak Ruler (the yin line in position 5), did not successfully deliver himself from inferior men. He is overthrown (changes to a yin line) and the yang line in position 2 of Hexagram 7 takes command; that is, the Army takes command of the government.

---

[4] There are five other hexagram that have the same probability as Hexagram 7 of turning into Hexagram 2. These five hexagrams are: 24, 100-000; 15, 001-000; 16, 000-100; 8, 000-010; and 23, 000-001.

[5] Legge (Dover), p. 98.

Hexagram 29, *Water,* symbolizes danger. In times of great danger it is easy for civil government to yield power to the military. The yang line in position 5 of Hexagram 29 (The Ruler) changes into a yin line and the only yang line left is in position 2, thus the military rules.

The yang line in position 6 in Hexagram 4, *The Young Shoot,* is the force which restrains and educates the immature young. When this yang line changes to a yin line then the only force left is Hexagram 7, *An Army.*

Hexagram 2, *Earth,* is a consequent of Hexagram 7, *An Army.* The army is composed of many who are receptive to commands and only a few who initiate commands. When these few disappear (symbolized by the yang line in Hexagram 7 changing to a yin line) then only receptiveness is left. A military government does not encourage creativity, thus it is always in danger of falling into passivity.

Hexagram Stories:[7] There is a simple algorithm for constructing a hexagram story for any hexagram. Change the line in the first position of the original hexagram—yang to yin, or yin to yang. This produces a second hexagram. Then change the second line of the second hexagram. This produces a third hexagram. The third line of this hexagram is changed and the process is repeated until the sixth line of the sixth hexagram is changed, producing the seventh hexagram. This seventh hexagram will be the opposite of the original hexagram. The process is continued. The first line of the seventh hexagram is changed producing an eighth hexagram, and the second line of the eighth hexagram is changed producing a ninth hexagram, until the sixth line of the twelfth hexagram is changed producing the thirteenth hexagram, which will be the original hexagram.

---

[7] Hexagram Stories are the discovery of the author, who did not find mention of them in English literature concerning the *I Ching.*

For example, the story of Hexagram 7, *An Army,* is:

	Hexagram	Text Number	Line Figure	Binary Number	Name
1	010-000	7		(16)	*An Army*
2	110-000	19		(48)	*Authority Approaches*
3	100-000	24		(32)	*Return*
4	101-000	36		(40)	*The Bright (Calling) Pheasant*
5	101-100	55		(44)	*Abundance*
6	101-110	49		(46)	*Revolution*
7	101-111	13		(47)	*Companions*
8	001-111	33		(15)	*The Piglet*
9	011-111	44		(31)	*Meeting/Subjugated*
10	010-111	6		(23)	*Grievance*
11	010-011	59		(19)	*Flood/Dispersion*
12	010-001	4		(17)	*The Young Shoot*
13	010-000	7		(16)	*An Army*

It should be noted that the seventh hexagram in each story is the opposite hexagram of the first. If a thirteenth hexagram is added to the sequence, as above, the sequence returns to the first hexagram.

It may be hypothesized that the formal sequence of thirteen for any hexagram represents a progression of meaning known as its **hexagram story**. The story tells how the situation represented by the first hexagram changes to its opposite situation and then changes back again. For example, in the story above of Hexagram 7, *The Army,* this hexagram may represent a group of people ruled by force, i.e., a military society. Next is Hexagram 19, *Authority Approaches,* which in this context may represent the consolidation of the military society. Hexagram 24, *Return,* signifies that the military society has reached its full strength. It is now starting to wane. A conflict of values is just beginning to appear. The fourth hexagram, *The Bright (Calling) Pheasant,* means a situation that is "favorable in a hardship determination"[8] and Wilhelm/Baynes says concerning this hexagram that "here a man of dark nature is in a position of authority and brings harm to the wise and able man."[9] Wilhelm/Baynes gives as the judgment for this hexagram, "In adversity it furthers one to be persevering."[10] In the context of this story, this hexagram can be interpreted to mean that the military regime, sensing that its power is waning, is becoming oppressive. Hexagram 55,

---

[8] [A] Kunst, p. 311.

[9] [A] Wilhelm/Baynes, p. 139.

[10] [A] Wilhelm/Baynes, p. 140.

Abundance, signifies that "the King arrives"[11] and that "brilliance is conjoined with movement."[12] It is a time not to be sad. In this context the hexagram signifies the appearance of a man who can rule by wisdom, not by force. It signifies that the people are aware that they want such a ruler. This awareness leads to revolution, which is represented by Hexagram 49, *Revolution.* Hexagram 13, *Companions,* is the opposite hexagram of Hexagram 7, *An Army.* Hexagram 13 represents a society whose cohesiveness is based on humaneness, not on force. Half of the story is now told: how a military society changes to a society where fellowship reigns.

Nothing is permanent. All things change. Yin changes to Yang and Yang to Yin. The next Hexagram is 33, *The Piglet;* in this hexagram dark lines are ascending. They occupy lines positions 1 and 2 and are pushing upwards. The society based on humaneness is starting to decay. Hexagram 44, *Meeting/Subjugated,* "indicates a situation in which the principle of darkness, after having been eliminated, furtively and unexpectedly obtrudes again from within and below."[13] In Hexagram 6, *Grievance,* the upper trigram, *Heaven,* is ascending; the lower trigram, *Water,* is descending. The two are moving apart, which signifies trouble, specifically that "allegiance is blocked and becomes cautious."[14] It is a time of distrust and ill feelings. Hexagram 59, *Flood/Dispersion,* signifies the "dispersing and dissolving of divisive egotism."[15] In this context this could signify that nationalism is increasing and private interests are less important. Hexagram 4, *The Young Shoot,* signifies the immaturity of the young. In this context, it may mean that the state does not believe that people are wise enough to take care of themselves or to take care of each other; discipline is needed. And discipline has to be backed up with force. The next Hexagram is 7, *An Army.* The story is complete. It ends where it begins.

---

[11] [A] Yu, no page numbers in this volume. Given in hexagram text for Hexagram 55.

[12] [A] Blofeld, p. 193.

[13] [A] Wilhelm/Baynes, p. 170.

[14] [A] Whincup, p. 39.

[15] [A] Wilhelm/Baynes, p. 227.

8

THE TEXTUAL SEQUENCE
OF THE I CHING

39. Obstruction

The Three Books of Changes: In ancient times—prior to Confucius—there were at least three Books of Changes: the *Lien Shan* (Manifestation of Change in the Mountains), the *Kuei Tsang* (Flow and Return to Womb and Tomb), and the *Chou I* (Book of Changes of the Chou Dynasty). Practically nothing is known about the first two books. The *I Ching* as known to Confucius, and readers up to the present, is the *Chou I* version.[1]

In the *Chou I* (the *I Ching* as we know it today) the textual sequence of hexagrams begins with *Heaven,* ☰, 111-111, but it is alleged that in the *Lien Shan* version it began with *Mountain,* ☶, 001-001, and in the *Kuei Tsang* version with *Earth,* ☷, 000-000. The oldest textual sequence we have of the hexagrams is the *Chou I* version, but at present scholars have found no method for generating this textual sequence.[2]

The textual sequence of the *Chou I* version of the *I Ching*—also known as the King Wen order—is:

HEXAGRAMS ARRANGED IN TEXTUAL SEQUENCE

HEXAGRAM	TEXT #	BINARY #	NAME
111-111	1	(63)	*Heaven*
000-000	2	(0)	*Earth*
100-010	3	(34)	*Sprouting*
010-001	4	(17)	*The Young Shoot*
111-010	5	(58)	*Getting Wet*
010-111	6	(23)	*Grievance*
010-000	7	(16)	*An Army*
000-010	8	(2)	*Alliance*
111-011	9	(59)	*Small Restraint/ Small Accumulation*
110-111	10	(55)	*Treading*
111-000	11	(56)	*Peace/Flowing*
000-111	12	(7)	*Standstill*
101-111	13	(47)	*Companions*
111-101	14	(61)	*Great Possessions*
001-000	15	(8)	*Modesty*
000-100	16	(4)	*Contentment*

---

[1] The information given in this paragraph and the succeeding paragraph on the three versions of the *I Ching* is based on information given by [A] Wilhelm/Baynes p. lviii and [A] Needham p. 307.

[2] The textual sequence of the hexagrams in the Mawangdui manuscript, which differs from the order given in the *Chou I* version, also goes back to antiquity. This sequence is discussed later in this chapter.

HEXAGRAMS ARRANGED IN TEXTUAL SEQUENCE

HEXAGRAM	TEXT #	BINARY #	NAME
100-110	17	(38)	*The Chase*
011-001	18	(25)	*Illness/Decay*
110-000	19	(48)	*Authority Approaches*
000-011	20	(3)	*Observing*
100-101	21	(37)	*Biting Through*
101-001	22	(41)	*Adornment*
000-001	23	(1)	*Falling*
100-000	24	(32)	*Return*
100-111	25	(39)	*No Error (No Expectations)*
111-001	26	(57)	*Big Restraint/*
			Big Accumulation
100-001	27	(33)	*Bulging Cheeks*
011-110	28	(30)	*Big in Excess*
010-010	29	(18)	*Water*
101-101	30	(45)	*Fire*
001-110	31	(14)	*Mutual Influence*
011-100	32	(28)	*Constancy*
001-111	33	(15)	*The Piglet*
111-100	34	(60)	*Big Uses Force*
000-101	35	(5)	*Advance*
101-000	36	(40)	*The Bright (Calling) Pheasant*
101-011	37	(43)	*The Family*
110-101	38	(53)	*Estrangement*
001-010	39	(10)	*Obstruction*
010-100	40	(20)	*Obstruction Removed*
110-001	41	(49)	*Decrease*
100-011	42	(35)	*Increase*
111-110	43	(62)	*Decisive*
011-111	44	(31)	*Meeting/Subjugated*
000-110	45	(6)	*Gathering Together*
011-000	46	(24)	*Pushing Upwards*
010-110	47	(22)	*Burdened/Exhausted*
011-010	48	(26)	*A Well*

HEXAGRAMS ARRANGED IN TEXTUAL SEQUENCE

HEXAGRAM	TEXT #	BINARY #	NAME
101-110	49	(46)	*Revolution*
011-101	50	(29)	*The Ritual Caldron*
100-100	51	(36)	*Thunder*
001-001	52	(9)	*Mountain*
001-011	53	(11)	*Gradual Advance*
110-100	54	(52)	*A Maiden Marries*
101-100	55	(44)	*Abundance*
001-101	56	(13)	*The Traveler*
011-011	57	(27)	*Wind*
110-110	58	(54)	*Lake*
010-011	59	(19)	*Flood/Dispersion*
110-010	60	(50)	*Restraint (Regulations)*
110-011	61	(51)	*Inmost Sincerity (Allegiance)*
001-100	62	(12)	*Small in Excess*
101-010	63	(42)	*Already Across the River*
010-101	64	(21)	*Not Yet Across the River*

The names in the above table are those recommended in Chapter 4, "English Names of the Hexagrams."

The Ninth Wing: An Explanation of the Textual Sequence. An explanation of the textual sequence is given in the ancient commentary called the Ninth Wing (*Hsu Kua*). For example, concerning Hexagram 7, *An Army*, and Hexagram 8, *Alliance*, respectively, the Ninth Wing says:

> When there is conflict, the masses are sure to rise up. Hence there follows the hexagram of THE ARMY. Army means mass.[3]

and

> Among the masses there is surely a reason for uniting. Hence there follows the hexagram of HOLDING TOGETHER. Holding together means uniting.[4]

The Ninth Wing attempts to explain the textual sequence by giving a variety of connections between the meanings of successive hexagrams. The connections seem to be somewhat arbitrary and loose enough to allow for a

---

[3] [A] Wilhelm/Baynes, p. 421.

[4] [A] Wilhelm/Baynes, p. 425. HOLDING TOGETHER is the Wilhelm/Baynes name for Hexagram 8.

multiplicity of sequences. Richard Wilhelm says, "The NINTH WING, *Hsu Kua,* the Sequence—or Order—of the Hexagrams, offers a rather unconvincing explanation of the present sequence of the hexagrams."[5] Derek Walters says, "The order of the hexagrams is...an apparently random one (at least no-one has yet convincingly explained the reason for the sequence)."[6] James Legge says, "The connexion between any two (hexagrams) is sufficiently close; but on the whole the essays, which I have said they form, resemble 'a heap of orient pearls at random strung.' "[7]

The Problem of the Textual Sequence. The question addressed in this chapter is, What is the evidence that the textual sequence of the hexagrams in the *I Ching* (*Chou I* version) was produced by an algorithm? (An algorithm is a set of clearly defined rules or processes for the solution of a problem.[8]) Another way of asking the question is: Does the textual sequence represent a formal order? By a formal order is meant an order that is not dependent upon the meanings of the hexagrams, but upon the kinds of lines (yin or yang, moving or static) and/or their positions in the hexagrams. An example of a formal order would be the **Fu Hsi Order** of the hexagrams. This order occurs when the hexagrams are arranged as ascending binary numbers: 000-000, 000-001, 000-010, 000-011, 000-100, 000-101, 000-110, 000-111, etc. (See **Binary Order** and **Fu Hsi's Arrangement**.) A discussion of Leibniz's discovery of the **Fu Hsi Sequence** is given by Needham. Needham also mentions that the **Fu Hsi Sequence** is not ancient and can be traced no further back than the Sung Dynasty (960–1279 A.D.).[9]

Rules of the Textual Sequence. The only apparent structure exhibited by the textual sequence (the **King Wen Order**) is that any odd-numbered hexagram and its even-numbered successor form either a pair of inverses or op-

---

[5] [A] Wilhelm/Baynes p. 260.

[6] [A] Derek Walters, *The T'ai Hsuan Ching: The Hidden Classic,* p. 8.

[7] [A] Legge (Dover), p. 54.

[8] The textual sequence can be generated by an algorithm consisting of 64 rules: a rule to assign a number to each hexagram. Rule 1 would assign numeral 1 to Hexagram 111-111, Rule 2 would assign numeral 2 to Hexagram 000-000, Rule 3 would assign numeral 3 to Hexagram 100-010, and so forth. Such an algorithm, of course, would be trivial as it would be nothing but a description of the textual sequence itself. What is sought is an algorithm which is simpler than the textual sequence; yet the concept of simplicity is not easily defined or measured. One might be tempted to define the simplicity of an algorithm in terms of the number of rules it contains: the fewer the rules, the simpler the algorithm. Thus an algorithm containing four rules is simpler than one containing twelve rules. But it is not this easy, since some rules seem to be more complex than others. For example, is a rule which states that two numbers are to be multiplied more complex than a rule which states that these two numbers are to be added? Also, are conjunctions and disjunctions allowed in rules? For example, can there be legitimate rules which state that two numbers are to be multiplied **and** added or that a number, if even, is to be multiplied by 2 **or** if odd is to be divided by 3?

[9] [A] Needham, p. 341.

posites. (Henceforth, the word "pair" shall refer to any odd-numbered hexagram and its immediate even-numbered successor in the textual sequence.) The inverse of a hexagram is found by turning the hexagram upside down.[10] The result is a pair of inverses. An example of a pair of inverses is Hexagrams 3 and 4, which are respectively 100-010 and 010-001. In four cases (Hexagrams 1, 27, 29, 61) the inverse of the odd-numbered hexagram would be identical to the original hexagram. In these cases, the successor of the odd-numbered hexagram is its opposite. The opposite of a hexagram is found by changing every line in it to its opposite. A yang line is changed to a yin line and vice-versa. For example, the opposite of Hexagram 27, 100-001, *Bulging Cheeks,* is Hexagram 28, 011-110, *Big in Excess.* For these four odd-numbered hexagrams, the even-numbered successor is its opposite; otherwise, the even-numbered successor of an odd-numbered hexagram is its inverse. Hence, given the form of an odd-numbered hexagram, we can determine the form of its even-numbered successor.[11]

From the above information the Rule of Pairs (**RPrs**) may be formulated.

> **RPrs.** A pair of hexagrams in the textual sequence is a pair
> of inverses where such pairs contain distinct hexagrams, where
> they cannot they are pairs of opposites.

But the question remains: What algorithm determines the overall sequence of the hexagrams? More specifically: What algorithm generates the sequence of pairs or, given *Heaven* as Hexagram 1, what algorithm explains how the other odd-numbered hexagrams are generated?.

The following three rules are of some interest. Rules **RCrt 1** and **RCrt 2** demonstrate that correctness has some bearing on the textual sequence. A line is correct if it is a yang line in position 1, 3, or 5 or else it is a yin line in position 2, 4, or 6. If a line is not correct, then it is incorrect. Rule **RCH** shows that correspondence and holding together also have some bearing on the textual sequence. See Glossary for explanation of **correctness of a line**, **correspondence**, and **holding together**.

> **RCrt 1.** A hexagram with correct lines in positions 1, 3, and
> 5 (that is, yang lines in all three positions) is an odd-numbered
> hexagram.

---

[10] The lines in positions 1 and 6 are interchanged as well as the lines in positions 2 and 5, and 3 and 4.

[11] Of course the converse also holds. Given the sequence of even-numbered hexagrams their odd-numbered predecessors can be determined.

Line Position:	1	2	3	4	5	6	
Hexagram 1	1	1	1	1	1	1	*Heaven*
Hexagram 5	1	1	1	0	1	0	*Getting Wet*
Hexagram 9	1	1	1	0	1	1	*Small Restraint/Small Accumulation*
Hexagram 13	1	0	1	1	1	1	*Companions*
Hexagram 37	1	0	1	0	1	1	*The Family*
Hexagram 43	1	1	1	1	1	0	*Decisive*
Hexagram 49	1	0	1	1	1	0	*Revolution*
Hexagram 63	1	0	1	0	1	0	*Already Across the River*

The converse, however, is not true. There are odd-numbered hexagrams—all the odd-numbered hexagrams not in the list above—that do not have yang lines in positions 1, 3, and 5.

> **RCrt 2.** A hexagram with correct lines in positions 2, 3, and 5 (that is, a yin line in position 2, yang lines in positions 3 and 5) is an odd-numbered hexagram.

Line Position:	1	2	3	4	5	6	
Hexagram 13	1	**0**	1	1	1	1	*Companions*
Hexagram 31	0	**0**	1	1	1	0	*Mutual Influence*
Hexagram 33	0	**0**	1	1	1	1	*The Piglet*
Hexagram 37	1	**0**	1	0	1	1	*The Family*
Hexagram 39	0	**0**	1	0	1	0	*Obstruction*
Hexagram 49	1	**0**	1	1	1	0	*Revolution*
Hexagram 53	0	**0**	1	0	1	1	*Gradual Advance*
Hexagram 63	1	**0**	1	0	1	0	*Already Across the River*

Once again the converse does not hold, since there are odd-numbered hexagrams that do not have correct lines in positions 2, 3, and 5.

Two lines in a hexagram **correspond** to each other if and only if the lines are opposite (one yin and the other yang) and they occupy line positions 1 and 4, 2 and 5, 3 and 6. Corresponding lines need not be correct lines. Correspondence is most significant between lines in positions 2 and 5. Line 2 is the position of the Great Official; line 5 is that of the Ruler. A Yang line in position 2 (Strong Official) with a yin line in position 5 (Weak Ruler) is considered a favorable combination.

Opposite lines occupying adjacent line positions are said to **hold together**. Holding together is most important between line positions 4 and 5 (providing that the Ruler is in the 5th position). The hexagram is generally favorable when a yin line in position 4 holds together with a yang line in position

5. The relationship of holding together is also important between line positions 5 and 6. In this case it is generally favorable when a yin line in position 5 holds together with a yang line in position 6.

> **RCH.** A hexagram with a yang line in positions 3 and 6 and a yin line in position 5 is an even-numbered hexagram in the textual sequence.

In other words, a yang line in position 3 corresponding with the yin line in 5 is favorable; a yin line in position 5 holding together with a yang line in position 6 is also favorable. The two occur together—lines 3 and 5 corresponding and lines 5 and 6 holding together—only in even-numbered hexagrams.

Line Position:	1	2	3	4	5	6	
Hexagram 14	1	1	1	1	0	1	*Great Possessions*
Hexagram 18	0	1	1	0	0	1	*Illness/Decay*
Hexagram 22	1	0	1	0	0	1	*Adornment*
Hexagram 26	1	1	1	0	0	1	*Big Restraint/Big Accumulation*
Hexagram 30	1	0	1	1	0	1	*Fire*
Hexagram 50	0	1	1	1	0	1	*The Ritual Caldron*
Hexagram 52	0	0	1	0	0	1	*Mountain*
Hexagram 56	0	0	1	1	0	1	*The Traveler*

According to the Rule of Pairs (**RPrs**), the even-numbered above are inverses of the following odd-numbered hexagrams.

Line Position:	1	2	3	4	5	6	
Hexagram 13	1	0	1	1	1	1	*Companions*
Hexagram 17	1	0	0	1	1	0	*The Chase*
Hexagram 21	1	0	0	1	0	1	*Biting Through*
Hexagram 25	1	0	0	1	1	1	*No Error (No Expectations)*
Hexagram 29	0	1	0	0	1	0	*Water*
Hexagram 49	1	0	1	1	1	0	*Revolution*
Hexagram 51	1	0	0	1	0	0	*Thunder*
Hexagram 55	1	0	1	1	0	0	*Abundance*

Combining the above odd-numbered hexagrams with those derived by **RCrt 1** and **RCrt 2** yields the following list of 18 odd-numbered hexagrams. (Their 18 even-numbered successors can be determined by the Rule of Pairs, but these are not listed.) It must be stressed that these rules do **not** determine the textual number of the hexagrams listed below or their relative positions to each other in the textual sequence; they merely determine whether the textual number of the hexagram is odd or even and they do so for only 36 hexagrams: the 18 odd-numbered hexagrams listed below and their eighteen even-numbered successors.

Line Position:	1	2	3	4	5	6	
Hexagram 1	1	1	1	1	1	1	*Heaven*
Hexagram 5	1	1	1	0	1	0	*Getting Wet*
Hexagram 9	1	1	1	0	1	1	*Small Restraint/Small Accumulation*
Hexagram 13	1	0	1	1	1	1	*Companions*
Hexagram 17	1	0	0	1	1	0	*The Chase*
Hexagram 21	1	0	0	1	0	1	*Biting Through*
Hexagram 25	1	0	0	1	1	1	*No Error (No Expectations)*
Hexagram 29	0	1	0	0	1	0	*Water*
Hexagram 31	0	0	1	1	1	0	*Mutual Influence*
Hexagram 33	0	0	1	1	1	1	*The Piglet*
Hexagram 37	1	0	1	0	1	1	*The Family*
Hexagram 39	0	0	1	0	1	0	*Obstruction*
Hexagram 43	1	1	1	1	1	0	*Decisive*
Hexagram 49	1	0	1	1	1	0	*Revolution*
Hexagram 51	1	0	0	1	0	0	*Thunder*
Hexagram 53	0	0	1	0	1	1	*Gradual Advance*
Hexagram 55	1	0	1	1	0	0	*Abundance*
Hexagram 63	1	0	1	0	1	0	*Already Across the River*

Dennis and Terence McKenna discovered some interesting facts concerning the textual sequence. They examined adjoining hexagrams (Hexagrams 1 and 2, 2 and 3, 3 and 4, etc.) and counted the number of lines that had to change to allow a hexagram to change to its successor. For example, the number of changing lines in the transition from Hexagrams 1 to 2 is 6, from 2 to 3 is 2, from 3 to 4 is 4, from 4 to 5 is 4. Their findings are presented below:

> Our conclusion is that the King Wen sequence was ordered, aside from the already stated rules which generate the hexagram pairs, on the following principles:
>
> (1) Order among the 32 pairs was also determined by a wish to absolutely exclude transition situations with a value of 5.
>
> (2) Order among the 32 pairs was secondarily determined by a similar wish to absolutely exclude transition situations with a value of 1 except in cases where this would interfere with rule (1). Only two instances of a transition of value 1 occur, and both in situations where reversing the members of the pair involved (pairs 53–54 and 61–62) would cause valuations of 5.

(3) All 3's were eliminated except where this would cause a value of 5, 6, 1, or double 3.[13]

Nuclear Hexagrams and the Textual Sequence. Another observation concerning the textual sequence is the fact that the first two hexagrams and the last two hexagrams of the sequence are the basic nuclear hexagrams: Hexagrams 1, 2, 63, and 64 (see Chapter 6, **Nuclear Hexagrams**). Unfortunately, the twelve intermediate nuclear hexagrams are not symmetrically distributed in the textual sequence. The table below gives the positions of all 16 nuclear hexagrams.

01	**02**	03	04	05	06	07	08
09	10	11	12	13	14	15	16
17	18	19	20	21	22	**23**	**24**
25	26	**27**	**28**	29	30	31	32
33	34	35	36	**37**	**38**	**39**	**40**
41	42	**43**	**44**	45	46	47	48
49	50	51	52	**53**	**54**	55	56
57	58	59	60	61	62	**63**	**64**

**Figure 1. Position of the Nuclear Hexagrams
in the Textual Sequence**
(Textual numbers of nuclear hexagrams are in **boldface** type.)

Olsvanger and the Textual Sequence. Evidence that the textual sequence—apart from its pairs of inverses and opposites—is not a completely random sequence was found by Dr. Immanuel Olsvanger.[14] Olsvanger gives the following diagram (the coordinate system of numbers along the y-axis and letters along the x-axis is added), which is the textual sequence of the hexagrams written from right to left in descending rows. The hexagrams are regarded as binary numbers and expressed as the binary number's decimal equivalent. For example, Hexagram 1, ☰, 111-111, is 63; Hexagram 2, ☷, 000-000, is 00; Hexagram 3, ䷂, 100-010, is 34, and so forth.

[13] [A] Dennis J. McKenna and Terence L. McKenna, p. 130.

[14] [B] Dr. Immanuel Olsvanger, *Fu-Hsi: The Sage of Ancient China*, Massadah Ltd. Jerusalem, 1948.

8	02	16	23	58	17	34	00	63
7	04	08	61	47	07	56	55	59
6	32	01	41	37	03	48	25	38
5	28	14	45	18	30	33	57	39
4	20	10	53	43	40	05	60	15
3	26	22	24	06	31	62	35	49
2	13	44	52	11	09	36	29	46
1	21	42	12	51	50	19	54	27
	a	b	c	d	e	f	g	h

Figure 2

Olsvanger points out that the group of cells c8, d8, e8, f8 as well as the group c1, d1, e1, f1 each total 132. And that the group d6, d5, d4, d3 and the group e6, e5, e4, e3 each total 104. Also the square formed by the six cells g8, g7, g6, h8, h7, h6 and the square formed by the cells g3, g2, g1, h3, h2, h1 each total 240.[15]

In addition Olsvanger shows that the diagram can be divided in several other ways into two symmetrical sections, each section having the same total, namely 1,008. One such division is given in Figure 2 above,[16] the others are given in Figures 3 and 4 below.[17] Numbers in the upper half of the division are set in boldfaced type for emphasis.

---

[15] Other symmetrically located groups of cells that have the same totals, not mentioned by Olsvanger, are the group a7, b7, c7, d7 and the group e2, f2, g2, h2, each of which totals 120. The group a1, b1 and the group g8, h8 each total 63. The group c2, d2 and the group e7, f7 each total 63.

[16] It is interesting to note that each division contains 14 pairs of inverses. Also, if the numbers in the square are rearranged in counting order (i.e., 0 to 7 in the first row, 8 to 15 in the second row, and so forth), then all the border numbers—numbers in columns a and h and in rows 1 and 8—of this newly formed square, except 3 (numbers 6, 24, and 62) are upper division numbers. See [B] Hacker, "Order in the Textual Sequence of the Hexagrams of the *I Ching*."

[17] It should be noted that the numbers in the cells a8, a7, a6, b8, b7, b6 (2, 4, 32, 16, 8, 1) are all powers of 2 and that all the other numbers in the square can be gotten from these six numbers by summing various combinations of them. Olsvanger gives special attention to these six numbers.

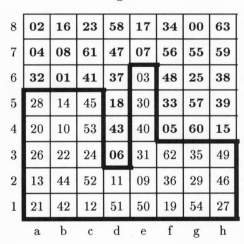

8	02	16	23	58	17	34	00	63
7	04	08	61	47	07	56	55	59
6	32	01	41	37	03	48	25	38
5	28	14	45	18	30	33	57	39
4	20	10	53	43	40	05	60	15
3	26	22	24	06	31	62	35	49
2	13	44	52	11	09	36	29	46
1	21	42	12	51	50	19	54	27
	a	b	c	d	e	f	g	h

Figure 3

8	02	16	23	58	17	34	00	63
7	04	08	61	47	07	56	55	59
6	32	01	41	37	03	48	25	38
5	28	14	45	18	30	33	57	39
4	20	10	53	43	40	05	60	15
3	26	22	24	06	31	62	35	49
2	13	44	52	11	09	36	29	46
1	21	42	12	51	50	19	54	27
	a	b	c	d	e	f	g	h

Figure 4

Two other symmetrical divisions, overlooked by Olsvanger, are shown in Figures 5 and 6. Yet another one may be formed from Figure 5 by redrawing the dividing line so that cells e7 and f7 are in the bottom division and cells c2 and d2 are in the top division. Each division totals 1,008.

	a	b	c	d	e	f	g	h
8	02	16	23	58	17	34	00	63
7	04	08	61	47	07	56	55	59
6	32	01	41	37	03	48	25	38
5	28	14	45	18	30	33	57	39
4	20	10	53	43	40	05	60	15
3	26	22	24	06	31	62	35	49
2	13	44	52	11	09	36	29	46
1	21	42	12	51	50	19	54	27

Figure 5

	a	b	c	d	e	f	g	h
8	02	16	23	58	17	34	00	63
7	04	08	61	47	07	56	55	59
6	32	01	41	37	03	48	25	38
5	28	14	45	18	30	33	57	39
4	20	10	53	43	40	05	60	15
3	26	22	24	06	31	62	35	49
2	13	44	52	11	09	36	29	46
1	21	42	12	51	50	19	54	27

Figure 6

Although Olsvanger's work does not produce an algorithm for generating the textual sequence of the hexagrams or their positions relative to each other in the textual sequence, his discoveries are, nevertheless, important for they suggest that there is a formal connection between the textual sequence (**King Wen's Arrangement**) and the binary sequence (**Fu Hsi's Arrangement**) of the hexagrams.[18] It would seem reasonable to assume that the **King Wen Sequence**—by some algorithm—was formed from the **Fu Hsi Sequence** since

---

[18] It would be more accurate to say that Olsvanger's discovery shows that there is a formal connection between *certain sections* of the textual sequence and the binary sequence of the hexagrams.

the algorithm for generating the **Fu Hsi Sequence** is known (the algorithm being the binary order) and Fu Hsi lived before King Wen. Unfortunately things are not always what they seem to be. Needham writes, "Actually the Fu-Hsi order...is not ancient at all, and cannot be traced further back than the Sung philosopher Shao Yung and his *Huang Chi Ching Shih Shu* (Book of the Sublime Principle which Governs All Things Within the World) of about 1060 A.D."[19]

On the other hand, the **Fu Hsi Arrangement (Earlier Heaven Sequence** or Primal Arrangement) of the trigrams does follow a binary order and this sequence is contained in the **Discussion of the Trigrams** (*Shuo Kua*), the Eighth Wing of the *Ten Wings* of the *I Ching*. According to Wilhelm/Baynes the **Fu Hsi Arrangement** of the trigrams "was already in existence at the time of the compilation of the Book of Changes under the Chou dynasty."[20] Hence, it can be argued that, since a binary order of the trigrams existed during the Chou dynasty, a binary order of the hexagrams probably existed at that time.

Another possibility is that both **King Wen's Arrangement** (textual sequence) and **Fu Hsi's Arrangement** (binary order) might be derived from a prior unknown arrangement of the hexagrams. As has been mentioned at the start of this chapter, there were in antiquity two other Books of Changes, each of which presented the hexagrams in an order that differs from the known textual sequence.

Lama Govinda and the Textual Sequence. Another attempt to show that the textual sequence is not a random one was presented by Lama Anagarika Govinda.[21] Concisely stated, Govinda's argument is that the sequence given below is the original textual sequence because when the hexagrams in each of the columns (given below) are represented as a line connecting its upper and lower primary trigrams on the **Fu Hsi Arrangement** of trigrams, the result is a symmetrical diagram.

Govinda's reconstructed arrangement of the sixty-four hexagrams—the sequence of "original purity"—is:

---

[19] [A] Joseph Needham, pp. 341–42.

[20] [A] Wilhelm/Baynes, pp. 265–66.

[21] [A] Lama Anagarika Govinda, Chapter XVII "Summary of Hexagram Arrangements" in *The Inner Structure of the I Ching: The Book of Transformations* (San Francisco: Wheelright Press, 1981).

Column 1	Column 2	Column 3	Column 4
Hexagram 1	Hexagram 17	Hexagram 33	Hexagram 49
Hexagram 2	Hexagram 18	Hexagram 34	Hexagram 50
Hexagram 35	Hexagram 19	**Hexagram 21**	Hexagram 51
Hexagram 36	Hexagram 20	**Hexagram 22**	Hexagram 52
Hexagram 5	Hexagram 23	Hexagram 37	Hexagram 53
Hexagram 6	Hexagram 24	Hexagram 38	Hexagram 54
Hexagram 7	Hexagram 25	Hexagram 39	Hexagram 55
Hexagram 8	Hexagram 26	Hexagram 40	Hexagram 56
Hexagram 9	Hexagram 27	Hexagram 41	**Hexagram 3**
Hexagram 10	Hexagram 28	Hexagram 42	**Hexagram 4**
Hexagram 11	Hexagram 29	Hexagram 43	Hexagram 57
Hexagram 12	Hexagram 30	Hexagram 44	Hexagram 58
Hexagram 13	Hexagram 31	Hexagram 45	Hexagram 59
Hexagram 14	Hexagram 32	Hexagram 46	Hexagram 60
Hexagram 15		Hexagram 47	Hexagram 61
Hexagram 16		Hexagram 48	Hexagram 62
			Hexagram 63
			Hexagram 64

The **boldface** hexagram numbers are those whose textual order Govinda changed.

Diagraming the sixteen hexagrams given in column 1 above yields Figure 7.

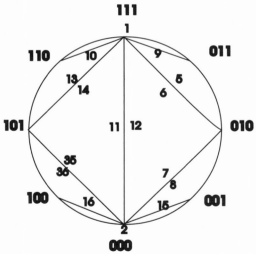

Figure 7.
Diagram of Column 1

In order to make this diagram symmetrical Govinda has to move Hexagrams 3 and 4 to a new position between Hexagrams 56 and 57 in column 4.

Diagraming the 14 hexagrams given in column 2 above yields Figure 8:

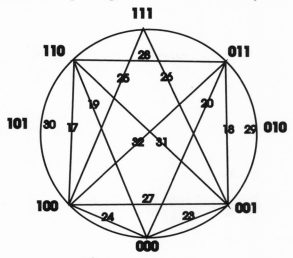

Figure 8.
Diagram of Column 2

By omitting Hexagrams 21 and 22, the resulting diagram is symmetrical.

Diagraming the 16 hexagrams given in column 3 above yields Figure 9:

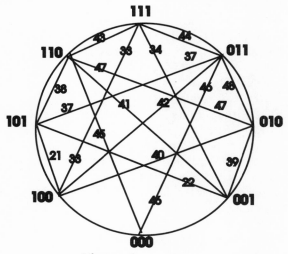

Figure 9.
Diagram of Column 3

In order to make this diagram symmetrical, Hexagrams 21 and 22 are substituted for Hexagrams 35 and 36. Hexagrams 35 and 36—as has been stated—are substituted for Hexagrams 3 and 4 in Column 1.

Diagraming the 18 hexagrams given in column 4 above yields Figure 10:

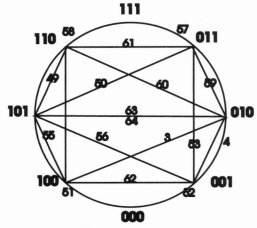

Figure 10.
Diagram of Column 4

In Column 4 Hexagrams 3 and 4 are inserted between Hexagrams 56 and 57. Column 4, when diagrammed, is symmetrical.

Govinda concludes that the symmetries that occur when his suggested changes are made demonstrates that these changes restore the textual sequence to its "original purity."[21] Although interesting and definitely a contribution to the literature on this topic, I do not think that Govinda's symmetrical diagrams prove his case.

Note that Figures 8 and 9 above have only horizontal symmetry (the left half of the circle is symmetrical with the right half of the circle), while Figures 7 and 10 are horizontally and vertically symmetrical (the left half of the circle is symmetrical with the right half of the circle and the top half of the circle is symmetrical with the bottom half of the circle). Hence, the type of symmetry is not consistent for all four circles. Would not an arrangement of the hexagrams that resulted in horizontal and vertical symmetry for all four circles be a stronger candidate for the original sequence?

If symmetry is the key to finding the "original order," then one would expect to find 16 hexagrams diagramed in each of the four figures. Such is not the case. In Figure 7, 16 hexagrams are diagramed (14 not counting hexagrams 1 and 2, which are double trigrams. These doubles are not represented by a line in the diagrams). In Figure 8, 14 are diagramed (12 not counting hexagrams 29 and 30, which are double trigrams). In Figure 9, 16 are diagramed, and in

---

[21] [A] Lama Anagarika Govinda, p. 151.

Figure 10, 18 (14 not counting hexagrams 51, 52, 57, and 58, which are double trigrams) are diagramed. Consequently, whether or not the double trigrams are counted, it is **not** the case that each diagram represents the same number of hexagrams, namely, sixteen. If there is no need for each diagram to represent the same number of hexagrams as the others, then there seems to be no need to have a number of diagrams that evenly divides into 64. In other words, why not have three diagrams or five diagrams or six diagrams?

The textual sequence of the *I Ching* is given in the *Sequence of the Hexagrams* (*Hsu Kua,* a commentary on the *I Ching* called the *Ninth Wing*). If Govinda's reconstructed sequence is correct then the *Sequence of the Hexagrams* is incorrect or has been incorrectly interpreted. But Govinda gives no evidence that would cause one to suspect the correctness of the *Sequence of the Hexagrams.*[22]

Also if Govinda's reconstructed sequence is correct then what happens to symmetries found by Olsvanger? Figure 10 below is the same kind of square as that given in Figure 2, except that it is based on Govinda's reconstructed sequence.

	a	b	c	d	e	f	g	h
8	02	16	23	58	40	05	00	63
7	04	08	61	47	07	56	55	59
6	57	39	32	01	03	48	25	38
5	60	15	28	14	45	18	30	33
4	35	49	20	10	53	43	41	37
3	29	46	26	22	24	06	31	62
2	17	34	13	44	32	11	09	36
1	21	42	12	51	50	19	54	27

Figure 11

The group of cells c8, d8, e8, f8 and c1, d1, e1, f1 no longer each total 132. Now the former totals 126 while the latter is still 132. The group d6, d5, d4, d3 and the group e6, e5, e4, e3 no longer each total 104. The former now totals 47 and the latter totals 125. Also the rectangle formed by the six cells g8, g7, g6, h8, h7, h6 and the rectangle formed by the cells g3, g2, g1, h3, h2, h1 instead of each totaling 240 now total, respectively, 240 and 219. Finally, none of the symmetrical divisions shown in Figures 2, 3, and 4 yield divisions that

---

[22] Although several scholars mention their dissatisfaction with the explanation given for the textual sequence by the *Hsu Kua* (see the beginning of this chapter), I know of none who have published in English any material casting doubt upon its correctness.

have the same total.

Hence, if Govinda's reconstructed sequence is correct, then the symmetries found by Olsvanger seem to be coincidental and, conversely, if Olsvanger's symmetries are not coincidental then Govinda's symmetries—based on his reconstructed sequence—are coincidental.

It is my opinion that Olsvanger's symmetries are more likely than Govinda's to be significant. My reasons are as follows:

> a. Olsvanger's symmetries are based on two orders that are part of the tradition of the *I Ching:* the textual sequence (**King Wen's Arrangement**) and the binary order (**Fu Hsi's Arrangement**). Olsvanger does not have to change the textual sequence in order to obtain his symmetries.

> b. Govinda's symmetries are based on three arbitrary assumptions: (i) That four and only four diagrams (the **Fu Hsi Arrangement** of the trigrams) are to be used to diagram the hexagrams; (ii) that it is permissible for one diagram to contain more hexagrams than another diagram; and (iii) that the type of symmetry (horizontal and/or vertical symmetry) may vary from one diagram to another.[23]

Neither Olsvanger's nor Govinda's symmetries can determine the textual number of a single hexagram or determine which hexagrams are odd-numbered or even-numbered. To date, however, no other researcher has done so.

Magic Squares and the *I Ching.* Dr. Schuyler Cammann writes that Yang Hui (a mathematician of the 13th century A.D.) gave the following magic square with the title "Plan of the I Ching":[24]

---

[23] Govinda's method seems to indicate that he is seeking a compromise between the degree of symmetry in his diagrams and the extent to which he is willing to change the traditional textual sequence, since a higher degree of horizontal and vertical symmetry would be achieved if hexagrams 23 and 24 were moved to a position between hexagrams 44 and 45. Govinda is quite right in trying to minimize textual changes, since the problem is to find an order in the traditional textual sequence, not to find orders into which the textual sequence can be changed. It should be noted that Govinda's new textual sequence differs considerably from the traditional one. More than half of the hexagrams would have to be renumbered.

[24] [B] Schuyler Cammann, "Old Chinese Magic Squares." Magic square is given, p. 44.

8	61	04	03	62	02	63	64	01
7	52	13	14	51	15	50	49	16
6	45	20	19	46	18	47	48	17
5	36	29	30	35	31	34	33	32
4	05	60	59	06	58	07	08	57
3	12	53	54	11	55	10	09	56
2	21	44	43	22	42	23	24	41
1	28	37	38	27	39	26	25	40
	a	b	c	d	e	f	g	h

Figure 12. Yang Hui's first magic square of eight.
(Each row, column and diagonal adds up to 260.)

Cammann states:

> It is not surprising that the Old Chinese should have tried to devise various systematic combinations employing the numbers from 1 to 64, because of their interest in the sixty-four hexagrams: linear symbols composed of six, whole or broken lines, which form the principle topic of the "Book of Changes." In fact, Yang Hui actually entitled this first square of eight the *I-shu t'u* or "Plan of the I (-Ching) Numbers." Perhaps this is just another indication of his background as a classical scholar; but it is quite possible that the name is an older one, and it may even preserve some memory of the use of a magic square of eight as a divination chart from which to select the numbers of specific hexagrams before looking them up in the *I Ching*.[25]

Cammann does not state whether or not the numbers in the square are the numbers in the textual sequence or the decimal equivalents of the hexagrams regarded as binary numbers. Also unclear is the expression "Plan of the I-(Ching) Numbers." One possible meaning is that the textual sequence is derived from this square. No other information on this square and its relation to the *I Ching* seems to be available in English.

Base 5 and the I Ching as a Calculator. René Barde, in an interesting paper,[26] makes a case for the following three points: (1) The ancient Chinese used a quinary—base 5—number system; (2) The hexagrams preceded

---

[25] [B] Schuyler Cammann, "Old Chinese Magic Squares," p. 45.

[26] [B] R. Barde, "Recherches sur les origines arithmetiques du *Yi-King*," *Archives internationales d'histoire des sciences*, 5 (1952): 234.

the trigrams; and (3) The *I Ching* is "a calculating procedure which permitted one to obtain, without knowledge of a multiplication table, the sums of 5 products of two numbers less than 10."[27]

Barde's case for his 3rd point is not entirely convincing, but it is not without merit. The *I Ching* may have had multiple functions. Further research in this direction may help solve the problem of the textual sequence.

Conclusion. In my opinion the textual sequence (**King Wen's Arrangement**) of the hexagrams has—at least in part—a formal order, and the strongest evidence for this are Olsvanger's discoveries, which are given above.[28]

Needham writes:

> Olsvanger and Barde translate the hexagrams of the Wen Wang (*I Ching* text) block order into ordinary numerals, by way of the binary system or otherwise, and find a variety of magic squares. While it is probably true that the discovery of the properties of magic squares occurred earlier in China than anywhere else, the magic squares obtained from the Book of Changes are rather complicated and it is hard to convince oneself that the Chinese mutationists ever had any such thought in mind when they arranged their hexagrams (Needham, p. 343.).

I agree with Needham that it is improbable that the Chinese mutationists consciously ordered the hexagrams so that their block arrangement would lead to the properties discovered by Olsvanger and others. What I contend is that the order discovered by Olsvanger—and perhaps others mentioned above— is derived from an algorithm used by the arrangers of the hexagrams. This original algorithm is still to be discovered.

The Textual Sequence in the Mawangdui *I Ching.* In 1973 at the Mawangdui site, Changsha, Hunan, a copy of the *I Ching* was found written on silk.[29] The sequence of the hexagrams in this manuscript differs radically from the traditional **King Wen Order.**

---

[27] [B] R. Barde, p. 264. Translation is mine.

[28] It may be that the order is part formal and part semantic, i.e., based on the meaning of the hexagrams.

[29] [B] Loewe, Michael A. N. "Manuscripts Found Recently in China: A Preliminary Survey." *T'oung Pao.*

1.	(1)	111-111	33.	(2)	000-000
2.	(12)	000-111	34.	(11)	111-000
3.	(33)	001-111	35.	(15)	001-000
4.	(10)	110-111	36.	(19)	110-000
5.	(6)	010-111	37.	(7)	010-000
6.	(13)	101-111	38.	(36)	101-000
7.	(25)	100-111	39.	(24)	100-000
8.	(44)	011-111	40.	(46)	011-000
9.	(52)	001-001	41.	(58)	110-110
10.	(26)	111-001	42.	(43)	111-110
11.	(23)	000-001	43.	(45)	000-110
12.	(41)	110-001	44.	(31)	001-110
13.	(4)	010-001	45.	(47)	010-110
14.	(22)	101-001	46.	(49)	101-110
15.	(27)	100-001	47.	(17)	100-110
16.	(18)	011-001	48.	(28)	011-110
17.	(29)	010-010	49.	(30)	101-101
18.	(5)	111-010	50.	(14)	111-101
19.	(8)	000-010	51.	(35)	000-101
20.	(39)	001-010	52.	(56)	001-101
21.	(60)	110-010	53.	(38)	110-101
22.	(63)	101-010	54.	(64)	010-101
23.	(3)	100-010	55.	(21)	100-101
24.	(48)	011-010	56.	(50)	011-101
25.	(51)	100-100	57.	(57)	011-011
26.	(34)	111-100	58.	(9)	111-011
27.	(16)	000-100	59.	(20)	000-011
28.	(62)	001-100	60.	(53)	001-011
29.	(54)	110-100	61.	(61)	110-011
30.	(40)	010-100	62.	(59)	010-011
31.	(55)	101-100	63.	(37)	101-011
32.	(32)	011-100	64.	(42)	100-011

Figure 13.
Textual Sequence of the Hexagrams in the
Mawangdui Manuscript

The numbers in parentheses are numbers of the hexagrams in the traditional
Ken Wen Sequence.

The Mawangdui sequence is mechanical and Shaughnessy gives the following method for generating it.

Group A	Group B
111	111
001	000
010	001
100	110
000	010
110	101
101	100
011	011

Figure 14

Each of the trigrams of Group A, serving as the upper or "outer" trigram, combines in turn with each of the trigrams of Group B (with the exception that each of the trigrams first combines with itself and then goes on to follow the prescribed order)...[30]

Shaughnessy's opinion is that the traditional sequence (**King Wen's Order**) "would seem to be the more authentic and should be retained."[31]

---

[30] [A] Shaughnessy, p. 168.

[31] [A] Shaughnessy, p. 174. Also see footnote 81, pp. 324-25.

9

PROBABILITY
AND THE HEXAGRAMS

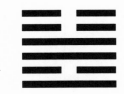

55. Abundance

The terminology used in the discussion of this chapter pertains to hexagrams considered solely in terms of their formal characteristics. Although these formal characteristics do have a bearing on the textual interpretation of the hexagram and its lines, such considerations will not be explored in this chapter.

Kinetic Lines. A line that is **moving** is changing to its opposite: yin changes to yang; yang changes to yin. A **static** line is one that is not moving. A **kinetic line** is a yin line or a yang line that is specified as either moving or static. If a yin or yang line is not defined as moving or static, it is called a **non-kinetic line.**

Kinetic Hexagrams. A **kinetic hexagram** is a hexagram composed of kinetic lines. It is a hexagram that has its lines specified as either moving or static. For example, Hexagram 3, ䷂, 100-010, *Sprouting,* or any other hexagram, would be a kinetic hexagram if each of its lines were described as either static or moving. For instance, to describe Hexagram 3 as having line 1 as static, lines 2 through 5 as moving, and line 6 as static makes Hexagram 3 a kinetic hexagram.

Number of Kinetic Hexagrams. There are two possibilities for each of the six lines in a hexagram: it is either static or moving. Hence for each hexagram there are sixty-four kinetic hexagrams ($2^6 = 64$), since there are sixty-four hexagrams and for each sixty-four kinetic hexagrams, the total number of kinetic hexagrams is $4,096$ (64×64).

The Yarrow-Stalk Method of Obtaining a Kinetic Hexagram.[1] The traditional way of obtaining a kinetic hexagram (for the purpose of seeking advice or divination) is by using fifty yarrow stalks. By tradition one of these stalks is returned to its container; only forty-nine are actually used. By a rather complicated process these forty-nine yarrow stalks are divided and counted until three numbers are yielded. (See **Chapter 10, Yarrow-Stalk Methods** for variations on these procedures.) These three numbers determine a single kinetic line of the hexagram; that is, these three numbers determine whether the line is yang or yin and whether it is moving or static. This process is repeated five times, until all six lines of the hexagram are formed.

In detail the process is as follows:

To determine the first number, perform Steps 1 and 2.

Step 1. The forty-nine stalks are placed in a heap on a table. In front of the heap is a tray. With one swift motion of the right hand the heap of stalks is divided into two piles: a right pile and a left pile.

Step 2. Then the following three operations are performed:

a. Take a stalk from the right pile and place it on a tray.

---

[1] With regard to using the *I Ching* as an oracle, a description of this yarrow-stalk method and (perhaps an older yarrow-stalk method) is in Chapter 10. See 1B Yarrow-Stalk Method: Version B.

b. Count the stalks in the left pile by fours until one, two, three, or four stalks remain. These remaining stalks are placed in the tray with the other stalk.

c. From the right pile take a number of stalks, but no more than four, which when added to the stalks on the tray will total either **five** or **nine**. Put these stalks on the tray. The number of stalks on the tray will be either five or nine. This number (five or nine) is the first number of three numbers that are needed to establish a line of the hexagram.

The numerical possibilities that the above three operations can produce are given in the table below:

Table 1. The First Number: 5 or 9

One Stalk from Right Pile		Remaining Stalks in Left Pile		Stalks Selected from Right Pile		Total Number of Stalks
1	+	1	+	3	=	5
1	+	2	+	2	=	5
1	+	3	+	1	=	5
1	+	4	+	4	=	9

To determine the second number, perform Steps 3 and 4.

Step 3. Combine the stalks in the right and left piles into one heap (leave the stalks on the tray) and then with one swift motion of the right hand divide the heap into two piles, a right pile and a left pile.

Step 4. Then perform the following three operations:

a. Take one stalk from the **right** pile and place it on the tray, but keep it separate from the group of 5 or 9 stalks already there. Start a second group on the tray.

b. Count the **left** pile by fours until one, two, three or four stalks remain. Place these remaining stalks on the tray with the one selected above, i.e., the second group.

c. From the **right** pile take a number of stalks, but no more than four, which when added to the stalks on the tray will total either **four** or **eight** (See Table 2). Put these stalks in the second group on the tray. The number of stalks in the second group on the tray will be either **four** or **eight**. This number (four or eight) is the second number of three numbers that are needed to establish a line of the hexagram.

Table 2. The Second and Third Number: 4 or 8

One Stalk from Right Pile		Remaining Stalks in Left Pile		Stalks Selected from Right Pile		Total Number of Stalks
1	+	1	+	2	=	4
1	+	2	+	1	=	4
1	+	3	+	4	=	8
1	+	4	+	3	=	8

Step 5. To determine the third number, perform Steps 5 and 6. Combine the stalks in the right and left piles into one heap (leave the two groups of stalks on the tray) and then swiftly divide with the right hand into two piles: a right pile and a left pile.

Step 6. Repeat the three operations given in Step 4 above, placing the stalks in a third group on the tray. The number of stalks in this third group on the tray will be **four** or **eight**.

Three numbers will now have been obtained: The first number must be a 5 or 9, the second number a 4 or 8 and the third number a 4 or 8. These three numbers determine a line in a hexagram.

Step 7. From the three numbers obtained find the kind of line they represented by using the table below:

Table 3. Determining the Kinetic Lines

Moving Yang	Moving Yin	Static Yang	Static Yin
5, 4, 4	9, 8, 8	9, 4, 8	9, 4, 4
		9, 8, 4	5, 4, 8
		5, 8, 8	5, 8, 4

Step 8. The above process determines the first (bottom) line of the hexagram. Steps 1 to 7 must be repeated five more times to determine the remaining five lines of the hexagram.

Table 4. The Probability of Obtaining a Kinetic Line by the Yarrow-Stalk Method

Probability of Obtaining a Moving Yin	Probability of Obtaining a Moving Yang	Probability of Obtaining a Static Yang	Probability of Obtaining a Static Yin
1/16	3/16	5/16	7/16

The probabilities in the above table are obtained by the following method of reasoning:

a) The probability of obtaining a 9 as first number is $\frac{1}{4}$ (.25) and the probability of obtaining a five as first number is $\frac{3}{4}$ (.75). Proof: It can be seen by looking at Table 1 above that there is only one way out of four $(\frac{1}{4})$ of obtaining a nine as the first number and three ways out of four $(\frac{3}{4})$ of obtaining a five as first number.

b) The probability of obtaining a 4 as second number is $\frac{1}{2}$ (.5); the probability of obtaining an 8 as second number is $\frac{1}{2}$ (.5). Proof: It can be seen from Table 2 that there are two ways out of four $(\frac{2}{4} = \frac{1}{2})$ of obtaining a 4 and two ways out of 4 $(\frac{2}{4} = \frac{1}{2})$ of obtaining an 8.

c) The probability of obtaining a 4 as third number is $\frac{1}{2}$ (.5) and the probability of obtaining an 8 as third number is $\frac{1}{2}$ (.5). Proof: Same as in (b) above.

d) The probability of obtaining a **moving yang line** is the probability of obtaining the numbers 5, 4, 4, which is obtained by multiplying the probabilities of each number together: $\frac{3}{4} \times \frac{1}{2} \times \frac{1}{2}$. The result is $\frac{3}{16}$.

e) The probability of obtaining a **static yang line** is found by adding together the probabilities of obtaining each of the following sequences: 9, 4, 8; 9, 8, 4 and 5, 8, 8 (the three sequences that yield a static yang line: see Table 3). The probability of obtaining each of these sequences is, respectively: $\frac{1}{16} = (\frac{1}{4} \times \frac{1}{2} \times \frac{1}{2})$, $\frac{1}{16} = (\frac{1}{4} \times \frac{1}{2} \times \frac{1}{2})$, $\frac{3}{16} = (\frac{3}{4} \times \frac{1}{2} \times \frac{1}{2})$. The sum of these probabilities is: $\frac{5}{16} = (\frac{1}{16} + \frac{1}{16} + \frac{3}{16})$.

f) The probability of obtaining a **moving yin line** is the probability of obtaining the numbers 9, 8, 8, which is obtained by multiplying together the separate probabilities, $\frac{1}{4} \times \frac{1}{2} \times \frac{1}{2}$. The result is $\frac{1}{16}$. It should be noted that a moving yin line is the most difficult (i.e., the least likely) line to obtain, which is consistent with the passive qualities associated with yin.

g) The probability of obtaining a **static yin line** is found by adding together the probabilities of obtaining each of the following sequences: 9, 4, 4; 5, 4, 8 and 5, 8, 4 (the three sequences that yield a static yin line: see Table 3). The probability of obtaining each of these sequences is, respectively: $\frac{1}{16} = (\frac{1}{4} \times \frac{1}{2} \times \frac{1}{2})$, $\frac{3}{16} = (\frac{3}{4} \times \frac{1}{2} \times \frac{1}{2})$, $\frac{3}{16} = (\frac{3}{4} \times \frac{1}{2} \times \frac{1}{2})$. The sum of these three probabilities is: $\frac{7}{16} = (\frac{1}{16} + \frac{3}{16} + \frac{3}{16})$. Note that a static yin line is the easiest (i.e., the most likely) line to obtain, which is consistent with the yin passive qualities.

h) The probability of getting a yang line, either moving or static, is $\frac{1}{2}$, since $\frac{3}{16} + \frac{5}{16} = \frac{1}{2}$. And the probability of getting a yin line, either moving or static, is $\frac{1}{2}$, since $\frac{1}{16} + \frac{7}{16} = \frac{1}{2}$.

Probability of Obtaining a Non-Kinetic Hexagram by the Yarrow-Stalk Method.[2] A **non-kinetic hexagram** is one whose lines are not kinetic, i.e., not specified as moving or static. Another way of stating it is to say a hexagram whose lines may be either static or moving. From (h) above we know that the probability of obtaining a non-kinetic yang line is the same as obtaining a non-kinetic yin line. Hence, each non-kinetic hexagram is as likely to occur as another. There are 64 non-kinetic hexagrams, and since each has an equal chance of being formed by the yarrow-stalk method, the chance of getting any specific one of them is $\frac{1}{64}$.

Probability of Obtaining a Kinetic Hexagram by the Yarrow-Stalk Method. The probability of obtaining a specific kinetic hexagram is found by multiplying together the probabilities of obtaining its six kinetic lines. For example, the probability of obtaining Hexagram 1, ☰, 111-111, with all of its yang lines static (the probability of obtaining a static yang line is $\frac{5}{16}$), is $\frac{5^6}{16^6}$ or $\frac{15,625}{16,777,216}$. The probability of obtaining Hexagram 24, ☳☷, 000-001, *Return*, with all lines static is $\frac{7^5 \times 5}{16^6}$, which is $\frac{84,035}{16,777,216}$. The probability of obtaining Hexagram 24 with all the yin lines moving and the yang line static is $\frac{1^5 \times 5}{16^6}$, which is $\frac{5}{16,777,216}$.

Calculating the probability of obtaining a hexagram which contains all four kinds of kinetic lines is easily done. For example, the probability of getting Hexagram 11, ☷☰, 111-000, *Peace*, with 2 moving yang lines, 1 static yang line, 2 moving yin lines, and 1 static yin line is $\frac{3}{16} \times \frac{3}{16} \times \frac{5}{16} \times \frac{1}{16} \times \frac{1}{16} \times \frac{7}{16}$, which is $\frac{315}{16^6}$.

---

[2] The original hexagram obtained by the yarrow-stalk method is always a kinetic hexagram; that is, each line is specified as moving or static. In this section we are determining the probability of getting one of the sixty-four hexagrams regardless of whether the lines are moving or static. For example, what is the probability that the yarrow-stalk method will yield Hexagram 13, regardless of what lines are moving or static?

The kinetic hexagram which is least likely to occur is Hexagram 2, ䷁, 000-000, *Earth,* with all of its yin lines moving. The probability of obtaining this kinetic hexagram by the yarrow-stalk method is $\frac{1}{16^6}$ or $\frac{1}{16,777,216}$. In other words there is only about 1 chance out of 16.7 million of going from *Earth* (Hexagram 2) to *Heaven* (Hexagram 1) in one step. The probability of getting Hexagram 1, ䷀, 111-111, *Heaven,* with all yang lines moving is considerably better: $\frac{3^6}{16^6}$ or $\frac{729}{16,777,216}$. Hence a change from Heaven to Earth in one step is 729 times more likely to occur than one from Earth to Heaven.

Probability of Obtaining a Kinetic Hexagram by the Three-Coin Method. This method requires that three coins be shaken in the hands and tossed onto a flat surface. This is done six times. Each toss determine a kinetic line of the divining hexagram according to the following combinations obtained:[3]

Table 5

3 Tails	Moving Yin Line (6)
3 Heads	Moving Yang Line (7)
2 Heads, 1 Tail	Static Yang Line (9)
2 Tails, 1 Head	Static Yin Line (8)

The following table shows the differences between the probability of obtaining a kinetic line by the yarrow-stalk method and the three-coin method.

Table 6

Kinetic Line	Yarrow Stalk Method	Three Coin Method
Moving Yin Line	1/16	2/16
Moving Yang Line	3/16	2/16
Static Yang Line	5/16	6/16
Static Yin Line	7/16	6/16

---

[3] This method is described in Chapter 10, *Methods of Divination.* Originally Chinese coins were used that were blank on one side and incribed on the other. I follow Blofeld in calling tails the inscribed side and heads the blank side ([A] Blofeld, p. 66.)

10

METHODS OF DIVINATION

50. Ritual Caldron

The *I Ching* **as Oracle.** There is little doubt that the *I Ching* was consulted in antiquity as an oracle. In the *Tso Chuan* (*Commentary on the Spring and Autumn Annals*), compiled between 430 B.C. and 250 B.C., there are recorded sixteen instances of the use of the *I Ching* for divination.[1] However, as early as 602 B.C. the *I Ching* assumed another function: that of expressing a world view and a method of categorizing and explaining the types of physical and social phenomena in the world.[2] These two functions are not necessarily exclusive. The extent to which one has a practical understanding of the world and the laws which govern it is a reflection of the extent to which one understands one's personal situation, one's relation to the present and to the future. Science and prediction go hand in hand, and philosophy and prophecy are often companions.

There are three basic ways in which the *I Ching* can be viewed and used:[3]

1. **Categorical Oracle.** In this view the *I Ching* is an oracle which will answer any question asked of it and whose advice is the best advice concerning the situation in question. To expect the *I Ching* to give definite answers to such questions as "Should I start looking for a new job?" or "Will the stock market go up by more than twenty points within a month?" is to view the *I Ching* as a **categorical** oracle.

2. **Conditional Oracle.** In this view the *I Ching* is an oracle whose answers and advice are applicable only **if** certain conditions occur. For example, if Hexagram 6, *Grievance,* is obtained when the *I Ching* is asked for advice concerning one's coworker, one interprets the advice given by Hexagram 6 as advice applicable to the situation only if there is or shortly will be a grievance (conflict) between the inquirer and his coworker. It is not interpreted as a prediction that there will be a grievance.

3. **Moral Guide.** In this view the *I Ching* is regarded as a book which gives moral guidance for any kind of situation. A particular Hexagram is not selected by any method of divination as an answer to a question, but instead, the inquirer selects a hexagram whose text describes his situation. This assumes that the inquirer is familiar with the text of all the hexagrams and is astute enough to select a hexagram whose text is applicable to his problem.

The process of divination—the first two uses of the *I Ching*—contains three parts: Formulation of the Question, Method of Divination, and Interpretation.

---

[1] These sixteen instances are listed and translated in Shchutskii, pp. 191–92. Shchutskii states, "Throughout the course of the seventh century B.C. the feudal lords used the *Book of Changes* exclusively as a divinatory text." [A] p. 192.

[2] [A] Shchutskii, p. 193.

[3] These three views are based on "three perspectives on the relationship of the *Yijing* to the world," described by [A] Smith, pp. 19-21.

Formulation of the Question.

Guideline 1. Every question should be **one** question. Do not ask two or more questions as one. The question "Will I get the job I applied for **and** will my uncle survive his operation?" is clearly a conjunction of two questions. Each part of this question should be asked separately. Also disjunctive questions such as "Should I take the job offered by Company X **or** take the one offered by Company Y?" are to be avoided.[4]

Guideline 2. Questions should be clear.[5] Avoid vagueness, ambiguity,[6] and high level abstractions.[7] The question "Will I find a good job?" is ambiguous, since a "good job" could mean a high salaried job (for example, an annual salary of over $40,000), or an interesting job (for example, a job that involves at least two months of travel a year to foreign countries).[8] Also the question is unsuitable because it has no time limit. Does the person asking this question want to know if he will find a 'good' job within a week, a month, a year, five years? The time limit, if relevant, should be made clear. Guideline 2 has to strike a balance with Guideline 3.

Guideline 3. If a clear and definite answer to your question is important then the question should be framed in such a way that one's ability in interpreting the *I Ching* is adequate to answer it. For example, if one does not know which hexagrams represent which months of the year, then one will have difficulty in obtaining an answer to the question "Within the forthcoming year, in what month is it advisable for me to get married?" Guideline 2 may conflict with Guideline 3. One's question may be too specific. In that case, one may not have the ability to interpret the text of the *I Ching* to the degree of specificity needed as an answer to the question. The more skilled one is at interpretation, the more specific the question can be.

Guideline 4. For the clearest answers, formulate your questions as requests for advice. Based on my own experience, I have found it more rewarding to ask the *I Ching* for advice, than to ask it for a prediction. I have had far

---

[4] Blofeld states that "Above all, the either/or type of question should be avoided." [A] Blofeld, p. 60. Hook writes, "An ambiguous either/or type of question must be avoided, otherwise, if the reply were to be 'yes' you would not know to which half of the question reference is being made." [A] Hook, *The I Ching And You,* pp. 12–13.

[5] This does not mean that the question has to be specific or detailed. General questions can be clear. For example, "What are the main things in my personal life I should be concerned about this coming year?"

[6] An expression is ambiguous if it has two or more meanings; it is vague if its meaning is unclear.

[7] Such questions as "What is the meaning of life?" "What is Truth?" "Is Love eternal?" involve high-level abstractions and are unsuitable questions. There is inherent vagueness in such abstractions.

[8] If the word "good" in the given question has two or more meanings then it is ambiguous. If the meaning of the word is unclear in this sentence, then it is vague. Generally such words as "good," "bad," "nice," "beautiful," and so forth are both ambiguous and vague.

better success with such general questions as "Should I take next summer off to do research on the *I Ching*?" than with questions such as "Will the stock for XYZ Company rise by two or more points within the next three months?"[9]

The following methods of divination, whenever possible, are explained in sufficient detail to allow the reader to perform them. However, the Plum Blossom Numerology Method is far too complicated to discuss in this work, and I have not been able to find any detailed explanation of the Forest of Change method in English. Hence, only a brief outline of these two methods is given here.

Methods of Divination

Traditional Methods

1. Yarrow-Stalk Method: Versions A and B
2. Spring and Autumn Method
3. Three-Coin Method
4. Six-Wands Method
5. The Plum Blossom Numerology of Shao Yung
6. Forest of Change

Modern Methods

7. Twelve-Wand Method
8. Eight-Coin Method (Pa Ch'ien Method)
9. Revised-Coin Method
10. Sixteen System
11. *I Ching* Cards (See Appendix L)
12. The Visual *I Ching* (See Appendix L)
13. *I Ching* Decision Science Computer (See Appendix L)

1. Yarrow-Stalk Methods. Versions A and B are both based on Chapter 9 of the **Great Treatise** (*Ta Chuan*), one of the **Ten Wings** of the *I Ching*. These two versions are mathematically equivalent; use of one over the other is a matter of preference alone.

1A. Yarrow-Stalk Method: Version A. This method is described in Greg Whincup's book and in a paper by Koon-Loon Leung. Whincup says that it is a reinterpretation of the traditional method described in other translations

---

[9] I do not believe that the *I Ching* advocates the view of an immutable future. The *I Ching,* I believe, advocates the view that our future is—for the most part—what we make it. Hence, such questions as "Will I die within ten years?" cannot be answered with a definite "yes" or "no," since our life expectancy depends—to a large extent— on many factors over which we have control. Hence, the *I Ching* can, at best, only give conditional answers to such questions, such as, "If one does so-and-so and avoids such-and-such then one may expect to be alive in ten years." It is my experience that the *I Ching* gives advice whether it is asked for or not.

([A] Whincup, p. 227). Leung says that this method is "the way practiced in ancient China" [B] (Leung, p. 244).

Equipment. Both methods start with fifty yarrow stalks. By tradition, one of these stalks is set aside. Only forty-nine are actually used in the divination. Blofeld states that the yarrow stalks should be between one to two feet long. Substitutes are allowed as long as the sticks are "clean and pleasing to the eye" ([A] Blofeld, p. 60). Pickup Sticks, toothpicks, even fifty coins of the same denomination, can be used.

Procedure. The following steps create the six kinetic lines of the divining hexagram.

> **Step 1.** With a quick motion of the hand divide the forty-nine stalks into two piles. (Note: when this step is repeated—Steps 6 and 7—there will be fewer than forty-nine stalks.) There are now a left and right pile with space right in between for the formation of a center pile.
>
> **Step 2.** Remove one stalk from the right pile and place it between the left and right piles. This is the start of the center pile.[10]
>
> **Step 3.** Count through the left pile by fours until there are 1, 2, 3, or 4 stalks left. Place these remaining stalks (1, 2, 3, or 4) in the center pile.
>
> **Step 4.** Count through the right pile by fours until there are 1, 2, 3, or 4 stalks left. Place these remaining stalks (1, 2, 3, or 4) in the center pile.[11]
>
> **Step 5.** Move the stalks in the center pile to one side (the discard pile) and combine the remaining stalks in the left and right piles into one pile. This pile now contains either 40 or 44 stalks. (Note when this step is repeated—Steps 6 and 7—there will be 40 or fewer in this pile. See steps 6 and 7 for the numbers).

---

[10] In the traditional method there is no center pile. The discard stalks are placed between the fingers of the left hand. The first stalk is kept between the little finger and the ring finger. The second time through, the stalks are placed between the ring finger and the middle finger. The third time through, the discard stalks and those in the left hand are placed in a discard pile.

[11] There is no need to count through the right pile by fours. The first time through steps 1 to 5 the center pile (which will be the discard pile) must total 5 or 9. Hence, if the center pile has 2, 3, or 4 in it after step 3, then add, respectively, 3, 2, or 1 to it from the right hand pile to total 5, and step 4 is completed. If the center pile has 5 in it, add 4 to it from the right hand pile to total 9, and step 4 is completed. The second and third times through steps 1 to 5 the center pile must total 4 or 8. Hence, if it has 2 or 3 in it after step 3, then add, respectively, 2 or 1 to it from the right hand pile to total 4, and step 4 is completed; if it has 4 or 5 in it, then add, respectively, 4 or 3 from the right hand pile to total 8 and step 4 is completed.

Step 6. Repeat steps 1 through 5. At step 1 the total number of stalks is either 40 or 44. After step 4 the new center pile will contain 4 or 8 stalks. After step 5 the remaining stalks—after the stalks in the center pile are placed in the discard pile—will total 32, 36, or 40.

Step 7. Repeat steps 1 through 5 again. At step 1 the pile now contains either 32, 36, or 40 stalks. After step 4 the new center pile will again contain 4 or 8 stalks. After step 5 the remaining stalks will now total 24, 28, 32, or 36.

Step 8. Divide the number of the remaining stalks by 4. The answer will be 6, 7, 8, or 9 groups.[12] This number determines the first (bottom) line of the divining hexagram.

6	Moving yin line.
7	Static yang line.
8	Static yin line.
9	Moving yang line.

Step 9. Starting with the 49 stalks, repeat steps 1 through 8 above five more times to determine the remaining five lines of the divining hexagram.

See the section *Interpreting the Divining Hexagram* at the end of 1B.

1B. Yarrow-Stalk Method: Version B. (This method was also explained in Chapter 9.)

Equipment. The same as for the Yarrow-Stalk Method A: fifty yarrow stalks, of which only forty-nine are used.

Procedure. The same procedure is used as in the Yarrow-Stalk Method A, except for Step 8. In the Yarrow-Stalk Method A the line is determined by the number of the **remaining** stalks. In Method B, the line is determined by the number of stalks in the discard pile after step 7. This discard pile will contain 13, 17, 21, or 25 stalks. The line is determined from Table 1 below.[13] There is no mathematical difference between Yarrow-Stalk Methods A and B. Method B

---

[12] This is the same as counting the number of stalks in the pile and dividing by 4.

[13] [A] Wilhelm/Baynes pp. 721–722 gives a device that replaces Table 1. For the number of stalks in the center pile let 9 = 2, 5 = 3, 4 = 3, and 8 = 2. Hence, if after the first run through steps 1 to 5 the center pile had 5, after the second run 8 and after the third run 4 (5 + 8 + 4), this would be regarded as 3 + 2 + 3, a total of 8, which is the number of a static yin line. The total will always be 6, 7, 8, or 9, which are the numbers traditionally assigned to the static and moving yin and yang lines. This device was investigated by [B] Koon-Loon Leung.

probably has become more popular than Method A, since the discard pile, being smaller than the remaining pile, is more easily counted.

Table 1. Determining the Kinetic[14] Lines

Moving Yang	Static Yin	Static Yang	Moving Yin
13 (5 + 4 + 4)	17 (9 + 4 + 4)	21 (9 + 8 + 4)	25 (9 + 8 + 8)
	17 (5 + 8 + 4)	21 (9 + 4 + 8)	
	17 (5 + 4 + 8)	21 (5 + 8 + 8)	

The probability of obtaining a kinetic line is given in the following table:

Table 2. Probability of Obtaining a Kinetic Line by Either Yarrow-Stalk Method[15]

Kinetic Line	Probability
Moving Yin Line	1/16
Moving Yang Line	3/16
Static Yang Line	5/16
Static Yin Line	7/16

Interpreting the Divining Hexagram. When six lines have been determined, a hexagram is formed which may or may not have moving lines. If there are no moving lines then all the material pertaining to the hexagram is read, but not any of the text that belongs to the lines. If there are moving lines then the material belonging to these lines is also read and a second hexagram is formed by changing all the moving lines to their **opposites** (yin changes to yang, yang changes to yin).[16] In this second divining hexagram, which represents the outcome of the situation, only the main text is read. The lines are not consulted.

---

[14] A **kinetic** line is a line which is specified as either moving or static

[15] Although it might seem from looking at Table 1 that the probability of getting a moving yang line is 1/8, since there is one favorable way of getting 13, namely 5 + 4 + 4, out of a total of 8 ways, this is incorrect. Not all of the eight ways shown in Table 1 are equally probable, since the probability of getting a 9, the first time one runs through steps 1 to 5, is 1/4 as compared to 3/4 for getting a 5. See Chapter 9, *Probability and the Hexagrams.*

[16] Whincup states that if there is exactly one moving line then **only** the text for this line is read (the text to the hexagram is read only to help one understand the text for the one moving line). If there are two or more moving lines, then a second hexagram is formed and the two hexagrams together is one's answer ([A] Whincup, p. 225).

2. Spring and Autumn Method.[17] This is similar to the yarrow-stalk method, but its method for determining static and moving lines is different.

Equipment. The same as the yarrow-stalk method.

Procedure.

Step 1. Use the yarrow-stalk method to obtain a hexagram. Make sure that you have recorded the number (6 = moving yin, 7 = static yang, 8 = static yin, and 9 = moving yang) of each line. If there are no moving lines, then one is finished; read only the text for the divining hexagram, not the text for the individual lines. If there are moving lines, continue to Step 2.

Step 2. Add all of the line numbers and subtract the sum from 55. The result is the **key number**. The key number will be between 1 and 19, inclusive.

Step 3. The object is to count the lines of the hexagram until the key number has been reached. Start counting from the bottom line of the hexagram upwards. If the key number is greater than 6 then count the top line of the hexagram twice and proceed counting downwards. If the key number is greater than 12, then count the bottom line of the hexagram twice and proceed upwards. Continue this method of counting until the key number is reached. Table 5 illustrates the counting procedure in full. Line 6 is designated by key numbers 6, 7, 18, etc. Line 5 by key numbers 5, 8, 17, etc. If the key number is 24 then line 1 is designated.

---

[17] The "Spring and Autumn Method" is my name for this divination procedure. Whincup is the only English-language source I have found. The description of this method is from [A] Whincup, pp. 228–229. Whincup's explanation of this ancient method does not cover all the possibilities, hence any description (especially in Step 4b) may contain inaccuracies. Whincup suggests that this may be the method used by ancient diviners at the time the *Commentary on the Spring and Autumn Annals* was written ([A] Whincup, p. 228). My description of the Spring and Autumn Method is based entirely on Whincup.

Table 3. Designating Line of Hexagram by Key Number

Lines of Hexagram		Locate Key Number and Determine What Line is on Same Row			
Line 6		6	7	18	19
Line 5		5	8	17	
Line 4		4	9	16	
Line 3		3	10	15	
Line 2		2	11	14	
Line 1		1	12	13	

Step 4. The information presented in this step comes from [A] Whincup, pp. 228–229. Whincup states that "No one has yet presented a complete hypothesis of how these earliest divinations were made." Hence, the following rules do not cover all possible causes. Sentences and words in parentheses are assumptions I have added.

a) If (one or) two lines in the hexagram are moving but neither is the designated line, then neither is allowed to move. In this case only the text of the hexagram is read. (If one of the two moving lines or the only moving line is the designated line, then this line is allowed to move. And the text for this line is read as the answer, while the text of the hexagram is read for a general background to the answer.)

b) If there are three or more moving yin lines or yang lines and none of them are designated, they all change. When (exactly) three lines change, both the text of the original and the new hexagram are read. If more than three lines change then the text of the new hexagram weighs far more than the text of the original. If the count falls on one of the moving lines, then only that line changes. (And the text of that line is the primary reading. The text of the hexagram is read for general background.)

3. Three-Coin Method.[18] The traditional coin method is popular because it is simple to use and takes far less time than the yarrow-stalk method. It is not recommended, however, by most serious practitioners of *I Ching* divination because it is not mathematically equivalent to the yarrow-stalk method in regards to the possibilities of determining the **kinetic** lines of the divining hexagram.

---

[18] Whincup states that the coin method "has been popular from the Tang and Song dynasties (600–1300 A.D.)" ([A] Whincup, p. 227).

Equipment. By tradition three Chinese coins are used: the kind that have a square hole in the center and are inscribed on one side only, the other side being blank. If Chinese coins of the kind described cannot be obtained then three United States pennies, or other coins with distinctively different sides, may be used.

Procedure. If Chinese coins as described above are used, then the blank side has a value of 3 and the inscribed side a value of 2. If other kinds of coins are used then one must decide which side to call inscribed and which side to call blank. Blofeld states that "...since the main function of coin inscriptions is to reveal their value, that side which indicates the value should be regarded as the inscribed side."[19] On American coins the value is inscribed on the side called "tails"; hence the "heads" side is regarded as blank.

Step 1. The three coins are shaken and thrown on a flat surface.

Step 2. From the sides of the coins that are face up, and using Table 4, the line is determined:

Table 4

Bl + Bl + Bl	(3 + 3 + 3 = 9)	Moving Yang
In + In + Bl	(2 + 2 + 3 = 7)	Static Yang
Bl + Bl + In	(3 + 3 + 2 = 8)	Static Yin
In + In + In	(2 + 2 + 2 = 6)	Moving Yin

(Bl = Blank Side, In = Inscribed Side)

Table 1 in terms of Heads and Tails is:

Table 5

H + H + H	(3 + 3 + 3 = 9)	Moving Yang
T + T + H	(2 + 2 + 3 = 7)	Static Yang
H + H + T	(3 + 3 + 2 = 8)	Static Yin
T + T + T	(2 + 2 + 2 = 6)	Moving Yin

(H = Heads, T = Tails)

Table 6. Probability of Obtaining a Kinetic Line by the Coin Method

Kinetic Line	Probability
Moving Yin Line	2/16
Moving Yang Line	2/16
Static Yang Line	6/16
Static Yin Line	6/16

---

[19] [A] Blofeld, p. 66.

A comparison of Tables 2 and 6 reveals that the coin method and the yarrow stalk method are different concerning their probabilities for obtaining a specific kinetic line. See Chapter 9, *Hexagrams and Probability*.

4. Six-Wand Method.[20] This method of forming a hexagram is as simple and fast as the coin method, but it does not indicate whether the lines are moving or static. The probability of obtaining any given hexagram by this method (ignoring whether or not it has moving or static lines) is 1/64, which is the same as with the yarrow-stalk and coin method.[21]

Equipment. Each wand—made from wood, ivory, or tortoise shell—is about eight inches long, one inch wide, and one-eighth inch thick. The wands are painted black on both sides, but painted across one side in the middle is a band of white one and one half inches wide.

Procedure. The side of the wand which has the white band across it represents a yin line (a black line with a gap in the middle). The solid black side of the wand represents a yang line.

Step 1. The wands are randomly shuffled sight unseen.

Step 2. The wands are rolled out on a table as if one were unrolling a scroll.

Step 3. The wands are then arranged as a hexagram. The wand nearest the person using them becomes the bottom line, the next nearest wand becomes the second line, and so forth, until the wand furthest from the person becomes the top line. The divination is the text for this hexagram, minus the text for the lines.

5. Plum Blossom Numerology of Shao Yung.

Da Liu describes these methods from *Plum Blossom Numerology (Kuan Mei Shu)*, a book written by Shao Yung (1011–1077 A.D.). The Plum Blossom system of divination is also explained in detail in [A] W. A. Sherrill and W. K. Chu, *An Anthology of I Ching*.

The outcome of the divination is not found in the text of the derived hexagram, but is determined mainly from the attributes of the primary trigrams and the cycles of the five elements. The interested reader is referred to Da Liu's book, [A] *I Ching Numerology*, as the methods are far too complicated and lengthy for inclusion in this chapter.

---

[20] I find the fullest description of the six wand method in [A] Douglas, pp. 39–40. No source is given.

[21] When it comes to determining which lines are moving and which are static the coin method is not equivalent to the yarrow-stalk method, but for both methods the probability of obtaining any given hexagram (regardless of whether or not its lines are static or moving) is 1/64.

6. Forest of Change.[22]

Equipment. The reader will need equipment to derive one solar-year hexagram, then one divining hexagram. A chart which gives the following correspondences: The four hexagrams (hexagrams 29, 51, 30, and 52) and the seasons to which each corresponds, and the sixty remaining hexagrams and the portion of the year to which each corresponds. (Each one of the sixty hexagrams would correspond to one degree of the zodiac—a 6.0875 day period($\frac{365.25}{60} = 6.0875$)— starting at the winter solstice.) Also needed is the equipment and method to divine a hexagram: yarrow stalks, or coins, and so forth.

Procedure. A hexagram is divined. One reads the text for the hexagram that corresponds to the period when the divination was made and then reads the text of the divining hexagram. The text of the first hexagram gives the general conditions affecting the situation; the text of the divining hexagram is the recommendation—the answer to the question.[23]

7. Twelve-Wand Method.[24] A variation of the six-wand method.

Equipment. Twelve wands. Six are marked yang and six are marked yin.

Procedure. The twelve wands are shuffled sight unseen, six are drawn one at a time. The first one drawn determines the bottom line of the hexagram. The second one drawn determines the second line of the hexagram, and so forth. This method yields no kinetic lines (i.e., moving or static lines.)

---

[22] The only description of this method I have encountered in English is given in [A] Schulz's unpublished dissertation, "Lai Chih-Te 1525–1604 and the Phenomenology of the *Classic of Change (I Ching),*" p. 15. The *Forest of Change (I Lin)* was written by Chiao Yen-shou (fl. 85–40 B.C.). The description given in the text is a simplified version of Schulz's outline.

[23] This is a simplified version of the procedure described by [A] Schulz, p. 15. Schulz writes: "One is supposed to employ the *Forest of Change* by finding the hexagram he has gotten in divination under the set of the hexagram that is assigned to the current 6.0875-day period and apply the information in its verse to the solution of his question. If, for example, on January sixteenth, during the period of AT ODDS (hex. 38), one divines the hexagram MEETING (hex. 44), he would consult the AT ODDS set of verses and read the verse under MEETING..."

[24] The only mention I have seen of this method in English is in Palmer, Ho, and O'Brien, *The Fortune Teller's I Ching.* The authors state that this method is currently used by the Chinese ([A] p. 38).

8. Eight-Coin Method (Pa Ch'ien Method).[25]

This method makes use of **Fu Hsi's Arrangement** of the trigrams and eight coins to obtain a divining hexagram with one line indicated. The judgment of the divining hexagram and its one indicated line is read to find the answer or advice sought.

Equipment. Eight coins of the same denomination. One of the coins is marked in some way to distinguish it from the others. The mark may be a scratch, a dab of paint or nail polish, etc. Also needed is **Fu Hsi's Arrangement** of the trigrams drawn on a piece of paper.

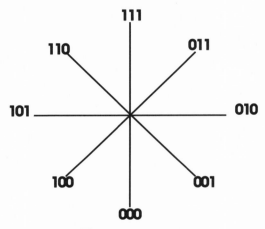

Figure 1.
Fu Hsi's Arrangement

Procedure.

Step 1. This step determines the bottom three lines of the divining hexagram. The eight coins are mixed randomly and then a coin is selected sight unseen and placed on the top trigram of the chart above (on Trigram 111). In a similar manner a second coin is selected and placed on the next trigram to the left (Trigram 110). This process is repeated (proceeding counter clockwise) until the marked coin is placed on a trigram. This trigram is the lower primary trigram of the divining hexagram.

---

[25] The eight coin method given here is based on the description of the Pa Ch'ien method in [A] Palmer, Ho, and O'Brien, *The Fortune Teller's I Ching,* pp. 41–45. According to Palmer, Ho, and O'Brien, the Pa Ch'ien method is the one most commonly used by the Chinese today (p. 40).

Step 2. This step determines the upper three lines of the divining hexagram. Repeat Step 1. The trigram on which the marked coin lands will be considered the upper primary trigram of the divining hexagram. The resulting hexagram is drawn on a piece of paper.

Step 3. Two of the unmarked coins are removed leaving six coins, one of which is marked. These six coins are mixed and they are selected, sight unseen, one at a time. The first is placed alongside the first line (bottom line) of the hexagram, the second along the second line of the hexagram, and so forth, until the last is alongside the sixth (top) line of the hexagram. Only the judgment of the hexagram and the commentary of the line indicated by the marked coin are read.

9. Revised-Coin Method.[26] This revised coin method has the same probabilities in regards to determining the kinetic lines of the divining hexagram as the yarrow-stalk method (See Table 2).

Equipment. Three coins.

Procedure.

Step 1. First Throw: Throw one coin. Record whether it comes up heads (H) or tails (T).

Step 2. Second Throw: Throw three coins. Record how many heads (H) and tails (T) come up.

Step 3. From the information in Step 1 and 2, look up the appropriate line in Table 7 and record. Note the expression "Not-(T,T,T)" in Table 7 means any combination **except** T,T,T and the expression "Not-(H,H,T)" means any combination **except** H,H,T. (The order in which H or T occurs is irrelevant).

Step 4. Repeat the above steps (1-3) five more times. Make sure that lines are recorded from bottom up.

Table 7. Determining the Kinetic[27] Lines by the Revised-Coin Method

First Throw	Second Throw	Kinetic Line	Probability
T	T + T + T	Moving Yin	1/16
T	Not–(T,T,T)	Static Yin	7/16
H	H + H + T	Moving Yang	3/16
H	Not–(H,H,T)	Static Yang	5/16

---

[26] [B] Hacker, "Brief Note on a Coin-Method..."

[27] A **kinetic** line is a line which is specified as either moving or static. See Glossary.

If there are no moving lines, then one reads the text for the hexagram, but not for the lines. If there are moving lines, one reads their texts as well as the hexagram text. One then obtains a second hexagram by changing all moving lines into their opposite (yin to yang, and yang to yin),[28] leaving the other lines the same. Only the main text of this second hexagram is read; it represents the outcome of the situation.

10. Sixteen System.

This method of forming a divinatory hexagram is extremely simple and yields the same probabilities of forming the kinetic lines of a hexagram as the yarrow-stalk method, versions A and B (See Table 2). The Sixteen System was invented by Larry Schoenholtz.[29]

Equipment: Sixteen beads (all the same size) of the following colors:[30]

1 black bead
3 red beads
5 yellow beads
7 white beads

Other objects may be used instead of beads as long as they are similar in all respects except color: buttons, marbles, pieces of paper, playing cards (where the different suits represent different colors), and so forth.

Procedure.

Step 1. The beads are placed in a container (a cup or small box) and shaken up. Schoenholtz recommends using more than sixteen beads as a larger number is easier to mix. If one multiplies the numbers listed above by three, then one has a total of forty-eight beads; the proportions remain the same.

Step 2. One bead is withdrawn sight unseen and the line is determined from Table 8 below. Record the line. (Remember that the lines are recorded from the bottom up.) **Return the bead to the container.**

Step 3. Repeat steps 1 and 2 five more times, thus obtaining six kinetic lines and forming the hexagram.

---

[28] Whincup states that if there is exactly one moving line then **only** the text for this line is read (the text to the hexagram is read only to help one understand the text for the one moving line). If there are two or more moving lines, then a second hexagram is formed and the two hexagrams together is one's answer. ([A] Whincup, p. 228).

[29] [A] Schoenholtz, pp. 82–83. It is also described by Whincup (pp. 227–28).

[30] Schoenholtz did not give any advice as to what colors should be used and I have not been able to find color attributes for the kinetic lines in English. My selection of colors was suggested by Table 13 on page 313 in [A] Needham, vol. 2. In this table black is the color of Trigram 000, *Mother.* Red is the color of Trigram 111, *Father.* Yellow is the color of Trigram 100, *Eldest Son,* and white is the color of Trigram 011, *Eldest Daughter.*

Table 8

Color	Kinetic Line	Probability
Black	Moving Yin Line	1/16
Red	Moving Yang Line	3/16
Yellow	Static Yang Line	5/16
White	Static Yin Line	7/16

Interpretation of the Divining Hexagram.

Interpreting the divining hexagram is an art as well as a science. It is a science because having a knowledge of **nuclear hexagrams, petals, cycles, stories, the five elements,** and so forth, is a tremendous aid in understanding the meaning of the hexagram.[31] It is an art because interpretation is not—nor can it ever be—a mechanical process. Interpretation requires a trained intuitive sense analogous to the diagnostic sense of a physician or the interpretative sense of a concert pianist. We do not all have this sense to the same degree, but we can develop what capacity we do have through practice.

Repetitive Expressions.

Below is a list of some expressions in the *I Ching*, with their interpretations. All of these expressions are from the Wilhelm/Baynes translation.

1. Perseverance. It might be better to substitute for "perseverance" the expression "It benefits one to follow the Way."[32]

The interpretation of "perseverance" as being in harmony with the Way, is my understanding of Lee's passage given in Footnote 32 below. Some expressions in the *I Ching* where "perseverance" occurs are:

Hexagram 1. Judgment. Furthering through perseverance.
Hexagram 2. Judgment. Perseverance brings success.
Hexagram 2. Judgment. Quiet perseverance brings good fortune.
Hexagram 3. Line 5. A little perseverance brings good fortune.
Hexagram 5. Judgment. Perseverance brings good fortune.
Hexagram 6. Line 3. To nourish oneself on ancient virtue induces perseverance.
Hexagram 7. Judgment. The army needs perseverance and a strong man.

---

[31] Of course the primary science in understanding the *I Ching* is sinology.

[32] My interpretation of Wilhelm/Baynes' word "perseverance" is based on Jung Young Lee's analysis of the Chinese words *li* and *chen*. Lee states: "To be correct means to be right with the principle of harmony through the help of divination. The advantageous or the furtherance can be attained, because of one's being in the right place and time." ([A] *Understanding the I Ching*, pp. 175–79).

2. Success. This word does not mean worldly success, but the benefits that come to a person who is in tune with the Way.[33] Some expressions in the *I Ching* where the word "success" occurs are:

Hexagram 4. Judgment. Youthful folly has success.
Hexagram 5. Judgment. If you are sincere, you have light and success.
Hexagram 9. Judgment. The taming power of the small has success.
Hexagram 12. Line 1. Perseverance brings good fortune and success.
Hexagram 12. Line 2. The standstill serves to help the great man to attain success.
Hexagram 15. Judgment. Modesty creates success.
Hexagram 17. Judgment. Following has supreme success.
Hexagram 18. Judgment. Work on what has been spoiled has supreme success.
Hexagram 19. Judgment. Approach has supreme success.

3. Great Water. When one or more of the primary trigrams in a hexagram is Trigram 5, 010, *Water,* generally the hexagram is unfavorable. When both primary trigrams are Trigram 5, then Hexagram 29, 010-010, *The Abysmal,* (Wilhelm/Baynes' name) is formed. In order for the Chou army to attack the Shang, it had to cross the Yellow River. Hence, the expression "crossing the great water" may be interpreted as a difficult, dangerous, or risky undertaking.[34] Some expressions in the *I Ching* containing the words "great water" are:

Hexagram 5. Judgment. It furthers one to cross the great water.
Hexagram 6. Judgment. It does not further one to cross the great water.
Hexagram 15. Line 1. A superior man modest about his modesty may cross the great water.
Hexagram 27. Line 5. One should not cross the great water.

4. West, Southwest, East, Northeast.

Wilhelm/Baynes says that "The southwest is the region of retreat, the northeast that of advance."[35] Therefore such expressions as "The southwest furthers" means it is favorable to retreat. Whincup saves himself the trouble of saying this by using the terms "retreat" and "advance" in his translation, instead of the terms southwest (west) and northeast (east).

---

[33] My interpretation is based on Lee's comment: "...we should not mean by success the accumulation of merits or the attainment of individual goals...(success) means one's will or desire is in accord with or in communion with the principle of the Great Harmony. Success here means one's conformity to the principle of changes" ([A] Lee, p. 172).

[34] Whincup uses "great river" in his translation instead of "great water." Whincup says, "In the *Changes,* fording a river symbolizes any difficult task or ordeal" ([A] Whincup, p. 36). No source is given.

[35] [A] Wilhelm/Baynes, p. 151.

The rationale for this interpretation is that before the Chou overthrew the Shang dynasty, the people of Chou and their supporters lived in the west and southwest, while the powerful Shang lived in the east and northeast. Hence, from the viewpoint of the Chou, to go west or southwest is to retreat, and to go northeast or east is to advance.[36] Of course such expressions as "the neighbor in the west" and "the neighbor in the east" (Hexagram 63, Line 5) refer to, respectively, Chou and Shang.

Some expressions using "west," "northwest," "east," or "northeast" are:

Hexagram 2. Judgment. It is favorable to find friends in the west and south, to forego friends in the east and north.

Hexagram 39. Judgment. The southwest furthers. The northeast does not further.

Hexagram 40. Judgment. The southwest furthers.

Hexagram 46. Judgment. Departure toward the south brings good fortune.

Hexagram 63. Line 5. The neighbor in the east who slaughters an ox does not attain as much real happiness as the neighbor in the west with his small offering.

5. Great Man, Superior Man, or **Seeing the Great Man.** Instead of "great man" and "superior man" Whincup uses "big man" and "lord." In general it is best to follow Blofeld's suggestion and interpret "great man" and "superior man" to mean a person who is superior in a moral and ethical sense (Blofeld, p. 81). However, the context of the question can certainly change this interpretation. For example, if the question is, "Should I have the operation that my family physician advised?" then it would be appropriate to interpret "see the great man" as advice to get a second opinion from the leading specialist in the area of your medical problem.

The expression "superior man" often occurs in the Images in the Wilhelm/Baynes translation. Examples are:

Hexagram 3. Image. Thus the superior man brings order out of confusion.

Hexagram 3. Line 3. The superior man understands the sign of the time and prefers to desist.

Hexagram 4. Image. Thus the superior man fosters his character by thoroughness in all that he does.

Hexagram 5. Image. Thus the superior man eats and drinks, is joyous and of good cheer.

---

[36] Legge writes that he takes "...the southwest as the regions in the south and west of the kingdom, which we know from the Shih were more especially devoted to Wan and his house, while the strength of the Kings of Shang lay in the north and east" ([A] Legge/Dover, p. 143). Whincup's chapter "Ancient China" should be read ([A] Whincup, pp. 9–14).

6. Good Fortune, Misfortune, and **No Blame.** Legge translates a paragraph of *The Great Treatise* to read:

> Therefore the good fortune and evil (mentioned in the explanations) are the indication of the right or wrong (in men's conduct of affairs), and the repentance and regret (similarly mentioned) are the indications of their sorrow and anxiety.[37]

and another to read:

> The expressions about good fortune or bad fortune are used with reference to (the figures and lines, as) being right or wrong (according to the conditions of time and place); those about repentance or regret refer to small faults (in the satisfying of those conditions); when it is said "there will be no error," or "no blame," there is a reference to (the subject) repairing an error by what is good.[38]

In Wilhelm/Baynes the translation says that good fortune means **gain** and misfortune means **loss**.[39] But in the commentary to the translation it is explained that "Always making the right choice in words and acts means gain; failing in this results in loss."[40] Good fortune is that which results from doing the correct thing at the correct time and place, and misfortune is that which results from incorrect (improper) behavior.[41]

The expression "no blame" is translated most of the time as "no mistake" or "no error" by Legge. Lee says, "In this respect Legge's translation can be more faithful than Wilhelm's to the original meaning of the text." ([A] Lee, *Understanding the I Ching,* p. 185). Whincup uses "comes to no harm." Blofeld uses, in various places "no blame," "free from error," and "preserves from harm." Cleary in *The Taoist I Ching* sometimes uses the expression "no fault."

In view of these multiple translations it is recommended that Legge be followed and the expression "no blame" be interpreted as meaning "no mistake," or "no error." Generally one should interpret these expressions as meaning that if one acts with propriety and ethical correctness in the situation, even if one's action leads to a detrimental materialistic situation (e.g., loss of money, and so forth), there is no error or mistake. Thus Whincup's translation "comes to no harm" is not recommended.

---

[37] [A] Legge/Dover, p. 352.

[38] [A] Legge/Dover, p. 352.

[39] [A] Wilhelm/Baynes, p. 288 and p. 291.

[40] [A] Wilhelm/Baynes, p. 291.

[41] I think that it is safe to say that good fortune is knowing and doing what is correct. This would be akin to the proverb "Virtue is its own reward."

A

THE BINARY SYSTEM

The Binary System of Counting: The system of arithmetic that we use to count is the decimal system which is based on the powers of 10. We use ten different numerals (e.g., 0, 1, 2, 3, 4, 5, 6, 7, 8, and 9) to write all numbers.

The binary system of arithmetic is based on the powers of 2 and uses only two numerals, 0 and 1, to write all numbers. The following table gives the binary equivalents for the first 16 numbers of the decimal system.

Table 1.

Decimal	Binary
0	0
1	1
2	10
3	11
4	100
5	101
6	110
7	111
8	1000
9	1001
10	1010
11	1011
12	1100
13	1101
14	1110
15	1111
16	10000

Hence 10 in the binary system is equivalent to 2 in the decimal system, 11 in the binary system is equivalent to 3 in the decimal system, 100 in the binary system is equivalent to 4 in the decimal system, etc.

Changing Binary Numbers to Decimal Numbers. To change a binary number to a decimal number use the following procedure.

Step 1. Using the decimal system write the numbers 1, 2, 4, 8, 16, 32, (each number is double its predecessor) below the digits of the binary number, writing from **right to left**. For example, take the binary number 1011:

$$1 \quad 0 \quad 1 \quad 1$$
$$8 \quad 4 \quad 2 \quad 1$$

Step 2. Add up all the numbers in the bottom row that are under 1's. These numbers are 8, 2, and 1. Their total is 11. Hence 1011 in the binary system equals 11 in the decimal system.

Another example, change binary number 011001 to its equivalent decimal number.

$$\begin{array}{cccccc} 0 & 1 & 1 & 0 & 0 & 1 \\ 32 & 16 & 8 & 4 & 2 & 1 \end{array}$$

Adding the numbers in the bottom row that are under 1's, we have $16+8+1 = 25$. Hence, 011001 in the binary system is equal to 25 in the decimal system.

Changing Decimal Numbers to Binary Numbers. The following procedure changes a decimal number to its binary equivalent.

Step 1. To derive the first digit (i.e., the digit on the extreme right) of the binary number, divide the decimal number by 2. If the number being divided is even, then the first digit is 0. If the number is odd, then the first digit is 1.

Step 2. If the result of Step 1 is one or greater then divide its integer part (drop the ".5" if there is one) by 2. If the integer part is even, the second digit will be 0. If the integer part is odd, the second digit will be 1. Keep dividing the integer part of each previous result by 2. If the integer part is even, the digit will be 0. If the integer part is odd, the digit will be 1. Stop when the result is less than one.

Example: Find the binary equivalent of 25.

Step 1.	25/2	=	12.5	First digit is : 1
Step 2.	12/2	=	6.0	Second digit is: 0
Step 3.	6/2	=	3.0	Third digit is: 0
Step 4.	3/2	=	1.5	Fourth digit is : 1
Step 5.	1/2	=	0.5	Fifth digit is: 1

Hence, 25 in the decimal system is 11001 in the binary system. Note that if the result is not even (i.e., ends in .5) the binary digit is 1, if the result is even the digit is 0.

Trigrams and Hexagrams as Binary Numbers. Each trigram and hexagram may be turned into a binary number by replacing its lines with numbers. Each yang line is replaced by 1 and each yin line is replaced by 0. The resulting digits are written horizontally. The digit on the extreme left is the bottom line (line 1) of the trigram or hexagram. The digit on the extreme right is the top line of the trigram or hexagram.

For example, Trigram 3, *Thunder,* which is two yin lines over one yang line would be written as 100. 100 as a binary number has 4 as a decimal equivalent. Note that all decimal numbers that are given as equivalents to binary numbers are in parentheses. In this book the expression "(4) is the binary number of Trigram 3" means that 4 is the decimal equivalent of the binary number which represents Trigram 3.

Hexagram 4, *The Young Shoot,* is expressed in digits as 010-001 (the hyphen is to make the number more readable). "010001" is equivalent to 17 in the decimal system. Hence, (17) is the binary number of Hexagram 4, which is short for saying that (17) is the decimal equivalent of Hexagram 4, expressed as a binary number.

B

TRIGRAM ATTRIBUTES
FROM THE EIGHTH WING

Trigram 1, 111 ☰. It is a symbol for heaven, for things which are round, for a ruler (prince), for a father, for jade, for metal, for cold, for ice, for deep red, for a good horse, for an old horse, for a thin horse, and for the fruit of trees.[1]

Trigram 2, 000 ☷. It is a symbol for earth, for a mother, for cloth, for a caldron, for thrift, for a young cow, for a large wagon, for the multitude, for a handle and support, and for black soil.

Trigram 3, 100 ☳. It is a symbol for thunder, for the dragon, for dark yellow, for spreading out, for a great road, for the eldest son, for decision and vehemence, for bamboo that is young, for reed and rushes, for a horse which can neigh well, for horses with white hind legs, for horses which gallop, for horses with a white star on their foreheads, for pod-bearing plants, strong plants and lush plants.

Trigram 4, 011 ☴. It is the symbol for wood, for wind, for the eldest daughter, for the plumb-line and a carpenter's square. It is the symbol for white, for the long, for the high, for advancing and retreating, for indecisiveness, for gray-haired men, for balding men, for men with broad foreheads, for men with much white in their eyes, for a tendency to desire large profits.

Trigram 5, 010 ☵. It is the symbol for water, channels and ditches (for draining and irrigation); for the hidden, for ambushes, for the straight and the crooked, for the bow and the wheel. It is the symbol for anxiety, distress of mind, pain in the ears, blood, and the color red; for horses with beautiful backs, horses with high spirits, horses with drooping heads, horses with thin hoofs, and horses that have a shambling step. It is a symbol for carriages (chariots) that are dangerous, for that which is penetrating, for the moon, for a thief, for a tree which is strong and has an inner firmness.

Trigram 6, 101 ☲. It is the symbol for fire, for the sun, for lightning, for the middle daughter, for armor and helmets, for spears and swords, for men with large bellies, for things which are dry, for turtles, crabs, mussels, and the tortoise. For trees which are hollow and rotten above.

Trigram 7, 001 ☶. It is the symbol for a mountain, for a bypath, for small stones, for doors, gates and openings; for fruits of trees and creeping plants; for a porter or eunuch, for the (ring) finger, for dogs, rats, birds with powerful bills; for trees that are strong with many knots (gnarled).

Trigram 8, 110 ☱. It is the symbol for a low-lying collection of water (lake), for the youngest daughter, for a sorceress, for the mouth and tongue; for the decay and putting down (of things in harvest); for the removal (of fruits) hanging (from the stems or branches); for soils that are strong and salty.

The Book of History describes the six ministries of the government. Each department is associated with one or more trigrams.[2]

---

[1] The traditional associations of the trigrams given below are from [A] Legge/Dover, Appendix V.

[2] See [A] Needham vol. 2, p. 337.

Ministry of	Duties	Trigram
Heaven	General Administration	111 Heaven
Earth	Education	000 Earth
Spring	Rites	100 Thunder
Summer	Executive	001 Mountain, 011 Wind, 101 Fire
Autumn	Justice and Punishment	110 Lake
Winter	Public Works	010 Water

Some Attributes of the Trigrams from Secondary Sources.[3]

Trigram 1. 111 ☰. Time: 7 p.m. to 10 p.m., late autumn, study rooms, clocks, tall buildings, clear and cold weather, fortifications, schools, universities, temples, stadiums, government offices, large city, cars, airplanes.

Trigram 2. 000 ☷. Time: 1 p.m. to 5 p.m., late summer to early autumn, kitchens, antiques, cloudy, clothing, mattresses, sheets, doctor, nurse, large groups of people, farms and farmers, fields.

Trigram 3. 100 ☳. Time: 5 a.m. to 7 a.m., spring, living rooms, storms, guns, explosives, radio stations, musicians, announcers, engineers.

Trigram 4. 011 ☴. Time: 7 a.m. to 11 a.m., late spring to early summer, hallways, windy, electric fans, ropes, wood, postmen, businessmen, publisher, libraries, research facilities.

Trigram 5. 010 ☵. Time: 10 p.m. to 1 a.m., mid-winter, bathrooms, pens, liquids, sleep, writers, philosophers, fishermen, bars, prostitutes.

Trigram 6. 101 ☲. Time: 11 a.m. to 1 p.m., summer, porch, warm and dry, library, guns, books, intelligence, electricity, theaters, department stores, writer, artist, teacher.

---

[3] The attributes of the trigrams given below are from [A] Tsung Hwa Jou, pp. 36–37 and [A] Sherrill and Chu, *An Anthology of I Ching,* Appendix A. Sherrill and Chu's list of attributes is ten pages in length.

Trigram 7. 001 ☶. Time: 1 a.m. to 5 a.m., early spring, bedrooms, cloudy and clearing, fixed or nonmoving objects, apartment buildings, hotels, motels, bridges, warehouses, priests, minister, family.

Trigram 8. 110 ☱. Time: 5 p.m. to 7 p.m., mid-autumn, playroom, kitchen, fog or rain, prostitutes, female singer, bars or taverns, tea, wine, coffee, things which give pleasure, entertainment, failures, sexual behavior, public relations, banker, things relating to the mouth and tongue: dentistry, laughter, and so forth.

Note that the times indicated by the trigrams follow the Later Heaven Sequence in a clockwise direction. The same applies to the months.

C

HEXAGRAMS:
THE NUMBER OF
YANG LINES

THE FOLLOWING HEXAGRAM CONTAINS 0 YANG LINES

Hexagram	Text #	Binary #	Name
000-000	2	(0)	Earth

THE FOLLOWING HEXAGRAMS CONTAIN 1 YANG LINE

Hexagram	Text #	Binary #	Name
000-001	23	(1)	Falling
000-010	8	(2)	Alliance
000-100	16	(4)	Contentment
001-000	15	(8)	Modesty
010-000	7	(16)	An Army
100-000	24	(32)	Return

THE FOLLOWING HEXAGRAMS CONTAIN 2 YANG LINES

Hexagram	Text #	Binary #	Name
000-011	20	(3)	Observing
000-101	35	(5)	Advance
000-110	45	(6)	Gathering Together
001-001	52	(9)	Mountain
001-010	39	(10)	Obstruction
001-100	62	(12)	Small in Excess
010-001	4	(17)	The Young Shoot
010-010	29	(18)	Water
010-100	40	(20)	Obstruction Removed
011-000	46	(24)	Pushing Upwards
100-001	27	(33)	Bulging Cheeks
100-010	3	(34)	Sprouting
100-100	51	(36)	Thunder
101-000	36	(40)	The Bright (Calling) Pheasant
110-000	19	(48)	Authority Approaches

THE FOLLOWING HEXAGRAMS CONTAIN 3 YANG LINES

Hexagram	Text #	Binary #	Name
000-111	12	(7)	Standstill
001-011	53	(11)	Gradual Advance
001-101	56	(13)	The Traveler
001-110	31	(14)	Mutual Influence
010-011	59	(19)	The Flood/Dispersion
010-101	64	(21)	Not Yet Across the River
010-110	47	(22)	Burdened/Exhausted
011-001	18	(25)	Illness/Decay
011-010	48	(26)	A Well
011-100	32	(28)	Constancy
100-011	42	(35)	Increase
100-101	21	(37)	Biting Through
100-110	17	(38)	The Chase
101-001	22	(41)	Adornment
101-010	63	(42)	Already Across the River
101-100	55	(44)	Abundance
110-001	41	(49)	Decrease
110-010	60	(50)	Restraint (Regulations)
110-100	54	(52)	A Maiden Marries
111-000	11	(56)	Peace/Flowing

THE FOLLOWING HEXAGRAMS CONTAIN 4 YANG LINES

Hexagram	Text #	Binary #	Name
001-111	33	(15)	The Piglet
010-111	6	(23)	Grievance
011-011	57	(27)	Wing
011-101	50	(29)	The Ritual Caldron
011-110	28	(30)	Big in Excess
100-111	25	(39)	No Error (No Expectations)
101-011	37	(43)	The Family
101-101	30	(45)	Fire
101-110	49	(46)	Revolution
110-011	61	(51)	Inmost Sincerity (Allegiance)
110-101	38	(53)	Estrangement
110-110	58	(54)	Lake
111-001	26	(57)	Big Restraint/Big Accumulation
111-010	5	(58)	Getting Wet
111-100	34	(60)	Big Uses Force

THE FOLLOWING HEXAGRAMS CONTAIN 5 YANG LINES

Hexagram	Text #	Binary #	Name
011-111	44	(31)	Meeting/Subjugated
101-111	13	(47)	Companions
110-111	10	(55)	Treading
111-011	9	(59)	Small Restraint/Small Accumulation
111-101	14	(61)	Great Possessions
111-110	43	(62)	Decisive

THE FOLLOWING HEXAGRAMS CONTAIN 6 YANG LINES

Hexagram	Text #	Binary #	Name
111-111	1	(63)	Heaven

D

PAIRS OF
HEXAGRAM OPPOSITES:
TEXTUAL SEQUENCE

The first hexagram in each pair in the textual # column is in textual sequence with the first hexagrams in the other pairs.

Hexagram Opposites	Textual #	Binary #	Name
111-111	1	(63)	Heaven
000-000	2	(0)	Earth
000-000	2	(0)	Earth
111-111	1	(63)	Heaven
100-010	3	(34)	Sprouting
011-101	50	(29)	The Ritual Caldron
010-001	4	(17)	The Young Shoot
101-110	49	(46)	Revolution
111-010	5	(58)	Getting Wet
000-101	35	(5)	Advance
010-111	6	(23)	Grievance
101-000	36	(40)	The Bright (Calling) Pheasant
010-000	7	(16)	An Army
101-111	13	(47)	Companions
000-010	8	(2)	Alliance
111-101	14	(61)	Great Possessions
111-011	9	(59)	Small Restraint/Small Accumulation
000-100	16	(4)	Contentment
110-111	10	(55)	Treading
001-000	15	(8)	Modesty
111-000	11	(56)	Peace/Flowing
000-111	12	(7)	Standstill
000-111	12	(7)	Standstill
111-000	11	(56)	Peace/Flowing
101-111	13	(47)	Companions
010-000	7	(16)	An Army
111-101	14	(61)	Great Possessions
000-010	8	(2)	Alliance
001-000	15	(8)	Modesty
110-111	10	(55)	Treading
000-100	16	(4)	Contentment
111-011	9	(59)	Small Restraint/Small Accumulation
100-110	17	(38)	The Chase
011-001	18	(25)	Illness/Decay
011-001	18	(25)	Illness/Decay
100-110	17	(38)	The Chase

Hexagram Opposites	Textual #	Binary #	Name
110-000	19	(48)	Authority Approaches
001-111	33	(15)	The Piglet
000-011	20	(3)	Observing
111-100	34	(60)	Big Uses Force
100-101	21	(37)	Biting Through
011-010	48	(26)	A Well
101-001	22	(41)	Adornment
010-110	47	(22)	Burdened/Exhausted
000-001	23	(1)	Falling
111-110	43	(62)	Decisive
100-000	24	(32)	Return
011-111	44	(31)	Meeting/Subjugated
100-111	25	(39)	No Error (No Expectations)
011-000	46	(24)	Pushing Upwards
111-001	26	(57)	Big Restraint/Big Accumulation
000-110	45	(6)	Gathering Together
100-001	27	(33)	Bulging Cheeks
011-110	28	(30)	Big in Excess
011-110	28	(30)	Big in Excess
100-001	27	(33)	Bulging Cheeks
010-010	29	(18)	Water
101-101	30	(45)	Fire
101-101	30	(45)	Fire
010-010	29	(18)	Water
001-110	31	(14)	Mutual Influence
110-001	41	(49)	Decrease
011-100	32	(28)	Constancy
100-011	42	(35)	Increase
001-111	33	(15)	The Piglet
110-000	19	(48)	Authority Approaches
111-100	34	(60)	Big Uses Force
000-011	20	(3)	Observing
000-101	35	(5)	Advance
111-010	5	(58)	Getting Wet
101-000	36	(40)	The Bright (Calling) Pheasant
010-111	6	(23)	Grievance
101-011	37	(43)	The Family
010-100	40	(20)	Obstruction Removed

Hexagram Opposites	Textual #	Binary #	Name
110-101	38	(53)	Estrangement
001-010	39	(10)	Obstruction
001-010	39	(10)	Obstruction
110-101	38	(53)	Estrangement
010-100	40	(20)	Obstruction Removed
101-011	37	(43)	The Family
110-001	41	(49)	Decrease
001-110	31	(14)	Mutual Influence
100-011	42	(35)	Increase
011-100	32	(28)	Constancy
111-110	43	(62)	Decisive
000-001	23	(1)	Falling
011-111	44	(31)	Meeting/Subjugation
100-000	24	(32)	Return
000-110	45	(6)	Gathering Together
111-001	26	(57)	Big Restraint/Big Accumulation
011-000	46	(24)	Pushing Upwards
100-111	25	(39)	No Error (No Expectations)
010-110	47	(22)	Burdened/Exhausted
101-001	22	(41)	Adornment
011-010	48	(26)	A Well
100-101	21	(37)	Biting Through
101-110	49	(46)	Revolution
010-001	4	(17)	The Young Shoot
011-101	50	(29)	The Ritual Caldron
100-010	3	(34)	Sprouting
100-100	51	(36)	Thunder
011-011	57	(27)	Wind
001-001	52	(9)	Mountain
110-110	58	(54)	Lake
001-011	53	(11)	Gradual Advance
110-100	54	(52)	A Maiden Marries
110-100	54	(52)	A Maiden Marries
001-011	53	(11)	Gradual Advance
101-100	55	(44)	Abundance
010-011	59	(19)	Flood/Dispersion
001-101	56	(13)	The Traveler
110-010	60	(50)	Restraint (Regulations)

Hexagram Opposites	Textual #	Binary #	Name
011-011	57	(27)	Wind
100-100	51	(36)	Thunder
110-110	58	(54)	Lake
001-001	52	(9)	Mountain
010-011	59	(19)	Flood/Dispersion
101-100	55	(44)	Abundance
110-010	60	(50)	Restraint (Regulations)
001-101	56	(13)	The Traveler
110-011	61	(51)	Inmost Sincerity (Allegiance)
001-100	62	(12)	Small in Excess
001-100	62	(12)	Small in Excess
110-011	61	(51)	Inmost Sincerity (Allegiance)
101-010	63	(42)	Already Across the River
010-101	64	(21)	Not Yet Across the River
010-101	64	(21)	Not Yet Across the River
101-010	63	(42)	Already Across the River

E

PAIRS OF
HEXAGRAM OPPOSITES:
BINARY SEQUENCE

First hexagram in each pair in the binary # column is in binary order with the first hexagrams in the other pairs.

Hexagram Opposites	Textual #	Binary #	Name
000-000	2	(0)	Earth
111-111	1	(63)	Heaven
000-001	23	(1)	Falling
111-110	43	(62)	Decisive
000-010	8	(2)	Alliance
111-101	14	(61)	Great Possessions
000-011	20	(3)	Observing
111-100	34	(60)	Big Uses Force
000-100	6	(4)	Contentment
111-011	9	(59)	Small Restraint/Small Accumulation
000-101	35	(5)	Advance
111-010	5	(58)	Getting Wet
000-110	45	(6)	Gathering Together
111-001	26	(57)	Big Restraint/Big Accumulation
000-111	12	(7)	Standstill
111-000	11	(56)	Peace/Flowing
001-000	15	(8)	Modesty
110-111	10	(55)	Treading
001-001	52	(9)	Mountain
110-110	58	(54)	Lake
001-010	39	(10)	Obstruction
110-101	38	(53)	Estrangement
001-011	53	(11)	Gradual Advance
110-100	54	(52)	A Maiden Marries
001-100	62	(12)	Small in Excess
110-011	61	(51)	Inmost Sincerity (Allegiance)
001-101	56	(13)	The Traveler
110-010	60	(50)	Restraint (Regulations)
001-110	31	(14)	Mutual Influence
110-001	41	(49)	Decrease
001-111	33	(15)	The Piglet
110-000	19	(48)	Authority Approaches
010-000	7	(16)	An Army
101-111	13	(47)	Companions

Hexagram Opposites	Textual #	Binary #	Name
010-001	4	(17)	The Young Shoot
101-110	49	(46)	Revolution
010-010	29	(18)	Water
101-101	30	(45)	Fire
010-011	59	(19)	Flood/Dispersion
101-100	55	(44)	Abundance
010-100	40	(20)	Obstruction Removed
101-011	37	(43)	The Family
010-101	64	(21)	Not Yet Across the River
101-010	63	(42)	Already Across the River
010-110	47	(22)	Burdened/Exhausted
101-001	22	(41)	Adornment
010-111	6	(23)	Grievance
101-000	36	(40)	The Bright (Calling) Pheasant
011-000	46	(24)	Pushing Upwards
100-111	25	(39)	No Error (No Expectations)
011-001	18	(25)	Illness/Decay
100-110	17	(38)	The Chase
011-010	48	(26)	A Well
100-101	21	(37)	Biting Through
011-011	57	(27)	Wind
100-100	51	(36)	Thunder
011-100	32	(28)	Constancy
100-011	42	(35)	Increase
011-101	50	(29)	The Ritual Caldron
100-010	3	(34)	Sprouting
011-110	28	(30)	Big in Excess
100-001	27	(33)	Bulging Cheeks
011-111	44	(31)	Meeting/Subjugated
100-000	24	(32)	Return
100-000	24	(32)	Return
011-111	44	(31)	Meeting/Subjugated
100-001	27	(33)	Bulging Cheeks
011-110	28	(30)	Big in Excess

Hexagram Opposites	Textual #	Binary #	Name
100-010	3	(34)	Sprouting
011-101	50	(29)	The Ritual Caldron
100-011	42	(35)	Increase
011-100	32	(28)	Constancy
100-100	51	(36)	Thunder
011-011	57	(27)	Wind
100-101	21	(37)	Biting Through
011-010	48	(26)	A Well
100-110	17	(38)	The Chase
011-001	18	(25)	Illness/Decay
100-111	25	(39)	No Error (No Expectations)
011-000	46	(24)	Pushing Upwards
101-000	36	(40)	The Bright (Calling) Pheasant
010-111	6	(23)	Grievance
101-001	22	(41)	Adornment
010-110	47	(22)	Burdened/Exhausted
101-010	63	(42)	Already Across the River
010-101	64	(21)	Not Yet Across the River
101-011	37	(43)	The Family
010-100	40	(20)	Obstruction Removed
101-100	55	(44)	Abundance
010-011	59	(19)	Flood/Dispersion
101-101	30	(45)	Fire
010-010	29	(18)	Water
101-110	49	(46)	Revolution
010-001	4	(17)	The Young Shoot
101-111	13	(47)	Companions
010-000	7	(16)	An Army
110-000	19	(48)	Authority Approaches
001-111	33	(15)	The Piglet
110-001	41	(49)	Decrease
001-110	31	(14)	Mutual Influence
110-010	60	(50)	Restraint (Regulations)
001-101	56	(13)	The Traveler
110-011	61	(51)	Inmost Sincerity (Allegiance)
001-100	62	(12)	Small in Excess

Hexagram Opposites	Textual #	Binary #	Name
110-100	54	(52)	A Maiden Marries
001-011	53	(11)	Gradual Advance
110-101	38	(53)	Estrangement
001-010	39	(10)	Obstruction
110-110	58	(54)	Lake
001-001	52	(9)	Mountain
110-111	10	(55)	Treading
001-000	15	(8)	Modesty
111-000	11	(56)	Peace/Flowing
000-111	12	(7)	Standstill
111-001	26	(57)	Big Restraint/Big Accumulation
000-110	45	(6)	Gathering Together
111-010	5	(58)	Getting Wet
000-101	35	(5)	Advance
111-011	9	(59)	Small Restraint/Small Accumulation
000-100	16	(4)	Contentment
111-100	34	(60)	Big Uses Force
000-011	20	(3)	Observing
111-101	14	(61)	Great Possessions
000-010	8	(2)	Alliance
111-110	43	(62)	Decisive
000-001	23	(1)	Falling
111-111	1	(63)	Heaven
000-000	2	(0)	Earth

F

THE NUCLEAR
HEXAGRAMS

LP = Lower Primary Trigram (Lines 1,2,3)
UP = Upper Primary Trigram (Lines 4,5,6)
LN = Lower Nuclear Trigram (Lines 2,3,4)
UN = Upper Nuclear Trigram (Lines 3,4,5)
The original hexagrams are given in binary order.

	HEXAGRAM	TEXT #	BINARY #	NAME
ORIGINAL	000-000	2	(0)	Earth
LN-UN	000-000	2	(0)	Earth
LN-UP	000-000	2	(0)	Earth
UN-UP	000-000	2	(0)	Earth
LP-UN	000-000	2	(0)	Earth
LP-LN	000-000	2	(0)	Earth
ORIGINAL	000-001	23	(1)	Falling
LN-UN	000-000	2	(0)	Earth
LN-UP	000-001	23	(1)	Falling
UN-UP	000-001	23	(1)	Falling
LP-UN	000-000	2	(0)	Earth
LP-LN	000-000	2	(0)	Earth
ORIGINAL	000-010	8	(2)	Alliance
LN-UN	000-001	23	(1)	Falling
LN-UP	000-010	8	(2)	Alliance
UN-UP	001-010	39	(10)	Obstruction
LP-UN	000-001	23	(1)	Falling
LP-LN	000-000	2	(0)	Earth
ORIGINAL	000-011	20	(3)	Observing
LN-UN	000-001	23	(1)	Falling
LN-UP	000-011	20	(3)	Observing
UN-UP	001-011	53	(11)	Gradual Advance
LP-UN	000-001	23	(1)	Falling
LP-LN	000-000	2	(0)	Earth
ORIGINAL	000-100	16	(4)	Contentment
LN-UN	001-010	39	(10)	Obstruction
LN-UP	001-100	62	(12)	Small in Excess
UN-UP	010-100	40	(20)	Obstruction Removed
LP-UN	000-010	8	(2)	Alliance
LP-LN	000-001	23	(1)	Falling

	HEXAGRAM	TEXT #	BINARY #	NAME
ORIGINAL	000-101	35	(5)	Advance
LN-UN	001-010	39	(10)	Obstruction
LN-UP	001-101	56	(13)	The Traveler
UN-UP	010-101	64	(21)	Not Yet Across the River
LP-UN	000-010	8	(2)	Alliance
LP-LN	000-001	23	(1)	Falling
ORIGINAL	000-110	45	(6)	Gathering Together
LN-UN	001-011	53	(11)	Gradual Advance
LN-UP	001-110	31	(14)	Mutual Influence
UN-UP	011-110	28	(30)	Big in Excess
LP-UN	000-011	20	(3)	Observing
LP-LN	000-001	23	(1)	Falling
ORIGINAL	000-111	12	(7)	Standstill
LN-UN	001-011	53	(11)	Gradual Advance
LN-UP	001-111	33	(15)	The Piglet
UN-UP	011-111	44	(31)	Meeting/Subjugation
LP-UN	000-011	20	(3)	Observing
LP-LN	000-001	23	(1)	Falling
ORIGINAL	001-000	15	(8)	Modesty
LN-UN	010-100	40	(20)	Obstruction Removed
LN-UP	010-000	7	(16)	An Army
UN-UP	100-000	24	(32)	Return
LP-UN	001-100	62	(12)	Small in Excess
LP-LN	001-010	39	(10)	Obstruction
ORIGINAL	001-001	52	(9)	Mountain
LN-UN	010-100	40	(20)	Obstruction Removed
LN-UP	010-001	4	(17)	The Young Shoot
UN-UP	100-001	27	(33)	Bulging Cheeks
LP-UN	001-100	62	(12)	Small in Excess
LP-LN	001-010	39	(10)	Obstruction

	HEXAGRAM	TEXT #	BINARY #	NAME
ORIGINAL	001-010	39	(10)	Obstruction
LN-UN	010-101	64	(21)	Not Yet Across the River
LN-UP	010-010	29	(18)	Water
UN-UP	101-010	63	(42)	Already Across the River
LP-UN	001-101	56	(13)	The Traveler
LP-LN	001-010	39	(10)	Obstruction
ORIGINAL	001-011	53	(11)	Gradual Advance
LN-UN	010-101	64	(21)	Not Yet Across the River
LN-UP	010-011	59	(19)	Flood/Dispersion
UN-UP	101-011	37	(43)	The Family
LP-UN	001-101	56	(13)	The Traveler
LP-LN	001-010	39	(10)	Obstruction
ORIGINAL	001-100	62	(12)	Small in Excess
LN-UN	011-110	28	(30)	Big in Excess
LN-UP	011-100	32	(28)	Constancy
UN-UP	110-100	54	(52)	A Maiden Marries
LP-UN	001-110	31	(14)	Mutual Influence
LP-LN	001-011	53	(11)	Gradual Advance
ORIGINAL	001-101	56	(13)	The Traveler
LN-UN	011-110	28	(30)	Big in Excess
LN-UP	011-101	50	(29)	The Ritual Caldron
UN-UP	110-101	38	(53)	Estrangement
LP-UN	001-110	31	(14)	Mutual Influence
LP-LN	001-011	53	(11)	Gradual Advance
ORIGINAL	001-110	31	(14)	Mutual Influence
LN-UN	011-111	44	(31)	Meeting/Subjugated
LN-UP	011-110	28	(30)	Big in Excess
UN-UP	111-110	43	(62)	Decisive
LP-UN	001-111	33	(15)	The Piglet
LP-LN	001-011	53	(11)	Gradual Advance

	HEXAGRAM	TEXT #	BINARY #	NAME
ORIGINAL	001-111	33	(15)	Piglet
LN-UN	011-111	44	(31)	Meeting/Subjugated
LN-UP	011-111	44	(31)	Meeting/Subjugated
UN-UP	111-111	1	(63)	Heaven
LP-UN	001-111	33	(15)	The Piglet
LP-LN	001-011	53	(11)	Gradual Advance
ORIGINAL	010-000	7	(16)	An Army
LN-UN	100-000	24	(32)	Return
LN-UP	100-000	24	(32)	Return
UN-UP	000-000	2	(0)	Earth
LP-UN	010-000	7	(16)	An Army
LP-LN	010-100	40	(20)	Obstruction Removed
ORIGINAL	010-001	4	(17)	The Young Shoot
LN-UN	100-000	24	(32)	Return
LN-UP	100-001	27	(33)	Bulging Cheeks
UN-UP	000-001	23	(1)	Falling
LP-UN	010-000	7	(16)	An Army
LP-LN	010-100	40	(20)	Obstruction Removed
ORIGINAL	010-010	29	(18)	Water
LN-UN	100-001	27	(33)	Bulging Cheeks
LN-UP	100-010	3	(34)	Sprouting
UN-UP	001-010	39	(10)	Obstruction
LP-UN	010-001	4	(17)	The Young Shoot
LP-LN	010-100	40	(20)	Obstruction Removed
ORIGINAL	010-011	59	(19)	Flood/Dispersion
LN-UN	100-001	27	(33)	Bulging Cheeks
LN-UP	100-011	42	(35)	Increase
UN-UP	001-011	53	(11)	Gradual Advance
LP-UN	010-001	4	(17)	The Young Shoot
LP-LN	010-100	40	(20)	Obstruction Removed

	HEXAGRAM	TEXT #	BINARY #	NAME
ORIGINAL	010-100	40	(20)	Obstruction Removed
LN-UN	101-010	63	(42)	Already Across the River
LN-UP	101-100	55	(44)	Abundance
UN-UP	010-100	40	(20)	Obstruction Removed
LP-UN	010-010	29	(18)	Water
LP-LN	010-101	64	(21)	Not Yet Across the River
ORIGINAL	010-101	64	(21)	Not Yet Across the River
LN-UN	101-010	63	(42)	Already Across the River
LN-UP	101-101	30	(45)	Fire
UN-UP	010-101	64	(21)	Not Yet Across the River
LP-UN	010-010	29	(18)	Water
LP-LN	010-101	64	(21)	Not Yet Across the River
ORIGINAL	010-110	47	(22)	Burdened/Exhausted
LN-UN	101-011	37	(43)	The Family
LN-UP	101-110	49	(46)	Revolution
UN-UP	011-110	28	(30)	Big in Excess
LP-UN	010-011	59	(19)	Flood/Dispersion
LP-LN	010-101	64	(21)	Not Yet Across the River
ORIGINAL	010-111	6	(23)	Grievance
LN-UN	101-011	37	(43)	The Family
LN-UP	101-111	13	(47)	Companions
UN-UP	011-111	44	(31)	Meeting/Subjugated
LP-UN	010-011	59	(19)	Flood/Dispersion
LP-LN	010-101	64	(21)	Not Yet Across the River
ORIGINAL	011-000	46	(24)	Pushing Upwards
LN-UN	110-100	54	(52)	A Maiden Marries
LN-UP	110-000	19	(48)	Authority Approaches
UN-UP	100-000	24	(32)	Return
LP-UN	011-100	32	(28)	Constancy
LP-LN	011-110	28	(30)	Big in Excess

	HEXAGRAM	TEXT #	BINARY #	NAME
ORIGINAL	011-001	18	(25)	Illness/Decay
LN-UN	110-100	54	(52)	A Maiden Marries
LN-UP	110-001	41	(49)	Decrease
UN-UP	100-001	27	(33)	Bulging Cheeks
LP-UN	011-100	32	(28)	Constancy
LP-LN	011-110	28	(30)	Big in Excess
ORIGINAL	011-010	48	(26)	A Well
LN-UN	110-101	38	(53)	Estrangement
LN-UP	110-010	60	(50)	Restraint (Regulations)
UN-UP	101-010	63	(42)	Already Across the River
LP-UN	011-101	50	(29)	The Ritual Caldron
LP-LN	011-110	28	(30)	Big in Excess
ORIGINAL	011-011	57	(27)	Wing
LN-UN	110-101	38	(53)	Estrangement
LN-UP	110-011	61	(51)	Inmost Sincerity (Allegiance)
UN-UP	101-011	37	(43)	The Family
LP-UN	011-101	50	(29)	The Ritual Caldron
LP-LN	011-110	28	(30)	Big in Excess
ORIGINAL	011-100	32	(28)	Constancy
LN-UN	111-110	43	(62)	Decisive
LN-UP	111-100	34	(60)	Big Uses Force
UN-UP	110-100	54	(52)	A Maiden Marries
LP-UN	011-110	28	(30)	Big in Excess
LP-LN	011-111	44	(31)	Meeting/Subjugated
ORIGINAL	011-101	50	(29)	The Ritual Caldron
LN-UN	111-110	43	(62)	Decisive
LN-UP	111-101	14	(61)	Great Possessions
UN-UP	110-101	38	(53)	Estrangement
LP-UN	011-110	28	(30)	Big in Excess
LP-LN	011-111	44	(31)	Meeting/Subjugation

	HEXAGRAM	TEXT #	BINARY #	NAME
ORIGINAL	011-110	28	(30)	Big in Excess
LN-UN	111-111	1	(63)	Heaven
LN-UP	111-110	43	(62)	Decisive
UN-UP	111-110	43	(62)	Decisive
LP-UN	011-111	44	(31)	Meeting/Subjugated
LP-LN	011-111	44	(31)	Meeting/Subjugated
ORIGINAL	011-111	44	(31)	Meeting/Subjugated
LN-UN	111-111	1	(63)	Heaven
LN-UP	111-111	1	(63)	Heaven
UN-UP	111-111	1	(63)	Heaven
LP-UN	011-111	44	(31)	Meeting/Subjugated
LP-LN	011-111	44	(31)	Meeting/Subjugated
ORIGINAL	100-000	24	(32)	Return
LN-UN	000-000	2	(0)	Earth
LN-UP	000-000	2	(0)	Earth
UN-UP	000-000	2	(0)	Earth
LP-UN	100-000	24	(32)	Return
LP-LN	100-000	24	(32)	Return
ORIGINAL	100-001	27	(33)	Bulging Cheeks
LN-UN	000-000	2	(0)	Earth
LN-UP	000-001	23	(1)	Falling
UN-UP	000-001	23	(1)	Falling
LP-UN	100-000	24	(32)	Return
LP-LN	100-000	24	(32)	Return
ORIGINAL	100-010	3	(34)	Sprouting
LN-UN	000-001	23	(1)	Falling
LN-UP	000-010	8	(2)	Alliance
UN-UP	001-010	39	(10)	Obstruction
LP-UN	100-001	27	(33)	Bulging Cheeks
LP-LN	100-000	24	(32)	Return

	HEXAGRAM	TEXT #	BINARY #	NAME
ORIGINAL	100-011	42	(35)	Increase
LN-UN	000-001	23	(1)	Falling
LN-UP	000-011	20	(3)	Observing
UN-UP	001-011	53	(11)	Gradual Advance
LP-UN	100-001	27	(33)	Bulging Cheeks
LP-LN	100-000	24	(32)	Return
ORIGINAL	100-100	51	(36)	Thunder
LN-UN	001-010	39	(10)	Obstruction
LN-UP	001-100	62	(12)	Small in Excess
UN-UP	010-100	40	(20)	Obstruction Removed
LP-UN	100-010	3	(34)	Sprouting
LP-LN	100-001	27	(33)	Bulging Cheeks
ORIGINAL	100-101	21	(37)	Biting Through
LN-UN	001-010	39	(10)	Obstruction
LN-UP	001-101	56	(13)	The Traveler
UN-UP	010-101	64	(21)	Not Yet Across the River
LP-UN	100-010	3	(34)	Sprouting
LP-LN	100-001	27	(33)	Bulging Cheeks
ORIGINAL	100-110	17	(38)	The Chase
LN-UN	001-011	53	(11)	Gradual Advance
LN-UP	001-110	31	(14)	Mutual Influence
UN-UP	011-110	28	(30)	Big in Excess
LP-UN	100-011	42	(35)	Increase
LP-LN	100-001	27	(33)	Bulging Cheeks
ORIGINAL	100-111	25	(39)	No Error (No Expectations)
LN-UN	001-011	53	(11)	Gradual Advance
LN-UP	001-111	33	(15)	The Piglet
UN-UP	011-111	44	(31)	Meeting/Subjugated
LP-UN	100-011	42	(35)	Increase
LP-LN	100-001	27	(33)	Bulging Cheeks

	HEXAGRAM	TEXT #	BINARY #	NAME
ORIGINAL	100-111	25	(39)	No Error (No Expectations)
LN-UN	001-011	53	(11)	Gradual Advance
LN-UP	001-111	33	(15)	The Piglet
UN-UP	011-111	44	(31)	Meeting/Subjugated
LP-UN	100-011	42	(35)	Increase
LP-LN	100-001	27	(33)	Bulging Cheeks
ORIGINAL	101-000	36	(40)	The Bright (Calling) Pheasant
LN-UN	010-100	40	(20)	Obstruction Removed
LN-UP	010-000	7	(16)	An Army
UN-UP	100-000	24	(32)	Return
LP-UN	101-100	55	(44)	Abundance
LP-LN	101-010	63	(42)	Already Across the River
ORIGINAL	101-001	22	(41)	Adornment
LN-UN	010-100	40	(20)	Obstruction Removed
LN-UP	010-001	4	(17)	The Young Shoot
UN-UP	100-001	27	(33)	Bulging Cheeks
LP-UN	101-100	55	(44)	Abundance
LP-LN	101-010	63	(42)	Already Across the River
ORIGINAL	101-010	63	(42)	Already Across the River
LN-UN	010-101	64	(21)	Not Yet Across the River
LN-UP	010-010	29	(18)	Water
UN-UP	101-010	63	(42)	Already Across the River
LP-UN	101-101	30	(45)	Fire
LP-LN	101-010	63	(42)	Already Across the River
ORIGINAL	101-011	37	(43)	The Family
LN-UN	010-101	64	(21)	Not Yet Across the River
LN-UP	010-011	59	(19)	Flood/Dispersion
UN-UP	101-011	37	(43)	The Family
LP-UN	101-101	30	(45)	Fire
LP-LN	101-010	63	(42)	Already Across the River

	HEXAGRAM	TEXT #	BINARY #	NAME
ORIGINAL	101-100	55	(44)	Abundance
LN-UN	011-110	28	(30)	Big in Excess
LN-UP	011-100	32	(28)	Constancy
UN-UP	110-100	54	(52)	A Maiden Marries
LP-UN	101-110	49	(46)	Revolution
LP-LN	101-011	37	(43)	The Family
ORIGINAL	101-101	30	(45)	Fire
LN-UN	011-110	28	(30)	Big in Excess
LN-UP	011-101	50	(29)	The Ritual Caldron
UN-UP	110-101	38	(53)	Estrangement
LP-UN	101-110	49	(46)	Revolution
LP-LN	101-011	37	(43)	The Family
ORIGINAL	101-110	49	(46)	Revolution
LN-UN	011-111	44	(31)	Meeting/Subjugated
LN-UP	011-110	28	(30)	Big in Excess
UN-UP	111-110	43	(62)	Decisive
LP-UN	101-111	13	(47)	Companions
LP-LN	101-011	37	(43)	The Family
ORIGINAL	101-111	13	(47)	Companions
LN-UN	011-111	44	(31)	Meeting/Subjugated
LN-UP	011-111	44	(31)	Meeting/Subjugated
UN-UP	111-111	1	(63)	Heaven
LP-UN	101-111	13	(47)	Companions
LP-LN	101-011	37	(43)	The Family
ORIGINAL	110-000	19	(48)	Authority Approaches
LN-UN	100-000	24	(32)	Return
LN-UP	100-000	24	(32)	Return
UN-UP	000-000	2	(0)	Earth
LP-UN	110-000	19	(48)	Authority Approaches
LP-LN	110-100	54	(52)	A Maiden Marries

	HEXAGRAM	TEXT #	BINARY #	NAME
ORIGINAL	110-001	41	(49)	Decrease
LN-UN	100-000	24	(32)	Return
LN-UP	100-001	27	(33)	Bulging Cheeks
UN-UP	000-001	23	(1)	Falling
LP-UN	110-000	19	(48)	Authority Approaches
LP-LN	110-100	54	(52)	A Maiden Marries
ORIGINAL	110-010	60	(50)	Restraint (Regulations)
LN-UN	100-001	27	(33)	Bulging Cheeks
LN-UP	100-010	3	(34)	Sprouting
UN-UP	001-010	39	(10)	Obstruction
LP-UN	110-001	41	(49)	Decrease
LP-LN	110-100	54	(52)	A Maiden Marries
ORIGINAL	110-011	61	(51)	Inmost Sincerity (Allegiance)
LN-UN	100-001	27	(33)	Bulging Cheeks
LN-UP	100-011	42	(35)	Increase
UN-UP	001-011	53	(11)	Gradual Advance
LP-UN	110-001	41	(49)	Decrease
LP-LN	110-100	54	(52)	A Maiden Marries
ORIGINAL	110-100	54	(52)	A Maiden Marries
LN-UN	101-010	63	(42)	Already Across the River
LN-UP	101-100	55	(44)	Abundance
UN-UP	010-100	40	(20)	Obstruction Removed
LP-UN	110-010	60	(50)	Restraint (Regulations)
LP-LN	110-101	38	(53)	Estrangement
ORIGINAL	110-101	38	(53)	Estrangement
LN-UN	101-010	63	(42)	Already Across the River
LN-UP	101-101	30	(45)	Fire
UN-UP	010-101	64	(21)	Not Yet Across the River
LP-UN	110-010	60	(50)	Restraint (Regulations)
LP-LN	110-101	38	(53)	Estrangement

	HEXAGRAM	TEXT #	BINARY #	NAME
ORIGINAL	110-110	58	(54)	Lake
LN-UN	101-011	37	(43)	The Family
LN-UP	101-110	49	(46)	Revolution
UN-UP	011-110	28	(30)	Big in Excess
LP-UN	110-011	61	(51)	Inmost Sincerity (Allegiance)
LP-LN	110-101	38	(53)	Estrangement
ORIGINAL	110-111	10	(55)	Treading
LN-UN	101-011	37	(43)	The Family
LN-UP	101-111	13	(47)	Companions
UN-UP	011-111	44	(31)	Meeting/Subjugated
LP-UN	110-011	61	(51)	Inmost Sincerity (Allegiance)
LP-LN	110-101	38	(53)	Estrangement
ORIGINAL	111-000	11	(56)	Peace/Flowing
LN-UN	110-100	54	(52)	A Maiden Marries
LN-UP	110-000	19	(48)	Authority Approaches
UN-UP	100-000	24	(32)	Return
LP-UN	111-100	34	(60)	Big Uses Force
LP-LN	111-110	43	(62)	Decisive
ORIGINAL	111-001	26	(57)	Big Restraint/Big Accumulation
LN-UN	110-100	54	(52)	A Maiden Marries
LN-UP	110-001	41	(49)	Decrease
UN-UP	100-001	27	(33)	Bulging Cheeks
LP-UN	111-100	34	(60)	Big Uses Force
LP-LN	111-110	43	(62)	Decisive
ORIGINAL	111-010	5	(58)	Getting Wet
LN-UN	110-101	38	(53)	Estrangement
LN-UP	110-010	60	(50)	Restraint (Regulations)
UN-UP	101-010	63	(42)	Already Across the River
LP-UN	111-101	14	(61)	Great Possessions
LP-LN	111-110	43	(62)	Decisive

	HEXAGRAM	TEXT #	BINARY #	NAME
ORIGINAL	111-011	9	(59)	Small Restraint/ Small Accumulation
LN-UN	110-101	38	(53)	Estrangement
LN-UP	110-011	61	(51)	Inmost Sincerity (Allegiance)
UN-UP	101-011	37	(43)	The Family
LP-UN	111-101	14	(61)	Great Possessions
LP-LN	111-110	43	(62)	Decisive
ORIGINAL	111-100	34	(60)	Big Uses Force
LN-UN	111-110	43	(62)	Decisive
LN-UP	111-100	34	(60)	Big Uses Force
UN-UP	110-100	54	(52)	A Maiden Marries
LP-UN	111-110	43	(62)	Decisive
LP-LN	111-111	1	(63)	Heaven
ORIGINAL	111-101	14	(61)	Great Possessions
LN-UN	111-110	43	(62)	Decisive
LN-UP	111-101	14	(61)	Great Possessions
UN-UP	110-101	38	(53)	Estrangement
LP-UN	111-110	43	(62)	Decisive
LP-LN	111-111	1	(63)	Heaven
ORIGINAL	111-110	43	(62)	Decisive
LN-UN	111-111	1	(63)	Heaven
LN-UP	111-110	43	(62)	Decisive
UN-UP	111-110	43	(62)	Decisive
LP-UN	111-111	1	(63)	Heaven
LP-LN	111-111	1	(63)	Heaven
ORIGINAL	111-111	1	(63)	Heaven
LN-UN	111-111	1	(63)	Heaven
LN-UP	111-111	1	(63)	Heaven
UN-UP	111-111	1	(63)	Heaven
LP-UN	111-111	1	(63)	Heaven
LP-LN	111-111	1	(63)	Heaven

G

HEXAGRAM STORIES

The first hexagrams of each story form a binary sequence. STORY OF HEXA-GRAM: 000-000

Hexagram	Text #	Binary #	Name
000-000	2	(0)	Earth
100-000	24	(32)	Return
110-000	19	(48)	Authority Approaches
111-000	11	(56)	Peace/Flowing
111-100	34	(60)	Big Uses Force
111-110	43	(62)	Decisive
111-111	1	(63)	Heaven
011-111	44	(31)	Meeting/Subjugated
001-111	33	(15)	The Piglet
000-111	12	(7)	Standstill
000-011	20	(3)	Observing
000-001	23	(1)	Falling
000-000	2	(0)	Earth

STORY OF HEXAGRAM: 000-001

Hexagram	Text #	Binary #	Name
000-001	23	(1)	Falling
100-001	27	(33)	Bulging Cheeks
110-001	41	(49)	Decrease
111-001	26	(57)	Big Restraint/Big Accumulation
111-101	14	(61)	Great Possessions
111-111	1	(63)	Heaven
111-110	43	(62)	Decisive
011-110	28	(30)	Big in Excess
001-110	31	(14)	Mutual Influence
000-110	45	(6)	Gathering Together
000-010	8	(2)	Alliance
000-000	2	(0)	Earth
000-001	23	(1)	Falling

STORY OF HEXAGRAM: 000-010

Hexagram	Text #	Binary #	Name
000-010	8	(2)	Alliance
100-010	3	(34)	Sprouting
110-010	60	(50)	Restraint (Regulations)
111-010	5	(58)	Getting Wet
111-110	43	(62)	Decisive
111-100	34	(60)	Big Uses Force
111-101	14	(61)	Great Possessions
011-101	50	(29)	The Ritual Caldron
001-101	56	(13)	The Traveler
000-101	35	(5)	Advance
000-001	23	(1)	Falling
000-011	20	(3)	Observing
000-010	8	(2)	Alliance

STORY OF HEXAGRAM: 000-011

Hexagram	Text #	Binary #	Name
000-011	20	(3)	Observing
100-011	42	(35)	Increase
110-011	61	(51)	Inmost Sincerity (Allegiance)
111-011	9	(59)	Small Restraint/Small Accumulation
111-111	1	(63)	Heaven
111-101	14	(61)	Great Possessions
111-100	34	(60)	Big Uses Force
011-100	32	(28)	Constancy
001-100	62	(12)	Small in Excess
000-100	16	(4)	Contentment
000-000	2	(0)	Earth
000-010	8	(2)	Alliance
000-011	20	(3)	Observing

STORY OF HEXAGRAM: 000-100

Hexagram	Text #	Binary #	Name
000-100	16	(4)	Contentment
100-100	51	(36)	Thunder
110-100	54	(52)	A Maiden Marries
111-100	34	(60)	Big Uses Force
111-000	11	(56)	Peace/Flowing
111-010	5	(58)	Getting Wet
111-011	9	(59)	Small Restraint/Small Accumulation
011-011	57	(27)	Wind
001-011	53	(11)	Gradual Advance
000-011	20	(3)	Observing
000-111	12	(7)	Standstill
000-101	35	(5)	Advance
000-100	16	(4)	Contentment

STORY OF HEXAGRAM: 000-101

Hexagram	Text #	Binary #	Name
000-101	35	(5)	Advance
100-101	21	(37)	Biting Through
110-101	38	(53)	Estrangement
111-101	14	(61)	Great Possessions
111-001	26	(57)	Big Restraint/Big Accumulation
111-011	9	(59)	Small Restraint/Small Accumulation
111-010	5	(58)	Getting Wet
011-010	48	(26)	A Well
001-010	39	(10)	Obstruction
000-010	8	(2)	Alliance
000-110	45	(6)	Gathering Together
000-100	16	(4)	Contentment
000-101	35	(5)	Advance

STORY OF HEXAGRAM: 000-110

Hexagram	Text #	Binary #	Name
000-110	45	(6)	Gathering Together
100-110	17	(38)	The Chase
110-110	58	(54)	Lake
111-110	43	(62)	Decisive
111-010	5	(58)	Getting Wet
111-000	11	(56)	Peace/Flowing
111-001	26	(57)	Big Restraint/Big Accumulation
011-001	18	(25)	Illness/Decay
001-001	52	(9)	Mountain
000-001	23	(1)	Falling
000-101	35	(5)	Advance
000-111	12	(7)	Standstill
000-110	45	(6)	Gathering Together

STORY OF HEXAGRAM: 000-111

Hexagram	Text #	Binary #	Name
000-111	12	(7)	Standstill
100-111	25	(39)	No Error (No Expectations)
110-111	10	(55)	Treading
111-111	1	(63)	Heaven
111-011	9	(59)	Small Restraint/Small Accumulation
111-001	26	(57)	Big Restraint/Big Accumulation
111-000	11	(56)	Peace/Flowing
011-000	46	(24)	Pushing Upwards
001-000	15	(8)	Modesty
000-000	2	(0)	Earth
000-100	16	(4)	Contentment
000-110	45	(6)	Gathering Together
000-111	12	(7)	Standstill

STORY OF HEXAGRAM: 001-000

Hexagram	Text #	Binary #	Name
001-000	15	(8)	Modesty
101-000	36	(40)	The Bright (Calling) Pheasant
111-000	11	(56)	Peace/Flowing
110-000	19	(48)	Authority Approaches
110-100	54	(52)	A Maiden Marries
110-110	58	(54)	Lake
110-111	10	(55)	Treading
010-111	6	(23)	Grievance
000-111	12	(7)	Standstill
001-111	33	(15)	The Piglet
001-011	53	(11)	Gradual Advance
001-001	52	(9)	Mountain
001-000	15	(8)	Modesty

STORY OF HEXAGRAM: 001-001

Hexagram	Text #	Binary #	Name
001-001	52	(9)	Mountain
101-001	22	(41)	Adornment
111-001	26	(57)	Big Restraint/Big Accumulation
110-001	41	(49)	Decrease
110-101	38	(53)	Estrangement
110-111	10	(55)	Treading
110-110	58	(54)	Lake
010-110	47	(22)	Burdened/Exhausted
000-110	45	(6)	Gathering Together
001-110	31	(14)	Mutual Influence
001-010	39	(10)	Obstruction
001-000	15	(8)	Modesty
001-001	52	(9)	Mountain

STORY OF HEXAGRAM: 001-010

Hexagram	Text #	Binary #	Name
001-010	39	(10)	Obstruction
101-010	63	(42)	Already Across the River
111-010	5	(58)	Getting Wet
110-010	60	(50)	Restraint (Regulations)
110-110	58	(54)	Lake
110-100	54	(52)	A Maiden Marries
110-101	38	(53)	Estrangement
010-101	64	(21)	Not Yet Across the River
000-101	35	(5)	Advance
001-101	56	(13)	The Traveler
001-001	52	(9)	Mountain
001-011	53	(11)	Gradual Advance
001-010	39	(10)	Obstruction

STORY OF HEXAGRAM: 001-011

Hexagram	Text #	Binary #	Name
001-011	53	(11)	Gradual Advance
101-011	37	(43)	The Family
111-011	9	(59)	Small Restraint/Small Accumulation
110-011	61	(51)	Inmost Sincerity (Allegiance)
110-111	10	(55)	Treading
110-101	38	(53)	Estrangement
110-100	54	(52)	A Maiden Marries
010-100	40	(20)	Obstruction Removed
000-100	16	(4)	Contentment
001-100	62	(12)	Small in Excess
001-000	15	(8)	Modesty
001-010	39	(10)	Obstruction
001-011	53	(11)	Gradual Advance

STORY OF HEXAGRAM: 001-100

Hexagram	Text #	Binary #	Name
001-100	62	(12)	Small in Excess
101-100	55	(44)	Abundance
111-100	34	(60)	Big Uses Force
110-100	54	(52)	A Maiden Marries
110-000	19	(48)	Authority Approaches
110-010	60	(50)	Restraint (Regulations)
110-011	61	(51)	Inmost Sincerity (Allegiance)
010-011	59	(19)	Flood/Dispersion
000-011	20	(3)	Observing
001-011	53	(11)	Gradual Advance
001-111	33	(15)	The Piglet
001-101	56	(13)	The Traveler
001-100	62	(12)	Small in Excess

STORY OF HEXAGRAM: 001-101

Hexagram	Text #	Binary #	Name
001-101	56	(13)	The Traveler
101-101	30	(45)	Fire
111-101	14	(61)	Great Possessions
110-101	38	(53)	Estrangement
110-001	41	(49)	Decrease
110-011	61	(51)	Inmost Sincerity (Allegiance)
110-010	60	(50)	Restraint (Regulations)
010-010	29	(18)	Water
000-010	8	(2)	Alliance
001-010	39	(10)	Obstruction
001-110	31	(14)	Mutual Influence
001-100	62	(12)	Small in Excess
001-101	56	(13)	The Traveler

STORY OF HEXAGRAM: 001-110

Hexagram	Text #	Binary #	Name
001-110	31	(14)	Mutual Influence
101-110	49	(46)	Revolution
111-110	43	(62)	Decisive
110-110	58	(54)	Lake
110-010	60	(50)	Restraint (Regulations)
110-000	19	(48)	Authority Approaches
110-001	41	(49)	Decrease
010-001	4	(17)	The Young Shoot
000-001	23	(1)	Falling
001-001	52	(9)	Mountain
001-101	56	(13)	The Traveler
001-111	33	(15)	The Piglet
001-110	31	(14)	Mutual Influence

STORY OF HEXAGRAM: 001-111

Hexagram	Text #	Binary #	Name
001-111	33	(15)	The Piglet
101-111	13	(47)	Companions
111-111	1	(63)	Heaven
110-111	10	(55)	Treading
110-011	61	(51)	Inmost Sincerity (Allegiance)
110-001	41	(49)	Decrease
110-000	19	(48)	Authority Approaches
010-000	7	(16)	An Army
000-000	2	(0)	Earth
001-000	15	(8)	Modesty
001-100	62	(12)	Small in Excess
001-110	31	(14)	Mutual Influence
001-111	33	(15)	The Piglet

STORY OF HEXAGRAM: 010-000

Hexagram	Text #	Binary #	Name
010-000	7	(16)	An Army
110-000	19	(48)	Authority Approaches
100-000	24	(32)	Return
101-000	36	(40)	The Bright (Calling) Pheasant
101-100	55	(44)	Abundance
101-110	49	(46)	Revolution
101-111	13	(47)	Companions
001-111	33	(15)	The Piglet
011-111	44	(31)	Meeting/Subjugated
010-111	6	(23)	Grievance
010-011	59	(19)	Flood/Dispersion
010-001	4	(17)	The Young Shoot
010-000	7	(16)	An Army

STORY OF HEXAGRAM: 001-001

Hexagram	Text #	Binary #	Name
010-001	4	(17)	The Young Shoot
110-001	41	(49)	Decrease
100-001	27	(33)	Bulging Cheeks
101-001	22	(41)	Adornment
101-101	30	(45)	Fire
101-111	13	(47)	Companions
101-110	49	(46)	Revolution
001-110	31	(14)	Mutual Influence
011-110	28	(30)	Big in Excess
010-110	47	(22)	Burdened/Exhausted
010-010	29	(18)	Water
010-000	7	(16)	An Army
010-001	4	(17)	The Young Shoot

STORY OF HEXAGRAM: 010-010

Hexagram	Text #	Binary #	Name
010-010	29	(18)	Water
110-010	60	(50)	Restraint (Regulations)
100-010	3	(34)	Sprouting
101-010	63	(42)	Already Across the River
101-110	49	(46)	Revolution
101-100	55	(44)	Abundance
101-101	30	(45)	Fire
001-101	56	(13)	The Traveler
011-101	50	(29)	The Ritual Caldron
010-101	64	(21)	Not Yet Across the River
010-001	4	(17)	The Young Shoot
010-011	59	(19)	Flood/Dispersion
010-010	29	(18)	Water

STORY OF HEXAGRAM: 010-011

Hexagram	Text #	Binary #	Name
010-011	59	(19)	Flood/Dispersion
110-011	61	(51)	Inmost Sincerity (Allegiance)
100-011	42	(35)	Increase
101-011	37	(43)	The Family
101-111	13	(47)	Companions
101-101	30	(45)	Fire
101-100	55	(44)	Abundance
001-100	62	(12)	Small in Excess
011-100	32	(28)	Constancy
010-100	40	(20)	Obstruction Removed
010-000	7	(16)	An Army
010-010	29	(18)	Water
010-011	59	(19)	Flood/Dispersion

STORY OF HEXAGRAM: 010-100

Hexagram	Text #	Binary #	Name
010-100	40	(20)	Obstruction Removed
110-100	54	(52)	A Maiden Marries
100-100	51	(36)	Thunder
101-100	55	(44)	Abundance
101-000	36	(40)	The Bright (Calling) Pheasant
101-010	63	(42)	Already Across the River
101-011	37	(43)	The Family
001-011	53	(11)	Gradual Advance
011-011	57	(27)	Wind
010-011	59	(19)	Flood/Dispersion
010-111	6	(23)	Grievance
010-101	64	(21)	Not Yet Across the River
010-100	40	(20)	Obstruction Removed

STORY OF HEXAGRAM: 010-101

Hexagram	Text #	Binary #	Name
010-101	64	(21)	Not Yet Across the River
110-101	38	(53)	Estrangement
100-101	21	(37)	Biting Through
101-101	30	(45)	Fire
101-001	22	(41)	Adornment
101-011	37	(43)	The Family
101-010	63	(42)	Already Across the River
001-010	39	(10)	Obstruction
011-010	48	(26)	A Well
010-010	29	(18)	Water
010-110	47	(22)	Burdened/Exhausted
010-100	40	(20)	Obstruction Removed
010-101	64	(21)	Not Yet Across the River

STORY OF HEXAGRAM: 010-110

Hexagram	Text #	Binary #	Name
010-110	47	(22)	Burdened/Exhausted
110-110	58	(54)	Lake
100-110	17	(38)	The Chase
101-110	49	(46)	Revolution
101-010	63	(42)	Already Across the River
101-000	36	(40)	The Bright (Calling) Pheasant
101-001	22	(41)	Adornment
001-001	52	(9)	Mountain
011-001	18	(25)	Illness/Decay
010-001	4	(17)	The Young Shoot
010-101	64	(21)	Not Yet Across the River
010-111	6	(23)	Grievance
010-110	47	(22)	Burdened/Exhausted

STORY OF HEXAGRAM: 010-111

Hexagram	Text #	Binary #	Name
010-111	6	(23)	Grievance
110-111	10	(55)	Treading
100-111	25	(39)	No Error (No Expectations)
101-111	13	(47)	Companions
101-011	37	(43)	The Family
101-001	22	(41)	Adornment
101-000	36	(40)	The Bright (Calling) Pheasant
001-000	15	(8)	Modesty
011-000	46	(24)	Pushing Upwards
010-000	7	(16)	An Army
010-100	40	(20)	Obstruction Removed
010-110	47	(22)	Burdened/Exhausted
010-111	6	(23)	Grievance

STORY OF HEXAGRAM: 011-000

Hexagram	Text #	Binary #	Name
011-000	46	(24)	Pushing Upwards
111-000	11	(56)	Peace/Flowing
101-000	36	(40)	The Bright (Calling) Pheasant
100-000	24	(32)	Return
100-100	51	(36)	Thunder
100-110	17	(38)	The Chase
100-111	25	(39)	No Error (No Expectations)
000-111	12	(7)	Standstill
010-111	6	(23)	Grievance
011-111	44	(31)	Meeting/Subjugated
011-011	57	(27)	Wind
011-001	18	(25)	Illness/Decay
011-000	46	(24)	Pushing Upwards

STORY OF HEXAGRAM: 011-001

Hexagram	Text #	Binary #	Name
011-001	18	(25)	Illness/Decay
111-001	26	(57)	Big Restraint/Big Accumulation
101-001	22	(41)	Adornment
100-001	27	(33)	Bulging Cheeks
100-101	21	(37)	Biting Through
100-111	25	(39)	No Error (No Expectations)
100-110	17	(38)	The Chase
000-110	45	(6)	Gathering Together
010-110	47	(22)	Burdened/Exhausted
011-110	28	(30)	Big in Excess
011-010	48	(26)	A Well
011-000	46	(24)	Pushing Upwards
011-001	18	(25)	Illness/Decay

STORY OF HEXAGRAM: 011-010

Hexagram	Text #	Binary #	Name
011-010	48	(26)	A Well
111-010	5	(58)	Getting Wet
101-010	63	(42)	Already Across the River
100-010	3	(34)	Sprouting
100-110	17	(38)	The Chase
100-100	51	(36)	Thunder
100-101	21	(37)	Biting Through
000-101	35	(5)	Advance
010-101	64	(21)	Not Yet Across the River
011-101	50	(29)	The Ritual Caldron
011-001	18	(25)	Illness/Decay
011-011	57	(27)	Wind
011-010	48	(26)	A Well

STORY OF HEXAGRAM: 011-011

Hexagram	Text #	Binary #	Name
011-011	57	(27)	Wind
111-011	9	(59)	Small Restraint/Small Accumulation
101-011	37	(43)	The Family
100-011	42	(35)	Increase
100-111	25	(39)	No Error (No Expectations)
100-101	21	(37)	Biting Through
100-100	51	(36)	Thunder
000-100	16	(4)	Contentment
010-100	40	(20)	Obstruction Removed
011-100	32	(28)	Constancy
011-000	46	(24)	Pushing Upwards
011-010	48	(26)	A Well
011-011	57	(27)	Wind

STORY OF HEXAGRAM: 011-100

Hexagram	Text #	Binary #	Name
011-100	32	(28)	Constancy
111-100	34	(60)	Big Uses Force
101-100	55	(44)	Abundance
100-100	51	(36)	Thunder
100-000	24	(32)	Return
100-010	3	(34)	Sprouting
100-011	42	(35)	Increase
000-011	20	(3)	Observing
010-011	59	(19)	Flood/Dispersion
011-011	57	(27)	Wind
011-111	44	(31)	Meeting/Subjugated
011-101	50	(29)	The Ritual Caldron
011-100	32	(28)	Constancy

STORY OF HEXAGRAM: 011-101

Hexagram	Text #	Binary #	Name
011-101	50	(29)	The Ritual Caldron
111-101	14	(61)	Great Possessions
101-101	30	(45)	Fire
100-101	21	(37)	Biting Through
100-001	27	(33)	Bulging Cheeks
100-011	42	(35)	Increase
100-010	3	(34)	Sprouting
000-010	8	(2)	Alliance
010-010	29	(18)	Water
011-010	48	(26)	A Well
011-110	28	(30)	Big in Excess
011-100	32	(28)	Constancy
011-101	50	(29)	The Ritual Caldron

STORY OF HEXAGRAM: 011-110

Hexagram	Text #	Binary #	Name
011-110	28	(30)	Big in Excess
111-110	43	(62)	Decisive
101-110	49	(46)	Revolution
100-110	17	(38)	The Chase
100-010	3	(34)	Sprouting
100-000	24	(32)	Return
100-001	27	(33)	Bulging Cheeks
000-001	23	(1)	Falling
010-001	4	(17)	The Young Shoot
011-001	18	(25)	Illness/Decay
011-101	50	(29)	The Ritual Caldron
011-111	44	(31)	Meeting/Subjugated
011-110	28	(30)	Big in Excess

STORY OF HEXAGRAM: 011-111

Hexagram	Text #	Binary #	Name
011-111	44	(31)	Meeting/Subjugated
111-111	1	(63)	Heaven
101-111	13	(47)	Companions
100-111	25	(39)	No Error (No Expectations)
100-011	42	(35)	Increase
100-001	27	(33)	Bulging Cheeks
100-000	24	(32)	Return
000-000	2	(0)	Earth
010-000	7	(16)	An Army
011-000	46	(24)	Pushing Upwards
011-100	32	(28)	Constancy
011-110	28	(30)	Big in Excess
011-111	44	(31)	Meeting/Subjugated

STORY OF HEXAGRAM: 100-000

Hexagram	Text #	Binary #	Name
100-000	24	(32)	Return
000-000	2	(0)	Earth
010-000	7	(16)	An Army
011-000	46	(24)	Pushing Upwards
011-100	32	(28)	Constancy
011-110	28	(30)	Big in Excess
011-111	44	(31)	Meeting/Subjugated
111-111	1	(63)	Heaven
101-111	13	(47)	Companions
100-111	25	(39)	No Error (No Expectations)
100-011	42	(35)	Increase
100-001	27	(33)	Bulging Cheeks
100-000	24	(32)	Return

STORY OF HEXAGRAM: 100-001

Hexagram	Text #	Binary #	Name
100-001	27	(33)	Bulging Cheeks
000-001	23	(1)	Falling
010-001	4	(17)	The Young Shoot
011-001	18	(25)	Illness/Decay
011-101	50	(29)	The Ritual Caldron
011-111	44	(31)	Meeting/Subjugated
011-110	28	(30)	Big in Excess
111-110	43	(62)	Decisive
101-110	49	(46)	Revolution
100-110	17	(38)	The Chase
100-010	3	(34)	Sprouting
100-000	24	(32)	Return
100-001	27	(33)	Bulging Cheeks

STORY OF HEXAGRAM: 100-010

Hexagram	Text #	Binary #	Name
100-010	3	(34)	Sprouting
000-010	8	(2)	Alliance
010-010	29	(18)	Water
011-010	48	(26)	A Well
011-110	28	(30)	Big in Excess
011-100	32	(28)	Constancy
011-101	50	(29)	The Ritual Caldron
111-101	14	(61)	Great Possessions
101-101	30	(45)	Fire
100-101	21	(37)	Biting Through
100-001	27	(33)	Bulging Cheeks
100-011	42	(35)	Increase
100-010	3	(34)	Sprouting

STORY OF HEXAGRAM: 100-011

Hexagram	Text #	Binary #	Name
100-011	42	(35)	Increase
000-011	20	(3)	Observing
010-011	59	(19)	Flood/Dispersion
011-011	57	(27)	Wind
011-111	44	(31)	Meeting/Subjugated
011-101	50	(29)	The Ritual Caldron
011-100	32	(28)	Constancy
111-100	34	(60)	Big Uses Force
101-100	55	(44)	Abundance
100-100	51	(36)	Thunder
100-000	24	(32)	Return
100-010	3	(34)	Sprouting
100-011	42	(35)	Increase

STORY OF HEXAGRAM: 100-100

Hexagram	Text #	Binary #	Name
100-100	51	(36)	Thunder
000-100	16	(4)	Contentment
010-100	40	(20)	Obstruction Removed
011-100	32	(28)	Constancy
011-000	46	(24)	Pushing Upwards
011-010	48	(26)	A Well
011-011	57	(27)	Wind
111-011	9	(59)	Small Restraint/Small Accumulation
101-011	37	(43)	The Family
100-011	42	(35)	Increase
100-111	25	(39)	No Error (No Expectations)
100-101	21	(37)	Biting Through
100-100	51	(36)	Thunder

STORY OF HEXAGRAM: 100-101

Hexagram	Text #	Binary #	Name
100-101	21	(37)	Biting Through
000-101	35	(5)	Advance
010-101	64	(21)	Not Yet Across the River
011-101	50	(29)	The Ritual Caldron
011-001	18	(25)	Illness/Decay
011-011	57	(27)	Wind
011-010	48	(26)	A Well
111-010	5	(58)	Getting Wet
101-010	63	(42)	Already Across the River
100-010	3	(34)	Sprouting
100-110	17	(38)	The Chase
100-100	51	(36)	Thunder
100-101	21	(37)	Biting Through

STORY OF HEXAGRAM: 100-110

100-110	17	(38)	The Chase
000-110	45	(6)	Gathering Together
010-110	47	(22)	Burdened/Exhausted
011-110	28	(30)	Big in Excess
011-010	48	(26)	A Well
011-000	46	(24)	Pushing Upwards
011-001	18	(25)	Illness/Decay
111-001	26	(57)	Big Restraint/Big Accumulation
101-001	22	(41)	Adornment
100-001	27	(33)	Bulging Cheeks
100-101	21	(37)	Biting Through
100-111	25	(39)	No Error (No Expectations)
100-110	17	(38)	The Chase

STORY OF HEXAGRAM: 100-111

Hexagram	Text #	Binary #	Name
100-111	25	(39)	No Error (No Expectations)
000-111	12	(7)	Standstill
010-111	6	(23)	Grievance
011-111	44	(31)	Meeting/Subjugated
011-011	57	(27)	Wind
011-001	18	(25)	Illness/Decay
011-000	46	(24)	Pushing Upwards
111-000	11	(56)	Peace/Flowing
101-000	36	(40)	The Bright (Calling) Pheasant
100-000	24	(32)	Return
100-100	51	(36)	Thunder
100-110	17	(38)	The Chase
100-111	25	(39)	No Error (No Expectations)

STORY OF HEXAGRAM: 101-000

Hexagram	Text #	Binary #	Name
101-000	36	(40)	The Bright (Calling) Pheasant
001-000	15	(8)	Modesty
011-000	46	(24)	Pushing Upwards
010-000	7	(16)	An Army
010-100	40	(20)	Obstruction Removed
010-110	47	(22)	Burdened/Exhausted
010-111	6	(23)	Grievance
110-111	10	(55)	Treading
100-111	25	(39)	No Error (No Expectations)
101-111	13	(47)	Companions
101-011	37	(43)	The Family
101-001	22	(41)	Adornment
101-000	36	(40)	The Bright (Calling) Pheasant

STORY OF HEXAGRAM: 101-001

Hexagram	Text #	Binary #	Name
101-001	22	(41)	Adornment
001-001	52	(9)	Mountain
011-001	18	(25)	Illness/Decay
010-001	4	(17)	The Young Shoot
010-101	64	(21)	Not Yet Across the River
010-111	6	(23)	Grievance
010-110	47	(22)	Burdened/Exhausted
110-110	58	(54)	Lake
100-110	17	(38)	The Chase
101-110	49	(46)	Revolution
101-010	63	(42)	Already Across the River
101-000	36	(40)	The Bright (Calling) Pheasant
101-001	22	(41)	Adornment

STORY OF HEXAGRAM: 101-010

Hexagram	Text #	Binary #	Name
101-010	63	(42)	Already Across the River
001-010	39	(10)	Obstruction
011-010	48	(26)	A Well
010-010	29	(18)	Water
010-110	47	(22)	Burdened/Exhausted
010-100	40	(20)	Obstruction Removed
010-101	64	(21)	Not Yet Across the River
110-101	38	(53)	Estrangement
100-101	21	(37)	Biting Through
101-101	30	(45)	Fire
101-001	22	(41)	Adornment
101-011	37	(43)	The Family
101-010	63	(42)	Already Across the River

STORY OF HEXAGRAM: 101-011

Hexagram	Text #	Binary #	Name
101-011	37	(43)	The Family
001-011	53	(11)	Gradual Advance
011-011	57	(27)	Wind
010-011	59	(19)	Flood/Dispersion
010-111	6	(23)	Grievance
010-101	64	(21)	Not Yet Across the River
010-100	40	(20)	Obstruction Removed
110-100	54	(52)	A Maiden Marries
100-100	51	(36)	Thunder
101-100	55	(44)	Abundance
101-000	36	(40)	The Bright (Calling) Pheasant
101-010	63	(42)	Already Across the River
101-011	37	(43)	The Family

STORY OF HEXAGRAM: 101-100

Hexagram	Text #	Binary #	Name
101-100	55	(44)	Abundance
001-100	62	(12)	Small in Excess
011-100	32	(28)	Constancy
010-100	40	(20)	Obstruction Removed
010-000	7	(16)	An Army
010-010	29	(18)	Water
010-011	59	(19)	Flood/Dispersion
110-011	61	(51)	Inmost Sincerity (Allegiance)
100-011	42	(35)	Increase
101-011	37	(43)	The Family
101-111	13	(47)	Companions
101-101	30	(45)	Fire
101-100	55	(44)	Abundance

STORY OF HEXAGRAM: 101-101

Hexagram	Text #	Binary #	Name
101-101	30	(45)	Fire
001-101	56	(13)	The Traveler
011-101	50	(29)	The Ritual Caldron
010-101	64	(21)	Not Yet Across the River
010-001	4	(17)	The Young Shoot
010-011	59	(19)	Flood/Dispersion
010-010	29	(18)	Water
110-010	60	(50)	Restraint (Regulations)
100-010	3	(34)	Sprouting
101-010	63	(42)	Already Across the River
101-110	49	(46)	Revolution
101-100	55	(44)	Abundance
101-101	30	(45)	Fire

STORY OF HEXAGRAM: 101-110

Hexagram	Text #	Binary #	Name
101-110	49	(46)	Revolution
001-110	31	(14)	Mutual Influence
011-110	28	(30)	Big in Excess
010-110	47	(22)	Burdened/Exhausted
010-010	29	(18)	Water
010-000	7	(16)	An Army
010-001	4	(17)	The Young Shoot
110-001	41	(49)	Decrease
100-001	27	(33)	Bulging Cheeks
101-001	22	(41)	Adornment
101-101	30	(45)	Fire
101-111	13	(47)	Companions
101-110	49	(46)	Revolution

STORY OF HEXAGRAM: 101-111

Hexagram	Text #	Binary #	Name
101-111	13	(47)	Companions
001-111	33	(15)	The Piglet
011-111	44	(31)	Meeting/Subjugated
010-111	6	(23)	Grievance
010-011	59	(19)	Flood/Dispersion
010-001	4	(17)	The Young Shoot
010-000	7	(16)	An Army
110-000	19	(48)	Authority Approaches
100-000	24	(32)	Return
101-000	36	(40)	The Bright (Calling) Pheasant
101-100	55	(44)	Abundance
101-110	49	(46)	Revolution
101-111	13	(47)	Companions

STORY OF HEXAGRAM: 101-000

Hexagram	Text #	Binary #	Name
110-000	19	(48)	Authority Approaches
010-000	7	(16)	An Army
000-000	2	(0)	Earth
001-000	15	(8)	Modesty
001-100	62	(12)	Small in Excess
001-110	31	(14)	Mutual Influence
001-111	33	(15)	The Piglet
101-111	13	(47)	Companions
111-111	1	(63)	Heaven
110-111	10	(55)	Treading
110-011	61	(51)	Inmost Sincerity (Allegiance)
110-001	41	(49)	Decrease
110-000	19	(48)	Authority Approaches

STORY OF HEXAGRAM: 101-001

Hexagram	Text #	Binary #	Name
110-001	41	(49)	Decrease
010-001	4	(17)	The Young Shoot
000-001	23	(1)	Falling
001-001	52	(9)	Mountain
001-101	56	(13)	The Traveler
001-111	33	(15)	The Piglet
001-110	31	(14)	Mutual Influence
101-110	49	(46)	Revolution
111-110	43	(62)	Decisive
110-110	58	(54)	Lake
110-010	60	(50)	Restraint (Regulations)
110-000	19	(48)	Authority Approaches
110-001	41	(49)	Decrease

STORY OF HEXAGRAM: 101-010

Hexagram	Text #	Binary #	Name
110-010	60	(50)	Restraint (Regulations)
010-010	29	(18)	Water
000-010	8	(2)	Alliance
001-010	39	(10)	Obstruction
001-110	31	(14)	Mutual Influence
001-100	62	(12)	Small in Excess
001-101	56	(13)	The Traveler
101-101	30	(45)	Fire
111-101	14	(61)	Great Possessions
110-101	38	(53)	Estrangement
110-001	41	(49)	Decrease
110-011	61	(51)	Inmost Sincerity (Allegiance)
110-010	60	(50)	Restraint (Regulations)

STORY OF HEXAGRAM: 101-011

Hexagram	Text #	Binary #	Name
110-011	61	(51)	Inmost Sincerity (Allegiance)
010-011	59	(19)	Flood/Dispersion
000-011	20	(3)	Observing
001-011	53	(11)	Gradual Advance
001-111	33	(15)	The Piglet
001-101	56	(13)	The Traveler
001-100	62	(12)	Small in Excess
101-100	55	(44)	Abundance
111-100	34	(60)	Big Uses Force
110-100	54	(52)	A Maiden Marries
110-000	19	(48)	Authority Approaches
110-010	60	(50)	Restraint (Regulations)
110-011	61	(51)	Inmost Sincerity (Allegiance)

STORY OF HEXAGRAM: 101-100

Hexagram	Text #	Binary #	Name
110-100	54	(52)	A Maiden Marries
010-100	40	(20)	Obstruction Removed
000-100	16	(4)	Contentment
001-100	62	(12)	Small in Excess
001-000	15	(8)	Modesty
001-010	39	(10)	Obstruction
001-011	53	(11)	Gradual Advance
101-011	37	(43)	The Family
111-011	9	(59)	Small Restraint/Small Accumulation
110-011	61	(51)	Inmost Sincerity (Allegiance)
110-111	10	(55)	Treading
110-101	38	(53)	Estrangement
110-100	54	(52)	A Maiden Marries

STORY OF HEXAGRAM: 110-101

Hexagram	Text #	Binary #	Name
110-101	38	(53)	Estrangement
010-101	64	(21)	Not Yet Across the River
000-101	35	(5)	Advance
001-101	56	(13)	The Traveler
001-001	52	(9)	Mountain
001-011	53	(11)	Gradual Advance
001-010	39	(10)	Obstruction
101-010	63	(42)	Already Across the River
111-010	5	(58)	Getting Wet
110-010	60	(50)	Restraint (Regulations)
110-110	58	(54)	Lake
110-100	54	(52)	A Maiden Marries
110-101	38	(53)	Estrangement

STORY OF HEXAGRAM: 110-110

Hexagram	Text #	Binary #	Name
110-110	58	(54)	Lake
010-110	47	(22)	Burdened/Exhausted
000-110	45	(6)	Gathering Together
001-110	31	(14)	Mutual Influence
001-010	39	(10)	Obstruction
001-000	15	(8)	Modesty
001-001	52	(9)	Mountain
101-001	22	(41)	Adornment
111-001	26	(57)	Big Restraint/Big Accumulation
110-001	41	(49)	Decrease
110-101	38	(53)	Estrangement
110-111	10	(55)	Treading
110-110	58	(54)	Lake

STORY OF HEXAGRAM: 110-111

Hexagram	Text #	Binary #	Name
110-111	10	(55)	Treading
010-111	6	(23)	Grievance
000-111	12	(7)	Standstill
001-111	33	(15)	The Piglet
001-011	53	(11)	Gradual Advance
001-001	52	(9)	Mountain
001-000	15	(8)	Modesty
101-000	36	(40)	The Bright (Calling) Pheasant
111-000	11	(56)	Peace/Flowing
110-000	19	(48)	Authority Approaches
110-100	54	(52)	A Maiden Marries
110-110	58	(54)	Lake
110-111	10	(55)	Treading

STORY OF HEXAGRAM: 111-000

Hexagram	Text #	Binary #	Name
111-000	11	(56)	Peace/Flowing
011-000	46	(24)	Pushing Upwards
001-000	15	(8)	Modesty
000-000	2	(0)	Earth
000-100	16	(4)	Contentment
000-110	45	(6)	Gathering Together
000-111	12	(7)	Standstill
100-111	25	(39)	No Error (No Expectations)
110-111	10	(55)	Treading
111-111	1	(63)	Heaven
111-011	9	(59)	Small Restraint/Big Accumulation
111-001	26	(57)	Big Restraint/Big Accumulation
111-000	11	(56)	Peace/Flowing

STORY OF HEXAGRAM: 111-001

Hexagram	Text #	Binary #	Name
111-001	26	(57)	Big Restraint/Big Accumulation
011-001	18	(25)	Illness/Decay
001-001	52	(9)	Mountain
000-001	23	(1)	Falling
000-101	35	(5)	Advance
000-111	12	(7)	Standstill
000-110	45	(6)	Gathering Together
100-110	17	(38)	The Chase
110-110	58	(54)	Lake
111-110	43	(62)	Decisive
111-010	5	(58)	Getting Wet
111-000	11	(56)	Peace/Flowing
111-001	26	(57)	Big Restraint/Big Accumulation

STORY OF HEXAGRAM: 111-010

Hexagram	Text #	Binary #	Name
111-010	5	(58)	Getting Wet
011-010	48	(26)	A Well
001-010	39	(10)	Obstruction
000-010	8	(2)	Alliance
000-110	45	(6)	Gathering Together
000-100	16	(4)	Contentment
000-101	35	(5)	Advance
100-101	21	(37)	Biting Through
110-101	38	(53)	Estrangement
111-101	14	(61)	Great Possessions
111-001	26	(57)	Big Restraint/Big Accumulation
111-011	9	(59)	Small Restraint/Small Accumulation
111-010	5	(58)	Getting Wet

STORY OF HEXAGRAM: 111-011

Hexagram	Text #	Binary #	Name
111-011	9	(59)	Small Restraint/Small Accumulation
011-011	57	(27)	Wind
001-011	53	(11)	Gradual Advance
000-011	20	(3)	Observing
000-111	12	(7)	Standstill
000-101	35	(5)	Advance
000-100	16	(4)	Contentment
100-100	51	(36)	Thunder
110-100	54	(52)	A Maiden Marries
111-100	34	(60)	Big Uses Force
111-000	11	(56)	Peace/Flowing
111-010	5	(58)	Getting Wet
111-011	9	(59)	Small Restraint/Small Accumulation

STORY OF HEXAGRAM: 111-100

Hexagram	Text #	Binary #	Name
111-100	34	(60)	Big Uses Force
011-100	32	(28)	Constancy
001-100	62	(12)	Small in Excess
000-100	16	(4)	Contentment
000-000	2	(0)	Earth
000-010	8	(2)	Alliance
000-011	20	(3)	Observing
100-011	42	(35)	Increase
110-011	61	(51)	Inmost Sincerity (Allegiance)
111-011	9	(59)	Small Restraint/Small Accumulation
111-111	1	(63)	Heaven
111-101	14	(61)	Great Possessions
111-100	34	(60)	Big Uses Force

STORY OF HEXAGRAM: 111-101

Hexagram	Text #	Binary #	Name
111-101	14	(61)	Great Possessions
011-101	50	(29)	The Ritual Caldron
001-101	56	(13)	The Traveler
000-101	35	(5)	Advance
000-001	23	(1)	Falling
000-011	20	(3)	Observing
000-010	8	(2)	Alliance
100-010	3	(34)	Sprouting
110-010	60	(50)	Restraint (Regulations)
111-010	5	(58)	Getting Wet
111-110	43	(62)	Decisive
111-100	34	(60)	Big Uses Force
111-101	14	(61)	Great Possessions

STORY OF HEXAGRAM: 111-110

Hexagram	Text #	Binary #	Name
111-110	43	(62)	Decisive
011-110	28	(30)	Big in Excess
001-110	31	(14)	Mutual Influence
000-110	45	(6)	Gathering Together
000-010	8	(2)	Alliance
000-000	2	(0)	Earth
000-001	23	(1)	Falling
100-001	27	(33)	Bulging Cheeks
110-001	41	(49)	Decrease
111-001	26	(57)	Big Restraint/Big Accumulation
111-101	14	(61)	Great Possessions
111-111	1	(63)	Heaven
111-110	43	(62)	Decisive

STORY OF HEXAGRAM: 111-111

Hexagram	Text #	Binary #	Name
111-111	1	(63)	Heaven
011-111	44	(31)	Meeting/Subjugated
001-111	33	(15)	The Piglet
000-111	12	(7)	Standstill
000-011	20	(3)	Observing
000-001	23	(1)	Falling
000-000	2	(0)	Earth
100-000	24	(32)	Return
110-000	19	(48)	Authority Approaches
111-000	11	(56)	Peace/Flowing
111-100	34	(60)	Big Uses Force
111-110	43	(62)	Decisive
111-111	1	(63)	Heaven

H

HEXAGRAM FLOWERS

The flower centers are given in binary order.

Hexagram	Text #	Binary #	Name
000-000	2	(0)	Earth
The petals of the center hexagram are:			
A 100-000	24	(32)	Return
A 010-000	7	(16)	An Army
A 001-000	15	(8)	Modesty
A 000-100	16	(4)	Contentment
A 000-010	8	(2)	Alliance
A 000-001	23	(1)	Falling

Hexagram	Text #	Binary #	Name
000-001	23	(1)	Falling
The petals of the center hexagram are:			
A 100-001	27	(33)	Bulging Cheeks
A 010-001	4	(17)	The Young Shoot
A 001-001	52	(9)	Mountain
A 000-101	35	(5)	Advance
A 000-011	20	(3)	Observing
C 000-000	2	(0)	Earth

Hexagram	Text #	Binary #	Name
000-010	8	(2)	Alliance
The petals of the center hexagram are:			
A 100-010	3	(34)	Sprouting
A 010-010	29	(18)	Water
A 001-010	39	(10)	Obstruction
A 000-110	45	(6)	Gathering Together
C 000-000	2	(0)	Earth
A 000-011	20	(3)	Observing

Hexagram	Text #	Binary #	Name
000-011	20	(3)	Observing
The petals of the center hexagram are:			
A 100-011	42	(35)	Increase
A 010-011	59	(19)	Flood/Dispersion
A 001-011	53	(11)	Gradual Advance
A 000-111	12	(7)	Standstill
C 000-001	23	(1)	Falling
C 000-010	8	(2)	Alliance

Hexagram	Text #	Binary #	Name
000-100	16	(4)	Contentment
The petals of the center hexagram are:			
A 100-100	51	(36)	Thunder
A 010-100	40	(20)	Obstruction Removed
A 001-100	62	(12)	Small in Excess
C 000-000	2	(0)	Earth
A 000-110	45	(6)	Gathering Together
A 000-101	35	(5)	Advance

Hexagram	Text #	Binary #	Name
000-101	35	(5)	Advance
The petals of the center hexagram are:			
A 100-101	21	(37)	Biting Through
A 010-101	64	(21)	Not Yet Across the River
A 001-101	56	(13)	The Traveler
C 000-001	23	(1)	Falling
A 000-111	12	(7)	Standstill
C 000-100	16	(4)	Contentment

Hexagram	Text #	Binary #	Name
000-110	45	(6)	Gathering Together
The petals of the center hexagram are:			
A 100-110	17	(38)	The Chase
A 010-110	47	(22)	Burdened/Exhausted
A 001-110	31	(14)	Mutual Influence
C 000-010	8	(2)	Alliance
C 000-100	16	(4)	Contentment
A 000-111	12	(7)	Standstill

Hexagram	Text #	Binary #	Name
000-111	12	(7)	Standstill
The petals of the center hexagram are:			
A 100-111	25	(39)	No Error (No Expectations)
A 010-111	6	(23)	Grievance
A 001-111	33	(15)	The Piglet
C 000-011	20	(3)	Observing
C 000-101	35	(5)	Advance
C 000-110	45	(6)	Gathering Together

Hexagram	Text #	Binary #	Name
001-000	15	(8)	Modesty
The petals of the center hexagram are:			
A 101-000	36	(40)	The Bright (Calling) Pheasant
A 011-000	46	(24)	Pushing Upwards
C 000-000	2	(0)	Earth
A 001-100	62	(12)	Small in Excess
A 001-010	39	(10)	Obstruction
A 001-001	52	(9)	Mountain

Hexagram	Text #	Binary #	Name
001-001	52	(9)	Mountain
The petals of the center hexagram are:			
A 101-001	22	(41)	Adornment
A 011-001	18	(25)	Illness/Decay
C 000-001	23	(1)	Falling
A 001-101	56	(13)	The Traveler
A 001-011	53	(11)	Gradual Advance
C 001-000	15	(8)	Modesty

Hexagram	Text #	Binary #	Name
001-010	39	(10)	Obstruction
The petals of the center hexagram are:			
A 101-010	63	(42)	Already Across the River
A 011-010	48	(26)	A Well
C 000-010	8	(2)	Alliance
A 001-110	31	(14)	Mutual Influence
C 001-000	15	(8)	Modesty
A 001-011	53	(11)	Gradual Advance

Hexagram	Text #	Binary #	Name
001-011	53	(11)	Gradual Advance

The petals of the center hexagram are:

Hexagram	Text #	Binary #	Name
A 101-011	37	(43)	The Family
A 011-011	57	(27)	Wind
C 000-011	20	(3)	Observing
A 001-111	33	(15)	The Piglet
C 001-001	52	(9)	Mountain
C 001-010	39	(10)	Obstruction

Hexagram	Text #	Binary #	Name
001-100	62	(12)	Small in Excess

The petals of the center hexagram are:

Hexagram	Text #	Binary #	Name
A 101-100	55	(44)	Abundance
A 011-100	32	(28)	Constancy
C 000-100	16	(4)	Contentment
C 001-000	15	(8)	Modesty
A 001-110	31	(14)	Mutual Influence
A 001-101	56	(13)	The Traveler

Hexagram	Text #	Binary #	Name
001-101	56	(13)	The Traveler

The petals of the center hexagram are:

Hexagram	Text #	Binary #	Name
A 101-101	30	(45)	Fire
A 011-101	50	(29)	The Ritual Caldron
C 000-101	35	(5)	Advance
C 001-001	52	(9)	Mountain
A 001-111	33	(15)	The Piglet
C 001-100	62	(12)	Small in Excess

Hexagram	Text #	Binary #	Name
001-110	31	(14)	Mutual Influence

The petals of the center hexagram are:

Hexagram	Text #	Binary #	Name
A 101-110	49	(46)	Revolution
A 011-110	28	(30)	Big in Excess
C 000-110	45	(6)	Gathering Together
C 001-010	39	(10)	Obstruction
C 001-100	62	(12)	Small in Excess
A 001-111	33	(15)	The Piglet

Hexagram	Text #	Binary #	Name
001-111	33	(15)	The Piglet
The petals of the center hexagram are:			
A 101-111	13	(47)	Companions
A 011-111	44	(31)	Meeting/Subjugated
C 000-111	12	(7)	Standstill
C 001-011	53	(11)	Gradual Advance
C 001-101	56	(13)	The Traveler
C 001-110	31	(14)	Mutual Influence

Hexagram	Text #	Binary #	Name
010-000	7	(16)	An Army
The petals of the center hexagram are:			
A 110-000	19	(48)	Authority Approaches
C 000-000	2	(0)	Earth
A 011-000	46	(24)	Pushing Upwards
A 010-100	40	(20)	Obstruction Removed
A 010-010	29	(18)	Water
A 010-001	4	(17)	The Young Shoot

Hexagram	Text #	Binary #	Name
010-001	4	(17)	The Young Shoot
The petals of the center hexagram are:			
A 110-001	41	(49)	Decrease
C 000-001	23	(1)	Falling
A 011-001	18	(25)	Illness/Decay
A 010-101	64	(21)	Not Yet Across the River
A 010-011	59	(19)	Flood/Dispersion
C 010-000	7	(16)	An Army

Hexagram	Text #	Binary #	Name
010-010	29	(18)	Water
The petals of the center hexagram are:			
A 110-010	60	(50)	Restraint (Regulations)
C 000-010	8	(2)	Alliance
A 011-010	48	(26)	A Well
A 010-110	47	(22)	Burdened/Exhausted
C 010-000	7	(16)	An Army
A 010-011	59	(19)	Flood/Dispersion

Hexagram	Text #	Binary #	Name
010-011	59	(19)	Flood/Dispersion
The petals of the center hexagram are:			
A 110-011	61	(51)	Inmost Sincerity (Allegiance)
C 000-011	20	(3)	Observing
A 011-011	57	(27)	Wind
A 010-111	6	(23)	Grievance
C 010-001	4	(17)	The Young Shoot
C 010-010	29	(18)	Water

Hexagram	Text #	Binary #	Name
010-100	40	(20)	Obstruction Removed
The petals of the center hexagram are:			
A 110-100	54	(52)	A Maiden Marries
C 000-100	16	(4)	Contentment
A 011-100	32	(28)	Constancy
C 010-000	7	(16)	An Army
A 010-110	47	(22)	Burdened/Exhausted
A 010-101	64	(21)	Not Yet Across the River

Hexagram	Text #	Binary #	Name
010-101	64	(21)	Not Yet Across the River
The petals of the center hexagram are:			
A 110-101	38	(53)	Estrangement
C 000-101	35	(5)	Advance
A 011-101	50	(29)	The Ritual Caldron
C 010-001	4	(17)	The Young Shoot
A 010-111	6	(23)	Grievance
C 010-100	40	(20)	Obstruction Removed

Hexagram	Text #	Binary #	Name
010-110	47	(22)	Burdened/Exhausted
The petals of the center hexagram are:			
A 110-110	58	(54)	Lake
C 000-110	45	(6)	Gathering Together
A 011-110	28	(30)	Big in Excess
C 010-010	29	(18)	Water
C 010-100	40	(20)	Obstruction Removed
A 010-111	6	(23)	Grievance

Hexagram	Text #	Binary #	Name
010-111	6	(23)	Grievance
The petals of the center hexagram are:			
A 110-111	10	(55)	Treading
C 000-111	12	(7)	Standstill
A 011-111	44	(31)	Meeting/Subjugated
C 010-011	59	(19)	Flood/Dispersion
C 010-101	64	(21)	Not Yet Across the River
C 010-110	47	(22)	Burdened/Exhausted

Hexagram	Text #	Binary #	Name
011-000	46	(24)	Pushing Upwards
The petals of the center hexagram are:			
A 111-000	11	(56)	Peace/Flowing
C 001-000	15	(8)	Modesty
C 010-000	7	(16)	An Army
A 011-100	32	(28)	Constancy
A 011-010	48	(26)	A Well
A 011-001	18	(25)	Illness/Decay

Hexagram	Text #	Binary #	Name
011-001	18	(25)	Illness/Decay
The petals of the center hexagram are:			
A 111-001	26	(57)	Big Restraint/Big Accumulation
C 001-001	52	(9)	Mountain
C 010-001	4	(17)	The Young Shoot
A 011-101	50	(29)	The Ritual Caldron
A 011-011	57	(27)	Wind
C 011-000	46	(24)	Pushing Upwards

Hexagram	Text #	Binary #	Name
011-010	48	(26)	A Well
The petals of the center hexagram are:			
A 111-010	5	(58)	Getting Wet
C 001-010	39	(10)	Obstruction
C 010-010	29	(18)	Water
A 011-110	28	(30)	Big in Excess
C 011-000	46	(24)	Pushing Upwards
A 011-011	57	(27)	Wind

Hexagram	Text #	Binary #	Name
011-011	57	(27)	Wind

The petals of the center hexagram are:

A 111-011	9	(59)	Small Restraint/Small Accumulation
C 001-011	53	(11)	Gradual Advance
C 010-011	59	(19)	Flood/Dispersion
A 011-111	44	(31)	Meeting/Subjugated
C 011-001	18	(25)	Illness/Decay
C 011-010	48	(26)	A Well

Hexagram	Text #	Binary #	Name
011-100	32	(28)	Constancy

The petals of the center hexagram are:

A 111-100	34	(60)	Big Uses Force
C 001-100	62	(12)	Small in Excess
C 010-100	40	(20)	Obstruction Removed
C 011-000	46	(24)	Pushing Upwards
A 011-110	28	(30)	Big in Excess
A 011-101	50	(29)	The Ritual Caldron

Hexagram	Text #	Binary #	Name
011-101	50	(29)	The Ritual Caldron

The petals of the center hexagram are:

A 111-101	14	(61)	Great Possessions
C 001-101	56	(13)	The Traveler
C 010-101	64	(21)	Not Yet Across the River
C 011-001	18	(25)	Illness/Decay
A 011-111	44	(31)	Meeting/Subjugated
C 011-100	32	(28)	Constancy

Hexagram	Text #	Binary #	Name
011-110	28	(30)	Big in Excess

The petals of the center hexagram are:

A 111-110	43	(62)	Decisive
C 001-110	31	(14)	Mutual Influence
C 010-110	47	(22)	Burdened/Exhausted
C 011-010	48	(26)	A Well
C 011-100	32	(28)	Constancy
A 011-111	44	(31)	Meeting/Subjugated

Hexagram	Text #	Binary #	Name
011-111	44	(31)	Meeting/Subjugated

The petals of the center hexagram are:

A 111-111	1	(63)	Heaven
C 001-111	33	(15)	The Piglet
C 010-111	6	(23)	Grievance
C 011-011	57	(27)	Wind
C 011-101	50	(29)	The Ritual Caldron
C 011-110	28	(30)	Big in Excess

Hexagram	Text #	Binary #	Name
100-000	24	(32)	Return

The petals of the center hexagram are:

C 000-000	2	(0)	Earth
A 110-000	19	(48)	Authority Approaches
A 101-000	36	(40)	The Bright (Calling) Pheasant
A 100-100	51	(36)	Thunder
A 100-010	3	(34)	Sprouting
A 100-001	27	(33)	Bulging Cheeks

Hexagram	Text #	Binary #	Name
100-001	27	(33)	Bulging Cheeks

The petals of the center hexagram are:

C 000-001	23	(1)	Falling
A 110-001	41	(49)	Decrease
A 101-001	22	(41)	Adornment
A 100-101	21	(37)	Biting Through
A 100-011	42	(35)	Increase
C 100-000	24	(32)	Return

Hexagram	Text #	Binary #	Name
100-010	3	(34)	Sprouting

The petals of the center hexagram are:

C 000-010	8	(2)	Alliance
A 110-010	60	(50)	Restraint (Regulations)
A 101-010	63	(42)	Already Across the River
A 100-110	17	(38)	The Chase
C 100-000	24	(32)	Return
A 100-011	42	(35)	Increase

Hexagram	Text #	Binary #	Name
100-011	42	(35)	Increase

The petals of the center hexagram are:

C 000-011	20	(3)	Observing
A 110-011	61	(51)	Inmost Sincerity (Allegiance)
A 101-011	37	(43)	The Family
A 100-111	25	(39)	No Error (No Expectations)
C 100-001	27	(33)	Bulging Cheeks
C 100-010	3	(34)	Sprouting

Hexagram	Text #	Binary #	Name
100-100	51	(36)	Thunder

The petals of the center hexagram are:

C 000-100	16	(4)	Contentment
A 110-100	54	(52)	A Maiden Marries
A 101-100	55	(44)	Abundance
C 100-000	24	(32)	Return
A 100-110	17	(38)	The Chase
A 100-101	21	(37)	Biting Through

Hexagram	Text #	Binary #	Name
100-101	21	(37)	Biting Through

The petals of the center hexagram are:

C 000-101	35	(5)	Advance
A 110-101	38	(53)	Estrangement
A 101-101	30	(45)	Fire
C 100-001	27	(33)	Bulging Cheeks
A 100-111	25	(39)	No Error (No Expectations)
C 100-100	51	(36)	Thunder

Hexagram	Text #	Binary #	Name
100-110	17	(38)	The Chase

The petals of the center hexagram are:

C 000-110	45	(6)	Gathering Together
A 110-110	58	(54)	Lake
A 101-110	49	(46)	Revolution
C 100-010	3	(34)	Sprouting
C 100-100	51	(36)	Thunder
A 100-111	25	(39)	No Error (No Expectations)

Hexagram	Text #	Binary #	Name
100-111	25	(39)	No Error (No Expectations)
The petals of the center hexagram are:			
C 000-111	12	(7)	Standstill
A 110-111	10	(55)	Treading
A 101-111	13	(47)	Companions
C 100-011	42	(35)	Increase
C 100-101	21	(37)	Biting Through
C 100-110	17	(38)	The Chase

Hexagram	Text #	Binary #	Name
101-000	36	(40)	The Bright (Calling) Pheasant
The petals of the center hexagram are:			
C 001-000	15	(8)	Modesty
A 111-000	11	(56)	Peace/Flowing
C 100-000	24	(32)	Return
A 101-100	55	(44)	Abundance
A 101-010	63	(42)	Already Across the River
A 101-001	22	(41)	Adornment

Hexagram	Text #	Binary #	Name
101-001	22	(41)	Adornment
The petals of the center hexagram are:			
C 001-001	52	(9)	Mountain
A 111-001	26	(57)	Big Restraint/Big Accumulation
C 100-001	27	(33)	Bulging Cheeks
A 101-101	30	(45)	Fire
A 101-011	37	(43)	The Family
C 101-000	36	(40)	The Bright (Calling) Pheasant

Hexagram	Text #	Binary #	Name
101-010	63	(42)	Already Across the River
The petals of the center hexagram are:			
C 001-010	39	(10)	Obstruction
A 111-010	5	(58)	Getting Wet
C 100-010	3	(34)	Sprouting
A 101-110	49	(46)	Revolution
C 101-000	36	(40)	The Bright (Calling) Pheasant
A 101-011	37	(43)	The Family

Hexagram	Text #	Binary #	Name
101-011	37	(43)	The Family
The petals of the center hexagram are:			
C 001-011	53	(11)	Gradual Advance
A 111-011	9	(59)	Small Restraint/Small Accumulation
C 100-011	42	(35)	Increase
A 101-111	13	(47)	Companions
C 101-001	22	(41)	Adornment
C 101-010	63	(42)	Already Across the River

Hexagram	Text #	Binary #	Name
101-100	55	(44)	Abundance
The petals of the center hexagram are:			
C 001-100	62	(12)	Small in Excess
A 111-100	34	(60)	Big Uses Force
C 100-100	51	(36)	Thunder
C 101-000	36	(40)	The Bright (Calling) Pheasant
A 101-110	49	(46)	Revolution
A 101-101	30	(45)	Fire

Hexagram	Text #	Binary #	Name
101-101	30	(45)	Fire
The petals of the center hexagram are:			
C 001-101	56	(13)	The Traveler
A 111-101	14	(61)	Great Possessions
C 100-101	21	(37)	Biting Through
C 101-001	22	(41)	Adornment
A 101-111	13	(47)	Companions
C 101-100	55	(44)	Abundance

Hexagram	Text #	Binary #	Name
101-110	49	(46)	Revolution
The petals of the center hexagram are:			
C 001-110	31	(14)	Mutual Influence
A 111-110	43	(62)	Decisive
C 100-110	17	(38)	The Chase
C 101-010	63	(42)	Already Across the River
C 101-100	55	(44)	Abundance
A 101-111	13	(47)	Companions

Hexagram	Text #	Binary #	Name
101-111	13	(47)	Companions
The petals of the center hexagram are:			
C 001-111	33	(15)	The Piglet
A 111-111	1	(63)	Heaven
C 100-111	25	(39)	No Error (No Expectations)
C 101-011	37	(43)	The Family
C 101-101	30	(45)	Fire
C 101-110	49	(46)	Revolution

Hexagram	Text #	Binary #	Name
110-000	19	(48)	Authority Approaches
The petals of the center hexagram are:			
C 010-000	7	(16)	An Army
C 100-000	24	(32)	Return
A 111-000	11	(56)	Peace/Flowing
A 110-100	54	(52)	A Maiden Marries
A 110-010	60	(50)	Restraint (Regulations)
A 110-001	41	(49)	Decrease

Hexagram	Text #	Binary #	Name
110-001	41	(49)	Decrease
The petals of the center hexagram are:			
C 010-001	4	(17)	The Young Shoot
C 100-001	27	(33)	Bulging Cheeks
A 111-001	26	(57)	Big Restraint/Big Accumulation
A 110-101	38	(53)	Estrangement
A 110-011	61	(51)	Inmost Sincerity (Allegiance)
C 110-000	19	(48)	Authority Approaches

Hexagram	Text #	Binary #	Name
110-010	60	(50)	Restraint (Regulations)
The petals of the center hexagram are:			
C 010-010	29	(18)	Water
C 100-010	3	(34)	Sprouting
A 111-010	5	(58)	Getting Wet
A 110-110	58	(54)	Lake
C 110-000	19	(48)	Authority Approaches
A 110-011	61	(51)	Inmost Sincerity (Allegiance)

Hexagram	Text #	Binary #	Name
110-011	61	(51)	Inmost Sincerity (Allegiance)

The petals of the center hexagram are:

C 010-011	59	(19)	Flood/Dispersion
C 100-011	42	(35)	Increase
A 111-011	9	(59)	Small Restraint/Small Accumulation
A 110-111	10	(55)	Treading
C 110-001	41	(49)	Decrease
C 110-010	60	(50)	Restraint (Regulations)

Hexagram	Text #	Binary #	Name
110-100	54	(52)	A Maiden Marries

The petals of the center hexagram are:

C 010-100	40	(20)	Obstruction Removed
C 100-100	51	(36)	Thunder
A 111-100	34	(60)	Big Uses Force
C 110-000	19	(48)	Authority Approaches
A 110-110	58	(54)	Lake
A 110-101	38	(53)	Estrangement

Hexagram	Text #	Binary #	Name
110-101	38	(53)	Estrangement

The petals of the center hexagram are:

C 010-101	64	(21)	Not Yet Across the River
C 100-101	21	(37)	Biting Through
A 111-101	14	(61)	Great Possessions
C 110-001	41	(49)	Decrease
A 110-111	10	(55)	Treading
C 110-100	54	(52)	A Maiden Marries

Hexagram	Text #	Binary #	Name
110-110	58	(54)	Lake

The petals of the center hexagram are:

C 010-110	47	(22)	Burdened/Exhausted
C 100-110	17	(38)	The Chase
A 111-110	43	(62)	Decisive
C 110-010	60	(50)	Restraint (Regulations)
C 110-100	54	(52)	A Maiden Marries
A 110-111	10	(55)	Treading

Hexagram	Text #	Binary #	Name
110-111	10	(55)	Treading
The petals of the center hexagram are:			
C 010-111	6	(23)	Grievance
C 100-111	25	(39)	No Error (No Expectations)
A 111-111	1	(63)	Heaven
C 110-011	61	(51)	Inmost Sincerity (Allegiance)
C 110-101	38	(53)	Estrangement
C 110-110	58	(54)	Lake

Hexagram	Text #	Binary #	Name
111-000	11	(56)	Peace/Flowing
The petals of the center hexagram are:			
C 011-000	46	(24)	Pushing Upwards
C 101-000	36	(40)	The Bright (Calling) Pheasant
C 110-000	19	(48)	Authority Approaches
A 111-100	34	(60)	Big Uses Force
A 111-010	5	(58)	Getting Wet
A 111-001	26	(57)	Big Restraint/Big Accumulation

Hexagram	Text #	Binary #	Name
111-001	26	(57)	Big Restraint/Big Accumulation
The petals of the center hexagram are:			
C 011-001	18	(25)	Illness/Decay
C 101-001	22	(41)	Adornment
C 110-001	41	(49)	Decrease
A 111-101	14	(61)	Great Possessions
A 111-011	9	(59)	Small Restraint/Small Accumulation
C 111-000	11	(56)	Peace/Flowing

Hexagram	Text #	Binary #	Name
111-010	5	(58)	Getting Wet
The petals of the center hexagram are:			
C 011-010	48	(26)	A Well
C 101-010	63	(42)	Already Across the River
C 110-010	60	(50)	Restraint (Regulations)
A 111-110	43	(62)	Decisive
C 111-000	11	(56)	Peace/Flowing
A 111-011	9	(59)	Small Restraint/Small Accumulation

Hexagram	Text #	Binary #	Name
111-011	9	(59)	Small Restraint/Small Accumulation

The petals of the center hexagram are:

C 011-011	57	(27)	Wind
C 101-011	37	(43)	The Family
C 110-011	61	(51)	Inmost Sincerity (Allegiance)
A 111-111	1	(63)	Heaven
C 111-001	26	(57)	Big Restraint/Big Accumulation
C 111-010	5	(58)	Getting Wet

Hexagram	Text #	Binary #	Name
111-100	34	(60)	Big Uses Force

The petals of the center hexagram are:

C 011-100	32	(28)	Constancy
C 101-100	55	(44)	Abundance
C 110-100	54	(52)	A Maiden Marries
C 111-000	11	(56)	Peace/Flowing
A 111-110	43	(62)	Decisive
A 111-101	14	(61)	Great Possessions

Hexagram	Text #	Binary #	Name
111-101	14	(61)	Great Possessions

The petals of the center hexagram are:

C 011-101	50	(29)	The Ritual Caldron
C 101-101	30	(45)	Fire
C 110-101	38	(53)	Estrangement
C 111-001	26	(57)	Big Restraint/Big Accumulation
A 111-111	1	(63)	Heaven
C 111-100	34	(60)	Big Uses Force

Hexagram	Text #	Binary #	Name
111-110	43	(62)	Decisive

The petals of the center hexagram are:

C 011-110	28	(30)	Big in Excess
C 101-110	49	(46)	Revolution
C 110-110	58	(54)	Lake
C 111-010	5	(58)	Getting Wet
C 111-100	34	(60)	Big Uses Force
A 111-111	1	(63)	Heaven

Hexagram	Text #	Binary #	Name
111-111	1	(63)	Heaven
The petals of the center hexagram are:			
C 011-111	44	(31)	Meeting/Subjugated
C 101-111	13	(47)	Companions
C 110-111	10	(55)	Treading
C 111-011	9	(59)	Small Restraint/Small Accumulation
C 111-101	14	(61)	Great Possessions
C 111-110	43	(62)	Decisive

I

HEXAGRAM CYCLES

The first hexagrams in each cycle are in binary sequence.

Hexagram	Text #	Binary #	Name
000-000	2	(0)	Earth

Hexagram	Text #	Binary #	Name
000-001	23	(1)	Falling
100-000	24	(32)	Return
010-000	7	(16)	An Army
001-000	15	(8)	Modesty
000-100	16	(4)	Contentment
000-010	8	(2)	Alliance

Hexagram	Text #	Binary #	Name
000-010	8	(2)	Alliance
000-001	23	(1)	Falling
100-000	24	(32)	Return
010-000	7	(16)	An Army
001-000	15	(8)	Modesty
000-100	16	(4)	Contentment

Hexagram	Text #	Binary #	Name
000-011	20	(3)	Observing
100-001	27	(33)	Bulging Cheeks
110-000	19	(48)	Authority Approaches
011-000	46	(24)	Pushing Upwards
001-100	62	(12)	Small in Excess
000-110	45	(6)	Gathering Together

Hexagram	Text #	Binary #	Name
000-100	16	(4)	Contentment
000-010	8	(2)	Alliance
000-001	23	(1)	Falling
100-000	24	(32)	Return
010-000	7	(16)	An Army
001-000	15	(8)	Modesty

Hexagram	Text #	Binary #	Name
000-101	35	(5)	Advance
100-010	3	(34)	Sprouting
010-001	4	(17)	The Young Shoot
101-000	36	(40)	The Bright (Calling) Pheasant
010-100	40	(20)	Obstruction Removed
001-010	39	(10)	Obstruction

Hexagram	Text #	Binary #	Name
000-110	45	(6)	Gathering Together
000-011	20	(3)	Observing
100-001	27	(33)	Bulging Cheeks
110-000	19	(48)	Authority Approaches
011-000	46	(24)	Pushing Upwards
001-100	62	(12)	Small in Excess

Hexagram	Text #	Binary #	Name
000-111	12	(7)	Standstill
100-011	42	(35)	Increase
110-001	41	(49)	Decrease
111-000	11	(56)	Peace/Flowing
011-100	32	(28)	Constancy
001-110	31	(14)	Mutual Influence

Hexagram	Text #	Binary #	Name
001-000	15	(8)	Modesty
000-100	16	(4)	Contentment
000-010	8	(2)	Alliance
000-001	23	(1)	Falling
100-000	24	(32)	Return
010-000	7	(16)	An Army

Hexagram	Text #	Binary #	Name
001-001	52	(9)	Mountain
100-100	51	(36)	Thunder
010-010	29	(18)	Water

Hexagram	Text #	Binary #	Name
001-010	39	(10)	Obstruction
000-101	35	(5)	Advance
100-010	3	(34)	Sprouting
010-001	4	(17)	The Young Shoot
101-000	36	(40)	The Bright (Calling) Pheasant
010-100	40	(20)	Obstruction Removed

Hexagram	Text #	Binary #	Name
001-011	53	(11)	Gradual Advance
100-101	21	(37)	Biting Through
110-010	60	(50)	Restraint (Regulations)
011-001	18	(25)	Illness/Decay
101-100	55	(44)	Abundance
010-110	47	(22)	Burdened/Exhausted

Hexagram	Text #	Binary #	Name
001-100	62	(12)	Small in Excess
000-110	45	(6)	Gathering Together
000-011	20	(3)	Observing
100-001	27	(33)	Bulging Cheeks
110-000	19	(48)	Authority Approaches
011-000	46	(24)	Pushing Upwards

Hexagram	Text #	Binary #	Name
001-101	56	(13)	The Traveler
100-110	17	(38)	The Chase
010-011	59	(19)	Flood/Dispersion
101-001	22	(41)	Adornment
110-100	54	(52)	A Maiden Marries
011-010	48	(26)	A Well

Hexagram	Text #	Binary #	Name
001-110	31	(14)	Mutual Influence
000-111	12	(7)	Standstill
100-011	42	(35)	Increase
110-001	41	(49)	Decrease
111-000	11	(56)	Peace/Flowing
011-100	32	(28)	Constancy

Hexagram	Text #	Binary #	Name
001-111	33	(15)	The Piglet
100-111	25	(39)	No Error (No Expectations)
110-011	61	(51)	Inmost Sincerity (Allegiance)
111-001	26	(57)	Big Restraint/Big Accumulation
111-100	34	(60)	Big Uses Force
011-110	28	(30)	Big in Excess

Hexagram	Text #	Binary #	Name
010-000	7	(16)	An Army
001-000	15	(8)	Modesty
000-100	16	(4)	Contentment
000-010	8	(2)	Alliance
000-001	23	(1)	Falling
100-000	24	(32)	Return

Hexagram	Text #	Binary #	Name
010-001	4	(17)	The Young Shoot
101-000	36	(40)	The Bright (Calling) Pheasant
010-100	40	(20)	Obstruction Removed
001-010	39	(10)	Obstruction
000-101	35	(5)	Advance
100-010	3	(34)	Sprouting

Hexagram	Text #	Binary #	Name
010-010	29	(18)	Water
001-001	52	(9)	Mountain
100-100	51	(36)	Thunder

Hexagram	Text #	Binary #	Name
010-011	59	(19)	Flood/Dispersion
101-001	22	(41)	Adornment
110-100	54	(52)	A Maiden Marries
011-010	48	(26)	A Well
001-101	56	(13)	The Traveler
100-110	17	(38)	The Chase

Hexagram	Text #	Binary #	Name
010-100	40	(20)	Obstruction Removed
001-010	39	(10)	Obstruction
000-101	35	(5)	Advance
100-010	3	(34)	Sprouting
010-001	4	(17)	The Young Shoot
101-000	36	(40)	The Bright (Calling) Pheasant

Hexagram	Text #	Binary #	Name
010-101	64	(21)	Not Yet Across the River
101-010	63	(42)	Already Across the River

Hexagram	Text #	Binary #	Name
010-110	47	(22)	Burdened/Exhausted
001-011	53	(11)	Gradual Advance
100-101	21	(37)	Biting Through
110-010	60	(50)	Restraint (Regulations)
011-001	18	(25)	Illness/Decay
101-100	55	(44)	Abundance

Hexagram	Text #	Binary #	Name
010-111	6	(23)	Grievance
101-011	37	(43)	The Family
110-101	38	(53)	Estrangement
111-010	5	(58)	Getting Wet
011-101	50	(29)	The Ritual Caldron
101-110	49	(46)	Revolution

Hexagram	Text #	Binary #	Name
011-000	46	(24)	Pushing Upwards
001-100	62	(12)	Small in Excess
000-110	45	(6)	Gathering Together
000-011	20	(3)	Observing
100-001	27	(33)	Bulging Cheeks
110-000	19	(48)	Authority Approaches

Hexagram	Text #	Binary #	Name
011-001	18	(25)	Illness/Decay
101-100	55	(44)	Abundance
010-110	47	(22)	Burdened/Exhausted
001-011	53	(11)	Gradual Advance
100-101	21	(37)	Biting Through
110-010	60	(50)	Restraint (Regulations)

Hexagram	Text #	Binary #	Name
011-010	48	(26)	A Well
001-101	56	(13)	The Traveler
100-110	17	(38)	The Chase
010-011	59	(19)	Flood/Dispersion
101-001	22	(41)	Adornment
110-100	54	(52)	A Maiden Marries

Hexagram	Text #	Binary #	Name
011-011	57	(27)	Wind
101-101	30	(45)	Fire
110-110	58	(54)	Lake

Hexagram	Text #	Binary #	Name
011-100	32	(28)	Constancy
001-110	31	(14)	Mutual Influence
000-111	12	(7)	Standstill
100-011	42	(35)	Increase
110-001	41	(49)	Decrease
111-000	11	(56)	Peace/Flowing

Hexagram	Text #	Binary #	Name
011-101	50	(29)	The Ritual Caldron
101-110	49	(46)	Revolution
010-111	6	(23)	Grievance
101-011	37	(43)	The Family
110-101	38	(53)	Estrangement
111-010	5	(58)	Getting Wet

Hexagram	Text #	Binary #	Name
011-110	28	(30)	Big in Excess
001-111	33	(15)	The Piglet
100-111	25	(39)	No Error (No Expectations)
110-011	61	(51)	Inmost Sincerity (Allegiance)
111-001	26	(57)	Big Restraint/Big Accumulation
111-100	34	(60)	Big Uses Force

Hexagram	Text #	Binary #	Name
011-111	44	(31)	Meeting/Subjugated
101-111	13	(47)	Companions
110-111	10	(55)	Treading
111-011	9	(59)	Small Restraint/Small Accumulation
111-101	14	(61)	Great Possessions
111-110	43	(62)	Decisive

Hexagram	Text #	Binary #	Name
100-000	24	(32)	Return
010-000	7	(16)	An Army
001-000	15	(8)	Modesty
000-100	16	(4)	Contentment
000-010	8	(2)	Alliance
000-001	23	(1)	Falling

Hexagram	Text #	Binary #	Name
100-001	27	(33)	Bulging Cheeks
110-000	19	(48)	Authority Approaches
011-000	46	(24)	Pushing Upwards
001-100	62	(12)	Small in Excess
000-110	45	(6)	Gathering Together
000-011	20	(3)	Observing

Hexagram	Text #	Binary #	Name
100-010	3	(34)	Sprouting
010-001	4	(17)	The Young Shoot
101-000	36	(40)	The Bright (Calling) Pheasant
010-100	40	(20)	Obstruction Removed
001-010	39	(10)	Obstruction
000-101	35	(5)	Advance

Hexagram	Text #	Binary #	Name
100-011	42	(35)	Increase
110-001	41	(49)	Decrease
111-000	11	(56)	Peace/Flowing
011-100	32	(28)	Constancy
001-110	31	(14)	Mutual Influence
000-111	12	(7)	Standstill

Hexagram	Text #	Binary #	Name
100-100	51	(36)	Thunder
010-010	29	(18)	Water
001-001	52	(9)	Mountain

Hexagram	Text #	Binary #	Name
100-101	21	(37)	Biting Through
110-010	60	(50)	Restraint (Regulations)
011-001	18	(25)	Illness/Decay
101-100	55	(44)	Abundance
010-110	47	(22)	Burdened/Exhausted
001-011	53	(11)	Gradual Advance

Hexagram	Text #	Binary #	Name
100-110	17	(38)	The Chase
010-011	59	(19)	Flood/Dispersion
101-001	22	(41)	Adornment
110-100	54	(52)	A Maiden Marries
011-010	48	(26)	A Well
001-101	56	(13)	The Traveler

Hexagram	Text #	Binary #	Name
100-111	25	(39)	No Error (No Expectations)
110-011	61	(51)	Inmost Sincerity (Allegiance)
111-001	26	(57)	Big Restraint/Big Accumulation
111-100	34	(60)	Big Uses Force
011-110	28	(30)	Big in Excess
001-111	33	(15)	The Piglet

Hexagram	Text #	Binary #	Name
101-000	36	(40)	The Bright (Calling) Pheasant
010-100	40	(20)	Obstruction Removed
001-010	39	(10)	Obstruction
000-101	35	(5)	Advance
100-010	3	(34)	Sprouting
010-001	4	(17)	The Young Shoot

Hexagram	Text #	Binary #	Name
101-001	22	(41)	Adornment
110-100	54	(52)	A Maiden Marries
011-010	48	(26)	A Well
001-101	56	(13)	The Traveler
100-110	17	(38)	The Chase
010-011	59	(19)	Flood/Dispersion

Hexagram	Text #	Binary #	Name
101-010	63	(42)	Already Across the River
010-101	64	(21)	Not Yet Across the River

Hexagram	Text #	Binary #	Name
101-011	37	(43)	The Family
110-101	38	(53)	Estrangement
111-010	5	(58)	Getting Wet
011-101	50	(29)	The Ritual Caldron
101-110	49	(46)	Revolution
010-111	6	(23)	Grievance

Hexagram	Text #	Binary #	Name
101-100	55	(44)	Abundance
010-110	47	(22)	Burdened/Exhausted
001-011	53	(11)	Gradual Advance
100-101	21	(37)	Biting Through
110-010	60	(50)	Restraint (Regulations)
011-001	18	(25)	Illness/Decay

Hexagram	Text #	Binary #	Name
101-101	30	(45)	Fire
110-110	58	(54)	Lake
011-011	57	(27)	Wind

Hexagram	Text #	Binary #	Name
101-110	49	(46)	Revolution
010-111	6	(23)	Grievance
101-011	37	(43)	The Family
110-101	38	(53)	Estrangement
111-010	5	(58)	Getting Wet
011-101	50	(29)	The Ritual Caldron

Hexagram	Text #	Binary #	Name
101-111	13	(47)	Companions
110-111	10	(55)	Treading
111-011	9	(59)	Small Restraint/Small Accumulation
111-101	14	(61)	Great Possessions
111-110	43	(62)	Decisive
011-111	44	(31)	Meeting/Subjugated

Hexagram	Text #	Binary #	Name
110-000	19	(48)	Authority Approaches
011-000	46	(24)	Pushing Upwards
001-100	62	(12)	Small in Excess
000-110	45	(6)	Gathering Together
000-011	20	(3)	Observing
100-001	27	(33)	Bulging Cheeks

Hexagram	Text #	Binary #	Name
110-001	41	(49)	Decrease
111-000	11	(56)	Peace/Flowing
011-100	32	(28)	Constancy
001-110	31	(14)	Mutual Influence
000-111	12	(7)	Standstill
100-011	42	(35)	Increase

Hexagram	Text #	Binary #	Name
110-010	60	(50)	Restraint (Regulations)
011-001	18	(25)	Illness/Decay
101-100	55	(44)	Abundance
010-110	47	(22)	Burdened/Exhausted
001-011	53	(11)	Gradual Advance
100-101	21	(37)	Biting Through

Hexagram	Text #	Binary #	Name
110-011	61	(51)	Inmost Sincerity (Allegiance)
111-001	26	(57)	Big Restraint/Big Accumulation
111-100	34	(60)	Big Uses Force
011-110	28	(30)	Big in Excess
001-111	33	(15)	The Piglet
100-111	25	(39)	No Error (No Expectations)

Hexagram	Text #	Binary #	Name
110-100	54	(52)	A Maiden Marries
011-010	48	(26)	A Well
001-101	56	(13)	The Traveler
100-110	17	(38)	The Chase
010-011	59	(19)	Flood/Dispersion
101-001	22	(41)	Adornment

Hexagram	Text #	Binary #	Name
110-101	38	(53)	Estrangement
111-010	5	(58)	Getting Wet
011-101	50	(29)	The Ritual Caldron
101-110	49	(46)	Revolution
010-111	6	(23)	Grievance
101-011	37	(43)	The Family

Hexagram	Text #	Binary #	Name
110-110	58	(54)	Lake
011-011	57	(27)	Wind
101-101	30	(45)	Fire

Hexagram	Text #	Binary #	Name
110-111	10	(55)	Treading
111-011	9	(59)	Small Restraint/Small Accumulation
111-101	14	(61)	Great Possessions
111-110	43	(62)	Decisive
011-111	44	(31)	Meeting/Subjugated
101-111	13	(47)	Companions

Hexagram	Text #	Binary #	Name
111-000	11	(56)	Peace/Flowing
011-100	32	(28)	Constancy
001-110	31	(14)	Mutual Influence
000-111	12	(7)	Standstill
100-011	42	(35)	Increase
110-001	41	(49)	Decrease

Hexagram	Text #	Binary #	Name
111-001	26	(57)	Big Restraint/Big Accumulation
111-100	34	(60)	Big Uses Force
011-110	28	(30)	Big in Excess
001-111	33	(15)	The Piglet
100-111	25	(39)	No Error (No Expectations)
110-011	61	(51)	Inmost Sincerity (Allegiance)

Hexagram	Text #	Binary #	Name
111-010	5	(58)	Getting Wet
011-101	50	(29)	The Ritual Caldron
101-110	49	(46)	Revolution
010-111	6	(23)	Grievance
101-011	37	(43)	The Family
110-101	38	(53)	Estrangement

Hexagram	Text #	Binary #	Name
111-011	9	(59)	Small Restraint/Small Accumulation
111-101	14	(61)	Great Possessions
111-110	43	(62)	Decisive
011-111	44	(31)	Meeting/Subjugated
101-111	13	(47)	Companions
110-111	10	(55)	Treading

Hexagram	Text #	Binary #	Name
111-100	34	(60)	Big Uses Force
011-110	28	(30)	Big in Excess
001-111	33	(15)	The Piglet
100-111	25	(39)	No Error (No Expectations)
110-011	61	(51)	Inmost Sincerity (Allegiance)
111-001	26	(57)	Big Restraint/Big Accumulation

Hexagram	Text #	Binary #	Name
111-101	14	(61)	Great Possessions
111-110	43	(62)	Decisive
011-111	44	(31)	Meeting/Subjugated
101-111	13	(47)	Companions
110-111	10	(55)	Treading
111-011	9	(59)	Small Restraint/Small Accumulation

Hexagram	Text #	Binary #	Name
111-110	43	(62)	Decisive
011-111	44	(31)	Meeting/Subjugated
101-111	13	(47)	Companions
110-111	10	(55)	Treading
111-011	9	(59)	Small Restraint/Small Accumulation
111-101	14	(61)	Great Possessions

Hexagram	Text #	Binary #	Name
111-111	1	(63)	Heaven

J

YARROW-STALK METHOD
PROBABILITIES

Table 1. Probability of Hexagrams 1–8 Moving to Hexagrams 1–32
Textual numbers of a hexagram cast by the yarrow-stalk method are shown along the
top line. Numbers in the left column represent the second hexagram formed by the
first hexagram's moving lines. (For Hexagrams 33–64, see Table 2.) Probability of
casting the first hexagram with moving lines forming the second hexagram is shown
in the table as a numerator over the denominator of 16,777,216 (16 to the sixth); only
the numerator is shown. The probability of casting Hexagram 4 with no moving lines
is 60,025/16,777,216.

	1	2	3	4	5	6	7	8
1	15625	1	25	25	625	625	5	5
2	729	117649	21609	21609	3969	3969	50421	50421
3	2025	2401	60025	441	11025	945	1029	12005
4	2025	2401	441	60025	945	11025	12005	1029
5	5625	49	1225	105	30625	225	245	245
6	5625	49	105	1225	225	30625	245	245
7	1215	16807	3087	36015	6615	6615	84035	7203
8	1215	16807	36015	3087	6615	6615	7203	84035
9	9375	7	175	175	4375	375	35	35
10	9375	7	175	175	375	4375	35	35
11	3375	343	735	735	18375	135	1715	147
12	3375	343	735	735	135	18375	147	1715
13	9375	7	175	15	375	375	3	35
14	9375	7	15	175	375	375	35	3
15	1215	16807	3087	3087	6615	567	7203	7203
16	1215	16807	3087	3087	567	6615	7203	7203
17	3375	343	8575	63	1575	1575	147	1715
18	3375	343	63	8575	1575	1575	1715	147
19	2025	2401	5145	5145	11025	945	12005	1029
20	2025	2401	5145	5145	945	11025	1029	12005
21	3375	343	735	735	135	1575	147	147
22	3375	343	735	735	1575	135	147	147
23	1215	16807	3087	36015	567	6615	7203	7203
24	1215	16807	36015	3087	6615	567	7203	7203
25	5625	49	1225	105	225	2625	21	245
26	5625	49	105	1225	2625	225	245	21
27	2025	2401	5145	5145	945	945	1029	1029
28	5625	49	105	105	2625	2625	245	245
29	2025	2401	5145	5145	11025	11025	12005	12005
30	5625	49	105	105	225	225	21	21
31	3375	343	735	63	1575	1575	147	1715
32	3375	343	63	735	1575	1575	1715	147

Table 1. Probability of Hexagrams 9–16 Moving to Hexagrams 1–32
Textual numbers of a hexagram cast by the yarrow-stalk method are shown along the top line. Numbers in the left column represent the second hexagram formed by the first hexagram's moving lines. (For Hexagrams 33–64, see Table 2.) Probability of casting the first hexagram with moving lines forming the second hexagram is shown in the table as a numerator over the denominator of 16,777,216 (16 to the sixth); only the numerator is shown.

	9	10	11	12	13	14	15	16
1	3125	3125	125	125	3125	3125	5	5
2	1701	1701	9261	9261	1701	1701	50421	50421
3	4725	4725	2205	2205	4725	405	1029	1029
4	4725	4725	2205	2205	405	4725	1029	1029
5	13125	1125	6125	45	1125	1125	245	21
6	1125	13125	45	6125	1125	1125	21	245
7	2835	2835	15435	1323	243	2835	7203	7203
8	2835	2835	1323	15435	2835	243	7203	7203
9	21875	1875	875	75	1875	1875	35	3
10	1875	21875	75	875	1875	1875	3	35
11	7875	675	42875	27	675	7875	1715	147
12	675	7875	27	42875	7875	675	147	1715
13	1875	1875	75	875	21875	1875	35	35
14	1875	1875	875	75	1875	21875	35	35
15	2835	243	15435	1323	2835	2835	84035	7203
16	243	2835	1323	15435	2835	2835	7203	84035
17	675	7875	315	3675	7875	675	147	1715
18	7875	675	3675	315	675	7875	1715	147
19	4725	4725	25725	189	405	4725	1029	1029
20	4725	4725	189	25725	4725	405	1029	1029
21	675	7875	315	3675	7875	7875	147	1715
22	7875	675	3675	315	7875	7875	1715	147
23	2835	2835	1323	15435	2835	2835	7203	7203
24	2835	2835	15435	1323	2835	2835	7203	7203
25	1125	13125	45	6125	13125	1125	21	245
26	13125	1125	6125	45	1125	13125	245	21
27	4725	4725	2205	2205	4725	4725	1029	1029
28	1125	1125	525	525	1125	1125	245	245
29	4725	4725	2205	2205	405	405	1029	1029
30	1125	1125	525	525	13125	13125	245	245
31	675	675	315	3675	7875	675	1715	1715
32	675	675	3675	315	675	7875	1715	1715

Table 1. Probability of Hexagrams 17–24 Moving to Hexagrams 1–32
Textual numbers of a hexagram cast by the yarrow-stalk method are shown along the top line. Numbers in the left column represent the second hexagram formed by the first hexagram's moving lines. (For Hexagrams 33–64, see Table 2.) Probability of casting the first hexagram with moving lines forming the second hexagram is shown in the table as a numerator over the denominator of 16,777,216 (16 to the sixth); only the numerator is shown.

	17	18	19	20	21	22	23	24
1	125	125	25	25	125	125	5	5
2	9261	9261	21609	21609	9261	9261	50421	50421
3	25725	189	5145	5145	2205	2205	1029	12005
4	189	25725	5145	5145	2205	2205	12005	1029
5	525	525	1225	105	45	525	21	245
6	525	525	105	1225	525	45	245	21
7	1323	15435	36015	3087	1323	1323	7203	7203
8	15435	1323	3087	36015	1323	1323	7203	7203
9	75	875	175	175	75	875	35	35
10	875	75	175	175	875	75	35	35
11	315	3675	8575	63	315	3675	147	1715
12	3675	315	63	8575	3675	315	1715	147
13	875	75	15	175	875	875	35	35
14	75	875	175	15	875	875	35	35
15	1323	15435	3087	3087	1323	15435	7203	7203
16	15435	1323	3087	3087	15435	1323	7203	7203
17	42875	27	735	735	3675	315	147	1715
18	27	42875	735	735	315	3675	1715	147
19	2205	2205	60025	441	2205	2205	1029	12005
20	2205	2205	441	60025	2205	2205	12005	1029
21	3675	315	735	735	42875	3675	1715	1715
22	315	3675	735	735	3675	42875	1715	1715
23	1323	15435	3087	36015	15435	15435	84035	7203
24	15435	1323	36015	3087	15435	15435	7203	84035
25	6125	45	105	1225	6125	525	245	245
26	45	6125	1225	105	525	6125	245	245
27	2205	2205	5145	5145	25725	25725	12005	12005
28	525	525	105	105	45	45	21	21
29	2205	2205	5145	5145	189	189	1029	1029
30	525	525	105	105	6125	6125	245	245
31	3675	315	63	735	315	315	147	147
32	315	3675	735	63	315	315	147	147

Table 1. Probability of Hexagrams 25–32 Moving to Hexagrams 1–32

Textual numbers of a hexagram cast by the yarrow-stalk method are shown along the top line. Numbers in the left column represent the second hexagram formed by the first hexagram's moving lines. (For Hexagrams 33–64, see Table 2.) Probability of casting the first hexagram with moving lines forming the second hexagram is shown in the table as a numerator over the denominator of 16,777,216 (16 to the sixth); only the numerator is shown.

	25	26	27	28	29	30	31	32
1	625	625	25	625	25	625	125	125
2	3969	3969	21609	3969	21609	3969	9261	9261
3	11025	945	5145	945	5145	945	2205	189
4	945	11025	5145	945	5145	945	189	2205
5	225	2625	105	2625	1225	225	525	525
6	2625	225	105	2625	1225	225	525	525
7	567	6615	3087	6615	36015	567	1323	15435
8	6615	567	3087	6615	36015	567	15435	1323
9	375	4375	175	375	175	375	75	75
10	4375	375	175	375	175	375	75	75
11	135	18375	735	1575	735	1575	315	3675
12	18375	135	735	1575	735	1575	3675	315
13	4375	375	175	375	15	4375	875	75
14	375	4375	175	375	15	4375	75	875
15	567	6615	3087	6615	3087	6615	15435	15435
16	6615	567	3087	6615	3087	6615	15435	15435
17	18375	135	735	1575	735	1575	3675	315
18	135	18375	735	1575	735	1575	315	3675
19	945	11025	5145	945	5145	945	189	2205
20	11025	945	5145	945	5145	945	2205	189
21	18375	1575	8575	135	63	18375	315	315
22	1575	18375	8575	135	63	18375	315	315
23	6615	6615	36015	567	3087	6615	1323	1323
24	6615	6615	36015	567	3087	6615	1323	1323
25	30625	225	1225	225	105	2625	525	45
26	225	30625	1225	225	105	2625	45	525
27	11025	11025	60025	81	441	11025	189	189
28	225	225	9	30625	1225	225	6125	6125
29	945	945	441	11025	60025	81	2205	2205
30	2625	2625	1225	225	9	30625	525	525
31	1575	135	63	18375	735	1575	42875	3675
32	135	1575	63	18375	735	1575	3675	42875

Table 1. Probability of Hexagrams 33–40 Moving to Hexagrams 1–32

Textual numbers of a hexagram cast by the yarrow-stalk method are shown along the top line. Numbers in the left column represent the second hexagram formed by the first hexagram's moving lines. (For Hexagrams 33–64, see Table 2.) Probability of casting the first hexagram with moving lines forming the second hexagram is shown in the table as a numerator over the denominator of 16,777,216 (16 to the sixth); only the numerator is shown.

	33	34	35	36	37	38	39	40
1	625	625	25	25	625	625	25	25
2	3969	3969	21609	21609	3969	3969	21609	21609
3	945	945	441	5145	11025	945	5145	441
4	945	945	5145	441	945	11025	441	5145
5	225	2625	9	1225	2625	225	1225	105
6	2625	225	1225	9	225	2625	105	1225
7	567	6615	3087	3087	567	6615	3087	36015
8	6615	567	3087	3087	6615	567	36015	3087
9	375	375	15	175	4375	375	175	15
10	375	375	175	15	375	4375	15	175
11	135	18375	63	8575	1575	1575	735	735
12	18375	135	8575	63	1575	1575	735	735
13	4375	375	175	175	4375	375	175	15
14	375	4375	175	175	375	4375	15	175
15	6615	6615	3087	36015	6615	567	36015	3087
16	6615	6615	36015	3087	567	6615	3087	36015
17	1575	1575	735	735	1575	1575	735	735
18	1575	1575	735	735	1575	1575	735	735
19	81	11025	441	5145	945	11025	441	5145
20	11025	81	5145	441	11025	945	5145	441
21	1575	1575	8575	735	1575	18375	63	735
22	1575	1575	735	8575	18375	1575	735	63
23	6615	567	36015	3087	6615	6615	3087	3087
24	567	6615	3087	36015	6615	6615	3087	3087
25	2625	225	1225	105	2625	2625	105	105
26	225	2625	105	1225	2625	2625	105	105
27	945	945	5145	5145	11025	11025	441	441
28	2625	2625	105	105	225	225	1225	1225
29	945	945	441	441	945	945	5145	5145
30	2625	2625	1225	1225	2625	2625	105	105
31	18375	1575	735	735	1575	135	8575	735
32	1575	18375	735	735	135	1575	735	8575

Table 1. Probability of Hexagrams 41–48 Moving to Hexagrams 1–32
Textual numbers of a hexagram cast by the yarrow-stalk method are shown along the top line. Numbers in the left column represent the second hexagram formed by the first hexagram's moving lines. (For Hexagrams 33–64, see Table 2.) Probability of casting the first hexagram with moving lines forming the second hexagram is shown in the table as a numerator over the denominator of 16,777,216 (16 to the sixth); only the numerator is shown.

	41	42	43	44	45	46	47	48
1	125	125	3125	3125	25	25	125	125
2	9261	9261	1701	1701	21609	21609	9261	9261
3	2205	25725	4725	405	5145	441	2205	2205
4	25725	2205	405	4725	441	5145	2205	2205
5	525	525	13125	1125	105	1225	525	6125
6	525	525	1125	13125	1225	105	6125	525
7	15435	1323	2835	2835	3087	36015	15435	15435
8	1323	15435	2835	2835	36015	3087	15435	15435
9	875	875	1875	1875	15	175	75	875
10	875	875	1875	1875	175	15	875	75
11	3675	315	7875	675	63	8575	315	3675
12	315	3675	675	7875	8575	63	3675	315
13	75	875	1875	1875	175	15	75	75
14	875	75	1875	1875	15	175	75	75
15	1323	1323	2835	2835	3087	36015	1323	15435
16	1323	1323	2835	2835	36015	3087	15435	1323
17	315	3675	7875	675	8575	63	3675	315
18	3675	315	675	7875	63	8575	315	3675
19	25725	2205	4725	405	441	5145	2205	2205
20	2205	25725	405	4725	5145	441	2205	2205
21	3675	3675	675	675	735	63	315	27
22	3675	3675	675	675	63	735	27	315
23	15435	15435	243	2835	3087	3087	1323	1323
24	15435	15435	2835	243	3087	3087	1323	1323
25	525	6125	1125	1125	1225	9	525	45
26	6125	525	1125	1125	9	1225	45	525
27	25725	25725	405	405	441	441	189	189
28	45	45	13125	13125	1225	1225	6125	6125
29	2205	2205	4725	4725	5145	5145	25725	25725
30	525	525	1125	1125	105	105	45	45
31	27	315	7875	7875	8575	735	3675	3675
32	315	27	7875	7875	735	8575	3675	3675

Table 1. Probability of Hexagrams 49–56 Moving to Hexagrams 1–32

Textual numbers of a hexagram cast by the yarrow-stalk method are shown along the top line. Numbers in the left column represent the second hexagram formed by the first hexagram's moving lines. (For Hexagrams 33–64, see Table 2.) Probability of casting the first hexagram with moving lines forming the second hexagram is shown in the table as a numerator over the denominator of 16,777,216 (16 to the sixth); only the numerator is shown.

	49	50	51	52	53	54	55	56
1	625	625	25	25	125	125	125	125
2	3969	3969	21609	21609	9261	9261	9261	9261
3	11025	81	5145	441	2205	2205	2205	189
4	81	11025	441	5145	2205	2205	189	2205
5	2625	225	105	105	525	525	525	45
6	225	2625	105	105	525	525	45	525
7	567	6615	3087	3087	1323	15435	1323	1323
8	6615	567	3087	3087	15435	1323	1323	1323
9	375	375	15	175	875	75	75	75
10	375	375	175	15	75	875	75	75
11	1575	1575	735	735	315	3675	3675	315
12	1575	1575	735	735	3675	315	315	3675
13	4375	375	175	175	875	75	875	875
14	375	4375	175	175	75	875	875	875
15	6615	6615	3087	36015	15435	1323	15435	15435
16	6615	6615	36015	3087	1323	15435	15435	15435
17	18375	135	8575	63	315	3675	3675	315
18	135	18375	63	8575	3675	315	315	3675
19	945	945	5145	441	189	25725	2205	189
20	945	945	441	5145	25725	189	189	2205
21	1575	1575	8575	735	315	3675	3675	3675
22	1575	1575	735	8575	3675	315	3675	3675
23	567	6615	3087	36015	15435	1323	1323	15435
24	6615	567	36015	3087	1323	15435	15435	1323
25	2625	225	1225	105	525	525	525	525
26	225	2625	105	1225	525	525	525	525
27	945	945	5145	5145	2205	2205	2205	2205
28	2625	2625	105	105	525	525	525	525
29	945	945	441	441	2205	2205	189	189
30	2625	2625	1225	1225	525	525	6125	6125
31	18375	1575	735	735	3675	315	3675	3675
32	1575	18375	735	735	315	3675	3675	3675

Table 1. Probability of Hexagrams 57–64 Moving to Hexagrams 1–32
Textual numbers of a hexagram cast by the yarrow-stalk method are shown along the
top line. Numbers in the left column represent the second hexagram formed by the
first hexagram's moving lines. (For Hexagrams 33–64, see Table 2.) Probability of
casting the first hexagram with moving lines forming the second hexagram is shown in
the table as a numerator over the denominator of 16,777,216 (16 to the sixth); only the
numerator is shown.

	57	58	59	60	61	62	63	64
1	625	625	125	125	625	25	125	125
2	3969	3969	9261	9261	3969	21609	9261	9261
3	945	11025	2205	25725	11025	441	25725	189
4	11025	945	25725	2205	11025	441	189	25725
5	2625	2625	525	6125	2625	105	6125	45
6	2625	2625	6125	525	2625	105	45	6125
7	6615	6615	15435	15435	6615	3087	1323	15435
8	6615	6615	15435	15435	6615	3087	15435	1323
9	4375	375	875	875	4375	15	875	75
10	375	4375	875	875	4375	15	75	875
11	1575	1575	315	3675	1575	735	3675	315
12	1575	1575	3675	315	1575	735	315	3675
13	375	375	75	75	375	175	875	75
14	375	375	75	75	375	175	75	875
15	6615	567	1323	1323	567	36015	15435	1323
16	567	6615	1323	1323	567	36015	1323	15435
17	135	18375	315	3675	1575	735	3675	315
18	18375	135	3675	315	1575	735	315	3675
19	945	11025	2205	25725	11025	441	2205	2205
20	11025	945	25725	2205	11025	441	2205	2205
21	135	1575	315	315	1575	735	315	3675
22	1575	135	315	315	1575	735	3675	315
23	6615	567	15435	1323	6615	3087	1323	15435
24	567	6615	1323	15435	6615	3087	15435	1323
25	225	2625	525	525	2625	105	525	525
26	2625	225	525	525	2625	105	525	525
27	945	945	2205	2205	11025	441	2205	2205
28	2625	2625	525	525	225	1225	525	525
29	11025	11025	25725	25725	11025	441	2205	2205
30	225	225	45	45	225	1225	525	525
31	1575	1575	315	315	135	8575	3675	315
32	1575	1575	315	315	135	8575	315	3675

Table 2. Probability of Hexagrams 1–8 Moving to Hexagrams 33–64

Textual numbers of a hexagram cast by the yarrow-stalk method are shown along the top line. Numbers in the left column represent the second hexagram formed by the first hexagram's moving lines. (For Hexagrams 1–32, see Table 1.) Probability of casting the first hexagram with moving lines forming the second hexagram is shown in the table as a numerator over the denominator of 16,777,216 (16 to the sixth); only the numerator is shown.

	1	2	3	4	5	6	7	8
33	5625	49	105	105	225	2625	21	245
34	5625	49	105	105	2625	225	245	21
35	2025	2401	441	5145	81	11025	1029	1029
36	2025	2401	5145	441	11025	81	1029	1029
37	5625	49	1225	105	2625	225	21	245
38	5625	49	105	1225	225	2625	245	21
39	2025	2401	5145	441	11025	945	1029	12005
40	2025	2401	441	5145	945	11025	12005	1029
41	3375	343	735	8575	1575	1575	1715	147
42	3375	343	8575	735	1575	1575	147	1715
43	9375	7	175	15	4375	375	35	35
44	9375	7	15	175	375	4375	35	35
45	2025	2401	5145	441	945	11025	1029	12005
46	2025	2401	441	5145	11025	945	12005	1029
47	3375	343	735	735	1575	18375	1715	1715
48	3375	343	735	735	18375	1575	1715	1715
49	5625	49	1225	9	2625	225	21	245
50	5625	49	9	1225	225	2625	245	21
51	2025	2401	5145	441	945	945	1029	1029
52	2025	2401	441	5145	945	945	1029	1029
53	3375	343	735	735	1575	1575	147	1715
54	3375	343	735	735	1575	1575	1715	147
55	3375	343	735	63	1575	135	147	147
56	3375	343	63	735	135	1575	147	147
57	5625	49	105	1225	2625	2625	245	245
58	5625	49	1225	105	2625	2625	245	245
59	3375	343	735	8575	1575	18375	1715	1715
60	3375	343	8575	735	18375	1575	1715	1715
61	5625	49	1225	1225	2625	2625	245	245
62	2025	2401	441	441	945	945	1029	1029
63	3375	343	8575	63	18375	135	147	1715
64	3375	343	63	8575	135	18375	1715	147

Table 2. Probability of Hexagrams 9–16 Moving to Hexagrams 33–64
Textual numbers of a hexagram cast by the yarrow-stalk method are shown along the top line. Numbers in the left column represent the second hexagram formed by the first hexagram's moving lines. (For Hexagrams 1–32, see Table 1.) Probability of casting the first hexagram with moving lines forming the second hexagram is shown in the table as a numerator over the denominator of 16,777,216 (16 to the sixth); only the numerator is shown.

	9	10	11	12	13	14	15	16
33	1125	1125	45	6125	13125	1125	245	245
34	1125	1125	6125	45	1125	13125	245	245
35	405	4725	189	25725	4725	4725	1029	12005
36	4725	405	25725	189	4725	4725	12005	1029
37	13125	1125	525	525	13125	1125	245	21
38	1125	13125	525	525	1125	13125	21	245
39	4725	405	2205	2205	4725	405	12005	1029
40	405	4725	2205	2205	405	4725	1029	12005
41	7875	7875	3675	315	675	7875	147	147
42	7875	7875	315	3675	7875	675	147	147
43	1875	1875	875	75	1875	1875	35	35
44	1875	1875	75	875	1875	1875	35	35
45	405	4725	189	25725	4725	405	1029	12005
46	4725	405	25725	189	405	4725	12005	1029
47	675	7875	315	3675	675	675	147	1715
48	7875	675	3675	315	675	675	1715	147
49	1125	1125	525	525	13125	1125	245	245
50	1125	1125	525	525	1125	13125	245	245
51	405	4725	2205	2205	4725	4725	1029	12005
52	4725	405	2205	2205	4725	4725	12005	1029
53	7875	675	315	3675	7875	675	1715	147
54	675	7875	3675	315	675	7875	147	1715
55	675	675	3675	315	7875	7875	1715	1715
56	675	675	315	3675	7875	7875	1715	1715
57	13125	1125	525	525	1125	1125	245	21
58	1125	13125	525	525	1125	1125	21	245
59	7875	7875	315	3675	675	675	147	147
60	7875	7875	3675	315	675	675	147	147
61	13125	13125	525	525	1125	1125	21	21
62	405	405	2205	2205	4725	4725	12005	12005
63	7875	675	3675	315	7875	675	1715	147
64	675	7875	315	3675	675	7875	147	1715

Table 2. Probability of Hexagrams 17–24 Moving to Hexagrams 33–64

Textual numbers of a hexagram cast by the yarrow-stalk method are shown along the top line. Numbers in the left column represent the second hexagram formed by the first hexagram's moving lines. (For Hexagrams 1–32, see Table 1.) Probability of casting the first hexagram with moving lines forming the second hexagram is shown in the table as a numerator over the denominator of 16,777,216 (16 to the sixth); only the numerator is shown.

	17	18	19	20	21	22	23	24
33	525	525	9	1225	525	525	245	21
34	525	525	1225	9	525	525	21	245
35	2205	2205	441	5145	25725	2205	12005	1029
36	2205	2205	5145	441	2205	25725	1029	12005
37	525	525	105	1225	525	6125	245	245
38	525	525	1225	105	6125	525	245	245
39	2205	2205	441	5145	189	2205	1029	1029
40	2205	2205	5145	441	2205	189	1029	1029
41	315	3675	8575	735	3675	3675	1715	1715
42	3675	315	735	8575	3675	3675	1715	1715
43	875	75	175	15	75	75	3	35
44	75	875	15	175	75	75	35	3
45	25725	189	441	5145	2205	189	1029	1029
46	189	25725	5145	441	189	2205	1029	1029
47	3675	315	735	735	315	27	147	147
48	315	3675	735	735	27	315	147	147
49	6125	45	105	105	525	525	21	245
50	45	6125	105	105	525	525	245	21
51	25725	189	5145	441	25725	2205	1029	12005
52	189	25725	441	5145	2205	25725	12005	1029
53	315	3675	63	8575	315	3675	1715	147
54	3675	315	8575	63	3675	315	147	1715
55	3675	315	735	63	3675	3675	147	1715
56	315	3675	63	735	3675	3675	1715	147
57	45	6125	105	1225	45	525	245	21
58	6125	45	1225	105	525	45	21	245
59	315	3675	735	8575	315	315	1715	147
60	3675	315	8575	735	315	315	147	1715
61	525	525	1225	1225	525	525	245	245
62	2205	2205	441	441	2205	2205	1029	1029
63	3675	315	735	735	315	3675	147	1715
64	315	3675	735	735	3675	315	1715	147

Table 2. Probability of Hexagrams 25–32 Moving to Hexagrams 33–64

Textual numbers of a hexagram cast by the yarrow-stalk method are shown along the top line. Numbers in the left column represent the second hexagram formed by the first hexagram's moving lines. (For Hexagrams 1–32, see Table 1.) Probability of casting the first hexagram with moving lines forming the second hexagram is shown in the table as a numerator over the denominator of 16,777,216 (16 to the sixth); only the numerator is shown.

	25	26	27	28	29	30	31	32
33	2625	225	105	2625	105	2625	6125	525
34	225	2625	105	2625	105	2625	525	6125
35	11025	945	5145	945	441	11025	2205	2205
36	945	11025	5145	945	441	11025	2205	2205
37	2625	2625	1225	225	105	2625	525	45
38	2625	2625	1225	225	105	2625	45	525
39	945	945	441	11025	5145	945	25725	2205
40	945	945	441	11025	5145	945	2205	25725
41	1575	18375	8575	135	735	1575	27	315
42	18375	1575	8575	135	735	1575	315	27
43	375	375	15	4375	175	375	875	875
44	375	375	15	4375	175	375	875	875
45	11025	81	441	11025	5145	945	25725	2205
46	81	11025	441	11025	5145	945	2205	25725
47	1575	135	63	18375	8575	135	3675	3675
48	135	1575	63	18375	8575	135	3675	3675
49	2625	225	105	2625	105	2625	6125	525
50	225	2625	105	2625	105	2625	525	6125
51	11025	945	5145	945	441	11025	2205	2205
52	945	11025	5145	945	441	11025	2205	2205
53	1575	1575	735	1575	735	1575	3675	315
54	1575	1575	735	1575	735	1575	315	3675
55	1575	1575	735	1575	63	18375	3675	3675
56	1575	1575	735	1575	63	18375	3675	3675
57	225	2625	105	2625	1225	225	525	525
58	2625	225	105	2625	1225	225	525	525
59	1575	1575	735	1575	8575	135	315	315
60	1575	1575	735	1575	8575	135	315	315
61	2625	2625	1225	225	1225	225	45	45
62	945	945	441	11025	441	11025	25725	25725
63	1575	1575	735	1575	735	1575	3675	315
64	1575	1575	735	1575	735	1575	315	3675

Table 2. Probability of Hexagrams 33–40 Moving to Hexagrams 33–64
Textual numbers of a hexagram cast by the yarrow-stalk method are shown along the top line. Numbers in the left column represent the second hexagram formed by the first hexagram's moving lines. (For Hexagrams 1–32, see Table 1.) Probability of casting the first hexagram with moving lines forming the second hexagram is shown in the table as a numerator over the denominator of 16,777,216 (16 to the sixth); only the numerator is shown.

	33	34	35	36	37	38	39	40
33	30625	225	1225	105	2625	225	1225	105
34	225	30625	105	1225	225	2625	105	1225
35	11025	945	60025	441	945	11025	441	5145
36	945	11025	441	60025	11025	945	5145	441
37	2625	225	105	1225	30625	225	1225	9
38	225	2625	1225	105	225	30625	9	1225
39	11025	945	441	5145	11025	81	60025	441
40	945	11025	5145	441	81	11025	441	60025
41	135	1575	735	735	1575	18375	63	735
42	1575	135	735	735	18375	1575	735	63
43	375	4375	15	175	375	375	175	175
44	4375	375	175	15	375	375	175	175
45	11025	945	5145	441	945	945	5145	5145
46	945	11025	441	5145	945	945	5145	5145
47	1575	1575	735	63	135	1575	735	8575
48	1575	1575	63	735	1575	135	8575	735
49	2625	2625	105	1225	2625	225	1225	105
50	2625	2625	1225	105	225	2625	105	1225
51	945	11025	5145	5145	945	11025	441	5145
52	11025	945	5145	5145	11025	945	5145	441
53	18375	135	735	735	18375	135	8575	63
54	135	18375	735	735	135	18375	63	8575
55	1575	18375	735	8575	1575	1575	735	735
56	18375	1575	8575	735	1575	1575	735	735
57	2625	225	105	105	2625	225	1225	105
58	225	2625	105	105	225	2625	105	1225
59	1575	135	735	63	1575	1575	735	735
60	135	1575	63	735	1575	1575	735	735
61	225	225	105	105	2625	2625	105	105
62	11025	11025	5145	5145	945	945	5145	5145
63	1575	1575	63	8575	18375	135	8575	63
64	1575	1575	8575	63	135	18375	63	8575

Table 2. Probability of Hexagrams 41–48 Moving to Hexagrams 33–64
Textual numbers of a hexagram cast by the yarrow-stalk method are shown along the top line. Numbers in the left column represent the second hexagram formed by the first hexagram's moving lines. (For Hexagrams 1–32, see Table 1.) Probability of casting the first hexagram with moving lines forming the second hexagram is shown in the table as a numerator over the denominator of 16,777,216 (16 to the sixth); only the numerator is shown.

	41	42	43	44	45	46	47	48
33	45	525	1125	13125	1225	105	525	525
34	525	45	13125	1125	105	1225	525	525
35	2205	2205	405	4725	5145	441	2205	189
36	2205	2205	4725	405	441	5145	189	2205
37	525	6125	1125	1125	105	105	45	525
38	6125	525	1125	1125	105	105	525	45
39	189	2205	4725	4725	5145	5145	2205	25725
40	2205	189	4725	4725	5145	5145	25725	2205
41	42875	3675	675	675	63	735	315	315
42	3675	42875	675	675	735	63	315	315
43	75	75	21875	1875	175	175	875	875
44	75	75	1875	21875	175	175	875	875
45	189	2205	4725	4725	60025	441	25725	2205
46	2205	189	4725	4725	441	60025	2205	25725
47	315	315	7875	7875	8575	735	42875	3675
48	315	315	7875	7875	735	8575	3675	42875
49	45	525	13125	1125	1225	105	525	525
50	525	45	1125	13125	105	1225	525	525
51	2205	2205	4725	405	5145	441	2205	189
52	2205	2205	405	4725	441	5145	189	2205
53	315	3675	675	7875	735	735	315	3675
54	3675	315	7875	675	735	735	3675	315
55	315	315	7875	675	735	735	315	315
56	315	315	675	7875	735	735	315	315
57	525	525	1125	13125	105	1225	525	6125
58	525	525	13125	1125	1225	105	6125	525
59	3675	3675	675	7875	735	735	3675	3675
60	3675	3675	7875	675	735	735	3675	3675
61	6125	6125	1125	1125	105	105	525	525
62	189	189	4725	4725	5145	5145	2205	2205
63	315	3675	7875	675	735	735	315	3675
64	3675	315	675	7875	735	735	3675	315

Table 2. Probability of Hexagrams 49–56 Moving to Hexagrams 33–64
Textual numbers of a hexagram cast by the yarrow-stalk method are shown along the
top line. Numbers in the left column represent the second hexagram formed by the first
hexagram's moving lines. (For Hexagrams 1–32, see Table 1.) Probability of casting
the first hexagram with moving lines forming the second hexagram is shown in the
table as a numerator over the denominator of 16,777,216 (16 to the sixth); only the
numerator is shown.

	49	50	51	52	53	54	55	56
33	2625	2625	105	1225	6125	45	525	6125
34	2625	2625	1225	105	45	6125	6125	525
35	945	11025	5145	5145	2205	2205	2205	25725
36	11025	945	5145	5145	2205	2205	25725	2205
37	2625	225	105	1225	6125	45	525	525
38	225	2625	1225	105	45	6125	525	525
39	11025	945	441	5145	25725	189	2205	2205
40	945	11025	5145	441	189	25725	2205	2205
41	135	1575	735	735	315	3675	315	315
42	1575	135	735	735	3675	315	315	315
43	4375	375	175	15	75	875	875	75
44	375	4375	15	175	875	75	75	875
45	11025	945	5145	441	2205	2205	2205	2205
46	945	11025	441	5145	2205	2205	2205	2205
47	1575	1575	735	63	315	3675	315	315
48	1575	1575	63	735	3675	315	315	315
49	30625	225	1225	105	525	525	6125	525
50	225	30625	105	1225	525	525	525	6125
51	11025	945	60025	441	189	25725	25725	2205
52	945	11025	441	60025	25725	189	2205	25725
53	1575	1575	63	8575	42875	27	315	3675
54	1575	1575	8575	63	27	42875	3675	315
55	18375	1575	8575	735	315	3675	42875	3675
56	1575	18375	735	8575	3675	315	3675	42875
57	225	2625	9	1225	6125	45	45	525
58	2625	225	1225	9	45	6125	525	45
59	135	1575	63	735	3675	315	27	315
60	1575	135	735	63	315	3675	315	27
61	225	225	105	105	525	525	45	45
62	11025	11025	5145	5145	2205	2205	25725	25725
63	18375	135	735	735	3675	315	3675	315
64	135	18375	735	735	315	3675	315	3675

Table 2. Probability of Hexagrams 57–64 Moving to Hexagrams 33–64

Textual numbers of a hexagram cast by the yarrow-stalk method are shown along the top line. Numbers in the left column represent the second hexagram formed by the first hexagram's moving lines. (For Hexagrams 1–32, see Table 1.) Probability of casting the first hexagram with moving lines forming the second hexagram is shown in the table as a numerator over the denominator of 16,777,216 (16 to the sixth); only the numerator is shown.

	57	58	59	60	61	62	63	64
33	2625	225	525	45	225	1225	525	525
34	225	2625	45	525	225	1225	525	525
35	945	945	2205	189	945	5145	189	25725
36	945	945	189	2205	945	5145	25725	189
37	2625	225	525	525	2625	105	6125	45
38	225	2625	525	525	2625	105	45	6125
39	11025	945	2205	2205	945	5145	25725	189
40	945	11025	2205	2205	945	5145	189	25725
41	1575	1575	3675	3675	18375	63	315	3675
42	1575	1575	3675	3675	18375	63	3675	315
43	375	4375	75	875	375	175	875	75
44	4375	375	875	75	375	175	75	875
45	945	11025	2205	2205	945	5145	2205	2205
46	11025	945	2205	2205	945	5145	2205	2205
47	1575	18375	3675	3675	1575	735	315	3675
48	18375	1575	3675	3675	1575	735	3675	315
49	225	2625	45	525	225	1225	6125	45
50	2625	225	525	45	225	1225	45	6125
51	81	11025	189	2205	945	5145	2205	2205
52	11025	81	2205	189	945	5145	2205	2205
53	18375	135	3675	315	1575	735	3675	315
54	135	18375	315	3675	1575	735	315	3675
55	135	1575	27	315	135	8575	3675	315
56	1575	135	315	27	135	8575	315	3675
57	30625	225	6125	525	2625	105	525	525
58	225	30625	525	6125	2625	105	525	525
59	18375	1575	42875	3675	18375	63	315	3675
60	1575	18375	3675	42875	18375	63	3675	315
61	2625	2625	6125	6125	30625	9	525	525
62	945	945	189	189	81	60025	2205	2205
63	1575	1575	315	3675	1575	735	42875	27
64	1575	1575	3675	315	1575	735	27	42875

K

A HEXAGRAM LINE
ANALYZER

The following program LINES.HEX, will list all the hexagrams that have a certain combination of yang or yin lines in certain line positions. For example, it will list all hexagrams that have a yang line in line position 1 and a yin line in position 4 or all the hexagrams that have a yang line in line positions 1, 3, and 5, or all the hexagrams that have a yang line in positions 1 and 2 and a yin line in position 6, and so forth.

The program is written in True BASIC ^{TM}, but may easily be rewritten in other forms of BASIC. The lines preceded by an "!" are remarks explaining the program and are not part of the program.

```
!  Name of Program:  LINES.HEX
!  First we clear the screen.
CLEAR
!  These window settings make it easy to use the BOX LINES later
!  in the program.
SET window -10,10,-10,10
!  In Hex_A the hexagrams are stored in textual order.
!  There is no known algorithm for generating the textual
!  sequence of the hexagrams.  Therefore, the textual sequence
!  is read into the array.
DIM Hex_A$(64)
MAT READ Hex_A$
DATA 111111,000000,100010,010001,111010,010111,010000,000010
DATA 111011,110111,111000,000111,101111,111101,001000,000100
DATA 100110,011001,110000,000011,100101,101001,000001,100000
DATA 100111,111001,100001,011110,010010,101101,001110,011100
DATA 001111,111100,000101,101000,101011,110101,001010,010100
DATA 110001,100011,111110,011111,000110,011000,010110,011010
DATA 101110,011101,100100,001001,001011,110100,101100,001101
DATA 011011,110110,010011,110010,110011,001100,101010,010101
!  In Hex_B$ the hexagrams are stored in binary order.
DIM Hex_B$(64)
!  This block generates the hexagrams in binary order (from "000000"
!  to "111111") and stores the binary numbers in array Hex_B$.
Let hex_0$ = "000000"
LET c = 1
LET Hex_B$(c) = hex_0$
DO
For x = 6 to 1 Step -1
    If hex_0$[x:x] = "0" then
      LET hex_0$[x:x] = "1"
LET c = c + 1
LET Hex_B$(c) = hex_0
```

```
        EXIT FOR
    ELSE
        LET hex_0$[x:x] = "0"
    END IF
NEXT x
LOOP until hex_0$ = "111111"
!
DO
Clear
!  These BOX LINES commands draw a double bordered box around the menu.
BOX LINES -7,7,0,9
BOX LINES -6.5,6.5,.5,8.5
Set cursor 4,1
!  This is the menu.
Print TAB(4,33); "Yang line = 1"
Print TAB(5,33); "Yin line = 0"
Print TAB(6,33); "Yang or Yin = ?"
Print TAB(8,22); "Below each line number enter 1, 0, or ?"
Print TAB(10,33); "Lines:  123-456"
Set cursor 11,38
!  An example of an input is:  "11?-0??."
Input string$
!  The input string has 7 places.  The 4th place (the hyphen) is not
!  used.
!
Let a$ = string$[1:1]
Let b$ = string$[2:2]
Let c$ = string$[3:3]
Let d$ = string$[5:5]
Let e$ = string$[6:6]
Let f$ = string$[7:7]
!  One has here the option of printing out the hexagrams in binary
!  or textual order.
PRINT TAB(15,28); "Press B for Binary Order."
PRINT TAB(16,28); "Press T for Textual Order."
!  When the "B" key or "T" key is pressed the program continues.
Get Key bt
!  A key is selected and the screen clears.
CLEAR
SET CURSOR 4,30
!  The original input is printed out on top of screen.
PRINT "INPUT WAS:"; " "; a$ & b$ & c$; "-"; d$ & e$ & f$
PRINT
SET CURSOR 6,1
```

```
!  The heading is printed.
PRINT "Hexagram Text # Binary # Name"
!  If either upper case "B" (ASCII 66) or lower case "b" (ASCII
!  98) is pressed, then and only then does this part of the
!  program run.  The appropriate hexagrams are printed out in
!  binary order.
IF bt = 66 or bt = 98 then
!  Binary Order
!  For each line position of the input, this program selects a hexagram
!  that has the same line in that position and any line in positions
!  marked with an "?."
For g = 1 to 64
     IF Hex_B$(g)[1:1] = a$ or a$ = "?" then
       IF Hex_B$(g)[2:2] = b$ or b$ = "?" then
         IF Hex_B$(g)[3:3] = c$ or c$ = "?" then
           IF Hex_B$(g)[4:4] = d$ or d$ = "?" then
             IF Hex_B$(g)[5:5] = e$ or e$ = "?" then
               IF Hex_B$(g)[6:6] = f$ or f$ = "?" then
!  IF this section of the program runs, then FLAG is set equal to 1.
!  If an input other then "1", "0", and "?" are used under the line
!  positions, then this section of the program will not run and Flag_B
!  will be equal to 0.  Hence, if binary order is selected and it does
!  not run, then an illegal symbol was entered.  The command
!  "IF Flag_B = 0" then" given below operates when an illegal symbol
!  prevents this part of the program from running.
                    Let Flag_B = 1
!  The command below is a counter.  Each time a line is printed by

!  the sub routine named,
!  Identify, d increases by 1.
                    Let d = d + 1
!  Sub routine, Identify, prints out the hexagram, its textual and binary
!  number, and its name.
                 CALL Identify(Hex_0$)
!  Here the counter is made use of to prevent information on the screen
!  from scrolling up out of sight.  When d = 17, 34, or 51 then the
!  Get Key command becomes operative and stops the program until
!  a key is pressed.
                 If d = 17 or d = 34 or d = 51 then
                    PRINT
                    PRINT "    (Press any key to continue)"
                    Get Key x
                    CLEAR
                    SET CURSOR 4,30
```

```
                              PRINT "INPUT WAS:"; " "; STRING$
                              PRINT
                             PRINT "Hexagram Text # Binary # Name"
                        END IF
                        END IF
                  END IF
               END IF
            END IF
         END IF
      END IF
NEXT g
PRINT
!  The counter d is also used in the print command below to give
!  the number of hexagrams printed.
PRINT "Number of hexagrams is:"; d
!  If binary order was selected, but that portion of the program did not
!  run, then Flag_B will equal 0, indicating that an illegal symbol was
!  used.
IF Flag_B = 0 then
   PRINT
   Set Cursor 13,1
   PRINT "                                      "
   PRINT "          Please try again.  You entered incorrect symbols."
   PRINT "                                      "
END IF
!
!  Textual Order
!  If upper case "T" (ASCII 84) or lower case "t" (ASCII 116) is selected
!  then and only then does this part of the program run, which prints out
!  the appropriate hexagrams in textual order.
ELSE IF bt = 84 or bt = 116 then
For g = 1 to 64
    IF Hex_A$(g)[1:1] = a$ or a$ = "?" then
       IF Hex_A$(g)[2:2] = b$ or b$ = "?" then
          IF Hex_A$(g)[3:3] = c$ or c$ = "?" then
             IF Hex_A$(g)[4:4] = d$ or d$ = "?" then
                IF Hex_A$(g)[5:5] = e$ or e$ = "?" then
                   LET HEX_0$ = Hex_A$(g)
!  IF Flag_T equals 1, then this part of the program ran.
                   Let Flag_T = 1
!  This counter increases by one each time a hexagram is printed.
                   Let e = e + 1
!  This sub routine prints out the hexagram, its textual and binary
!  number, and its name.
```

```
                    CALL Identify(Hex_0$)
! Here the counter is used to keep information from scrolling up out of
! sight on the screen.
                    If e = 17 or e = 34 or e = 51 then
                      PRINT
                      PRINT " (Press any key to continue)
                      Get Key x
                      CLEAR
                      SET CURSOR 4,30
                      PRINT "INPUT WAS:"; " "; STRING$
                      PRINT
                      PRINT "Hexagram Text # Binary # Name"
                    END IF
                    END IF
                END IF
              END IF
            END IF
          END IF
        END IF
NEXT g
PRINT
PRINT "Number of hexagrams is:"; e
! If Flag_T equals 0 then an illegal symbol prevented the textual sequence
! from running.
IF Flag_T = 0 then
  PRINT
  Set Cursor 13,1
  PRINT "                              "
  PRINT "          Please try again.  You entered incorrect symbols."
  PRINT "                              "
END IF
ELSE
SET CURSOR 13,1
! If neither the binary nor textual part of the program ran, then
! neither the "B" nor "T" key was pressed.
PRINT " YOU MUST PRESS EITHER THE ""B"" OR ""T"" KEY. "
PRINT " PRESS F1 AND TRY AGAIN. "
PRINT "                              "
END IF
! Variables are initialized (set back to zero), in preparation for
! another cycle.
Let g = 0
Let Flag_B = 0
Let Flag_T = 0
```

```
Let d = 0
Let e = 0
PRINT
PRINT " F1 = For another cycle.  Esc = Escape to DOS."
Get Key x
If x = 27 then
   EXIT DO
Else
END IF
LOOP
END
!
!This is the Sub Routine Identify.
SUB Identify(HEX$)
SELECT CASE HEX$
  Case "000000"
      PRINT "000-000    2     (0)     Earth"
  Case "000001"
      PRINT "000-001   23     (1)     Falling"
  Case "000010"
      PRINT "000-010    8     (2)     Alliance"
  Case "000011"
      PRINT "000-011   20     (3)     Observing"
  Case "000100"
      PRINT "000-100   16     (4)     Contentment"
  Case "000101"
      PRINT "000-101"  35     (5)     Advance"
  Case "000110"
      PRINT "000-110   45     (6)     Gathering Together"
  Case "000111"
      PRINT "000-111   12     (7)     Standstill"
  Case "001000"
      PRINT "001-000   15     (8)     Modesty"
  Case "001001"
      PRINT "001-001   52     (9)     Mountain"
  Case "001010"
      PRINT "001-010   39     (10)    Obstruction"
  Case "001011"
      PRINT "001-011   53     (11)    Gradual Advance"
  Case "001100"
      PRINT "001-100   62     (12)    Small in Excess"
  Case "001101"
      PRINT "001-101   56     (13)    The Traveler"
  Case "001110"
```

```
        PRINT "001-110    31    (14)    Mutual Influence"
Case "001111"
        PRINT "001-111    33    (15)    The Piglet"
Case "010000"
        PRINT "010-000     7    (16)    An Army"
Case "010001"
        PRINT "010-001     4    (17)    The Young Shoot"
Case "010010"
        PRINT "010-010    29    (18)    Water"
Case "010011"
        PRINT "010-011    59    (19)    Flood/Dispersion"
Case "010100"
        PRINT "010-100    40    (20)    Obstruction Removed"
Case "010101"
        PRINT "010-101    64    (21)    Not Yet Across the River"
Case "010110"
        PRINT "010-110    47    (22)    Burdened/Exhausted"
Case "010111"
        PRINT "010-111     6    (23)    Grievance"
Case "011000"
        PRINT "011-000    46    (24)    Pushing Upwards"
Case "011001"
        PRINT "011-001    18    (25)    Illness/Decay"
Case "011010"
        PRINT "011-010    48    (26)    A Well"
Case "011011"
        PRINT "011-011    57    (27)    Wind"
Case "011100"
        PRINT "011-100    32    (28)    Constancy"
Case "011101"
        PRINT "011-101    50    (29)    Ritual Caldron"
Case "011110"
        PRINT "011-110    28    (30)    Big in Excess"
Case "011111"
        PRINT "011-111    44    (31)    Meeting/Subjugation"
Case "100000"
        PRINT "100-000    24    (32)    Return"
Case "100001"
        PRINT "100-001    27    (33)    Bulging Cheeks"
Case "100010"
        PRINT "100-010     3    (34)    Sprouting"
Case "100011"
        PRINT "100-011    42    (35)    Increase"
Case "100100"
```

```
        PRINT "100-100    51   (36)   Thunder"
Case "100101"
        PRINT "100-101    21   (37)   Biting Through"
Case "100110"
        PRINT "100-110    17   (38)   The Chase"
Case "100111"
        PRINT "100-111    25   (39)   No Error (No Expectations)"
Case "101000"
        PRINT "101-000    36   (40)   The Bright (Calling) Pheasant"
Case "101001"
        PRINT "101-001    22   (41)   Adornment"
Case "101010"
        PRINT "101-010    63   (42)   Already Across the River"
Case "101011"
        PRINT "101-011    37   (43)   The Family"
Case "101100"
        PRINT "101-100    55   (44)   Abundance"
Case "101101"
        PRINT "101-101    30   (45)   Fire"
Case "101110"
        PRINT "101-110    49   (46)   Revolution"
Case "101111"
        PRINT "101-111    13   (47)   Companions"
Case "110000"
        PRINT "110-000    19   (48)   Authority Approaches"
Case "110001"
        PRINT "110-001    41   (49)   Decrease"
Case "110010"
        PRINT "110-010    60   (50)   Restraint/Regulations"
Case "110011"
        PRINT "110-011    61   (51)   Inmost Sincerity (Allegiance)"
Case "110100"
        PRINT "110-100    54   (52)   A Maiden Marries"
Case "110101"
        PRINT "110-101    38   (53)   Estrangement"
Case "110110"
        PRINT "110-110    58   (54)   Lake"
Case "110111"
        PRINT "110-111    10   (55)   Treading"
Case "111000"
        PRINT "111-000    11   (56)   Peace/Flowing"
Case "111001"
        PRINT "111-001    26   (57)   Big Restraint/Big Accumulation"
Case "111010"
```

```
      PRINT "111-010     5    (58)   Getting Wet"
Case "111011"
      PRINT "111-011     9    (59)   Small Restraint/Small Accumulation"
Case "111100"
      PRINT "111-100    34    (60)   Big Uses Force"
Case "111101"
      PRINT "111-101    14    (61)   Great Possessions"
Case "111110"
      PRINT "111-110    43    (62)   Decisive"
Case "111111"
      PRINT "111-111     1    (63)   Heaven"
END SELECT
END SUB
```

L

I CHING DEVICES AND EQUIPMENT

An Audio Exploration of I-Ching. Audio Renaissance Tapes, Inc. 9110 Sunset Boulevard, Los Angeles, CA 90069, 1988.

Contains three specially-minted I Ching coins, a 72-page booklet which explains the coin oracle method, a translation of the *I Ching,* and an hour-long cassette.

The cassette gives a brief explanation of the attributes of the eight trigrams and explains how to use the coin oracle method.

Book of Changes. R. K. West Consulting, P.O. Box 8059, Mission Hills, CA, 91346.

Requires DOS 2.1 or later; 512KB RAM. This is a new version of the *I Ching* program **Oracle**. Both programs are by Rosemary West.

The *Book of Changes* is "completely menu-driven so that you never need to enter long command sequences." The author states:

> You can edit the text for each hexagram on the screen, so that Book of Changes can incorporate your favorite translation and commentaries. You can also add your own comments separately from the regular text, and choose whether or not to include them in the readings. Readings can be printed or saved on disk for reference and editing.

The menu also allows user to display the attributes of the trigrams and to view the text of any hexagram and its lines. Screen colors, system and printing defaults can be changed by user. There is also an option to allow user to reduce file size.

Menu gives user choice of coin method or yarrow-stalk method or of letting the program make the choice. Registration fee is $29.00. This program is shareware, but is copyrighted by the author.

Huang's I Ching. Kerson Huang, P.O. Box 1083, Marblehead, MA 01945, 1987. Obtainable from author.

This is *I Ching* software. Program comes on a 5 1/4" disk for IBM compatible personal computers. A primer of nineteen screens is given which covers the concept of yin and yang, the eight trigrams, and a brief history of the *I Ching.* A sub-program allows one to combine trigrams and the text number and name of the resulting hexagrams is given. The main program offers the following menu: Automatic hexagram casting, Manual hexagram casting, Read I Ching, DateMark On/Off, Exit to DOS. The text of the moving lines of the cast hexagram are given and an explanation of this text. The opportunity is given to print the cast hexagram and line text obtained. If the option Read I Ching is selected it lists the hexagrams either by textual sequence or alphabetically by name. A hexagram is selected and the text is given for every line. An explanation of each line text may also be obtained.

I Ching Cards. University Books, Inc. 1615 Hillside Avenue, New Hyde Park, N. Y. 11040, 1972.

A deck of 69 cards (3" x 5"). Each of the 64 hexagrams is portrayed on a card. On one side is its Chinese and English name, the hexagram symbol, and the names and natural attribute of its primary trigrams. On the reverse side of the card the judgment is given in a short paragraph, as is the text for the lines. Of the remaining 5 cards, one is an introduction to the *I Ching,* one explains the coin method of divination, one gives the King Wen (Textual) sequence of the hexagrams, one gives the King Wen and Fu Hsi arrangement of the trigrams, and the last gives some of the common attributes of the trigrams.

I Ching Cards. Made in Switzerland by Agmüller. Distributed exclusively by U. S. Games Systems, Inc. New York, N. Y. 10016. Copyright 1971, I Ching Productions.

A deck of eighty cards (2.75" x 4.75"). There are five instruction cards which give the background of the *I Ching* and the coin method, one card for the emblems, four explaining the trigrams, one card giving the Fu Hsi sequence of the hexagrams, five blank cards for notes, and sixty-four cards for the hexagrams. On the back of the first instruction card it states: "Commentaries about *I Ching* from Encyclopedia, C. G. Jung, Ta Chuan, and Hermann Hesse." Also included are three metallic coins marked "yang 3" on one side and "yin 2" on the other.

I Ching Decision Science Computer. Solfan, 665 Clyde Avenue, Mountain View, CA 94043, 1977.

This electronic device, which weighs only 2 and 1/2 ounces without its 9-volt battery, is manufactured by Solfan. In size it is about 3 1/2" x 2 1/2" x 1 1/4." It has three lights, each of which can be red or green. In addition two of the lights are capable of alternating between red and green and one of these lights is capable of flashing red or flashing green. The 19-page owner's manual explains three ways in which the I Ching Decision Science Computer can be used to answer questions. A quick answer can be obtained by interpreting the color of the lights, whether they're flashing or not, etc., or by using a table in the owner's manual, the color of the lights can be interpreted as the textual number of a hexagram. Finally, the manual gives instruction for determining the divining hexagram line by line with the same probabilities as the yarrow-stalk method.

Oracle. R. K. West, P.O. Box 8044, Mission Hills, CA, 91346. Distributed by Public Brand Software, P.O. Box 51315, Indianapolis, IN 46251, 1988.

This software, written for personal computers, contains two programs: ICHING.EXE and TAROT.EXE and seven pages of documentation, which may be printed out. The documentation covers both of the executable programs. This *I Ching* program is an earlier version of the **Book of Changes** listed above and is no longer available.

The *I Ching* program will cast a hexagram using either the coin method or the yarrow-stalk method. Both methods are visually represented. It takes seven consecutive presses of the <enter> key to obtain a hexagram by the coin method and 85 consecutive presses of the <enter> key to obtain a hexagram by the yarrow-stalk method.

The hexagram is displayed and the text for the Judgment, the Image, and the moving lines are given. The Wilhelm/Baynes translation is used. Whether the cast hexagram has moving lines or not, only the cast hexagram is given.

Oracle-East: Secrets of the I Ching Revealed. Zephyr Services, 306 S. Homewood Ave. Pittsburgh, PA, 15208.

Oracle-East is *I Ching* software. Can be bought for IBM compatibles, Apple and C64/128. The main menu offers the following choices: 1. How to Use Oracle-East; 2. Cast the I Ching; 3. Table of 8 Trigrams; 4. Table of 64 Hexagrams; 5. Meaning and History of I Ching; 6. The Computer and I Ching; and 7. Exit Oracle-East. Three screens are devoted to instructions. A hexagram may be cast by the probabilities of the coin method or the yarrow-stalk method. The Image, Judgement, and text of the moving lines are given for the hexagram obtained. The Image and Judgement of the final hexagram is given. All of this may be printed. The table of the trigrams gives the eight trigrams and their names, the table of the hexagrams gives the sixty-four hexagrams and their names. An argument is given—under the heading of The Computer and the I Ching—that using the computer to cast a hexagram is compatible with the traditional yarrow-stalk method (or the coin method depending upon option chosen).

The Visual I Ching: A New Approach to the Ancient Chinese Oracle. Salem House Publishers, Topsfield, Massachusetts, 1987.

Comes in a cardboard box and contains: a deck of sixty-four cards (each card has a hexagram on it and is illustrated); a deck of eight cards (each card has a trigram on it and is illustrated); a blue ritual cloth on which the cards may be placed in certain positions; a small note pad; and a 112-page hardcover instruction book. The book gives the background of the *I Ching* and explains various games and exercises that can be performed by the cards on the ritual cloth.

The method of forming the divinatory hexagram is to mix the eight trigram cards (face down) on the blue cloth and place the cards at random in a circle. At random one is selected and its name recorded. This card is then turned face down and the procedure is repeated five more times. A male card (Trigram 1. *Father*, Trigram 3. *Eldest Son*, Trigram 5. *Middle Son*, or Trigram 7. *Youngest Son*) indicates a yang line. A female card (Trigram 2. *Mother*, Trigram 4. *Eldest Daughter*, Trigram 6. *Middle Daughter*, Trigram 8. *Youngest Daughter*) indicates a yin line. Moving lines are indicated by Trigrams 1 and 2.

Also given are numerous games and exercises.

M

GLOSSARY OF TERMS
AND PROPER NAMES

Antecedent Hexagram

Given two hexagrams, the first is antecedent and the second is consequent, if and only if, they differ in exactly one line position such that the first has a yang line in this position and the second has a yin line in this position. Since it is more probable for a yang line to change into a yin line, than vice-versa, it is more probable for an antecedent hexagram to change into its consequent, than vice-versa. For example, Hexagram 1, 111-111 is antecedent to Hexagram 44, 011-111. The terms antecedent and consequent hexagrams are generally used to describe the petals of a hexagram. See **Consequent Hexagram**, **Petals**, **Flower**, **Flower Center**.

Basic Nuclear Hexagram

A **hexagram** which has itself or its **opposite** as its **nuclear hexagram**. There are four basic nuclear hexagrams. They are hexagrams 1, 2, 63, and 64.

Binary Number

A number expressed using only the digits 1 and 0. Such numbers are used in the **binary system**. In this book we shall use the expression "binary number" to mean a decimal number that is equivalent to a hexagram (or trigram) viewed as a binary number.

Binary Order

Counting in the binary system is as follows: 0, 1, 10, 11, 100, 101, 110, 111, 1000, 1001, 1010, 1011, 1100, 1101, 1110, 1111, 10000, etc. When the hexagrams are regarded as binary numbers (yang line = 1, yin line = 0, leftmost digit = line position 1) there may be initial 0's, e.g., 000-001. These 0's have no numerical value. The trigrams in binary order are: 000, 001, 010, 011, 100, 101, 110, and 111.

Binary Order of the Hexagrams

See **Fu Hsi's Arrangement** of the hexagrams.

Binary System

A number system based on the powers of 2. See **Binary Order**.

Book of Changes

See **I Ching**, **Five Classics**, and **Six Classics**.

Book of Documents

See **Book of History**. See **Shu Ching**.

Book of History
See **Shu Ching**, **Five Classics**, and **Six Classics**.

Book of Odes
See **Shih Ching**, **Five Classics**, and **Six Classics**. Also called **Book of Songs**.

Book of Rites
See **Li Chi**, **Five Classics**, and **Six Classics**.

Center
See **Flower Center**.

Central Line
A line in a **hexagram** is central if and only if it is in **line position** 3 or 5.

Character of a Line
A line's character in a **hexagram** is determined by whether it is a **yin** or **yang** line, a **central** or not central line, or a **correct** or incorrect line. Two lines have the same character only if they are both yin or both yang, both central or not, **and** both correct or not. (See **Correspondence**, **Correctness of a Line**, **Holding Together**.)

Ch'en T'uan (ca. 906–989).
A Taoist who originated the **Lo River Map** and the **Yellow River Map** and was the source for many numerologists of the Sung Dynasty.

Ch'un Ch'iu *Spring and Autumn Annals.*
One of the **Five Classics**. A partial record of historical events from 722 B.C. to 481 B.C. Compiled by Confucius from records from Lu, his native state.

Ching Fang (77–37 B.C.)
A member of the **Hsian Shu** school of interpretation of the **I Ching**. He developed the arrangement of the hexagrams called the Eight Houses. (See **Houses of the Hexagrams**.)

Chou I
See **Lien Shan**.

Chou Dynasty (jo) (1122 B.C.–256 A.D.)

1122 B.C. is the traditional date for the beginning of the Chou Dynasty. A safer estimate would be circa 1000 B.C. Founded by **King Wen**, his son **King Wu**, and the **Duke of Chou**.

Chu Hsi (1130–1200 A.D.)

A Neo-Confucianist. Called by Fung Yu-Lan "the greatest synthesizer in Chinese thought." ([A] Fung Yu-Lan, vol. 2, p. xxiii). Tried to unite the **Hsiang shu** and **I Li** schools as well as various other cosmologies.

Classic

See **Five Classics** and **Six Classics**.

Commentary on the Images (*Hsiang Chuan*)

A commentary in two parts which comprises the Third and Fourth Wings of the **Ten Wings**. The commentary gives an image for each of the **primary trigrams** in each **hexagram** and attempts to determine the meaning of the **hexagram** from the relationship between these two images. Also given in this commentary are brief comments on the line texts.

Commentary on the Judgment (*T'uan Chuan*)

A commentary in two parts which comprises the First and Second Wings of the **Ten Wings**. The commentary gives an interpretation for each **hexagram**. Traditionally authorship is attributed to Confucius.

Commentary on the Words of the Text (*Wen Yen*)

The Seventh Wing (commentary) of the **Ten Wings**. Part of multiple commentaries from the Confucian school. Covers only the first two **hexagrams**.

Complementary Opposites

Qualities or attributes that are thought of as opposites, but neither can exist without the other. Thus, complementary opposites are qualities or entities that do not strive with one another, but complement one another and by so doing form a whole that cannot exist without both complements. Such opposites not only may exist side by side, but often must exist in such a state. Examples of complementary opposites are: man/woman, concave/convex, inside/outside, etc. See **Polar Opposites**.

Confucius (kǒn fū shǔs)

Latinized form of Chinese **Kung Fu-tze** (koong foo dzu). Dates are: 551–479 B.C. Influential Chinese philosopher who considered himself to be a transmitter of the traditions of the Sage-Kings. Regarded by some scholars

as the author of the **Great Treatise**, a commentary on the **I Ching**. One
of the four men associated with the **I Ching**. The others are **Fu Hsi**, **King
Wen**, and the **Duke of Chou**.

Consequent Hexagram

Given two hexagrams, the first is consequent and the second is antecedent
in relation to each other, if and only if they differ in exactly one line position
such that the first hexagram has a yin line in this position where the second
has a yang line. Since it is more probable for a yang line to turn into a
yin line than vice-versa, it is more probable for the second hexagram to
turn into the first. For example, Hexagram 44, 011-111 is a consequent
of Hexagram 1, 111-111. See **Antecedent Hexagram**, **Petals**, **Flower**,
Flower Center.

Constituting Ruler of Hexagram

Every hexagram has at least one line which is its constituting ruler. The
constituting ruler (or rulers) of a hexagram is the line (or lines) which char-
acterizes the hexagram's meaning. For example, in Hexagram 43, 111-110,
Decisive, line 6—the yin at the top—is the Constituting Ruler. It is this
line that the five yang lines determine to overthrow. Thus the meaning of
the hexagram is exemplified by the 6th line. The same line may be both a
Constituting and Governing Ruler. See **Governing Ruler of Hexagram**
and **Rulers of a Hexagram**.

Converse

The converse of a **hexagram** is another hexagram which is found by inter-
changing the **primary trigrams** of the original. For example, the converse
of Hexagram 23, 000-001, *Falling,* is Hexagram 15, 001-000, *Modesty.*

Correctness of a Line

A line in a **hexagram** is correct if and only if it is a **yang line** in line
position 1, 3, or 5 or if it is a **yin line** in line position 2, 4, or 6. If a line is
not correct then it is incorrect.

Correspondence

Two lines in a **hexagram** correspond to each other if and only if the lines
are **opposite** (one yin and the other yang) and they occupy **line positions**
1 and 4, 2 and 5, or 3 and 6. Correspondence is most important between
line positions 2 and 5, the line positions of the Great Official and the Ruler
respectively. It is generally favorable when the correspondence is that of a
strong official to weak ruler (i.e., a yang line in position 3 and a yin line in
position 5). (See **Holding Together** and **Character of a Line**.)

Cycle

The cycle of a **hexagram** is found by moving the line in **line position** 6 to line position 1 and moving all the other lines up one. This process is repeated as long as it generates a hexagram not already in the cycle. Hexagram 1, 111-111 and Hexagram 2, 000-000 have no cycles. All the other hexagrams have either 2, 3, or 6 hexagrams in a cycle.

Discussion of the Trigrams (*Shuo Kua*)

The Eighth Wing of the **Ten Wings**. Predates Confucius. Explains the eight trigrams.

Divining Hexagram

The **hexagram** which is obtained by one of the many divining methods used to consult the **I Ching** as an oracle or advisor. Two traditional methods are the **Yarrow Stalk Method** and the **Three Coin Method**.

Double Hexagram

Sometimes called a **Double** or a **House Hexagram**. A **hexagram** whose primary trigrams are the same. The upper primary trigram is the same as the lower primary trigram. Example is Hexagram 29, 101-101, *Water*. There are eight Doubles: Hexagrams 1, 2, 29, 30, 51, 52, 57, and 58. Sometimes called a Double or a House Hexagram.

Duke of Chou (jo)

Son of **King Wen**. One of the founders of the Chou Dynasty and one of the four men associated with the **I Ching**. The other three are **Fu Hsi**, **King Wen**, and **Confucius**.

Earlier Heaven Sequence (or **Fu Hsi's Arrangement** of trigrams, **Sequence of Earlier Heaven**, **Primal Arrangement**, **World of Thought Arrangement**)

A circular arrangement of the trigrams arranged in **binary order**. 000, 001, 010, and 011 are positions on a circle at 180°, 135°, 90°, 45°, respectively. 100, 101, 110, and 111 are at 225°, 270°, 315°, and 360°, respectively. The result is that all pairs of **opposites** are opposite each other on the circle. Also if a line is drawn connecting all the trigrams on the circle in binary order the result is a diagram that approximates the Yin-Yang Symbol.

Eight Houses

See **Houses of the Hexagrams**.

Emblems
See **Four Images**.

Family Member
See **Family Relation**.

Family Relation
The following table gives the family relationships for the trigrams in the **Earlier** and **Later Heaven Sequence**.

Trigram	Earlier Heaven	Later Heaven
111	Father	Father
000	Mother	Mother
100	Eldest Son	Eldest Son
010	Middle Daughter	Middle Son
001	Youngest Daughter	Youngest Son
011	Eldest Daughter	Eldest Daughter
101	Middle Son	Middle Daughter
110	Youngest Son	Youngest Daughter

In the **Earlier Heaven Sequence** the bottom line of the **trigram** is the sex determinant. In the **Later Heaven Sequence** sex is determined by the kind of line (yin or yang) which occurs an odd number of times.

Fifth Nuclear Hexagram
Formed from a **hexagram** by placing the hexagram's **upper primary trigram** over its **lower nuclear trigram**.

Five Agents
Also called the Five Elements. The five agents in productive (or generative) order are: Earth, Metal, Water, Wood, Fire. In order of conquest (or destructive) order they are: Earth, Water, Fire, Metal, Wood. These agents represent different stages of cosmic and social activity. They are **not** to be thought of as the elemental components of matter. Each of the Five Agents has associated with it a color, a taste, an odor, an animal, a grain, an organ of the body, a sense organ, a planet, a musical note, a heavenly body, and so forth. Four of the Five Agents are associated with a season, a direction, and an **emblem** of the **I Ching**. The Five Agents are a classificatory system first known to be systematized by Tsou Yen (350?–270? B.C.). ([A] Needham, p. 232). The traditional view is that the Five Agents system can be traced back to 2,000 B.C.

Five Classics

The five Confucian Classics are: the *I Ching* (*Book of Changes*), the *Shih Ching* (*Book of Odes* or *Book of Songs*), the *Shu Ching* (*Book of History* or *Book of Documents*), the *Li Chi* (*Book of Rites* or *Record of Rites*), and the *Ch'un Ch'iu* (*Spring and Autumn Annals*). If the lost classic, the *Yo Ching* (*Book of Music*), is counted then there are **Six Classics**. The *Yo Ching* was lost in or before the 3rd century B.C. and was replaced by the **I Ching**. See **Six Classics, I Ching, Shih Ching, Shu Ching, Li Chi, Spring and Autumn Annals**.

Flower

A **hexagram** and its six **petals** constitute a flower. See **Antecedent Hexagram** and **Consequent Hexagram**.

Flower Center

A **hexagram** in relation to its six **petals** is a flower center. See **Flower**.

Four Images

The names of the Four Images (also called the Four Emblems) are: Great Yang, Lesser Yang, Great Yin, and Lesser Yin. They are also called: Old Yang, Young Yang, Old Yin and Young Yin. They are symbolized as 11, 10, 00, and 01, respectively. (A yang line is 1, and a yin line is 0, left digit is bottom line, right digit is top line.) Hence the Great Yang is a yang line over a yang line, Lesser Yang is a yin line over a yang line, and so forth. The bottom line is the sex determinant. ([A] Wilhelm/Baynes, p. 319). The numbers associated with the Images are: Old Yang = 9, Lesser Yang = 7, Old Yin = 6, Lesser Yin = 8. See **Moving Line** and **Static Line**.

Fourth Nuclear Hexagram

Formed from a **hexagram** by placing the hexagram's **upper nuclear trigram** over its **lower nuclear trigram**.

Fu Hsi (foō shē)

A legendary emperor and cultural hero of China who lived about 2800 B.C. Achievements accredited to him include the invention of writing, formulation of marriage laws, and introduction of hunting, fishing, and cooking methods to the Chinese. His name is given to the **Earlier Heaven Sequence** and to an arrangement of the **hexagrams** that reflects a binary order when a **yang line** is regarded as 1 and **yin line** is regarded as 0. Many authorities doubt that the **hexagrams** can be traced back to the time of Fu Hsi. One of the four men associated with the **I Ching**. The others are **King Wen**, the **Duke of Chou**, and **Confucius**.

Fu Hsi's Arrangement (or **Order**)

A particular order of trigrams (see **Earlier Heaven Sequence**) or hexagrams. There are two arrangements of the hexagrams named after **Fu Hsi.** One is an eight by eight square formed by the 64 hexagrams arranged in **binary order**. Hexagram 2, 000-000 is in the upper left hand corner of the square and the hexagrams in binary order are written from left to right ending with Hexagram 1, 111-111 in the lower right hand corner. The second arrangement is circular. The 64 hexagrams are evenly distributed in a circle. At the bottom is Hexagram 2, 000-000 and the hexagrams in **binary order** ascend counter clockwise to Hexagram 44, 011-111 (binary value 31), then Hexagram 24, 100-000 (binary value 32) occurs immediately to the left of Hexagram 2 and the rest of the hexagrams in **binary order** ascend clockwise. The result is a circular arrangement of hexagrams such that each pair of opposites is opposite the other on the circle. If a line is drawn connecting the hexagrams in **binary order** the resulting diagram resembles a Yin-Yang symbol. The **Fu Hsi Arrangement** of the hexagrams (a circular arrangement of the hexagrams around their square arrangement) was invented by **Shao Yung**.

Governing Ruler of Hexagram

Each hexagram has one or more lines which are its Governing Rulers. Generally, it is the line in line position 5 (the position of the Ruler), but not always. The Governing Ruler is the line which rules the hexagram by virtue of its strength, place, and time in the hexagram. The same line may be both a Governing Ruler and a Constituting Ruler. See **Constituting Ruler of Hexagram** and **Rulers of a Hexagram**.

Gray Code

A way of writing the digits of numbers such that when these numbers are in counting order (e.g., 1, 2, 3 and so forth) any two successive numbers in this order will be identical to each other in all digit positions except one and the digits in this one position will differ from each other by one unit. A number of different Gray Codes may be written for a number system in any base, but it is usually used for the binary system. (An example of a binary Gray Code sequence is: 0, 1, 11, 10, 110, 111, 101, 100, 1100, 1101, 1111.) It is usually the **reflected** Gray Code that is used. For an attempt to meaningfully present the hexagrams in the order of a Gray Code, see [B] McKenna, Dennis J. and Victor H. Mair.

Great Treatise (*Hsi T'zu Chuan* or *Ta Chuan*)

The largest and—according to some scholars—the most significant commentary of the group of commentaries to the **I Ching** known as the **Ten Wings**. The two parts of the *Great Treatise* form the Fifth and Sixth Wings of the

Ten Wings. Tradition attributes the authorship of the **Great Treatise** to Confucius (551–479 B.C.). Although some scholars dispute this tradition it is generally agreed that the **Great Treatise** was written not later than 90 B.C. Sometimes referred to as *The Commentary on Appended Judgments.*

Hexagram
A symbol composed of six horizontal lines. A line is either a **yang line** or a **yin line**. There are 64 hexagrams. Each hexagram has a name and a text number and represents a particular state of change: cosmic, political, social, or personal. See **Kinetic Hexagram, Non-Kinetic Hexagram.**

Hexagram Cycle
See **Cycle.**

Hexagram Flower
See **Flower.**

Hexagram Pair (or **Pair**)
A pair is any odd-numbered hexagram and its even-numbered successor in the textual sequence (**King Wen's Arrangement**). For example, Hexagrams 1 and 2, Hexagrams 3 and 4, and Hexagrams 5 and 6 are all pairs.

Hexagram Story
See **Story.**

Hexagram Text
See **Judgment.**

Ho T'u
See **Yellow River Map**

Holding Together
Two lines in a **hexagram** may hold together when they are **opposites** and occupy adjacent **line positions**. Holding together is of most importance between line positions 4 and 5 (providing that the ruler is in the 5th position). The hexagram is generally favorable when a yin line in position 4 holds together with a yang line in position 5. The relationship of holding together is also important between line positions 5 and 6. In this case it is generally favorable when a yin line in position 5 holds together with a yang line in position 6.

House Hexagram

Sometimes called a **Double Hexagram** or **Pure Hexagram**. A hexagram whose **primary trigrams** are the same (upper primary trigram identical with lower primary trigram). There are eight House Hexagrams: Hexagrams 1, 2, 29, 30, 51, 52, 57, and 58. Each House Hexagram heads (and is part of) a unique group of 8 hexagrams known as a House. Collectively these divisions are called the **Houses of the Hexagrams**.

Houses of the Hexagrams

An arrangement of the sixty-four hexagrams by **Ching Fang** (77–37 B.C.). Its purpose was probably part of some divinatory method. The arrangement is a division of the hexagrams into eight groups, each containing eight hexagrams. Each group is called a House (or Mansion) and is named after the first Hexagram (**House Hexagram**) in the group. The first hexagram in each group is a **double hexagram** (one in which both primary trigrams are the same). The First House, headed by Hexagram 1, is called The House of the Great Creative, the other houses are numbered in the clockwise order of their primary trigrams in the **Later Heaven Sequence**. Hence the Second House is headed by Hexagram 29; it is called the House of Water. The Third House is headed by Hexagram 52; it is called House of the Mountain, and so forth. The second through eighth hexagram in each House is formed from the first by the following process. The line in the first place of the first hexagram is changed to its opposite; this forms the second hexagram. The line in the second place of the second hexagram is changed to its opposite; this forms the third hexagram. The line in the third place of the third hexagram is changed to its opposite; this forms the fourth hexagram. This process is continued until the sixth hexagram is the first hexagram with its first five lines changed to its opposite. The seventh hexagram is formed from the sixth by changing its fifth line to its opposite. Finally, the eighth hexagram is formed from the seventh by changing the first three lines of the seventh hexagram to its opposite. For example, the hexagrams in the House of the Great Creative are:

The House of the Great Creative

1.	Hex. 1.	111-111
2.	Hex. 44.	011-111
3.	Hex. 33.	001-111
4.	Hex. 12.	000-111
5.	Hex. 20.	000-011
6.	Hex. 23.	000-001
7.	Hex. 35.	000-101
8.	Hex. 14.	111-101

The Houses are listed in [A] Wilhelm/Baynes, pp. 725–27.

Hsiang Shu School of Interpretation

Translated as Symbol (Image) and Number School of Interpretation of the **I Ching**. This school was active in the Han dynasty (206 B.C.–220 A.D.). One of its foremost proponents was **Shao Yung** (1011–1077 A.D.) in the Sung dynasty. The **Hsiang Shu** school emphasized the formal, transformational and numerical aspects of the hexagrams and their component trigrams. Members of this school assigned the hexagrams to periods of the calendar, to the **Five Agents**, to the four directions, and so forth. The **Hsiang Shu** school is in contrast to the **I Li** school; the latter emphasized textual analysis. See **Meng Hsi** , **Ching Fang**, and **Chu Shi**.

I Ching (ē jing)

See **Lien Shan**. Literally means "The Classic Book of Changes" or "The Classic Book of Change." An ancient Chinese book—the main part of which predates Confucius—consisting of 64 symbols called **hexagrams**. Each of these hexagrams may represent a cosmic, social, or personal situation. Advice is given concerning proper conduct for this situation. These symbols were used for purposes of divination, but the book is also studied for its wisdom. Generally included with the **I Ching** are its **Ten Wings**, which are a collection of commentaries.

I Li School of Interpretation

Translated as the Meaning and Principle (or Moral Principle) School of Interpretation. An interpretation of the **I Ching** that stresses textual analysis and attempts to find moral guidance from such analysis. This **I Li** school is in contrast to the **Hsiang Shu** school of interpretation. The latter school emphasizes the formal and numerical aspects of the hexagrams. One of the foremost proponents of the **I Li** school was **Wang Pi** (226–249 A.D.). See **Chu Shi**.

Images

See **Commentary on the Images**.

Inner World Arrangement

See **Later Heaven Sequence**.

Intermediate Nuclear Hexagram

The **nuclear hexagram** of a **non-nuclear hexagram**. There are twelve intermediate hexagrams: hexagrams 23, 24, 27, 28, 37, 38, 39, 40, 43, 44, 53 and 54.

Inverse

The inverse of a **trigram** is the trigram formed by writing its lines in reverse order. For example, the inverse of trigram "100" is "001." The inverse of a **hexagram** is the hexagram formed by writing its lines in reverse order. For example, the inverse of Hexagram 46, 011-000, is Hexagram 45, 000-110. And, of course, Hexagram 45 is the inverse of Hexagram 46. See **Opposite**.

Judgment Also called **Hexagram Text**

The text which follows the name of the hexagram and precedes the **line text**. The Judgment describes a situation related to the hexagram and its name. The Judgment is an interpretation of the hexagram and a recommendation for action or non-action. (See [A] Lee, *Understanding the I Ching*, p. 154–59.)

Kinetic Hexagram

A **hexagram** defined by six **kinetic lines** and their **line positions**. In short, a hexagram in which each line is specified as either moving or static. See **Kinetic Line**, **Non-Kinetic Hexagram**, and **Non-Kinetic Line**.

Kinetic Line

A **yin** or **yang line** which is specified as a **moving line** or a **static line**.

King Wen

(Born about 1231 B.C.) Founder of the **Chou Dynasty**. King Wen is alleged to have combined the **trigrams** to form the **hexagrams** while in prison.

King Wen's Arrangement (Sequence, or Order)

A particular order of trigrams (see **Later Heaven Sequence**) or hexagrams (see **Textual Sequence**).

Kuei Tsang

See **Lien Shan**.

Kung Fu-tze

The Chinese name of **Confucius**.

Kuo Yu (Conversations from the States or Discourses on the States)

Covers the same period as the **Tso Chuan** and is similar to it. Parts of the text of the **I Ching** appear in the **Kuo Yu**. See **Tso Chuan**.

Later Heaven Sequence
(Also known as **King Wen's Arrangement** of trigrams, **Sequence of Later Heaven**, **World of Phenomena**, **World of Senses**, **Inner World Arrangement**). A circular arrangement of the eight trigrams representing the cycle of the seasons. Starting with spring the arrangement is: 100, 110, 101, 000, 110, 111, 010, 001.

Li Chi
The **Li Chi** (*Record of Rites*) contains forty-nine chapters, and of the three classics on rites (*I Li, Chou Li,* and *Li Chi*) is the most widely read and studied book. The *Li Chin* (*Classic Book of Rites*) was one of the original Five Confucian Classics, of which only fragments remain.
Ch'en Shou-Yi writes:

> All the three Li books were later compilations which had not been worked on by Confucius. That the *Li Chi* was a Han compilation had always been admitted. The *Chou Li,* instead of being the handiwork of the Duke of Chou, was most probably a projection of the mind of a group of political utopianists in the Warring States period, and the *I Li* was not what Confucius had taught his own disciples, but the salvaging of a number of etiquette manuals which had been handed down privately among members of the Confucian school. In other words, with the original *Li Chin* lost, these three purported classics filled the gap psychologically, if not documentarily, for two thousand years. ([A] Ch'en, *Chinese Literature: A Historical Introduction*, p. 82.)

Keeping in mind Ch'en's above commentary on the three works on rites, I have used the name *Li Chi* to designate a Confucian Classic. The term *Li Chin* has not been used by the Confucianists since the Han dynasty.

Lien Shan (*Manifestation of Change in the Mountains*)
The name of one of the three systems (versions) of the **I Ching**. The three systems are the **Lien Shan**, **Kuei Tsang** (*Flow and Return to Womb and Tomb*), and the **Chou I** (*Book of Changes of the Chou Dynasty*). Only fragments of the first two works remain. The **I Ching** as we know it today is the **Chou I**. A short account of these three versions of the **I** is given by Needham p. 307.

Line Position
Every **hexagram** has 6 line positions. They are numbered from the bottom up. Hence, the bottom line of a **hexagram** is in line position 1, the top line in line position 6. Line positions 1, 3, and 5 are yang positions. Line positions 2, 4, and 6 are yin positions (see **Correctness of a Line**). When the **hexagram** is expressed as a binary number using 1's and 0's (e.g.,

101-000) then the line positions are numbered from left to right.

Line Text

The text attached to each of the six lines for each of the sixty-four hexagrams. Hexagrams 1 and 2 have an extra line text apiece. The total number of line texts is 386: $(64 \times 6) + 2$. The line text follows the **hexagram text**.

Lo River Map (Lo Shu)

Said to have originated in antiquity, but was attached to **I Ching** by Ch'en T'uan (ca. 906–989). Nine groups of dots are arranged so that if they are numbered they form a square.

$$
\begin{array}{ccc}
4 & 9 & 2 \\
3 & 5 & 7 \\
8 & 1 & 6
\end{array}
$$

This is a magic square whose rows, columns, and diagonals add up to 15. See **Yellow River Map** and **Ch'en T'uan**.

Lo Shu

See **Lo River Map**.

Lower Nuclear Hexagram

Formed from a **hexagram** by placing the hexagram's **lower nuclear trigram** over its **lower primary trigram**.

Lower Nuclear Trigram

The **trigram** formed by the lines of a **hexagram** in **line positions** 2, 3, and 4.

Lower Primary Trigram

The bottom three lines of a **hexagram**. The lines of a **hexagram** in **line positions** 2, 3, and 4.

Mawangdui Manuscript

In 1973 at the Mawangdui site in Changsha a copy of the **I Ching** was found written on silk. The grave was made in 168 B.C. Thus this is, by several centuries, the oldest known copy of the **I Ching**. The Mawangdui **I Ching** seems to be from a different tradition, since its hexagrams do not follow the **King Wen Textual Sequence**.

Meng Hsi (fl. 51 B.C.)
Assigned hexagrams to the four cardinal directions, the four seasons, and periods of the year. Belonged to the **Hsiang Shu** school of interpretation of the **I Ching**.

Miscellaneous Notes on the Hexagrams (*Tsa Kua*)
The Tenth Wing (commentary) of the **Ten Wings**. Consists of interpretations of the **hexagrams** in mnemonic verses.

Moving Line
A line is moving if it is changing into its **opposite**. A moving **yang line** (symbolized by the number 9) changes to a **yin line**. A moving **yin line** (symbolized by the number 6) changes to a **yang line**.

Non-Kinetic Hexagram
A **hexagram** defined only by **non-kinetic lines** and their **line positions**. In other words, a **non-kinetic** hexagram is a hexagram whose lines are not specified as either **moving** or **static**. Unless otherwise indicated **hexagram** shall mean non-kinetic hexagram. See **Kinetic Hexagram**.

Non-Kinetic Line
A **yin** or **yang line** which is not specified as either **moving** or **static**. See **Kinetic Line**.

Non-Nuclear Hexagram
A hexagram which is not the **nuclear hexagram** of any hexagram. There are 48 non-nuclear hexagrams. See **Basic Nuclear Hexagram** and **Intermediate Nuclear Hexagram**.

Nuclear Hexagram
Formed from a **hexagram** by placing the hexagram's **upper nuclear trigram** over its **lower nuclear trigram**. If the lines of a hexagram are written in the following line position order—2, 3, 4, 3, 4, 5—a nuclear hexagram is formed. Sometimes called **primary nuclear hexagram** to distinguish it from other kinds of nuclear hexagrams.

Nuclear Trigram
Either the **upper** or **lower nuclear trigram** of a **hexagram**.

Opposite

The opposite of a **yang line** is a **yin line** and vice-versa. The opposite of a **trigram** is another **trigram** which is found by changing all the lines in the original to their opposites. The opposite of a **hexagram** is another hexagram which is found by changing all the lines in the original to their opposites. For example, the opposite of Hexagram 7, 010-000, *An Army* is Hexagram 13, 101-111, *Companions.* See **Complementary Opposites**, **Polar Opposites**, **Inverse**.

Outer World Arrangement

See **Earlier Heaven Sequence**.

Pair

See **Hexagram Pair**.

Petals

The six **hexagrams** that differ from a given hexagram (the **flower center**) by one **opposite** line. The **petals** of the **center** Hexagram 7, *Army*, 010-000 are:

Hexagram 19	110-000	Authority Approaches
Hexagram 2	000-000	Earth
Hexagram 46	011-000	Pushing Upwards
Hexagram 40	010-100	Obstruction Removed
Hexagram 29	010-010	Water
Hexagram 4	010-001	The Young Shoot

Polar Opposites

Qualities or attributes that cannot co-exist in union with one another, that is, the existence of one tends to negate the existence of the other. Polar opposites are thought of as being in strife with one another. Examples are: hot/cold, smart/stupid, heavy/light, bold/timid, etc. See **Complementary Opposites**.

Primal Arrangement

See **Earlier Heaven Sequence**.

Primary Nuclear Hexagram

See **Nuclear Hexagram**.

Primary Trigram

The top or bottom three lines of a **hexagram**, respectively, the **upper** or **lower primary trigram**.

Record of Rites

See **Li Chi**.

River Map

See **Writing from the River Lo** and **Yellow River Map**.

Rulers of a Hexagram

There are two kinds of ruling lines in a hexagram: **Constituting Ruler** and **Governing Ruler**. [A] Wilhelm/Baynes gives the ruling lines for each hexagram (Book III) and states that the ruling lines of the hexagrams can be determined from the text of the Commentary on the Judgment (First Wing of the **I Ching**), p. 364. It is not made clear how this determination was made, as the [A] Legge/Dover translation of the Commentary of the Judgment (pp. 213–66) does not give the Constituting nor Governing Ruler of any hexagram.

Sequence of the Trigrams (*Hsu Kua*)

The Ninth Wing (Commentary) of the **Ten Wings**. Not authored by the Confucianists. Attempts to explain the **textual sequence** of the **hexagrams**.

Shao Yung (1011–1077 A.D.)

Leading proponent of the **Hsiang Shu** school of interpretation of the **I Ching** in the Shang dynasty. Developed many diagrams among which is the circular arrangement of the sixty-four hexagrams around the square arrangement of the hexagrams, both arrangements being in binary order. Also developed the Plum Blossom Numerology, a method of divination using the **I Ching** and numerology.

Shih Ching

Book of Odes or *Book of Songs*. One of the **Five Classics**. Contains 305 poems (songs), some of which were written in the 9th century B.C. A Han historian reports that Confucius compiled the collection from over three thousand odes and worked on their musical accompaniments. See **Five Classics** and **Six Classics**.

Shu Ching

Book of History or *Book of Documents*. One of the **Five Classics**. An incomplete record of four Chinese dynasties: Yao (2200–2000 B.C.), Hsia (2000–1750 B.C.), Shang (1750–1000 B.C.), and Chou (1000 to 628 B.C.). According to tradition Confucius arranged these historical documents and wrote a short introduction to each one. See **Five Classics** and **Six Classics**.

Six Classics

The five original classics were the *Yo Ching* (*Book of Music*), the *Li Chi* (*Record of Rites*), the *Shih Ching* (*Book of Odes*), the *Shu Ching* (*Book of History*), and the *Ch'un Ch'iu* (*Spring and Autumn Annals*). In the 3rd century B.C. the **I Ching** took the place of the lost Music Classic. The first mention of the **I Ching** as one of the classics is in Chapter 14 of *Chuang Tzu* (*The Book of Master Chuang*), written about 290 B.C. ([A] Swanson, p. 4.) See the **Five Classics**.

Spring and Autumn Annals

See **Ch'un Ch'iu**.

Static Line

A yang or yin line is static if the line is not changing to its **opposite**, i.e., if it is not a **moving line**. A static **yang line** is symbolized by the number 7, a static **yin line** is symbolized by the number 8.

Story

The story of a **hexagram** is found by changing the line in **line position** 1 of the first (original) hexagram to its **opposite** (this forms the second hexagram of the story) then changing the line in the second line position of the second hexagram to its opposite (this forms the third hexagram of the story). This process is repeated until the seventh hexagram is formed by changing the line in the sixth position of the sixth hexagram. The process is continued by changing the line in the first line position of the seventh hexagram to its opposite until the 12th hexagram is reached which will be identical to the first hexagram.

For example, the story of Hexagram 15. *Modesty,* is:

Hexagram 15	001-000	Modesty
Hexagram 36	101-000	The Bright (Calling) Pheasant
Hexagram 11	111-000	Peace/Flowing
Hexagram 19	110-000	Authority Approaches
Hexagram 54	110-100	A Maiden Marries
Hexagram 58	110-110	Lake
Hexagram 10	110-111	Treading
Hexagram 6	010-111	Grievance
Hexagram 12	000-111	Standstill
Hexagram 33	001-111	The Piglet
Hexagram 53	001-011	Gradual Advance
Hexagram 15	001-000	Modesty

Ten Wings

A collection of commentaries to the **I Ching**. The First and Second Wings are called the **Commentary on the Judgment** (*T'uan Chuan*), which is in two parts. The Third and Fourth Wings are called the **Commentary on the Images** (*Hsiang Chuan*), which is in two parts. The Fifth and Sixth Wings are called the **Great Treatise** (*Hsi Tz'u Chuan* or *Ta Chuan*), which is also in two parts. The Seventh Wing is called **Commentary on Words of the Text** (*Wen Yen*). The Eighth Wing is the **Discussion of the Trigrams** (*Shuo Kua*). The Ninth Wing is the **Sequence of the Hexagrams** (*Hsu Kua*). The Tenth Wing is the **Miscellaneous Notes on the Hexagrams** (*Tsa Kua*).

Textual Sequence

Also known as the **King Wen Order**. The traditional order in which the **hexagrams** are presented and numbered in the **I Ching**. In the textual sequence every even-numbered hexagram is either the **inverse** or **opposite** of its preceding odd-numbered hexagram. It is opposite when the inverse—due to the symmetry of the preceding hexagram—would result in the same hexagram.

Three Coin Method

An easy and fast method of consulting the **I Ching** as an oracle or advisor. Three coins are thrown six times. Each throw, depending upon the number of heads and tails obtained, determines a line of a hexagram. The text of this hexagram and the text of any moving lines obtained is supposed to contain the answer to one's question or be the advice sought.

Trigram

A symbol composed of three horizontal lines. A line is either a **yang line** or a **yin line**. There are 8 trigrams. Each trigram is symbolic of a **family member** (e.g., Father, Mother, Eldest Son, etc.), a natural image (e.g., Thunder, Mountain, Lake, etc.), parts of the body (e.g., head, trunk, feet, etc.), and so forth.

Tso Chuan *Tso Commentary.*

A *Commentary on the Spring and Autumn Annals (Ch'un Ch'iu)* compiled about 350 B.C., plus or minus a century. Author said to be Tso Ch'iu. Additions and changes were made by the Confucians about 100 B.C. The **Tso Chuan** contains certain passages from the **I Ching** which according to Hellmut Wilhelm are older than other versions of the **I Ching**. ([A] Hellmut Wilhelm, "I-ching Oracles in the Tso-chuan and the Kyo-yu"). See **Ch'un Ch'iu** and **Kuo Yu**.

Upper Nuclear Hexagram

Formed from a **hexagram** by placing the hexagram's **upper primary trigram** over its **upper nuclear trigram**.

Upper Nuclear Trigram

The **trigram** formed by the lines of a **hexagram** in **line positions** 3, 4, and 5.

Upper Primary Trigram

The top three lines of a **hexagram**. The lines of a **hexagram** in **line positions** in 4, 5, and 6.

Wang Pi (226–249 A.D.)

One of the main proponents of the **I Li** school of interpretation of the **I Ching**. Emphasized that it is the text, not the hexagram that is the correct method of understanding the **I Ching**. Wang Pi changed the emphasis on the **I Ching**, from divination to metaphysics. He stated that the hexagram symbol was only a means to an end. Once the end—the idea—was grasped the symbol could be forgotten. See **Shao Yung** and **Chu Hsi**.

World of Phenomena

See **Later Heaven Sequence**.

World of Senses

See **Later Heaven Sequence**.

World of Thought Arrangement
See **Earlier Heaven Arrangement**.

Yang Line
A yang line is represented as an unbroken horizontal line, "━" or as "1." A yang line is either a **moving line** or a **static line**. It is symbolic of the male principle, of activity, creativity, and warmth.

Yarrow-Stalk Method
An ancient and traditional method of consulting the **I Ching** as an oracle or an advisor. By a rather complicated process of manipulating 49 yarrow stalks six kinetic lines are selected and a hexagram is determined. The text of this **divining hexagram** and the text to any moving lines is supposed to contain the answer to one's question or to be the advice sought.

Yellow River Map (*Ho T'u*)
Said to have originated with **Fu Hsi**, but was attached to **I Ching** by Ch'en T'uan (ca. 906–989). It is a diagram consisting of groups of dots. The groups represent the numbers 1 to 9 and are correlated with the **Five Agents** and with the four directions. The correlations are: Earth (Center) = 5; Metal (West) = 4 and 9; Water (North) = 1 and 6; Wood (East) = 3 and 8; Fire (South) = 2 and 7.

$$
\begin{matrix}
 & & 7 & & \\
 & & 2 & & \\
 & & 5 & & \\
8 & 3 & 5 & 4 & 9 \\
 & & 5 & & \\
 & & 1 & & \\
 & & 6 & &
\end{matrix}
$$

Note that 5 occupies the center. South is the top (7) and North is the bottom (6). See **Lo River Map** and **Ch'en T'uan**.

Yin Line

A yin line is represented as a broken horizontal line, "━━" or (in this book) as "0." A yin line is either a **moving line** or a **static line**. It is symbolic of the female principle, of passivity, receptiveness, and coldness.

Yo Ching

Translated as the *Book of Music*. See **Five Classics**.

N

WILHELM/BAYNES
CONCORDANCE

1. ANCESTOR, ANCESTORS, ANCESTRESS

Hexagram 16, Image. Thus the ancient kings made music in order to honor merit, and offered it with splendor to the Supreme Deity, inviting their **ancestors** to be present.

Hexagram 35, Line 2. Progressing, but in sorrow. Perseverance brings good fortune. Then one obtains great happiness from one's **ancestress**.

Hexagram 62, Line 2. She passes by her **ancestor** and meets her **ancestress**.

Hexagram 63, Line 3. The Illustrious **Ancestor** (Emperor Wu Ting of the Yin dynasty) disciplines the Devil's Country. After three years he conquers it.

2. ARM Also listed under **PARTS OF THE BODY**

Hexagram 55, Line 3. He breaks his right **arm**.

3. ARMED, ARMS See also **ARROW, WEAPONS**

Hexagram 26, Line 3. Practice chariot driving and **armed** defense daily.

Hexagram 43, Judgment. It does not further to resort to **arms**.

Hexagram 43, Line 2. A cry of alarm. **Arms** at evening and at night.

Hexagram 63, Image. Thus the superior man takes thought of misfortune and **arms** himself against it in advance.

4. ARMIES, ARMY, ATTACK

Hexagram 7, Image. In the middle of the earth is water: The image of the **army**.

Hexagram 7, Judgment. The **army** needs perseverance and a strong man.

Hexagram 7, Line 1. An **army** must set forth in proper order.

Hexagram 7, Line 2. In the midst of the **army**. Good fortune. No blame.

Hexagram 7, Line 3. Perchance the **army** carries corpses in the wagon. Misfortune.

Hexagram 7, Line 4. The **army** retreats. No blame.

Hexagram 7, Line 5. Let the eldest lead the **army**. The youngest transports corpses.

Hexagram 11, Line 6. The wall falls back into the moat. Use no **army** now. Make your commands known within your own town. Perseverance brings humiliation.

Hexagram 13, Line 4. He climbs up on his wall; he cannot **attack**.

Hexagram 15, Line 5. It is favorable to **attack** with force. Nothing that would not further.

Hexagram 15, Line 6. Modesty that comes to expression. It is favorable to set **armies** marching to chastise one's own city and one's country.

Hexagram 16, Judgment. ENTHUSIASM. It furthers one to install helpers and to set **armies** marching.

Hexagram 24, Line 6. If **armies** are set marching in this way, one will in the end suffer a great defeat, disastrous for the ruler of the country. For ten years it will not be possible to **attack** again.

Hexagram 64, Line 3. Before completion, **attack** brings misfortune.

5. ARROW, ARROWS See also ARMS, WEAPONS, BOW

Hexagram 21, Line 4. Bites on dried gristly meat. Receives metal **arrows**.

Hexagram 40, Line 2. One kills three foxes in the field and receives a yellow **arrow**.

Hexagram 56, Line 5. He (the wanderer) shoots a pheasant. It drops with the first **arrow**.

6. AXE

Hexagram 56, Line 4. He obtains his property and an **axe**.
Hexagram 57, Line 6. He loses his property and his **axe**.

7. AXLE

Hexagram 34, Line 4. Power depends upon the **axle** of a big cart.

8. AXLETREES

Hexagram 26, Line 2. The **axletrees** are taken from the wagon.

9. BACK Also listed under PARTS OF THE BODY

Hexagram 40, Line 3. If a man carries a burden on his **back** and nonetheless rides in a carriage, he thereby encourages robbers to draw near.

Hexagram 52, Judgment. Keeping his **back** still so that he no longer feels his body.

10. BAD LUCK

Hexagram 62, Line 6. The flying bird leaves him. Misfortune. This means **bad luck** and injury.

11. BASKET

Hexagram 54, Line 6. The woman holds the **basket**, but there are no fruits in it.

12. BEARD

Hexagram 22, Line 2. Lends grace to the **beard** on his chin.

13. BED

Hexagram 23, Line 1. The leg of the **bed** is split.
Hexagram 23, Line 2. The **bed** is split at the edge.
Hexagram 23, Line 4. The **bed** is split up to the skin.
Hexagram 57, Line 2. Penetration under the **bed**.
Hexagram 57, Line 6. Penetration under the **bed**.

14. BELLY Also listed under **PARTS OF THE BODY**

Hexagram 36, Line 4. He penetrates the left side of the **belly**.

15. BELT See **LEATHER BELT**

16. BEREAVEMENT, GRIEF, GRIEVE

Hexagram 19, Line 3. If one is induced to **grieve** over it, one becomes free of blame.
Hexagram 62, Image. In **bereavement** he (the superior man) gives preponderance to **grief**.

17. BIRD

Hexagram 56, Line 6. The **bird**'s nest burns up.
Hexagram 62, Judgment. The flying **bird** brings the message: It is not well to strive upward, it is well to remain below.
Hexagram 62, Line 1. The **bird** meets with misfortune through flying.
Hexagram 62, Line 6. The flying **bird** leaves him. Misfortune.

18. BLOOD, BLOODY

Hexagram 2, Line 6. Dragons fight in the meadow. Their **blood** is black and yellow.
Hexagram 3, Line 6. **Bloody** tears flow.
Hexagram 5, Line 4. Waiting in **blood**.
Hexagram 9, Line 4. If you are sincere, **blood** vanishes and fear gives way.
Hexagram 54, Line 6. The man stabs the sheep, but no **blood** flows.
Hexagram 59, Line 6. He dissolves his **blood**.

19. BOAR

Hexagram 26, Line 5. The tusk of a gelded **boar**.

20. BODY Also listed under **PARTS OF THE BODY**

Hexagram 51, Line 6. Going ahead brings misfortune. If it has not yet touched one's **body** but has reached one's neighbor first, there is no blame.
Hexagram 52, Judgment. KEEPING STILL. Keeping his back still so that he no longer feels his **body**.

21. BOWL, BOWLS, EARTHEN BOWL, EARTHEN VESSELS

Hexagram 8, Line 1. Truth, like a full **earthen bowl**: Thus in the end good fortune comes from without.
Hexagram 29, Line 4. A jug of wine, a **bowl** of rice with it; **earthen vessels** simply handed through the window.
Hexagram 41, Judgment. One may use two small **bowls** for the sacrifice.

22. BOW See also **ARMS, ARROW, WEAPONS**

Hexagram 38, Line 6. First one draws a **bow** against him, then one lays the **bow** aside.

23. BOY See **LITTLE BOY**

24. BOYLIKE

Hexagram 20, Line 1. **Boylike** contemplation. For an inferior man, no blame. For a superior man, humiliation.

25. BRAKE, BRAKES

Hexagram 44, Line 1. It must be checked with a **brake** of bronze.
Hexagram 63, Line 1. He **brakes** his wheels.
Hexagram 64, Line 2. He **brakes** his wheels.

26. BRANCH See TREE

27. BRONZE

Hexagram 4, Line 3. Take not a maiden who, when she sees a man of **bronze**, loses possession of herself.
Hexagram 44, Line 1. It must be checked with a brake of **bronze**.

28. BULL

Hexagram 26, Line 4. The headboard of a young **bull**. Great good fortune.

29. CALDRON See also TING

Hexagram 50, Judgment. THE **CALDRON**. Supreme good fortune. Success.
Hexagram 50, Image. Fire over wood: The image of the **CALDRON**.

30. CALVES OF THE LEGS Also listed under PARTS OF THE BODY

Hexagram 31, Line 2. The influence shows itself in the **calves** of the legs. Misfortune.
Hexagram 52, Line 2. Keeping his **calves** still.

31. CANGUE

Hexagram 21, Line 6. His neck is fastened in the wooden **cangue**, so that his ears disappear.

32. CAPITAL

Hexagram 42, Line 4. It furthers one to be used in the removal of the **capital**.

33. CARRIAGE See also CART, CHARIOT, WAGON

Hexagram 22, Line 1. He lends grace to his toes, leaves the **carriage**, and walks.

Hexagram 23, Line 6. The superior man receives a **carriage**.

Hexagram 40, Line 3. If a man carries a burden on his back and nonetheless rides in a **carriage**, he thereby encourages robbers to draw near.

Hexagram 47, Line 4. He comes very quietly, oppressed in a golden **carriage**.

Hexagram 63, Line 2. The woman loses the curtain of her **carriage**.

34. CART See also CARRIAGE, CHARIOT, WAGON

Hexagram 34, Line 4. Power depends upon the axle of a big **cart**.

35. CAVE

Hexagram 62, Line 5. The prince shoots and hits him who is in the **cave**.

36. CHALICE See also SACRIFICE

Hexagram 51, Judgment. The shock terrified for a hundred miles, and he does not let fall the sacrificial spoon and **chalice**.

37. CHARIOT See also CARRIAGE, CART, WAGON

Hexagram 26, Line 3. Practice **chariot** driving and armed defense daily.

38. CHEEKS, CHEEKBONES See also PARTS OF THE BODY

Hexagram 31, Line 6. The influence shows itself in the jaws, **cheeks**, and tongue.

Hexagram 43, Line 3. To be powerful in the **cheekbones** brings misfortune.

39. CHILD

Hexagram 37, Line 3. When woman and **child** dally and laugh, it leads in the end to humiliation.

Hexagram 53, Line 3. The woman carries a **child** but does not bring it forth. Misfortune.

Hexagram 53, Line 5. For three years the woman has no **child**. In the end nothing can hinder her. Good fortune.

40. CHILDLIKE

Hexagram 4, Line 5. **Childlike** folly brings good fortune.

41. CHIN Also listed under **PARTS OF THE BODY**

Hexagram 22, Line 2. Lends grace to the beard on his **chin.**

42. CITIZENS

Hexagram 8, Line 5. In the hunt the king uses beaters on three sides only and foregoes game that runs off in front. The **citizens** need no warning. Good fortune.
Hexagram 25, Line 3. Undeserved misfortune. The cow that was tethered by someone is the wanderer's gain, the **citizen**'s loss.

43. CITY See **TOWN**

44. CLAN, CLANS

Hexagram 13, Image. Thus the superior man organizes the **clans** and makes distinctions between things.
Hexagram 13, Line 2. Fellowship with men in the **clan**. Humiliation.

45. CLOTHES See **GARMENTS**

46. CLOUD, CLOUDS Occurrences in Images not listed

Hexagram 9, Judgment. Dense **clouds**, no rain from the western region.
Hexagram 53, Line 6. The wild goose gradually draws near the **cloud** heights.
Hexagram 62, Line 5. Dense **clouds**, no rain from our western territory.

47. COCKCROW

Hexagram 61, Line 6. **Cockcrow** penetrating to heaven.

48. COLORS

Hexagram 2, Line 5. A **yellow** lower garment brings supreme good fortune.
Hexagram 2, Line 6. Dragons fight in the meadow. Their blood

is **black** and **yellow**.

Hexagram 21, Line 5. Bites on dried lean meat. Receives **yellow** gold.

Hexagram 22, Line 4. A **white** horse comes as if on wings.

Hexagram 28, Line 1. To spread **white** rushes underneath. No blame.

Hexagram 30, Line 2. **Yellow** light. Supreme good fortune.

Hexagram 33, Line 2. He holds him fast with **yellow** oxhide. No one can tear him loose.

Hexagram 40, Line 2. One kills three foxes in the field and receives a **yellow** arrow.

Hexagram 47, Line 2. The man with the **scarlet** knee bands is just coming.

Hexagram 47, Line 4. He comes very quietly, oppressed in a **golden** carriage.

Hexagram 47, Line 5. Oppression at the hands of the man with the **purple** knee bands.

Hexagram 49, Line 1. Wrapped in the hide of a **yellow** cow.

Hexagram 50, Line 5. The ting has **yellow** handles, **golden** carrying rings.

49. COMPANION, COMPANIONS, COMPANY

Hexagram 11, Line 2. Bearing with the uncultured in gentleness, fording the river with resolution, not neglecting what is distant, not regarding one's **companions**; thus one may manage to walk in the middle.

Hexagram 17, Line 1. To go out of the door in **company** produces deeds.

Hexagram 38, Line 5. The **companion** bites his way through the wrappings.

Hexagram 38, Line 6. Isolated through opposition, one sees one's **companion** as a pig covered with dirt, as a wagon full of devils.

Hexagram 40, Line 4. Deliver yourself from your great toe. Then the **companion** comes, and him you can trust.

Hexagram 41, Line 3. When one man journeys alone, he finds a **companion**.

50. COMRADES See FRIENDS

51. CONCUBINE

Hexagram 50, Line 1. One takes a **concubine** for the sake of her son.

Hexagram 54, Line 1. The marrying maiden as a **concubine.**

Hexagram 54, Line 3. The marrying maiden as a slave. She marries as a **concubine.**

52. CORPSES

Hexagram 7, Line 3. Perchance the army carries **corpses** in the wagon. Misfortune.

Hexagram 7, Line 5. Let the eldest lead the army. The youngest transports **corpses.**

53. COUNTRY, KINGDOM

Hexagram 15, Line 6. It is favorable to set armies marching to chastise one's own city and one's **country.**

Hexagram 20, Line 4. Contemplation of the light of the **kingdom.**

Hexagram 24, Line 6. If armies are set marching in this way, one will in the end suffer a great defeat, disastrous for the ruler of the **country.**

Hexagram 63, Line 3. The Illustrious Ancestor disciplines the Devil's **Country.**

Hexagram 64, Line 4. Shock, thus to discipline the Devil's **Country.**

54. COURT LADIES See also MAIDEN

Hexagram 23, Line 5. A shoal of fishes. Favor comes through the **court ladies.**

55. COURTYARD

Hexagram 36, Line 4. One gets at the very heart of the darkening of the light, and leaves gate and **courtyard.**

Hexagram 52, Judgment. He goes into his **courtyard** and does not see his people.

Hexagram 60, Line 1. Not going out of the door and the **courtyard** is without blame.

Hexagram 60, Line 2. Not going out of the gate and the **courtyard** brings misfortune.

56. COW

Hexagram 25, Line 3. Undeserved misfortune. The **cow** that was tethered by someone is the wanderer's gain, the citizen's loss.

Hexagram 30, Judgment. Care of the **cow** brings good fortune.

Hexagram 49, Line 1. Wrapped in the hide of a yellow **cow**.

Hexagram 56, Line 6. Through carelessness he (the wanderer) loses his **cow.** Misfortune.

57. CRANE

Hexagram 61, Line 2. A **crane** calling in the shade. Its young answers it.

58. CRIPPLED MEN: ONE-EYED MAN, LAME MAN

Hexagram 10, Line 3. A **one-eyed man** is able to see, a **lame man** is able to tread, he treads on the tail of the tiger. The tiger bites the man. Misfortune.

Hexagram 54, Line 1. A **lame man** who is able to tread.

Hexagram 54, Line 2. A **one-eyed** man who is able to see.

59. CRIES, CRY

Hexagram 43, Line 2. A **cry** of alarm.

Hexagram 43, Line 6. No **cry**.

Hexagram 59, Line 5. His loud **cries** are as dissolving as sweat. Dissolution!

60. CROSS THE GREAT WATER See also WATER

Hexagram 5, Judgment. It furthers one to **cross the great water**.

Hexagram 6, Judgment. It does not further one to **cross the great water**.

Hexagram 13, Judgment. It furthers one to **cross the great water**.

Hexagram 15, Line 1. A superior man modest about his modesty may **cross the great water**. Good fortune.

Hexagram 18, Image. It furthers one to **cross the great water**.

Hexagram 26, Judgment. It furthers one to **cross the great water**.

Hexagram 27, Line 5. One should not **cross the great water**.

Hexagram 27, Line 6. It furthers one to **cross the great water**.

Hexagram 42, Judgment. It furthers one to **cross the great water**.

Hexagram 59, Judgment. It furthers one to **cross the great water**.

Hexagram 61, Judgment. It furthers one to **cross the great water**.

Hexagram 64, Line 3. It furthers one to **cross the great water**.

61. CURTAIN, CURTAINS

Hexagram 55, Line 2. The **curtains** are of such fullness that the polestars can be seen at noon.

Hexagram 55, Line 4. The **curtain** is of such fullness that the polestars can be seen at noon.

Hexagram 63, Line 2. The woman loses the **curtain** of her carriage.

62. DANCE See SACRED DANCE

63. DARK MAN

Hexagram 10, Line 2. The perseverance of a **dark man** brings good fortune.

64. DECORATION

Hexagram 7, Line 2. The king bestows, a triple **decoration**.

65. DEER

Hexagram 3, Line 3. Whoever hunts the **deer** without the forester only loses his way in the forest.

66. DEVIL, DEVILS

Hexagram 38, Line 6. Isolated through opposition, one sees one's companion as a pig covered with dirt, as a wagon full of **devils**.

Hexagram 63, Line 3. The Illustrious Ancestor (Emperor Wu Ting of the Yin dynasty) disciplines the **Devil**'s Country. After three years he conquers it.

Hexagram 64, Line 4. Shock, thus to discipline the **Devil**'s Country.

67. DIRECTIONS: EAST, NORTH, NORTHEAST, SOUTH, SOUTHWEST, WEST, WESTERN

Hexagram 2, Judgment. It is favorable to find friends in the **west** and **south**, to forego friends in the **east** and **north**.

Hexagram 9, Judgment. Dense clouds, no rain from the **western** region.

Hexagram 17, Line 6. The king introduces him to the **Western Mountain**.

Hexagram 36, Line 3. Darkening of the light during the hunt in the **south**.

Hexagram 39, Judgment. OBSTRUCTION. The **southwest** furthers. The **northeast** does not further.

Hexagram 40, Judgment. DELIVERANCE. The **southwest** furthers.

Hexagram 46, Judgment. Departure towards the **south** brings good fortune.

Hexagram 62, Line 5. Dense clouds, no rain from our **western** territory.

Hexagram 63, Line 5. The neighbor in the **east** who slaughters an ox does not attain as much real happiness as the neighbor in the **west** with his small offering.

68. DISCIPLINE, DISCIPLINES

Hexagram 4, Line 1. To make a fool develop it furthers one to apply **discipline**.

Hexagram 63, Line 3. The Illustrious Ancestor (Emperor Wu Ting of the Yin dynasty) **disciplines** the Devil's Country. After three years he conquers it.

Hexagram 64, Line 4. Shock, thus to **discipline** the Devil's Country.

69. DOOR See also **GATE**

Hexagram 17, Line 1. To go out of the **door** in company produces deeds.

Hexagram 20, Line 2. Contemplation through the crack of the **door**.

Hexagram 60, Line 1. Not going out of the **door** and the courtyard is without blame.

70. DRAGONS

Hexagram 1, Line 1. Hidden **dragon**. Do not act.

Hexagram 1, Line 2. **Dragon** appearing in the field.

Hexagram 1, Line 5. Flying **dragon** in the heavens.

Hexagram 1, Line 6. Arrogant **dragon** will have cause to repent.

Hexagram 1, Lines 1–6. There appears a flight of **dragons** without heads.

Hexagram 2, Line 6. **Dragons** fight in the meadow. Their blood is black and yellow.

71. DRINK, DRINKING, EATING, EATING and DRINKING, FRUIT, MEAT, MEAT AND DRINK, FOOD

Hexagram 5, Image. Thus the superior man **eats and drinks**, is joyous and of good cheer.

Hexagram 5, Line 5. Waiting at **meat and drink**.

Hexagram 21, Line 2. Bites through tender **meat**, so that his nose disappears.

Hexagram 21, Line 3. Bites on old dried **meat** and strikes on something poisonous.

Hexagram 21, Line 4. Bites on dried gristly **meat**. Receives metal arrows.

Hexagram 21, Line 5. Bites on dried lean **meat**.

Hexagram 23, Line 6. There is a large **fruit** still uneaten.

Hexagram 26, Judgment. Not **eating** at home brings good fortune.

Hexagram 27, Image. Thus the superior man is careful of his words and temperate in **eating and drinking**.

Hexagram 37, Line 2. She (wife) should not follow her whims. She must attend within to the **food**.

Hexagram 47, Line 2. One is oppressed while at **meat and drink**.

Hexagram 48, Line 1. One does not **drink** the mud of the well. No animals come to an old well.

Hexagram 48, Line 3. The well is cleaned, but no one **drinks** from it.

Hexagram 48, Line 5. In the well there is a clear, cool spring from which one can **drink**.

Hexagram 50, Line 2. There is **food** in the ting.

Hexagram 53, Line 2. **Eating and drinking** in peace and concord.

Hexagram 54, Line 6. The woman holds the basket, but there are no **fruits** in it.

Hexagram 64, Line 6. There is **drinking** of wine in genuine confidence.

72. DRUM

Hexagram 61, Line 3. Now he beats the **drum**, now he stops.

73. EARS Also listed under PARTS OF THE BODY

Hexagram 21, Line 6. His neck is fastened in the wooden cangue so that his **ears** disappear. Misfortune.

74. EARTHEN BOWL See **BOWL**

75. EAST See **DIRECTIONS**

76. ELDEST See **YOUNGER**

77. ENEMY

> Hexagram 5, Line 3. Waiting in the mud. Brings about the arrival of the **enemy**.

78. ESTABLISHED ORDER

> Hexagram 34, Image. Thus the superior man does not tread upon paths that do not accord with **established order**.

79. EVIL PEOPLE, WRONG PEOPLE See also **INFERIOR PEOPLE**

> Hexagram 8, Line 3. You hold together with the **wrong people**.
> Hexagram 12, Judgment. **Evil people** do not further the perseverance of the superior man.
> Hexagram 38, Line 1. When you see **evil people** guard yourself against mistakes.

80. EYES See also **PARTS OF THE BODY**

> Hexagram 9, Line 3. The spokes burst out of the wagon wheels. Man and wife roll their **eyes**.
> Hexagram 27, Line 4. Spying about with sharp **eyes** like a tiger with insatiable craving. No blame.

81. FAMILIES, FAMILY

> Hexagram 7, Line 6. The great prince issues commands, founds states, vests **families** with fiefs.
> Hexagram 37, Judgment. THE **FAMILY**. The perseverance of the woman furthers.
> Hexagram 37, Image. Wind comes forth from fire: the image of THE **FAMILY**.
> Hexagram 37, Line 1. Firm seclusion within the **family**.
> Hexagram 37, Line 3. When tempers flare up in the **family**, too great severity brings remorse.

Hexagram 37, Line 5. As a king approaches his **family**.
Hexagram 55, Line 6. He screens off his **family**.

82. FATHER, MOTHER See also SON

Hexagram 18, Line 1. Setting right what has been spoiled by the **father**. If there is a son, no blame rests upon the departed **father**.
Hexagram 18, Line 2. Setting right what has been spoiled by the **mother**.
Hexagram 18, Line 3. Setting right what has been spoiled by the **father**.
Hexagram 18, Line 4. Tolerating what has been spoiled by the **father**.
Hexagram 18, Line 5. Setting right what has been spoiled by the **father**.

83. FEATHERS

Hexagram 53, Line 6. Its (wild goose) **feathers** can be used for the sacred dance. Good fortune.

84. FEET Also listed under PARTS OF THE BODY

Hexagram 21, Line 1. His **feet** are fastened in the stocks, so that his toes disappear. No blame.
Hexagram 47, Line 5. His nose and **feet** are cut off.

85. FEUDAL LORDS See LORDS

86. FIELD See MEADOW

87. FISH, FISHES

Hexagram 23, Line 5. A shoal of **fishes**.
Hexagram 44, Line 2. There is a **fish** in the tank.
Hexagram 44, Line 4. No **fish** in tank.
Hexagram 48, Line 2. At the wellhole one shoots **fishes**.
Hexagram 61, Judgment. Pigs and **fishes**.

88. FOOL, FOOLS, FOLLY

Hexagram 4, Judgment. Youthful **folly** has success. It is not I who seek the young **fool**; the young **fool** seeks me.
Hexagram 4, Line 1. To make a **fool** develop it furthers one to apply discipline.

Hexagram 4, Line 2. To bear with **fools** in kindness brings good fortune.
Hexagram 4, Line 4. Entangled **folly** brings humiliation.
Hexagram 4, Line 5. Childlike **folly** brings good fortune.
Hexagram 4, Line 6. In punishing **folly** it does not further one to commit transgressions.

89. FOOTPRINTS

Hexagram 30, Line 1. The **footprints** run crisscross.

90. FOREST, FORESTER

Hexagram 3, Line 3. Whoever hunts the deer without the **forester** only loses his way in the **forest**.

91. FORESTER See FOREST

92. FOUR QUARTERS OF THE WORLD, FOUR QUARTERS OF HEAVEN

Hexagram 30, Image. Thus the great man, by perpetuating this brightness, illumines the **four quarters of the world**.
Hexagram 44, Image. Thus does the prince act when disseminating his commands and proclaiming them to the **four quarters of heaven**.

93. FOX, FOXES

Hexagram 40, Line 2. One kills three **foxes** in the field and receives a yellow arrow.
Hexagram 64, Judgment. But if the little **fox**, after nearly completing the crossing, gets his tail in the water, there is nothing that would further.

94. FRIENDS, FRIENDLY, COMRADES See also COMPANION

Hexagram 2, Judgment. It is favorable to find **friends** in the west and south, to forego **friends** in the east and north.
Hexagram 8, Image. Thus the kings of antiquity bestowed the different states as fiefs and cultivated **friendly** relations with the feudal lords.
Hexagram 16, Line 4. You gather **friends** around you as a hair clasp gathers the hair.
Hexagram 24, Judgment. **Friends** come without blame.
Hexagram 31, Line 4. If a man is agitated in mind, and his

thoughts go hither and thither, only those **friends** on whom he fixes his conscious thoughts will follow.

Hexagram 33, Line 5. **Friendly** retreat.

Hexagram 39, Line 5. In the midst of the greatest obstructions, **friends** come.

Hexagram 50, Line 2. My **comrades** are envious, but they cannot hurt me.

Hexagram 51, Line 2. One's **comrades** have something to talk about.

Hexagram 58, Image. Thus the superior man joins with his **friends** for discussion and practice.

Hexagram 61, Line 3. He finds a **comrade**.

95. FRUIT See DRINK

96. GAME See HUNT

97. GARDENS

Hexagram 22, Line 5. Grace in hills and **gardens**.

98. GARMENT, CLOTHES

Hexagram 2, Line 5. A yellow lower **garment** brings supreme good fortune.

Hexagram 54, Line 5. The embroidered **garments** of the princess were not as gorgeous as those of the servingmaid.

Hexagram 63, Line 4. The finest **clothes** turn to rags.

99. GATE See also DOOR

Hexagram 13, Line 1. Fellowship with men at the **gate**. No blame.

Hexagram 36, Line 4. One gets at the very heart of the darkening of the light, and leaves **gate** and courtyard.

Hexagram 55, Line 6. He peers through the **gate** and no longer perceives anyone.

Hexagram 60, Line 2. Not going out of the **gate** and the courtyard brings misfortune.

100. GOAT

Hexagram 34, Line 3. A **goat** butts against a hedge and gets its horns entangled.
Hexagram 34, Line 5. Loses the **goat** with ease. No remorse.
Hexagram 34, Line 6. A **goat** butts against a hedge. It cannot go forward, it cannot go backward.

101. GOBLET

Hexagram 61, Line 2. I have a good **goblet**. I will share it with you.

102. GOD See **SUPREME DEITY**

103. GOLD, GOLDEN See also **COLOR**

Hexagram 21, Line 5. Bites on dried lean meat. Receives yellow **gold**.
Hexagram 47, Line 4. He comes very quietly, oppressed in a **golden** carriage.
Hexagram 50, Line 5. The ting has yellow handles, **golden** carrying rings.

104. GOOSE See **WILD GOOSE**

105. GOSSIP

Hexagram 36, Line 1. The host has occasion to **gossip** about him (the superior man).
Hexagram 5, Line 2. There is some **gossip**.
Hexagram 6, Line 1. There is a little **gossip**.

106. GOVERNMENT

Hexagram 49, Line 4. Changing the form of **government** brings good fortune.

107. GRASS, SOD

Hexagram 11, Line 1. When ribbon **grass** is pulled up, the **sod** comes with it.
Hexagram 12, Line 1. When ribbon **grass** is pulled up, the **sod** comes with it.

108. GREAT, GREAT LEADER, GREAT MAN See also KING, PRINCE, SUPERIOR MAN

Hexagram 11, Judgment. The small departs, the **great** approaches.

Hexagram 12, Judgment. The **great** departs; the small approaches.

Hexagram 12, Line 2. The standstill serves to help the **great man** to attain success.

Hexagram 12, Line 5. Good fortune for the **great man**. "What if it should fail, what if it should fail?" In this way he ties it to a cluster of mulberry shoots.

Hexagram 26, Judgment. THE TAMING POWER OF THE **GREAT**.

Hexagram 26, Image. Heaven within the mountain: THE TAMING POWER OF THE **GREAT**.

Hexagram 28, Judgment. PREPONDERANCE OF THE **GREAT**.

Hexagram 28, Image. THE IMAGE OF PREPONDERANCE OF THE **GREAT**.

Hexagram 30, Image. Thus the **great man**, by perpetuating this brightness, illumines the four quarters of the world.

Hexagram 34, Judgment. THE POWER OF THE **GREAT**.

Hexagram 34, Image. THE IMAGE OF THE POWER OF THE **GREAT**.

Hexagram 36, Line 3. Their **great leader** is captured.

Hexagram 47, Judgment. The **great man** brings about good fortune.

Hexagram 49, Line 5. The **great man** changes like a tiger.

Hexagram 1, Line 2. It furthers one to see the **great man**.

Hexagram 1, Line 5. It furthers one to see the **great man**.

Hexagram 6, Judgment. It furthers one to see the **great man**.

Hexagram 39, Judgment. It furthers one to see the **great man**.

Hexagram 39, Line 6. It furthers one to see the **great man**.

Hexagram 45, Judgment. It furthers one to see the **great man**.

Hexagram 46, Judgment. One must see the **great man**.

Hexagram 57, Judgment. It furthers one to see the **great man**.

109. GRIEF See BEREAVEMENT

110. GUEST, GUESTS

Hexagram 5, Line 6. Three uninvited **guests** arrive. Honor them, and in the end there will be good fortune.

Hexagram 20, Line 4. Contemplation of the light of the kingdom. It furthers one to exert influence as the **guest** of a king.
Hexagram 44, Line 2. Does not further **guests**.

111. HAIR, HAIR CLASP See also PARTS OF THE BODY

Hexagram 16, Line 4. You gather friends around you as a **hair clasp** gathers the hair.
Hexagram 38, Line 3. One sees the wagon dragged back, the oxen halted, a man's **hair** and nose cut off.

112. HAND, HANDS Also listed under PARTS OF THE BODY

Hexagram 26, Line 1. Danger is at **hand**.
Hexagram 45, Line 1. If you call out, then after one grasp of the **hand** you can laugh again.
Hexagram 47, Line 5. Oppression at the **hands** of the man with the purple knee bands.

113. HAMSTER

Hexagram 35, Line 4. Progress like a **hamster**. Perseverance brings danger.

114. HARVEST

Hexagram 25, Line 2. If one does not count on the **harvest** while plowing, nor on the use of the ground while clearing it, it furthers one to undertake something.

115. HAWK

Hexagram 40, Line 6. The prince shoots at a **hawk** on a high wall. He kills it.

116. HEAD See also PARTS OF THE BODY

Hexagram 1, Lines 1–6. There appears a flight of dragons without **heads**.
Hexagram 8, Line 6. He finds no **head** for holding together.
Hexagram 28, Line 6. It (water) goes over one's **head**.
Hexagram 63, Line 6. He gets his **head** in the water.
Hexagram 64, Line 6. But if one wets his **head**, he loses it, in truth.

117. HEADBOARD

Hexagram 26, Line 4. The **headboard** of a young bull. Great good fortune.

118. HEART See also PARTS OF THE BODY

Hexagram 29, Judgment. If you are sincere, you have success in your **heart**, and whatever you do succeeds.

Hexagram 35, Line 5. Take not gain and loss to **heart**.

Hexagram 36, Line 4. One gets at the very **heart** of the darkening of the light, and leaves gate and courtyard.

Hexagram 42, Line 5. If in truth you have a kind **heart**, ask not.

Hexagram 42, Line 6. He does not keep his **heart** constantly steady.

Hexagram 48, Line 3. This is my **heart's** sorrow, for one might draw from it (the well).

Hexagram 52, Line 2. His **heart** is not glad.

Hexagram 52, Line 3. The **heart** suffocates.

Hexagram 56, Line 4. He obtains his property and an ax. My **heart** is not glad.

119. HEAVEN, HEAVENS Occurrences in Images not listed

Hexagram 1, Line 5. Flying dragons in the **heavens**.

Hexagram 14, Line 3. A prince offers it to the Son of **Heaven**.

Hexagram 14, Line 6. He is blessed by **heaven**.

Hexagram 26, Line 6. One attains the way of **heaven**.

Hexagram 36, Line 6. First he climbed up to **heaven**, then he plunged into the depths of the earth.

Hexagram 44, Line 5. A melon covered with willow leaves. Hidden lines. Then it drops down to one from **heaven**.

Hexagram 61, Line 6. Cockcrow penetrating to **heaven**.

120. HEDGE

Hexagram 29, Line 6. Bound with cords and ropes, shut in between thorn-**hedged** prison walls: For three years one does not find the way.

Hexagram 34, Line 3. A goat butts against a **hedge** and gets its horns entangled.

Hexagram 34, Line 4. The **hedge** opens; there is no entanglement.

Hexagram 34, Line 6. A goat butts against a **hedge**. It cannot go forward, it cannot go backward.

121. HELPERS

Hexagram 3, Judgment. It furthers one to appoint **helpers**.
Hexagram 3, Line 1. It furthers one to appoint **helpers**.
Hexagram 16, Judgment. It furthers one to install **helpers** and to set armies marching.

122. HIDE See also OXHIDE

Hexagram 49, Line 1. Wrapped in the **hide** of a yellow cow.

123. HILL, HILLS, NINE HILLS

Hexagram 13, Line 3. He hides weapons in the thicket; he climbs the high **hill** in front of it.
Hexagram 22, Line 5. Grace in **hills** and gardens.
Hexagram 27, Line 2. Turning to the summit for nourishment, deviating from the path to seek nourishment from the **hill**.
Hexagram 51, Line 2. A hundred thousand times you lose your treasures and must climb the **nine hills**.

124. HIPS See also PARTS OF THE BODY

Hexagram 52, Line 3. Keeping his **hips** still.

125. HITS See STRIKE

126. HOARFROST, ICE

Hexagram 2, Line 1. When there is **hoarfrost** underfoot, solid **ice** is not far off.

127. HOME, HOUSE, HOUSEHOLD, HOUSEHOLDS

Hexagram 4, Line 2. The son is capable of taking charge of the **household**.
Hexagram 6, Line 2. One returns **home**, gives way.
Hexagram 6, Line 2. The people of his town, three hundred **households**, remain free of guilt.
Hexagram 23, Line 6. The **house** of the inferior man is split apart.
Hexagram 26, Judgment. Not eating at **home** brings good fortune.
Hexagram 37, Line 4. She (wife) is the treasure of the **house**.
Hexagram 41, Line 6. One obtains servants but no longer has a separate **home**.

Hexagram 47, Line 3. He enters his **house** and does not see his wife.
Hexagram 55, Line 6. His **house** is in a state of abundance. Misfortune.

128. HORNS

Hexagram 34, Line 3. A goat butts against a hedge and gets its **horns** entangled.
Hexagram 35, Line 6. Making progress with the **horns** is permissible only for the purpose of punishing one's own city.
Hexagram 44, Line 6. He comes to meet with his **horns**.

129. HORSE

Hexagram 3, Line 2. **Horse** and wagon part.
Hexagram 3, Line 4. **Horse** and wagon part.
Hexagram 3, Line 6. **Horse** and wagon part.
Hexagram 22, Line 4. A white **horse** comes as if on wings.
Hexagram 26, Line 3. A good **horse** that follows others.
Hexagram 35, Judgment. The powerful prince is honored with **horses** in large numbers.
Hexagram 36, Line 2. He gives aid with the strength of a **horse**. Good fortune.
Hexagram 38, Line 1. If you lose your **horse**, do not run after it; it will come back of its own accord.
Hexagram 59, Line 1. He brings help with the strength of a **horse**. Good fortune.
Hexagram 61, Line 4. The team **horse** goes astray. No blame.

130. HOUSE See HOME

131. HUNT, HUNTS, GAME

Hexagram 3, Line 3. Whoever **hunts** deer without the forester only loses his way in the forest.
Hexagram 7, Line 5. There is **game** in the field. It furthers one to catch it.
Hexagram 8, Line 5. In the **hunt** the king uses beaters on three sides only and foregoes **game** that runs off in front.
Hexagram 32, Line 4. No **game** in field.
Hexagram 36, Line 3. Darkening of the light during the **hunt** in the south.
Hexagram 57, Line 4. During the **hunt** three kinds of **game** are caught.

132. HUSBAND See MAN, HUSBAND AND WIFE

133. ILL, ILLNESS, DIE

Hexagram 16, Line 5. Persistently **ill**, and still does not **die**.
Hexagram 25, Line 5. Use no medicine in an **illness** incurred through no fault of your own. It will pass of itself.

134. INFERIOR MAN, INFERIOR MEN, INFERIOR PEOPLE, PETTY MAN See also EVIL PEOPLE, ORDINARY MEN, SMALL, WRONG PEOPLE

Hexagram 7, Line 6. **Inferior people** should not be employed.
Hexagram 12, Line 2. They bear and endure; this means good fortune for **inferior people**.
Hexagram 14, Line 3. A prince offers it to the Son of Heaven. A **petty man** cannot do this.
Hexagram 20, Line 1. Boylike contemplation. For an **inferior man**, no blame. For a superior man, humiliation.
Hexagram 23, Line 6. The house of the **inferior man** is split apart.
Hexagram 33, Image. Thus the superior man keeps the **inferior man** at a distance, not angrily but with reserve.
Hexagram 33, Line 4. Voluntary retreat brings good fortune to the superior man and downfall to the **inferior man**.
Hexagram 34, Line 3. The **inferior man** works through power. The superior man does not act thus.
Hexagram 40, Line 5. If only the superior man can deliver himself, it brings good fortune. Thus he proves to **inferior men** that he is in earnest.
Hexagram 49, Line 6. The **inferior man** molts in the face.
Hexagram 63, Line 3. **Inferior people** must not be employed.

135. INJURY See also ILL

Hexagram 62, Line 6. The flying bird leaves him. Misfortune. This means bad luck and **injury**.

136. INN

Hexagram 56, Line 2. The wanderer comes to an **inn**.
Hexagram 56, Line 3. The wanderer's **inn** burns down.

137. JADE

Hexagram 50, Line 6. The ting has rings of **jade**.

138. JAWS Also listed under **PARTS OF THE BODY**

Hexagram 31, Line 6. The influence shows itself in the **jaws**, cheeks, and tongue.
Hexagram 52, Line 5. Keeping his **jaws** still. The words have order.

139. JOY, JOYOUS, JOYOUSNESS

Hexagram 5, Image. Thus the superior man eats and drinks, is **joyous** and of good cheer.
Hexagram 47, Line 5. **Joy** comes softly.
Hexagram 58, Judgment. THE **JOYOUS**. Success.
Hexagram 58, Image. Lakes resting one on the other: The image of THE **JOYOUS**.
Hexagram 58, Image. Lakes resting one on the other: The image of THE **JOYOUS**.
Hexagram 58, Line 1. Contented **joyousness**. Good fortune.
Hexagram 58, Line 2. Sincere **joyousness**. Good fortune. Remorse disappears.
Hexagram 58, Line 3. Coming **joyousness**. Misfortune.
Hexagram 58, Line 4. **Joyousness** that is weighed is not at peace. After ridding himself of mistakes a man has **joy**.
Hexagram 58, Line 6. Seductive **joyousness**.

140. JUG

Hexagram 29, Line 4. A **jug** of wine, a bowl of rice with it; earthen vessels simply handed through the window.
Hexagram 48, Judgment. If one gets down almost to the water (in the well) and the rope does not go all the way, or the **jug** breaks, it brings misfortune.
Hexagram 48, Line 2. The **jug** is broken and leaks.

141. JUSTICE

Hexagram 21, Judgment. It is favorable to let **justice** be administered.

142. KILL, KILLS

Hexagram 30, Line 6. Then it is best to **kill** the leaders and take captive the followers. No blame.
Hexagram 40, Line 2. One **kills** three foxes in the field and receives a yellow arrow.
Hexagram 40, Line 6. The prince shoots at a hawk on a high wall. He **kills** it.

143. KING, RULER, SON OF HEAVEN, SOVEREIGN See also LORD

Hexagram 2, Line 3. If by chance you are in the service of a **king**, seek not works, but bring to completion.

Hexagram 6, Line 3. If by chance you are in the service of a **king**, seek not works.

Hexagram 7, Line 2. The **king** bestows a triple decoration.

Hexagram 8, Image. Thus the **kings** of antiquity bestowed the different states as fiefs and cultivated friendly relations with the feudal lords.

Hexagram 8, Line 5. In the hunt the **king** uses beaters on three sides only and foregoes game that runs off in front.

Hexagram 11, Image. Thus the **ruler** divides and completes the course of heaven and earth; he furthers and regulates the gifts of heaven and earth, and so aids the people.

Hexagram 11, Line 5. The **sovereign** I gives his daughter in marriage.

Hexagram 12, Line 4. He who acts at the command of **the highest** remains without blame.

Hexagram 14, Line 3. A prince offers it to the **Son of Heaven**.

Hexagram 16, Image. Thus the ancient **kings** made music in order to honor merit, and offered it with splendor to the Supreme Deity, inviting their ancestors to be present.

Hexagram 17, Line 6. The **king** introduces him to the Western Mountain.

Hexagram 18, Line 6. He does not serve **kings** and princes, sets himself higher goals.

Hexagram 20, Image. Thus the **kings** of old visited the regions of the world, contemplated the people and gave them instruction.

Hexagram 20, Line 4. It furthers one to exert influence as the guest of a **king**.

Hexagram 21, Image. Thus the **kings** of former times made firm the laws through clearly defined penalties.

Hexagram 24, Image. Thus the **kings** of antiquity closed the passes at the time of solstice. Merchants and strangers did not go about, and the **ruler** did not travel through the provinces.

Hexagram 24, Line 6. If armies are set marching in this way, one will in the end suffer a great defeat, disastrous for the **ruler** of the country.

Hexagram 25, Image. Thus the **kings** of old, rich in virtue, and in harmony with the time, fostered and nourished all beings.

Hexagram 30, Line 6. The **king** uses him to march forth and chastise.

Hexagram 37, Line 5. As a **king** he approaches his family.

Hexagram 39, Line 2. The **king's** servant is beset by obstruction upon obstruction, but it is not his own fault.

Hexagram 42, Line 2. The **king** presents him before God. Good fortune.

Hexagram 43, Judgment. One must resolutely make the matter known at the court of the **king**.

Hexagram 45, Judgment. The **king** approaches his temple.

Hexagram 46, Line 4. The **king** offers him Mount Ch'i.

Hexagram 48, Line 3. If the **king** were clear-minded, good fortune might be enjoyed in common.

Hexagram 54, Line 5. The **sovereign** I gave his daughter in marriage.

Hexagram 55, Judgment. The **king** attains abundance.

Hexagram 55, Line 1. When a man meets his destined **ruler**, they can be together ten days, and it is not a mistake.

Hexagram 55, Line 4. He meets his **ruler**, who is of like kind. Good fortune.

Hexagram 59, Judgment. The **king** approaches his temple.

Hexagram 59, Image. Thus the **kings** of old sacrificed to the Lord and built temples.

Hexagram 59, Line 5. A **king** abides without blame.

144. KNEE Also listed under **PARTS OF THE BODY**

Hexagram 47, Line 2. The man with the scarlet **knee** bands is just coming.

Hexagram 47, Line 5. Oppression at the hands of the man with the purple **knee** bands.

145. LAME MAN See, **CRIPPLED MAN**

146. LAMENT See also **TEARS** and **LAUGHTER**

147. LAWS See also **PENALTIES**

148. LAWSUITS

Hexagram 55, Image. Thus the superior man decides **lawsuits** and carries out punishments.

Hexagram 56, Image. Thus the superior man is clear-minded and cautious in imposing penalties and protracts no **lawsuits**.

149. LAUGHTER, LAUGHING See also **TEARS AND LAUGHTER**

150. LEADER See also **GREAT**

151. LEATHER BELT

> Hexagram 6, Line 6. Even if by chance a **leather belt** is bestowed on one, by the end of the morning it will have been snatched away three times.

152. LEAVES See **WILLOW LEAVES**

153. LIMITATION

> Hexagram 60, Judgment. LIMITATION. Success. Galling **limitation** must not be persevered in.
> Hexagram 60, Image. Water over lake: the image of **LIMITATION**.
> Hexagram 60, Line 3. He who knows no **limitation** will have cause to lament. No blame.
> Hexagram 60, Line 4. Contented **limitation**. Success.
> Hexagram 60, Line 5. Sweet **limitation** brings good fortune. Going brings esteem.
> Hexagram 60, Line 5. Galling **limitation**.

154. LINES

> Hexagram 2, Line 3. Hidden **lines**.
> Hexagram 55, Line 5. **Lines** are coming, blessing and fame draw near. Good fortune.

155. LITTLE BOY See also **BOYLIKE**

> Hexagram 17, Line 2. If one clings to the **little boy**, one loses the strong man.
> Hexagram 17, Line 3. If one clings to the strong man, one loses the **little boy**.

156. LORD, LORDS See also **KING, SUPREME DEITY**

> Hexagram 8, Image. Thus the kings of antiquity bestowed the different states as fiefs and cultivated friendly relations with the feudal **lords**.
> Hexagram 38, Line 2. One meets his **lord** in a narrow street.

157. MAGICIANS

Hexagram 57, Line 2. Priests and **magicians** are used in great number.

158. MAIDEN, WOMAN, COURT LADIES

Hexagram 3, Line 2. The **maiden** is chaste, she does not pledge herself. Ten years—then she pledges herself.

Hexagram 4, Line 2. To know how to take **women** brings good fortune.

Hexagram 4, Line 3. Take not a **maiden** who, when she sees a man of bronze, loses possession of herself.

Hexagram 9, Line 6. Perseverance brings the **woman** into danger. The moon is nearly full. Misfortune comes.

Hexagram 20, Line 2. Contemplation through the crack of the door. Furthering for the perseverance of a **woman**.

Hexagram 23, Line 5. A shoal of fishes. Favor comes through the **court ladies**.

Hexagram 28, Line 5. An older **woman** takes a husband.

Hexagram 31, Judgment. To take a **maiden** to wife brings good fortune.

Hexagram 32, Line 5. Giving duration to one's character through perseverance. This is good fortune for a **woman**, misfortune for a man.

Hexagram 37, Judgment. The perseverance of the **woman** furthers.

Hexagram 37, Line 3. When **woman** and child dally and laugh, it leads in the end to humiliation.

Hexagram 44, Judgment. The **maiden** is powerful. One should not marry such a **maiden**.

Hexagram 53, Judgment. The **maiden** is given in marriage.

Hexagram 53, Line 3. The **woman** carries a child but does not bring it forth. Misfortune.

Hexagram 53, Line 5. For three years the **woman** has no child. In the end nothing can hinder her. Good fortune.

Hexagram 54, Judgment. THE MARRYING **MAIDEN**.

Hexagram 54, Image. Thunder over the lake: The image of the marrying **maiden**.

Hexagram 54, Line 1. The marrying **maiden** as a concubine.

Hexagram 54, Line 3. The marrying **maiden** as a slave.

Hexagram 54, Line 4. The marrying **maiden** draws out the allotted time.

Hexagram 54, Line 6. The **woman** holds the basket, but there are no fruits in it.

Hexagram 63, Line 2. The **woman** loses the curtain of her carriage.

159. MAIDSERVANTS, SERVINGMAID See also SERVANT

Hexagram 33, Line 3. To retain people as men and **maidservants** brings good fortune.

Hexagram 54, Line 5. The embroidered garments of the princess were not as gorgeous as those of the **servingmaid**.

160. MAN AND WIFE, HUSBAND AND WIFE, WIFE See also MARRY, OLDER MAN

Hexagram 9, Line 3. The spokes burst out of the wagon wheels. **Man and wife** roll their eyes.

Hexagram 28, Line 2. An older man **takes a young wife**.

Hexagram 31, Judgment. To take a maiden to **wife** brings good fortune.

Hexagram 37, Line 2. She (**wife**) should not follow her whims. She must attend within to the food.

Hexagram 37, Line 4. She (**wife**) is the treasure of the house.

Hexagram 37, Line 5. As a king he (**husband**) approaches his family.

Hexagram 47, Line 3. He (**husband**) enters his house and does not see his **wife**.

161. MARRY, MARRIAGE, TAKES A HUSBAND, TAKES A MAIDEN TO WIFE, TAKES A WIFE, TAKES A YOUNG WIFE See also WIFE

Hexagram 11, Line 5. The sovereign I gives his daughter in **marriage**. This brings blessing and supreme good fortune.

Hexagram 28, Line 2. An older man **takes a young wife**.

Hexagram 28, Line 5. An older woman **takes a husband.**

Hexagram 31, Judgment. To **take a maiden to wife** brings good fortune.

Hexagram 44, Judgment. The maiden is powerful. One should not **marry** such a maiden.

Hexagram 53, Judgment. The maiden is given in **marriage**.

Hexagram 54, Judgment. THE **MARRYING** MAIDEN.

Hexagram 54, Image. Thunder over the lake: The image of the **marrying** maiden.

Hexagram 54, Line 1. The **marrying** maiden as a concubine.

Hexagram 54, Line 3. The **marrying** maiden as a slave. She **marries** as a concubine.

Hexagram 54, Line 4. The **marrying** maiden draws out the allotted time. A late **marriage** comes in due course.

Hexagram 54, Line 5. The sovereign I gave his daughter in **marriage**.

162. MEADOW, FIELD

Hexagram 1, Line 2. Dragons appearing in the **field**.

Hexagram 2, Line 6. Dragons fight in the **meadow**.

Hexagram 5, Line 1. Waiting in the **meadow**.

Hexagram 7, Line 5. There is game in the **field**.

Hexagram 13, Line 6. Fellowship with men in the **meadow**.

Hexagram 32, Line 4. No game in the **field**.

Hexagram 40, Line 2. One kills three foxes in the **field**.

163. MEAT See DRINK

164. MEDICINE See also ILL

Hexagram 25, Line 5. Use no **medicine** in an illness incurred through no fault of your own. It will pass of itself.

165. MELON

Hexagram 44, Line 5. A **melon** covered with willow leaves.

166. MEET, MEETING, MEETS

Hexagram 8, Judgment. Whoever comes too late **meets** with misfortune.

Hexagram 13, Line 5. Men bound in fellowship first weep and lament, but afterwards they laugh. After great struggles they succeed in **meeting**.

Hexagram 17, Line 6. He **meets** with firm allegiance and is still further bound.

Hexagram 18, Line 5. Setting right what has been spoiled by the father. One **meets** with praise.

Hexagram 32, Line 3. He who does not give duration to his character **meets** with disgrace.

Hexagram 35, Image. If one **meets** with no confidence, one should remain calm.

Hexagram 38, Line 2. One **meets** his lord in a narrow street.

Hexagram 38, Line 4. Isolated through opposition, one **meets** a like-minded man with whom one can associate in good faith.

Hexagram 39, Line 1. Going leads to obstructions, coming **meets** with praise.

Hexagram 44, Judgment. Coming to **meet**. The maiden is powerful.

Hexagram 44, Image. Under heaven, wind: The image of coming to **meet**.

Hexagram 44, Line 6. He comes to **meet** with his horns.

Hexagram 45, Image. Thus the superior man renews his weapons in order to **meet** the unforeseen.

Hexagram 46, Line 1. Pushing upward that **meets** with confidence brings great good fortune.

Hexagram 55, Line 1. When a man **meets** his destined ruler, they can be together ten days, and it is not a mistake. Going **meets** with recognition.

Hexagram 55, Line 2. Through going one **meets** with mistrust and hate.

Hexagram 55, Line 4. He **meets** his ruler, who is of like kind.

Hexagram 62, Line 1. The bird **meets** with misfortune through flying.

Hexagram 62, Line 2. She passes by her ancestor and **meets** her ancestress. He does not reach his prince and **meets** the official.

Hexagram 62, Line 4. No blame. He **meets** him without passing by.

Hexagram 62, Line 6. He passes him by, not **meeting** him.

167. MISTAKE, MISTAKES

Hexagram 35, Line 1. If one meets with no confidence, one should remain calm. No **mistake**.

Hexagram 38, Line 1. When you see evil people, guard yourself against **mistakes**.

Hexagram 38, Line 5. If one goes to him, how could it be a **mistake**.

Hexagram 40, Image. Thus the superior man pardons **mistakes** and forgives misdeeds.

Hexagram 43, Line 1. When one goes and is not equal to the task, one makes a **mistake.**

Hexagram 44, Line 3. If one is mindful of the danger, no great **mistake** is made.

Hexagram 55, Line 1. When a man meets his destined ruler, they can be together ten days, and it is not a **mistake**.
Hexagram 58, Line 4. After ridding himself of **mistakes** a man has joy.

168. MOAT

Hexagram 11, Line 6. The wall falls back into the **moat**.

169. MOON

Hexagram 9, Line 6. The **moon** is nearly full.
Hexagram 54, Line 5. The **moon** that is nearly full brings good fortune.
Hexagram 61, Line 4. The **moon** nearly at the full.

170. MOTHER See **FATHER**

171. MOUTH Also listed under **PARTS OF THE BODY**

Hexagram 27, Judgment. The CORNERS OF THE **MOUTH**. Perseverance brings good fortune. Pay heed to the providing of nourishment and to what a man seeks to fill his own **mouth** with.
Hexagram 27, Line 1. You let your magic tortoise go, and look at me with the corners of your **mouth** drooping.

172. MUD

Hexagram 5, Line 3. Waiting in the **mud**.
Hexagram 48, Line 1. One does not drink the **mud** of the well.

173. MULBERRY SHOOTS

Hexagram 12, Line 5. Standstill is giving way. Good fortune for the great man. "What if it should fail, what if it should fail?" In this way he ties it to a cluster of **mulberry shoots**.

174. NECK Also listed under **PARTS OF THE BODY**

Hexagram 21, Line 6. His **neck** is fastened in the wooden cangue, so that his ears disappear.
Hexagram 31, Line 5. The influence shows itself in the back of the **neck**.

175. NEIGHBOR

Hexagram 9, Line 5. If you are sincere and loyally attached, you are rich in your **neighbor**.

Hexagram 11, Line 4. He flutters down, not boasting of his wealth, together with his **neighbor**, guileless and sincere.

Hexagram 14, Line 4. He makes a difference between himself and his **neighbor**.

Hexagram 15, Line 5. No boasting of wealth before one's **neighbor**.

Hexagram 51, Line 6. If it has not yet touched one's own body but has reached one's **neighbor** first, there is no blame.

Hexagram 63, Line 5. The **neighbor** in the east who slaughters an ox does not attain as much real happiness as the **neighbor** in the west with his small offering.

176. NEST

Hexagram 56, Line 6. The bird's **nest** burns up.

177. NINE HILLS See HILL

178. NORTH See DIRECTIONS

179. NOSE Also listed under PARTS OF THE BODY

Hexagram 21, Line 2. Bites through tender meat, so that his **nose** disappears. No blame.

Hexagram 38, Line 3. One sees the wagon dragged back, the oxen halted, a man's hair and **nose** cut off.

Hexagram 47, Line 5. His **nose** and feet are cut off.

180. OFFERING See SACRIFICE

181. OFFICIAL

Hexagram 62, Line 2. He does not reach his prince and meets the **official**.

182. OLD AGE

Hexagram 30, Line 3. In the light of the setting sun, men either beat the pot and sing or loudly bewail the approach of **old age**.

183. OLDER MAN See also **YOUNG**

Hexagram 28, Line 2. An **older man** takes a young wife.

184. OLDER WOMAN See also **MAIDEN**

Hexagram 28, Line 5. An **older woman** takes a husband.

185. ONE-EYED MAN See **CRIPPLED MAN**

186. ORACLE

Hexagram 4, Judgment. At the first **oracle** I inform him.
Hexagram 8, Judgment. Inquire of the **oracle** again whether you possess sublimity, constancy, and perseverance; then there is no blame.
Hexagram 49, Line 5. Even before he questions the **oracle** he (the great man) is believed.

187. ORDINARY MEN See also **INFERIOR MAN**

Hexagram 59, Line 4. Dispersion leads in turn to accumulation. This is something that **ordinary men** do not think of.

188. OX, OXEN

Hexagram 38, Line 3. One sees the wagon dragged back, the **oxen** halted, a man's hair and nose cut off.
Hexagram 63, Line 5. The neighbor in the east who slaughters an **ox** does not attain as much real happiness as the neighbor in the west with his small offering.

189. OXHIDE

Hexagram 33, Line 2. He holds him fast with yellow **oxhide**.

190 PANTHER

Hexagram 49, Line 6. The superior man changes like a **panther**.

191. PARTS OF THE BODY Also listed separately under individual headings: **ARM, BACK, BELLY, CALVES OF THE LEGS, CHEEKS, CHEEKBONES, CHIN, EARS, FEET, HAND, HEAD, HEART, HIPS,**

JAWS, KNEE, MOUTH, NECK, NOSE, THIGHS, TOES, TONGUE, TRUNK, SACRUM, SKIN See also BODY, HAIR

Hexagram 1, Lines 1–6. There appears a flight of dragons without **heads**.

Hexagram 8, Line 6. He finds no **head** for holding together.

Hexagram 21, Line 1. His **feet** are fastened in the stocks, so that his **toes** disappear.

Hexagram 21, Line 2. Bites through tender meat, so that his **nose** disappears.

Hexagram 21, Line 6. His **neck** is fastened in the wooden cangue, so that his **ears** disappear.

Hexagram 22, Line 1. He lends grace to his **toes,** leaves the carriage, and walks.

Hexagram 22, Line 2. Lends grace to the beard on his **chin**.

Hexagram 23, Line 4. The bed is split up to the **skin**.

Hexagram 27, Judgment. The CORNERS OF THE **MOUTH**. Perseverance brings good fortune. Pay heed to the providing of nourishment and to what a man seeks to fill his own **mouth** with.

Hexagram 27, Line 1. You let your magic tortoise go, and look at me with the corners of your **mouth** drooping.

Hexagram 28, Line 6. It goes over one's **head**.

Hexagram 29, Judgment. If you are sincere, you have success in your **heart**, and whatever you do succeeds.

Hexagram 31, Line 1. The influence shows itself in the big **toe.**

Hexagram 31, Line 2. The influence shows itself in the **calves** of the legs.

Hexagram 31, Line 3. The influence shows itself in the **thighs**.

Hexagram 31, Line 5. The influence shows itself in the back of the **neck**.

Hexagram 31, Line 6. The influence shows itself in the **jaws, cheeks**, and **tongue**.

Hexagram 35, Line 5. Take not gain and loss to **heart.**

Hexagram 36, Line 2. Darkening of the light injures him in the left **thigh**.

Hexagram 36, Line 4. He penetrates the left side of the **belly**. One gets at the very **heart** of the darkening of the light, and leaves gate and courtyard.

Hexagram 38, Line 3. One sees the wagon dragged back, the oxen halted, a man's hair and **nose** cut off.

Hexagram 40, Line 3. If a man carries a burden on his **back** and nonetheless rides in a carriage, he thereby encourages robbers to draw near.

Hexagram 40, Line 4. Deliver yourself from your great **toe**. Then the companion comes, and him you can trust.

Hexagram 43, Line 1. Mighty in the forward-striding **toes**.

Hexagram 42, Line 5. If in truth you have a kind **heart**, ask not.

Hexagram 42, Line 6. He does not keep his **heart** constantly steady.

Hexagram 43, Line 3. To be powerful in the **cheekbones** brings misfortune.

Hexagram 43, Line 4. There is no **skin** on his **thighs**, and walking comes hard.

Hexagram 44, Line 3. There is no **skin** on his **thighs**, and walking comes hard.

Hexagram 45, Line 1. If you call out, then after one grasp of the **hand** you can laugh again.

Hexagram 47, Line 2. The man with the scarlet **knee** bands is just coming.

Hexagram 47, Line 5. His **nose** and **feet** are cut off.

Hexagram 47, Line 5. Oppression at the **hands** of the man with the purple **knee** bands.

Hexagram 48, Line 3. This is my **heart**'s sorrow, for one might draw from it (the well).

Hexagram 52, Judgment. Keeping his **back** still so that he no longer feels his **body**.

Hexagram 52, Line 1. Keeping his **toe** still. No blame.

Hexagram 52, Line 2. Keeping his **calves** still.

Hexagram 52, Line 2. His **heart** is not glad.

Hexagram 52, Line 3. Keeping his **hips** still.

Hexagram 52, Line 3. Making his **sacrum** stiff.

Hexagram 52, Line 3. The **heart** suffocates.

Hexagram 52, Line 4. Keeping his **trunk** still.

Hexagram 52, Line 5. Keeping his **jaws** still. The words have order.

Hexagram 55, Line 3. He breaks his right **arm**.

Hexagram 56, Line 4. He (the wanderer) obtains his property and an ax. My **heart** is not glad.

Hexagram 63, Line 6. He gets his **head** in the water.

Hexagram 64, Line 6. But if one wets his **head**, he loses it, in truth.

192. PATH, PATHS See also WAY

Hexagram 27, Line 2. Turning to the summit for nourishment, deviating from the **path** to seek nourishment from the hill.

Hexagram 27, Line 5. Turning away from the **path**.
Hexagram 34, Image. Thus the superior man does not tread upon **paths** that do not accord with established order.

193. PENALTIES, LAWS

Hexagram 21, Image. Thus the kings of former times made firm the **laws** through clearly defined **penalties**.
Hexagram 56, Image. Thus the superior man is clear-minded and cautious in imposing **penalties** and protracts no lawsuits.

194. PETTY MAN See INFERIOR MAN

195. PHEASANT

Hexagram 50, Line 3. The fat of the **pheasant** is not eaten.
Hexagram 56, Line 5. He (the wanderer) shoots a **pheasant.** It drops with the first arrow.

196. PIG, PIGS

Hexagram 38, Line 6. Isolated through opposition, one sees one's companion as a **pig** covered with dirt, as a wagon full of devils.
Hexagram 44, Line 1. Even a lean **pig** has it in him to rage around.
Hexagram 61, Judgment. **Pigs** and fishes.

197. PIT

Hexagram 5, Line 4. Get out of the **pit**.
Hexagram 5, Line 6. One falls into the **pit**.
Hexagram 29, Line 1. In the abyss one falls into a **pit**.
Hexagram 29, Line 3. In danger like this, pause at first and wait, otherwise you will fall into a **pit** in the abyss.

198. PLOWING

Hexagram 25, Line 2. If one does not count on the harvest while **plowing**, nor on the use of the ground while clearing it, it furthers one to undertake something.

199. POISONOUS

Hexagram 21, Line 3. Bites on old dried meat and strikes on something **poisonous**.

200. POLESTARS

Hexagram 55, Line 2. The curtain is of such fullness that the **polestars** can be seen at noon.
Hexagram 55, Line 4. The curtain is of such fullness that the **polestars** can be seen at noon.

201. POPLAR

Hexagram 28, Line 2. A dry **poplar** sprouts at the root.
Hexagram 28, Line 5. A withered **poplar** puts forth flowers.

202. POT

Hexagram 30, Line 3. In the light of the setting sun, men either beat the **pot** and sing or loudly bewail the approach of old age.

203. PRIESTS

Hexagram 57, Line 2. **Priests** and magicians are used in great number. Good fortune.

204. PRINCE, PRINCES, PRINCESS See also KING

Hexagram 7, Line 6. The great **prince** issues commands, founds states, vests families with fiefs.
Hexagram 10, Line 3. Thus does a warrior act on behalf of his great **prince**.
Hexagram 14, Line 3. A **prince** offers it to the Son of Heaven. A petty man cannot do this.
Hexagram 18, Line 6. He does not serve kings and **princes**, sets himself higher goals.
Hexagram 19, Line 5. Wise approach. This is right for a great **prince**.
Hexagram 35, Judgment. The powerful **prince** is honored with horses in large numbers.
Hexagram 40, Line 6. The **prince** shoots at a hawk on a high wall. He kills it.
Hexagram 42, Line 3. No blame, if you are sincere and walk in the middle, and report with a seal to the **prince**.
Hexagram 42, Line 4. If you walk in the middle and report to the **prince**, he will follow.
Hexagram 44, Image. Thus does the **prince** act when disseminating his commands and proclaiming them to the four quarters of heaven.

Hexagram 50, Line 4. The **prince**'s meal is spilled and his person is soiled.

Hexagram 54, Line 5. The embroidered garments of the **princess** were not as gorgeous as those of the servingmaid.

Hexagram 62, Line 2. He does not reach his **prince** and meets the official. No blame.

Hexagram 62, Line 5. The **prince** shoots and hits him who is in the cave.

205. PRINCE CHI

Hexagram 36, Line 6. Darkening of the light as with **Prince Chi**.

206. PRINCESS See PRINCE

207. PRISON

Hexagram 29, Line 6. Bound with cords and ropes, shut in between thorn-hedged **prison** walls: for three years one does not find the way.

208. PROPERTY

Hexagram 56, Line 2. The wanderer comes to an inn. He has his **property** with him.

Hexagram 56, Line 4. He (the wanderer) obtains his **property** and an ax.

Hexagram 57, Line 6. He loses his **property** and his ax.

209. PUNISHMENT, PUNISHING

Hexagram 4, Line 6. In **punishing** folly it does not further one to commit transgressions.

Hexagram 35, Line 6. Making progress with the horns is permissible only for the purpose of **punishing** one's own city.

Hexagram 55, Image. Thus the superior man decides lawsuits and carries out **punishments.**

210. RAGS See GARMENTS

211. RAIN

Hexagram 9, Image. Dense clouds, no **rain** from our western region.

Hexagram 9, Line 6. The **rain** comes, there is rest.

Hexagram 38, Line 6. As one goes, **rain** falls; then good fortune comes.

Hexagram 40, Image. Thunder and **rain** set in: The image of deliverance.

Hexagram 43, Line 3. He walks alone and is caught in the **rain.**

Hexagram 50, Line 3. Once **rain** falls, remorse is spent.

Hexagram 62, Line 5. Dense clouds, no **rain** from our western territory.

212. RICE

Hexagram 29, Line 4. A jug of wine, a bowl of **rice** with it; earthen vessels simply handed through the window.

213. RIDGEPOLE

Hexagram 28, Judgment. The **ridgepole** sags to the breaking point.

Hexagram 28, Line 3. The **ridgepole** sags to the breaking point.

Hexagram 28, Line 4. The **ridgepole** is braced.

214. RIVER

Hexagram 11, Line 2. Bearing with the uncultured in gentleness, fording the **river** with resolution, not neglecting what is distant, not regarding one's companions; thus one may manage to walk in the middle.

215. ROBBER, ROBBERS

Hexagram 3, Line 2. He is not a **robber**; he wants to woo when the time comes.

Hexagram 22, Line 4. He is not a **robber**; he will woo at the right time.

Hexagram 38, Line 6. He is not a **robber**; he will woo at the right time.

Hexagram 40, Line 3. If a man carries a burden on his back and nonetheless rides in a carriage, he thereby encourages **robbers** to draw near.

Hexagram 53, Line 3. It furthers one to fight off **robbers**.

216. ROCK

Hexagram 16, Line 2. Firm as a **rock**.

217. ROPE, ROPES

Hexagram 29, Line 6. Bound with cords and **ropes**, shut in between thorn-hedged prison walls: For three years one does not find the way.

Hexagram 48, Judgment. If one gets down almost to the water (in the well) and the **rope** does not go all the way, or the jug breaks, it brings misfortune.

218. RULER See KING

219. RUSHES

Hexagram 28, Line 1. To spread white **rushes** underneath.

220. SACK

Hexagram 2, Line 4. A tied-up **sack.**

221. SACRED DANCE

Hexagram 53, Line 6. Its (wild goose) feathers can be used for the **sacred dance**. Good fortune.

222. SACRIFICE, SACRIFICIAL SPOON, OFFERING, OFFERINGS, SMALL OFFERING See also CHALICE

Hexagram 20, Judgment. The ablution has been made, but not yet the **offering.**

Hexagram 41, Judgment. One may use two small bowls for the **sacrifice.**

Hexagram 45, Judgment. To bring great **offerings** creates good fortune.

Hexagram 45, Line 2. If one is sincere, it furthers one to bring even a **small offering.**

Hexagram 46, Line 2. If one is sincere, it furthers one to bring even a **small offering.**

Hexagram 47, Line 2. It furthers one to offer **sacrifice.**

Hexagram 47, Line 5. It furthers one to make **offerings** and libations.

Hexagram 51, Judgment. Laughing words—"Ha, ha!" The shock terrifies for a hundred miles, and he does not let fall the **sacrificial spoon** and chalice.

Hexagram 59, Image. Thus the kings of old **sacrificed** to the Lord and built temples.

Hexagram 63, Line 5. The neighbor in the east who slaughters an ox does not attain as much real happiness as the neighbor in the west with his **small offering.**

223. SACRUM Also listed under **PARTS OF THE BODY**

Hexagram 52, Line 3. Making his **sacrum** stiff.

224. SAND

Hexagram 5, Line 2. Waiting on the **sand**.

225. SEAL

Hexagram 42, Line 3. No blame, if you are sincere and walk in the middle, and report with a **seal** to the prince.

226. SECRET

Hexagram 61, Line 1. If there are **secret** designs, it is disquieting.

227. SERVANT, SERVANTS See also **MAIDSERVANTS**

Hexagram 39, Line 2. The king's **servant** is beset by obstruction upon obstruction, but it is not his own fault.
Hexagram 41, Line 6. One obtains **servants** but no longer has a separate home.
Hexagram 56, Line 2. He wins the steadfastness of a young **servant**.
Hexagram 56, Line 3. He loses the steadfastness of his young **servant**.

228. SERVINGMAID See **MAIDSERVANT, SERVANT**

229. SHEEP

Hexagram 43, Line 4. If a man were to let himself be led like a **sheep**, remorse would disappear.
Hexagram 54, Line 6. The man stabs the **sheep**, but no blood flows.

230. SHELTER

Hexagram 56, Line 4. The wanderer rests in a **shelter**.

231. SHOCK

Hexagram 51, Judgment. **SHOCK** brings success. **Shock** comes—"Oh, oh!" Laughing words—"Ha, ha!" The **shock** ter-

rifies for a hundred miles, and he does not let fall the sacrificial spoon and chalice.
Hexagram 51, Image. Thunder repeated: the image of **shock.**
Hexagram 51, Line 1. **Shock** comes—"Oh, oh!" Then follow laughing words—"Ha, ha!"
Hexagram 51, Line 2. **Shock** comes bringing danger.
Hexagram 51, Line 3. **Shock** comes and makes one distraught.
Hexagram 51, Line 4. **Shock** is mired.
Hexagram 51, Line 5. **Shock** goes hither and thither. Danger.
Hexagram 51, Line 6. **Shock** brings ruin and terrified gazing around.
Hexagram 64, Line 4. **Shock**, thus to discipline the Devil's Country.

232. SHOOTS See **STRIKE**

233. SIGHING See **TEARS**

234. SILK

Hexagram 22, Line 5. The roll of **silk** is meager and small.

235. SING, SINGS

Hexagram 30, Line 3. In the light of the setting sun, men either beat the pot and **sing** or loudly bewail the approach of old age. Misfortune.
Hexagram 61, Line 3. Now he sobs, now he **sings**.

236. SKIN Also listed under **PARTS OF THE BODY**

Hexagram 23, Line 4. The bed is split up to the **skin**.
Hexagram 43, Line 4. There is no **skin** on his thighs, and walking comes hard.
Hexagram 44, Line 3. There is no **skin** on his thighs, and walking comes hard.

237. SLAVE

Hexagram 54, Line 3. The marrying maiden as a **slave**.

238. SMALL OFFERING See **SACRIFICE**

239. SMALL (used as noun)

Hexagram 9, Judgment. The taming power of the **small** has success.
Hexagram 9, Image. The wind drives across heaven: The image of the taming power of the **small**.
Hexagram 11, Judgment. The **small** departs, the great approaches.

Hexagram 12, Judgment. The great departs; the **small** approaches.

Hexagram 62, Judgment. Preponderance of the **small**.

Hexagram 62, Image. Thunder on the mountain: Thus the image of preponderance of the **small**.

240. SOD See GRASS

241. SON See also FATHER

Hexagram 4, Line 2. The **son** is capable of taking charge of the household.

Hexagram 18, Line 1. Setting right what has been spoiled by the father. If there is a **son**, no blame rests upon the departed father.

Hexagram 50, Line 1. One takes a concubine for the sake of her **son**.

Hexagram 53, Line 1. The young **son** is in danger.

242. SOUTH See DIRECTIONS

243. SPOKES See WAGON

244. SPOON See SACRIFICE

245. SPRING

Hexagram 4, Image. A **spring** wells up at the foot of the mountain: The image of youth.

Hexagram 48, Line 5. In the well there is a clear, cool **spring** from which one can drink.

246. SQUARE See FORMS

247. STARS See also POLESTARS

Hexagram 55, Line 3. The underbrush is of such abundance that the small **stars** can be seen at noon.

248. STEPS

Hexagram 46, Line 5. One pushes upward by **steps**.

249. STONE

Hexagram 47, Line 3. A man permits himself to be oppressed by **stone**, and leans on thorns and thistles.

250. STREET

Hexagram 38, Line 2. One meets his lord in a narrow **street**.

251. STRIKE, STRIKES, HITS

Hexagram 21, Line 3. Bites on old dried meat and **strikes** on something poisonous.

Hexagram 42, Line 6. He brings increase to no one. Indeed, someone even **strikes** him.

Hexagram 62, Line 3. If one is not extremely careful, somebody may come up from behind and **strike** him.

Hexagram 62, Line 5. The prince shoots and **hits** him who is in the cave.

252. STRONG MAN See also GREAT

Hexagram 7, Judgment. The army needs perseverance and a **strong man**.

Hexagram 17, Line 2. If one clings to the little boy, one loses the **strong man**.

Hexagram 17, Line 3. If one clings to the **strong man**, one loses the little boy.

253. SUN

Hexagram 30, Line 3. In the light of the setting **sun**, men either beat the pot and sing or loudly bewail the approach of old age. Misfortune.

Hexagram 35, Image. The **sun** rises over the earth: The image of PROGRESS.

Hexagram 55, Image. Be not sad. Be like the **sun** at midday.

254. SUPERIOR MAN See also GREAT, GREAT MAN, STRONG MAN Occurrences in the Images, not given.

Hexagram 1, Line 3. All day long the **superior man** is creatively active.

Hexagram 2, Judgment. If the **superior man** undertakes something and tries to lead, he goes astray; but if he follows, he finds guidance.

Hexagram 3, Line 3. The **superior man** understands the signs of the time and prefers to desist.

Hexagram 9, Line 6. If the **superior man** persists, misfortune comes.

Hexagram 12, Judgment. Evil people do not further the perseverance of the **superior man**.

Hexagram 13, Judgment. The perseverance of the **superior man** furthers.

Hexagram 15, Judgment. The **superior man** carries things through.

Hexagram 15, Line 1. A **superior man** modest about his modesty may cross the great water.

Hexagram 15, Line 3. A **superior man** of modesty and merit carries things to conclusion.

Hexagram 20, Line 1. Boylike contemplation. For an inferior man, no blame. For a **superior man**, humiliation.

Hexagram 20, Line 5. Contemplation of my life. The **superior man** is without blame.

Hexagram 20, Line 6. Contemplation of his life. The **superior man** is without blame.

Hexagram 23, Line 6. The **superior man** receives a carriage.

Hexagram 33, Line 4. Voluntary retreat brings good fortune to the **superior man** and downfall to the inferior man.

Hexagram 34, Line 3. The inferior man works through power. The **superior man** does not act thus.

Hexagram 36, Line 1. The **superior man** does not eat for three days on his wanderings.

Hexagram 40, Line 5. If only the **superior man** can deliver himself, it brings good fortune. Thus he proves to inferior men that he is in earnest.

Hexagram 43, Line 3. The **superior man** is firmly resolved. He walks alone and is caught in the rain. He is bespattered, and people murmur against him.

Hexagram 49, Line 6. The **superior man** changes like a panther.

Hexagram 64, Line 5. The light of the **superior man** is true. Good fortune.

255. SUPREME DEITY, GOD, LORD

Hexagram 16, Image. Thus the ancient kings made music in order to honor merit, and offered it with splendor to the **Supreme Deity**, inviting their ancestors to be present.

Hexagram 42, Line 2. The king presents him before **God**.

Hexagram 59, Image. Thus the kings of old sacrificed to the **Lord** and built temples.

256. SWEAT

Hexagram 59, Line 5. His loud cries are as dissolving as **sweat**.

257. TAIL

Hexagram 10, Judgment. Treading upon the **tail** of the tiger.
Hexagram 10, Line 3. He treads on the **tail** of the tiger.
Hexagram 10, Line 4. He treads on the **tail** of the tiger.
Hexagram 33, Line 1. At the **tail** in retreat. This is dangerous.
Hexagram 63, Line 1. He gets his **tail** in the water.
Hexagram 64, Judgment. But if the little fox, after nearly completing the crossing, gets his **tail** in the water, there is nothing that would further.
Hexagram 64, Line 1. He gets his **tail** in the water.

258. TANK

Hexagram 44, Line 2. There is a fish in the **tank**.
Hexagram 44, Line 4. No fish in **tank**.

259. TAO Not listed. See PATH, WAY

260. TEACH, TEACHING

Hexagram 19, Image. Thus the superior man is inexhaustible in his will to **teach**, and without limits in his tolerance and protection of the people.
Hexagram 29, Image. Thus the superior man walks in lasting virtue and carries on the business of **teaching**.

261. TEARS, LAUGH, LAMENT, LAMENTING, SIGHING, SIGHS, SOBS, WEEP

Hexagram 3, Line 6. Bloody **tears** flow.
Hexagram 13, Line 5. Men bound in fellowship first **weep** and **lament**, but afterwards they **laugh**.
Hexagram 30, Line 6. **Tears** in floods, **sighing** and **lamenting**. Good fortune.
Hexagram 37, Line 3. When woman and child dally and **laugh**, it leads in the end to humiliation.
Hexagram 45, Line 1. If you call out, then after one grasp of the hand you can **laugh** again.
Hexagram 45, Line 3. Gathering together amid **sighs**.
Hexagram 45, Line 6. **Lamenting** and **sighing**, floods of **tears**.
Hexagram 51, Judgment. **Laughing** words—"Ha, ha!"
Hexagram 51, Line 1. Shock comes—"Oh, oh!" then follow **laughing** words—"Ha, ha!"
Hexagram 56, Line 6. The wanderer **laughs** at first, then must needs **lament** and **weep**.

Hexagram 60, Line 3. He who knows no limitation will have cause to **lament**.

Hexagram 61, Line 3. Now he **sobs**, now he sings.

262. TEMPLE, TEMPLES

Hexagram 45, Judgment. The king approaches his **temple**.

Hexagram 59, Judgment. The king approaches his **temple**.

Hexagram 59, Image. Thus the kings of old sacrificed to the Lord and built **temples**.

263. THIGH, THIGHS Also listed under **PARTS OF THE BODY**

Hexagram 31, Line 3. The influence shows itself in the **thighs**.

Hexagram 36, Line 2. Darkening of the light injures him in the left **thigh**.

Hexagram 43, Line 4. There is no skin on his **thighs**, and walking comes hard.

Hexagram 44, Line 3. There is no skin on his **thighs**.

264. THISTLES

Hexagram 47, Line 3. A man permits himself to be oppressed by stone, and leans on thorns and **thistles**.

265. THORNS, THORN-HEDGE

Hexagram 29, Line 6. Bound with cords and ropes, shut in between **thorn-hedged** prison walls: For three years one does not find the way.

Hexagram 47, Line 3. A man permits himself to be oppressed by stone, and leans on **thorns** and thistles.

266. THRIFT

Hexagram 62, Image. In his expenditures he (the superior man) gives preponderance to **thrift**.

267. TIGER

Hexagram 10, Judgment. Treading upon the tail of the **tiger**.

Hexagram 10, Line 3. He treads on the tail of the **tiger**. The **tiger** bites the man.

Hexagram 10, Line 4. He treads on the tail of the **tiger**.

Hexagram 27, Line 4. Spying about with sharp eyes like a **tiger** with insatiable craving.

Hexagram 49, Line 5. The great man changes like a **tiger**.

268. TING

Hexagram 50, Line 1. A **ting** with legs upturned.
Hexagram 50, Line 2. There is food in the **ting**.
Hexagram 50, Line 3. The handle of the **ting** is altered.
Hexagram 50, Line 4. The legs of the **ting** are broken.
Hexagram 50, Line 5. The **ting** has yellow handles, golden carrying rings.
Hexagram 50, Line 6. The **ting** has rings of jade.

269. TOES Also listed under **PARTS OF THE BODY**

Hexagram 21, Line 1. His feet are fastened in the stocks, so that his **toes** disappear.
Hexagram 22, Line 1. He lends grace to his **toes**, leaves the carriage, and walks.
Hexagram 31, Line 1. The influence shows itself in the big **toe**.
Hexagram 34, Line 1. Power in the **toes**.
Hexagram 40, Line 4. Deliver yourself from your great **toe**. Then the companion comes, and him you can trust.
Hexagram 43, Line 1. Mighty in the forward-striding **toes**.
Hexagram 52, Line 1. Keeping his **toes** still.

270. TONGUE Also listed under **PARTS OF THE BODY**

Hexagram 31, Line 6. The influence shows itself in the jaws, cheeks, and **tongue**.

271. TORTOISE

Hexagram 27, Line 1. You let your magic **tortoise** go, and look at me with the corners of your mouth drooping.
Hexagram 41, Line 5. Someone does indeed increase him. Ten pairs of **tortoises** cannot oppose it.
Hexagram 42, Line 2. Someone does indeed increase him; ten pairs of **tortoises** can not oppose it.

272. TOWN, TOWN'S PEOPLE, CITY

Hexagram 6, Line 2. The people of his **town**, three hundred households, remain free of guilt.
Hexagram 11, Line 6. Make your commands known within your own **town**.
Hexagram 15, Line 6. It is favorable to set armies marching to chastise one's own **city** and one's country.

Hexagram 35, Line 6. Making progress with the horns is only for the purpose of punishing one's own **city**.

Hexagram 43, Judgment. It is necessary to notify one's own **city**.

Hexagram 46, Line 3. One pushes upward into an empty **city**.

Hexagram 48, Judgment. The **town** may be changed, but the well cannot be changed.

273. TRADITION See ESTABLISHED ORDER

274. TREASURE, TREASURES

Hexagram 37, Line 4. She is the **treasure** of the house.

Hexagram 51, Line 2. A hundred thousand times you lose your **treasures** and must climb the nine hills.

275. TREE, TREES, BRANCH

Hexagram 28, Image. The lake rises above the **trees**: The image of preponderance of the great.

Hexagram 47, Line 1. One sits oppressed under a bare **tree** and strays into a gloomy valley.

Hexagram 53, Image. On the mountain a **tree**: the image of development.

Hexagram 53, Line 4. The wild goose gradually draws near the **tree**. Perhaps it will find a flat **branch**.

276. TRUNK Also listed under PARTS OF THE BODY

Hexagram 52, Line 4. Keeping his **trunk** still.

277. TRUTH, TRUTHFULLY

Hexagram 8, Line 1. Hold to him in **truth** and loyalty; this is without blame.

Hexagram 11, Line 3. Do not complain about this **truth**; enjoy the good fortune you possess.

Hexagram 14, Line 5. He whose **truth** is accessible, yet dignified, has good fortune.

Hexagram 42, Line 5. If in truth you have a kind **heart**, ask not.

Hexagram 43, Judgment. It must be announced **truthfully**.

Hexagram 55, Line 2. If one rouses him through **truth**, good fortune comes.

Hexagram 61, Judgment. Inner **truth**.

Hexagram 61, Image. Wind over lake: the image of INNER **TRUTH**.

Hexagram 61, Line 5. He possesses **truth**, which links together.

Hexagram 64, Line 1. But if one wets his head, he loses it, in **truth**.

278. TUSK

Hexagram 26, Line 5. The **tusk** of a gelded boar.

279. UNDERBRUSH

Hexagram 55, Line 3. The **underbrush** is of such abundance that the small stars can be seen at noon.

280. VALLEY

Hexagram 47, Line 1. One sits oppressed under a bare tree and strays into a gloomy **valley**.

281. VINES

Hexagram 47, Line 6. He is oppressed with creeping **vines**.

282.   WAGON, WHEELS, SPOKES See also CARRIAGE, CART, CHARIOT

Hexagram 3, Line 2. Horse and **wagon** part.

Hexagram 3, Line 4. Horse and **wagon** part.

Hexagram 3, Line 6. Horse and **wagon** part.

Hexagram 7, Line 3. Perchance the army carries corpses in the **wagon**.

Hexagram 9, Line 3. The **spokes** burst out of the **wagon wheels**.

Hexagram 14, Line 2. A big **wagon** for loading.

Hexagram 26, Line 2. The axletrees are taken from the **wagon**.

Hexagram 38, Line 3. One sees the **wagon** dragged back, the oxen halted, a man's hair and nose cut off.

Hexagram 38, Line 6. Isolated through opposition, one sees one's companion as a pig covered with dirt, as a **wagon** full of devils.

Hexagram 63, Line 1. He brakes his **wheels**.

Hexagram 64, Line 2. He brakes his **wheels**.

283. WAIT, WAITING

Hexagram 5, Judgment. **Waiting**. If you are sincere, you have light and success.
Hexagram 5, Image. Clouds rise up to heaven: The image of **waiting**.
Hexagram 5, Line 1. **Waiting** in the meadow.
Hexagram 5, Line 2. **Waiting** on the sand.
Hexagram 5, Line 3. **Waiting** in the mud.
Hexagram 5, Line 4. **Waiting** in blood.
Hexagram 5, Line 5. **Waiting** at meat and drink.
Hexagram 29, Line 3. In danger like this, pause at first and **wait**, otherwise you will fall into a pit in the abyss.

284. WALL, WALLS

Hexagram 11, Line 6. The **wall** falls back into the moat.
Hexagram 13, Line 4. He climbs up on his **wall**; he cannot attack.
Hexagram 29, Line 6. Bound with cords and ropes, shut in between thorn-hedged prison **walls**: For three years one does not find the way.
Hexagram 40, Line 6. The prince shoots at a hawk on a high **wall**.

285. WANDERER

Hexagram 25, Line 3. The cow that was tethered by someone is the **wanderer's** gain, the citizen's loss.
Hexagram 56, Judgment. THE **WANDERER**. Success through smallness. Perseverance brings good fortune to the **wanderer**.
Hexagram 56, Image. Fire on the mountain. The image of THE **WANDERER**.
Hexagram 56, Line 1. If the **wanderer** busies himself with trivial things, he draws down misfortune upon himself.
Hexagram 56, Line 2. The **wanderer** comes to an inn.
Hexagram 56, Line 3. The **wanderer's** inn burns down.
Hexagram 56, Line 4. The **wanderer** rests in a shelter.
Hexagram 56, Line 5. He (the **wanderer**) shoots a pheasant.
Hexagram 56, Line 6. The **wanderer** laughs at first, then must needs lament and weep.

286. WARRIOR

Hexagram 10, Line 3. Thus does a **warrior** act on behalf of his great prince.
Hexagram 57, Line 1. In advancing and in retreating, the perseverance of a **warrior** furthers.

287. WATER See also CROSSING THE GREAT WATER

Hexagram 6, Image. Heaven and **water** go their opposite ways: The image of CONFLICT.
Hexagram 7, Image. In the middle of the earth is **water**: The image of THE ARMY.
Hexagram 8, Image. On the earth is **water**: The image of HOLDING TOGETHER.
Hexagram 28, Line 6. One must go through the **water**. It goes over one's head.
Hexagram 29, Image. **Water** flows on uninterruptedly and reaches its goal: The image of the Abysmal repeated.
Hexagram 39, Image. **Water** on the mountain: The image of OBSTRUCTION.
Hexagram 48, Judgment. If one gets down almost to the **water** (in the well) and the rope does not go all the way, or the jug breaks, it brings misfortune.
Hexagram 47, Image. There is no **water** in the lake: The image of EXHAUSTION.
Hexagram 48, Image. **Water** over wood: the image of THE WELL.
Hexagram 59, Image. The wind drives over the **water**: The image of DISPERSION.
Hexagram 60, Image. **Water** over lake: the image of LIMITATION.
Hexagram 63, Image. **Water** over fire: the image of the condition in AFTER COMPLETION.
Hexagram 63, Line 1. He gets his tail in the **water**.
Hexagram 63, Line 6. He gets his head in the **water**.
Hexagram 64, Judgment. But if the little fox, after nearly completing the crossing, gets his tail in the **water**, there is nothing that would further.
Hexagram 64, Image. Fire over **water**: The image of the condition before transition.
Hexagram 64, Line 1. He (the little fox) gets his tail in the **water**.

288. WAY

Hexagram 3, Line 3. Whoever hunts deer without the forester only loses his **way** in the forest.

Hexagram 4, Line 1. To go on in this **way** brings humiliation.

Hexagram 6, Image. Heaven and water go their opposite **ways**: The image of CONFLICT.

Hexagram 6, Line 2. One cannot engage in conflict; one returns home, gives **way.**

Hexagram 9, Line 1. Return to the **way.**

Hexagram 12, Line 5. Standstill is giving **way**.

Hexagram 24, Judgment. To and fro goes the **way**.

Hexagram 26, Line 6. One attains the **way** of heaven.

Hexagram 29, Line 6. For three years one does not find the **way**.

Hexagram 37, Image. Thus the superior man has substance in his words and duration in his **way** of life.

Hexagram 50, Line 3. One is impeded in his **way** of life.

289. WEALTH

Hexagram 11, Line 4. He flutters down, not boasting of his **wealth**, together with his neighbor, guileless and sincere.

Hexagram 15, Line 5. No boasting of **wealth** before one's neighbor.

290. WEAPONS See also ARMS, ARROWS, BOW

Hexagram 13, Line 3. He hides **weapons** in the thicket; he climbs the high hill in front of it.

Hexagram 45, Image. Thus the superior man renews his **weapons** in order to meet the unforeseen.

291. WEED

Hexagram 43, Line 5. In dealing with **weeds**, firm resolution is necessary.

292. WEEP See, TEARS

293. WELL, WELLHOLE

Hexagram 48, Judgment. THE **WELL**. The town may be changed, but the **well** cannot be changed. It neither decreases nor increases. They come and go and draw from the **well**.

Hexagram 48, Image. Water over wood: the image of THE

WELL.

Hexagram 48, Line 1. One does not drink the mud of the **well**. No animals come to an old **well**.

Hexagram 48, Line 2. At the **wellhole** one shoots fishes.

Hexagram 48, Line 3. The **well** is cleaned, but no one drinks from it.

Hexagram 48, Line 4. The **well** is being lined.

Hexagram 48, Line 5. In the **well** there is a clear, cool spring from which one can drink.

Hexagram 48, Line 6. One draws from the **well** without hindrance.

294. WEST See **DIRECTIONS**

295. WIFE See **MAN, HUSBAND AND WIFE**

296. WILD GOOSE

Hexagram 53, Line 1. The **wild goose** gradually draws near the shore.

Hexagram 53, Line 2. The **wild goose** gradually draws near the cliff.

Hexagram 53, Line 3. The **wild goose** gradually draws near the plateau.

Hexagram 53, Line 4. The **wild goose** gradually draws near the tree.

Hexagram 53, Line 5. The **wild goose** gradually draws near the summit.

Hexagram 53, Line 6. The **wild goose** gradually draws near the cloud heights.

297. WILLOW LEAVES

Hexagram 44, Line 5. A melon covered with **willow leaves**.

298. WINE

Hexagram 29, Line 4. A jug of **wine**, a bowl of rice with it; earthen vessels simply handed through the window.

Hexagram 64, Line 6. There is drinking of **wine** in genuine confidence.

299. WINGS

Hexagram 22, Line 4. A white horse comes as if on **wings**.
Hexagram 36, Line 1. Darkening of the light during flight. He lowers his **wings**.

300. WOMAN See MAIDEN

301. WORDS

Hexagram 27, Image. Thus the superior man is careful of his **words** and temperate in eating and drinking.
Hexagram 37, Image. Thus the superior man has substance in his **words** and duration in his way of life.
Hexagram 43, Line 4. But if these **words** are heard they will not be believed.
Hexagram 51, Judgment. Laughing **words**—"Ha, ha!"
Hexagram 51, Line 1. Then follow laughing **words**—"Ha, ha!"
Hexagram 52, Line 5. Keeping his jaws still. The **words** have order.

302. WRONG PEOPLE See EVIL PEOPLE

303. YOUNG, YOUNGER, ELDEST

Hexagram 4, Judgment. It is not I who seek the **young** fool. The **young** fool seeks me.
Hexagram 7, Line 5. Let the **eldest** lead the army. The **younger** transports corpses.
Hexagram 26, Line 4. The headboard of a **young** bull.
Hexagram 28, Line 2. An older man takes a **young** wife.
Hexagram 53, Line 1. The **young** son is in danger.
Hexagram 56, Line 2. He wins the steadfastness of a **young** servant.
Hexagram 56, Line 3. He loses the steadfastness of his **young** servant.
Hexagram 61, Line 2. Its **young** answers it.

ANNOTATED
BIBLIOGRAPHY: BOOKS

All references to books in this work are listed in this bibliography. All books listed here are in English. The annotations may prove useful in identifying works of interest.

Adler, Joseph Alan. "Divination and Philosophy: Chu Hsi's Understanding of the *I Ching*." Ph.D. diss. in Religious Studies: University of California, Santa Barbara, 1984.

> The author states:

>> My chief aims are: (1) to determine how and in what religious and intellectual-historical context Chu Hsi understood divination to be relevant to the Confucian quest for Sagehood; (2) to identify and pursue the cosmological and (especially) epistemological assumptions and claims underlying his views of the **I** and divination; and (3) to explore, by means of this case, the parameters of "Confucian rationalism...." (p. 10).

Aero, Rita. *The I Ching Coloring Book*. R. L. Wing, trans. Garden City, New York: Doubleday & Company, Inc., 1984.

> On the right hand pages are pictures suitable for coloring. On the opposite pages are the hexagrams, their text (no line text is given), and an explanation of how the picture relates to the hexagram. Also given is the coin method of divination and the Chinese meaning of the colors.

Albertson, Edward. *The Complete I Ching for the Millions*. Los Angeles: Sherbourne Press Inc., 1969.

> No bibliography or references given. Perhaps a paraphrase of Legge's translation.

Anthony, Carol K. *A Guide to the I Ching*. Stow, Massachusetts: Anthony Publishing Company, 1980.

> Anthony intends her book to be a guide to the Wilhelm/Baynes translation. For each hexagram (including the lines) the author quotes selected passages from Wilhelm/Baynes (indicated by placing the quoted material in italics) and then gives her interpretation.

_____. *The Philosophy of the I Ching*. Stow, Massachusetts: Anthony Publishing Company, 1981.

> The theme of the book is how to use the *I Ching* as a daily guide to "...lead us through a process of self-development that satisfies our innate search for the meaning of existence" (p. vii).

Blofeld, John, trans. *The Book of Change*. New York: E. P. Dutton & Co., Inc., 1965.

> A simplified translation of the *I Ching*. In my opinion the book cannot stand alone, but is useful in conjunction with the Wilhelm/Baynes and Legge translations. Has a clear set of instructions for using the yarrow-stalk method to consult the *I Ching* as an oracle and has an interesting description of the author's experience in consulting the *I Ching*.

Ch'en, Shour-Yi. *Chinese Literature: A Historical Introduction*. New York: The Ronald Press Company, 1961.

> Good descriptions of the five Confucian Classics. See Chapter 5.

Chu, W. K. and W. A. Sherrill. *The Astrology of the I Ching*. New York: Samuel Weiser, Inc., 1976.

> Over four-hundred pages of divination procedures using astrology and the *I Ching*. The only reference given for the source of all this material is in the Preface, where the first author states: "*The Astrology of I Ching* is based on a manuscript in ancient classical Chinese, the title of which, translated literally, is 'Ho Map Lo Map Rational Number' " (p. ix). The book contains a short index, but no bibliography.

Cleary, Thomas, trans. *The Taoist I Ching*. Boston & London: Shambhala, 1986.

> The first of four books. Worthwhile reading for a Taoist perspective on the *I Ching*. A translation of a work written in 1796 A.D. by a Taoist named Liu I-ming. The work consisted of the *I Ching* and explanations and commentaries by Liu I-ming, a member of the Clear Serene branch of the Complete Reality School of Taoism. Cleary's translation also contains a thirty-three page introduction on a Taoist interpretation of the *I Ching* and a glossary of Taoist alchemical terms found in Liu's commentaries on the *I Ching*. Cleary uses the name "Joy" for

both Hexagrams 16 and 58; he avoids this in his other book, *The Buddhist I Ching.* (See below.)

_____, trans. *The Buddhist I Ching.* Boston & London: Shambhala, 1987.

      The second of four books. A good presentation of a Buddhist perspective on the *I Ching* and a translation of the *I Ching* and commentaries written by a Chinese Buddhist Chih-hsu Ou-i (1599–1655 A.D.). Translator's introduction is eleven pages. It is worthwhile comparing the names and explanations of the hexagrams with those in Cleary's first book, *The Taoist I Ching.* (See above.)

_____, trans. *I Ching: The Tao of Organization.* Boston & London: Shambhala, 1988.

      The third in a series of translations of the *I Ching.* This work contains the commentaries of Cheng I (1033–1108 A.D.), one of the great Neo-Confucianists.

      In the ten-page introduction a program of learning a deliberate method of consulting the *I Ching* is set forth and valuable information is given for practical use of the *I Ching.*

      The author claims that:

> *The Tao of Organization* analyzes relationships and power configurations within groups . . . The relationship between interpersonal and intra-personal forces, the crucial point on which the Tao—the Way, or inner pattern or design—of organization hinges, is the central focus of the explanation. This makes the commentary un-usually versatile in terms of studying both personal and collective life (p. ix).

_____, trans. *I Ching Mandalas.* Boston & London: Shambhala, 1989.

      The fourth book and presented by Cleary as a companion volume to his other three translations of the *I Ching.*

      Cleary writes:

> There are various sets of *I Ching* mandalas, with common and different designs. Generally speaking, there are two major functions associated with these mandalas. One is to encapsulate the foundation of the ideas underlying the *I Ching,* the other is to encapsulate

models of *I Ching* organizational patterns or
study courses... This volume uses both of these
functions; the Readings chapter, on the outer
teachings, employs programs abstracted from
the mandalas with readings of the text of the *I
Ching* as tools for consulting, coordinating, and
augmenting my earlier translations from Taoist,
Buddhist, and Confucian interpretations; the
Arcana sections, on the inner teachings, presents
a series of essays on the foundation of ideas represented by the mandalas, based on the teaching of Liu-I-Ming, master of Taoism, Confucianism, and Chang Buddhism (p. 2).

————, trans. *I Ching: The Book of Changes*. Boston & London: Shambhala,
1992. Pocket Classics.

This book measures 3 by $4\frac{1}{2}$ inches and is probably the
smallest English translation of the *I Ching*. It contains 169 pages
and a twenty page introduction. The text for each hexagram and
its lines are given as well as a list which gives for each hexagram
its nuclear hexagram and its opposite—in Cleary's terminology,
its correlate and its complement.

Crowley, Aleister. *The Book of Changes: A New Translation of the Book of
Changes by the Master Therion*. MRG: Archer's Court, Hastings, Sussex,
England.

No copyright or publication date given. Crowley uses
rhythms in his translation. Line text not given. Diagram in back
of book places the yin and yang line and the eight trigrams on
the Tree of Life. No references, bibliography or index.

Culling, Louis T. *The Incredible I Ching*. New York: Samuel Weiser, 1965.

Forty-six pages attempting to explain the *I Ching*. Aleister Crowley is often quoted. No bibliography, index, or references.

Damian-Knight, Guy. *The I Ching on Love*. Poole, Dorset: Blandford Press,
1984. Distributed in United States by Sterling Publishing Co., New York,
N.Y.

Author acknowledges his indebtedness to the Wilhelm/Baynes
edition of the *I Ching*. The resemblance is very slight.

Dhiegh, Khigh Alx, ed. *I Ching: Taoist Book of Days Calendar–Diary.* [Published yearly. See annotation for full publishing data.]

> Contains articles of uneven scholarship in the back of the Calendar-Diary. I have seen only years 1975–1981. The 1975 issue was published by Shambhala, the rest by Ballantine Books.

Dhiegh, Khigh Alx. *The Eleventh Wing: An Exposition of the Dynamics of I Ching for Now.* New York: Dell Publishing Co., 1973.

> Although this book is written for the popular press and has as its theme, "What the *I Ching* can do for you," it is interesting reading. Listed and depicted by photographs are a number of *I Ching* study devices patented by the author: the I Ching Universe-Cube, the Eight Houses Study Cubes, and the I Ching Oracle Disc. Also shown and described are the I Ching-Dex, I Ching Cards, and the I Ching Pyramid Kua. Of note is a fourteen-page bibliography which includes an annotated list of books in English (the titles are given in English and there is no indication that they are in Chinese), published in China, Hong Kong, and Taipei.

Douglas, Alfred. *How to Consult the I Ching.* New York: Berkeley Medallion Books, 1971. Published by arrangement with G. P. Putnam & Sons.

> Gives three methods for consulting the *I Ching* as an oracle: the Yarrow-Stalk Method, the Three-Coin Method, and the Six-Wand Method. The source of the translation is not made clear. Decision, Commentary, and the Lines are given for each hexagram. The three brief Appendices are entitled: Mathematical Aspect of the I Ching, The Development of the I Ching in China, and European Translations of the I Ching.

Fendos, George Jr. "Fei Chih's Place in the Development of I-Ching Studies." Ph.D. diss. in Chinese Studies: University of Wisconsin, Madison. 1988.

> This dissertation accomplishes two tasks: First it presents "a sound account of the development of the I-ching from its inception through the Early Han (206 B.C.–A.D. 1)..." (p. 10), and second, it analyzes Fei Chih's *I Ching* philosophy and accurately locates it in the development of *I Ching* studies.
>
> This work presents an excellent summary of the various theories for the origin of the *I Ching* and for each of the seven commentaries that compose the Ten Wings. The author points out the strengths and weaknesses of each theory and gives his opinion.

A 228–page bibliography (books and articles) of *I Ching* studies is given in Chinese, Japanese, Korean, Western languages, and three entries in the Vietnamese language.

Fox, Judy, Karen Hughes, and John Tampion. *An Illuminated I Ching.* New York: Arco Publishing, Inc., 1982.

A translation of the *I Ching* illustrated with black and white drawings. No source for translation given. Explains coin method of divination. Eight books listed in bibliography.

Fults, John Lee. *Magic Squares.* La Salle, Illinois: Open Court, 1974.

This book is listed for those interested in the *I Ching* and magic squares. This book does not mention the *I Ching* but is a fine introduction to the theory of magic squares. Covers diabolic squares (perfect squares). No index and a twelve-item bibliography. See Jim Moran, *The Wonders of Magic Squares.*

Gia-fu, Feng and Hugh L. Wilkerson. *Tai Chi: A Way of Centering and I Ching.* New York: Collier Books, 1970.

Translation by Gia-fu Feng and Jerome Kirk. Photographs by Hugh L. Wilkerson. The first ninety pages of the book is a new translation of the *I Ching*. The word "groovy" is sprinkled throughout the hexagram texts. Line text is also given. Pages 91 to 157 gives the basic steps and twenty-four positions of Tai Chi Ch'uan. Positions are illustrated by photographs and described.

Goodman, Howard Lazar. "Exegets and Exegeses of the Book of Changes in the Third Century AD: Historical and Scholastic Contexts for Wang Pi." Ph.D. diss. in East Asian Studies: Princeton University, 1985.

In the author's own words:

I have desired to study Wang Pi with the intention of interpreting the words of his commentary to the *Book of Changes*. I have started, however, by establishing groups and drawing inferences about those groupings. I place his family with other ones which had interests in the same classic and consider their roles in political and intellectual life. Next I collected all extant third-century comments to the text of the *Book of Changes* and its Ten Wings (the earliest written exegeses). I analyzed those

comments in relation to developments in the
exegetical genres themselves and in relation to
the interpretive approaches taken by earlier ex-
egetes. The method that all of this involves
has never been attempted for early Chinese intellectual history (p. xviii).

Govinda, Lama Anagarika. *The Inner Structure of the I Ching: The Book of Transformations*. San Francisco: Wheelwright Press, 1981.

Contains many diagrams in shades of red and black.
Much space is devoted to diagramming the Houses of the Hexagrams. Most interesting is Govinda's attempt to reconstruct the
textual sequence of the hexagrams. For those interested in the
problem of determining the order of the textual sequence, Chapter XVII Summary of Hexagram Arrangements, pp. 143–53, is
worthwhile reading.

Graham, Charles M. *The Concept of Cycle in Modern Science, Astrology, and I Ching*. Green Bay, Wisconsin: Cambridge Circle Limited, 1976.

The author writes:

This paper was originally prepared in 1974 as a
conventional University research project in the
history and methodology of science, bearing the
title *Historical and Contemporary Foundations
of the Study of Cycles* (Author's Note, first unnumbered page).

There is an 18-page bibliography with major works annotated,
but few deal with the *I Ching*. Total number of pages is 59.

Green, Michael. *The I Ching Records*. Philadelphia, Pennsylvania: Running Press, 1985.

Contains a three-page introduction, by Michael Green,
giving the coin method of divination. The other unnumbered
pages (about ninety), have diagrams for recording the obtained
hexagrams and headings under which one may record the Judgment and Image, Moving lines, and so forth.

Hirth, Friedrich. *The Ancient History of China: To the End of the Chou Dynasty*. Freeport, New York: Books for Libraries Press, 1908.

Gives the historical background of the period in which
the *I Ching* was written. Hirth was a professor of Chinese and
head of the Chinese department at Columbia University from
1902 to 1917.

Hook, Diana ffarington. *The I Ching and You.* New York: E. P. Dutton & Co., Inc., 1973.

> Better than most of the popular books that attempt to explain and analyse the *I Ching.* Explains the Earlier Heaven and Later Heaven Arrangement of the trigrams, gives examples of interpreting the hexagrams and much more. Contains an adequate index, a one-page bibliography, and forty-eight pages of appendices. In the appendices there is a clear guide to the yarrow-stalk method of divining, a list of the various titles for each hexagram, the attributes of the eight trigrams, a glossary of terms used in the *I Ching,* and so forth. References are few, but Hook is the only English author I know of who acknowledges her source for the concept of nuclear hexagrams and their use in analyzing hexagrams. The source is [A] Wilhelm/Baynes, p. 451.

_____. *The I Ching and Mankind.* London, Boston and Henley: Routledge & Kegan Paul Ltd., 1975.

> Hook relates the *I Ching* to numerology, astrology, the Tarot, the Kabbalah, the Ten Commandments, and so forth. There is a two-page bibliography, which includes books from the areas listed above. There is a six-page chart of mutating hexagrams (pp. 142–47) and numerous other tables and charts.

_____. *The I Ching and its Associations.* London, Boston and Henley: Routledge & Kegan Paul Ltd., 1980.

> Part I of the book deals with the relation of the *I Ching* to such topics as dowsing and geomancy, the Great Pyramid, the Golden Section, etc. Part II of the book gives twenty-five case histories where the *I Ching* was consulted as an oracle to answer a question. For example, "Case number 1. Should a child be moved to a new school?" (p. 70).

Huang, Kerson, *I Ching: The Oracle.* Singapore: World Scientific Publishing Co Pte Ltd., 1984.

> This book has been superceded by his second one. See Kerson Huang and Rosemary Huang, *The I Ching.*

Huang, Kerson and Rosemary Huang. *The I Ching.* New York: Workman Publishing Company Inc., 1985. First printing August 1987.

> Kerson Huang is a Professor of Physics at the Massachusetts Institute of Technology. He has had a life-long inter-

est in the *I Ching* and has kept abreast of the latest scholarly research concerning its interpretation and origin.

Huang's translation is based on the work of modern scholars summarized by Gao Heng in his works (in Chinese): *Modern Annotation to the Old Classic Zhou Yi* and *Discourses on the Old Classic Zhou Yi.* Huang translates only the original Chinese text of the hexagrams. He does not translate the Ten Wings.

There is material in this book which does not occur in many other English translations. For example, historical events referred to by the original Chinese text of the hexagrams, the *I Ching* as poetry, a brief account of the significance of the discovery of the Shang oracle bones, and so forth. Professor Huang also sells software which allows a person to consult (or study) the *I Ching* on a personal computer. For description see Appendix L.

Innes, Brian, Francis King and Neil Powell. *Fate and Fortune.* New York: Crescent Books. Copyright Macdonald & Co. (Publishers) Ltd. 1989.

The book is divided into four sections: Part 1, HORO-SCOPES, by Brian Innes; Part 2, THE BOOK OF CHANGES: THE I CHING, by Neil Powell; Part 3, PALMISTRY, by Francis King; and Part 4, THE TAROT, by Brian Innes.

The section on the *I Ching* (pp. 90–179) starts with a five-page discussion on "Tao: The Chinese Way." The rest of the section gives the Coin Method and the Six Wands Method of casting a hexagram. A translation of the hexagram text and line text is given for the sixty-four hexagrams. Almost each page is illustrated with a Chinese painting or sketch.

Johnson, Willard. *A Beginner's Guide to the I Ching.* Berkeley, California: Shambhala Booksellers, 1969.

A thirteen-page pamphlet which advocates the coin method for consulting the *I Ching* as an oracle. Recommends the Wilhelm/Baynes edition. Johnson says, "Many people would benefit from using it in as many ways. Wives could decide what cakes to bake with it, radio stations, what sorts of music to play at various times..." (p. 13).

Jou, Tsung Hwa. *The Tao of I Ching: Way to Divination.* Taiwan, 1984. Published by Tai Chi Foundation. Distributed by Charles E. Tuttle Co.

A translation of the *I Ching.* Gives a unique yarrow-stalk method of divination—called the Traditional Approach—

which is not described in any other book listed in this bibliography. Gives the coin method of divination and a lengthy discussion of the Plum Flower Mind I Ching. (Called elsewhere the Plum Blossom numerology system.) Traditional Chinese wood block prints are used to illustrate the qualities of each hexagram. No source is given for translation. No references, bibliography, or index.

Jung, Carl G. *Synchronicity: An Acausal Connecting Principle.* R. F. C. Hull, trans. Princeton N.J.: Bollingen Series: Princeton University Press, 1960.

> The material in this 135-page book is an extract from *The Structure and Dynamics of the Psyche,* Vol. 8 of the *Collected Works of C. G. Jung.*
>
> Jung first used the word "synchronicity" in the forward to the Wilhelm/Baynes translation of the *I Ching.* Jung—who assumes the validity of the divinatory function of the *I Ching*—offers the principle of synchronicity as an explanation. See F. David Peat, *Synchronicity: The Bridge Between Matter and Mind.*

Jung, Sinling. "Psychotherapeutic Implications of Consulting the Yi Jing (I Ching): A Phenomenological Approach." Ph.D. diss. in Professional Psychology: California School of Professional Psychology, Berkeley, 1985.

> The author states that:
>
> > The purpose of the present study is to explore, through qualitative analysis, the psychotherapeutic implications of consulting the Yi Jing, an area lacking completeness in the literature. Emphasis is on the enquirer's intrapsychic process of consulting the oracle (p. 3).
> >
> > The author concludes that the *I Ching* has therapeutic value although he admits that his study was limited to eight subjects and that his study did not "specifically reveal exactly how or why the Yi Jing works. . ." (p. 150).

Kaplan, Charles David. "Method as Phenomenon: The Case of the *I Ching.*" Ph.D. diss. in Sociology: University of California, Los Angeles, 1973.

> The author concludes that the "*I Ching* is a method of inquiry that is essentially subjective and unreliable. But these features of the *I Ching* are not sufficient to refuse it the status of a rational methodology for interpreting complex and veiled

situations" (p. 170). The author also points out that the *I Ching* "is as much a phenomenon as the subjective and unreliable procedures exhibited by practitioners of sociology in the data analysis experiment carried out by Hirschi and Selvin" (p. 170).

Kegan, Frank R. *I Ching Primer.* Chicago: The Aries Press, 1979.

The following description appears on the title page: "An Introduction to the Relevant-Process Perspective Upon the Occult in General and the Flux Tome (I Ching) in Particular." There are sixty-four pages on how to consult the *I Ching* as an oracle.

Kunst, Richard Alan. "The Original *Yijing:* A Text, Phonetic Transcription, Translation, and Indexes, with Sample Glosses." Ph.D. diss. in Oriental Languages: University of California, Berkeley, 1985.

Scholarship at its best. In the words of the author:

> This study includes tools to assist in understanding the original diviner's manual: first, a text which indicates probable emendations and the modern graphic counterparts for archaic orthography; second, a transcription of the entire text into standard *pinyin* romanization, also giving the Old Chinese readings where useful for syntactic or phonological analysis—for example, for rhyme and onomatopoeia; third, two translations, literal word-for-word and a more interpretive version; fourth, several introductory studies on the relation of the *Yijing* to primitive systematic thought, oral-formulaic literature, and the Early Old Chinese language; fifth, numerous reference aids, such as a glossary, a type-list and frequency count, and a concordance to graphs appearing in the text, all computer-generated; sixth, sample glosses for two complete hexagram-chapters; and finally, a photographic reproduction of the transcription of the Mawangdui manuscript of the text discovered in 1973, which was used in reconstructing the original text and its meaning. (From the Abstract, in front of Contents).

The book contains all this and more. It has thirteen tables, some of which are: "The Color Vocabulary of the *Yi*," "The Number Vocabulary of the *Yi*," "Paired Words of Opposite Meanings," "Reduplicated Expressions."

Of special interest is the author's attention to the Mawangdui manuscript, a copy of the *I Ching* found in the Hunan province in 1973. The manuscript was entombed in 168 B.C., which makes it, by several centuries, the oldest known version of the *I Ching*. The difference in the order of the hexagrams and the text from later versions is noted by the author.

Lee, Jung Young. *The Principle of Changes: Understanding the I Ching*. New Hyde Park, New York: University Books, 1971.

Worthwhile reading. Of special interest is Lee's explanation of the difficulties involved in translating the *I Ching*. Lee gives his interpretations of the Chinese words in the *I Ching* which have been translated by Wilhelm/Baynes as "judgment," "success," "nothing furthers," "furthering through perseverance," and so forth. The Chinese words are given. Also covered in some detail are the four cardinal virtues, which are repeatedly mentioned in the *I Ching*: yüan, heng, li, and chen. No bibliography or index. References are given in footnotes.

————. *The I Ching and Modern Man: Essays on Metaphysical Implications of Change*. Secaucus, New Jersey: University Books, 1975.

Some of the topics mentioned in the table of contents are The *I Ching* and Acupuncture; the *I Ching* and New Self-Therapy; the *I Ching* and the New Concept of God; the *I Ching* and New Styles of Living; and so forth.

Legge/Chai. Legge, James, trans. *I Ching: Book of Changes*. Edited by Ch'u Chai and Winberg Chai. New York: Bantam Books, 1964.

James Legge (1815–1897) was born in Huntly, Aberdeenshire. He served as a missionary at Malacca and Hongkong (1839–73). Was a professor of Chinese at Oxford (1876). Legge's earliest translation of the *I Ching* into English was in 1854–55. It was published in Hongkong in 1882 as part of the *Sacred Books of the East* series edited by Friedrich Max Müller.[1]

Ch'u and Winberg Chai have written a seventy-eight page introduction and study guide to this edition. This inexpensive little paperback contains the text of a 2nd edition published by the Clarendon Press in 1899 as Vol. XVI of *The Sacred*

---

[1] Legge (Ch'u Chai and Winberg Chai, eds.), p. xxxiv.

Books of the East. In 1986 the Legge/Chai edition was in its 16th printing. See Legge (Dover) and Legge/Van Over.

Up to the time that the Wilhelm/Baynes translation was published in 1950, Legge's translation was the only version of the *I Ching* available in English. The Legge translation belongs in the library of every serious *I Ching* scholar. Needham states that probably the best translation was that of Richard Wilhelm "though in many ways that of Legge is more useful" ([A] Needham, vol. 2, p. 308).

Legge (Dover). Legge, James, trans. *I Ching: Book of Changes.* New York: Dover Publications, Inc., 1963.

The same as the Bantam Books edition, minus the introduction by Ch'u Chai and Winberg Chai. However, the Dover edition has larger type and is much easier to read. See Legge/Chai, above, for publication history.

Legge/Van Over. Legge, James, trans. *I Ching.* Edited and introduction by Raymond Van Over. New York and Scarborough, Ontario: The New American Library, Inc., 1971.

Differs from the original edition of Legge's translation as follows: 1. The relevant material in the Ten Wings is placed with its appropriate hexagrams; 2. The Wade-Giles system of writing Chinese characters is used; and 3. The names of the hexagrams are added. Van Over states, "Where I was in doubt as to Legge's preference for a hexagram's name, I followed a comparative list of the traditional names given by other translators (including the valuable transcription table for each of the sixty-four hexagrams in another edition of Legge's translation by Ch'u and Winberg Chai)" (p. 40). See Legge/Chai, above, for publication history.

Liu, Da. *T'ai Chi Ch'uan and I Ching: A Choreography of Body and Mind.* New York: Harper & Row Publishers, 1972.

The T'ai Chi Ch'uan forms are briefly described and illustrated and then the correspondence between each hexagram and a T'ai Chi Ch'uan form is explained.

_____. *I Ching Coin Prediction.* New York: Harper & Row, 1975.

A translation of the *I Ching* which Liu claims is his own. Source is not given. No bibliography. Yarrow-stalk method of divination also given.

_____. *I Ching Numerology*. Published in San Francisco. New York: Harper & Row, 1979.

> Liu states that his book is based on Shao Yung's *I Ching Plum Blossom Numerology* (*Shao K'ang Chieh I Ching Mei Hwa Shu,* Hong Kong: Popular Publisher, no date) (Liu, p. 119). For many the book will be worthwhile reading. Specific instructions are given for different kinds of predictions: weather, marriage, travel, and so forth. A seven-page chapter gives the life of Shao Yung (1011–1077 A.D.) and briefly describes his works. The appendix gives the attributes of the eight trigrams, the cycles of the five elements, and instructions for using the Chinese animal calendar. Seven pages of end notes. No index except to the trigrams and hexagrams. See W. A. Sherrill and W. K. Chu, *An Anthology of I Ching.*

Loewe, Michael. "China." An article in *Oracles and Divination*. Edited by Michael Loewe and Carmen Blacker. Boulder, Colorado: Shambhala Publications, Inc., 1981.

> About seven pages of this article is devoted to the *I Ching*. Gives a brief history of the book. Mentioned is Wang Pi, Shao Yung, Leibniz, and Chou Tun-i.

MacHovec, Frank J., trans. *I Ching: The Book of Changes*. Mount Vernon, New York: The Peter Pauper Press, 1971.

> For each hexagram a short paragraph is given, which reads like a horoscope in the daily papers. For example, the opening sentences for Hexagram 27 are "You have a tendency to be selfish, to envy others, to unjustly use others. Nothing good can come from this attitude..." (p. 30). The lines are not mentioned. There is no bibliography or references.

Markert, Christopher. *I Ching the No. 1 Success Formula*. Wellingborough, Northamptonshire: The Aquarian Press, 1986.

> Translation of the *I Ching*. No source given, but author acknowledges his quotes from Legge's translation. Coin method of divination is explained as well as the yarrow-stalk method, and pebble method (no source given).

McKenna, Dennis J. and Terence K. McKenna. *The Invisible Landscape: Mind, Hallucinogens, and the I Ching*. New York: The Seabury Press, 1975.

> Contains three chapters on the *I Ching:* Chapter 8, The *I Ching* as Lunar Calendar and Astronomical Calendar;

Chapter 9, Order in the *I Ching;* and Chapter 10, Order in the World. The relation of the King Wen Sequence to DNA and the electromagnetic spectrum is suggested. Worthwhile reading, even though highly speculative. Contains some interesting observations on the textual sequence of the *I Ching* that I have not found elsewhere in the English literature. Also discussed is the holographic theory of mind.

Mears, I. and L. E. Mears. *Creative Energy: A Study of the I-Ching.* Burbank, California: Ohara Publications, Inc., 1976.

> An introduction to the *I Ching* and a translation. Authors state that "the explanatory statements marked by quotations are literal translations made directly from the Chinese text" (p. 51), but the source is not made clear. No index or bibliography.

Melyan, Gary and Wen-kuang Chu. *I-Ching: The Hexagrams Revealed.* Rutland, Vermont and Tokyo, Japan: Charles E. Tuttle Company. Copyright in Japan, 1977.

> Melyan writes: "It is to fill the need for a practical and simple introduction to consulting the *I Ching* as an oracle that Dr. Wen-kuang Chu and I have collaborated on this text" (p. 7). The lines of the hexagrams are not given, but for each hexagram there is a section entitled The Fortune, which contains outcomes in the following categories: Wish, Marriage, Love, Family, Children, Capital Loan, Business, Stock Market, Life Span, Sickness, Waiting for Someone, Looking for Someone, Lost Article, Travel, Lawsuit and Disputes, Employment, Examination, New Business, Change of Occupation or Specialization, Moving, and Weather. A bibliography is given listing *I Ching* translations, articles and papers on the *I Ching,* and secondary sources about the *I Ching.*

_____. *The Pocket I-CHING.* First YENBOOKS edition, 1988. Copyright 1977 by Charles E. Tuttle Co. Inc.

> This book is a reprint of the *I-Ching: The Hexagrams Revealed.* No revisions were made.

Moran, Jim. *The Wonders of Magic Squares.* New York: Vintage Books, A Division of Random House, 1982.

> This reference is given as a research aid for those who are interested in the *I Ching* and magic squares. The book does not mention the *I Ching* but is a good introduction to magic

squares. Martin Gardner, who wrote the introduction, says "It is the only book I know that manages to explain magic squares to mathematical illiterates but also to hook their interest in these fascinating curiosities" (p. xii). No index and a seven-entry bibliography. See John L. Fults, *Magic Squares.*

Murphy, Joseph. *Secret of the I Ching.* West Nyack, New York: Parker Publishing Company, 1970.

Murphy acknowledges in the Forward that he used the Wilhelm/Baynes edition, although his version of the *I Ching* has little resemblance to it. Murphy lavishly distributes Biblical quotations throughout his interpretation; there are about eight to a hexagram.

Needham, Joseph. *History of Scientific Thought,* vol. 2, and *Mathematics and the Sciences of the Heavens and the Earth,* vol. 3, of *Science and Civilization in China.* Cambridge University Press, 1956.

Volume 2 of Needham's monumental work devotes forty two pages to "The System of the Book of Changes" (pp. 304–45). In the same volume is the "Enumeration Orders and Symbolic Correlations" (pp. 253–73) of the Five-Element theory. Also of interest to *I Ching* scholars will be his section on Taoism, Chinese Naturalism, and the pseudo-sciences.

Volume 3 has two topics of possible interest to *I Ching* scholars: ancient Chinese mathematics and astrology.

Needham's volumes are extensively indexed and each has three bibliographies. The first is to Chinese books before 1800 A.D., the second is to Chinese and Japanese books and journal articles since 1800 A.D., and the third is to books and journal articles in Western languages.

Ni, Hua Ching. *The Book of Changes and the Unchanging Truth.* Malibu, California: The Shrine of the Eternal Breath of Tao, and Los Angeles, California: College of Tao and Traditional Chinese Healing, 1983.

Master Ni, the dustcover asserts, is a Taoist who has spent twenty-eight years in Asia teaching and practicing T'ai Chi Chuan, Kung Fu, Taoist meditation, internal alchemy, acupuncture and herbal medicine. The book, which claims to contain a new translation of the Book of Changes (p. iii), has no index or bibliography. It also contains no reference notes. The translation seems to contain no surprises and is fairly standard.

Norvell [No other name given]. *Miracle Power of the I Ching.* West Nyack, New York: Parker Publishing Company, 1980.

> Only relation to the *I Ching* is the name "*I Ching*" in the title and its occurrence throughout the book.

Palmer, Martin, Mak Hin Chung, Kwok Man Ho, and Angela Smith, eds. *T'ung Shu: The Ancient Chinese Almanac.* Boston: Shambhala Publications, Inc., 1986.

> Contains information on the Chinese calendar. States that in China the equinoxes and solstices occur in the middle of a season. Hence, in China each season starts about a month and a half earlier than by Western standards (p. 64).

Palmer, Martin, Kwok Man Ho, and Joanne O'Brien. *The Fortune Teller's I Ching.* New York: Ballantine Books, 1986.

> Originally published in Great Britain by Rider and Co. Ltd, an imprint of Century Hutchinson Ltd. The authors are all members of the International Consultancy on Religion, Education and Culture (ICOREC). Kwok Man Ho is the head of the Chinese section of the ICOREC and a practicing astrologer. The book claims to be the "first **new** interpretation" of the *I Ching*, one that is "closer to the original Chinese than previous translations" (From back cover). There is a 52-page preface containing four chapters. The first chapter gives the traditional account of the origin of the *I Ching*. The second chapter gives some interesting background information on the Legge and Richard Wilhelm Translations. The authors state that their own translation is based mainly on four contemporary commentaries of the *I Ching*. Unfortunately these commentaries are not clearly referenced. The third chapter gives three divinatory methods: the twelve-stick method, the three-coin method, and the eight-coin (Pa Ch'ien) method. The authors claim that the Pa Ch'ien method is the one most commonly used. I have not found any other account of the Pa Ch'ien method in English. The last chapter stresses that the *I Ching* does **not** foretell the future, it "gives you a fairly clear idea of **how you will go if you continue along the path you are now on**" (Palmer, Ho, and O'Brien, p. 52). In an appendix the Chinese text of the *I Ching* is given. Its source is Sun Tsai Shang's *Chou I Yuan I Hsin Cheng Shih*, a modern Chinese commentary.

Pattee, Rowena. *Moving with Change.* London, New York: Arkana (an imprint of Routledge & Kegan Paul, Ltd., 1968.)

> A bibliography that lists a surprising number of reputable works and papers on the *I Ching.* However, the sources used for the translation are not made clear. Several card methods of divination related to the *I Ching* are described by the author.

Peat, F. David. *Synchronicity: The Bridge Between Matter and Mind.* Toronto, New York, London: Bantam Books, 1987.

> A sympathetic treatment of the principle of synchronicity: the hypothesis that meaningful coincidences occur that can not be explained by chance or causality. Synchronicity as an acausal connecting principle is offered as an explanation of such coincidences. Carl Jung was the first to advance this theory. In the foreward to the Wilhelm/Baynes edition of the *I Ching,* Jung offers the theory of synchronicity as an explanation of the divinatory functions of the *I Ching.* Peat, following Jung, assumes that the *I Ching* does function as a reliable oracle and also offers the theory of synchronicity as an explanation. Approximately ten pages of the 245-page book is devoted to the *I Ching.* See Carl Jung, *Synchronicity.*

Poncé, Charles. *The Nature of the I Ching: Its Usage and Interpretation.* New York: Award Books (A547S) published by Universal Publishing and Distributing Corporation, 1970.

> Worthwhile reading! The only book in English that gives a variety of examples showing in some detail how to interpret a hexagram using its primary, upper, and lower nuclear hexagrams. Also of interest is the examples showing how to use the emblems (old yang, young yang, old yin, young yin) and the elements (Fire, Wood, Water, Metal) to analyze the meaning of a hexagram. There are practically no references and no index or bibliography.

Porter, Rosemary Macias. "Visual Metaphors from the *I Ching.*" M.A. diss. in Art: California State University, Long Beach, 1977.

> Total length is twenty-six pages. Drawings not available. Author states:
>
>> This project involved the extension of ideas from an auditory art form to a visual art form by creating visual images based upon methods used

by John Cage in the production of auditory musical and poetic compositions (pp. 1–2).

In essence the project is a method for creating drawings
by chance. By the use of the coin method six hexagrams are
selected. The numbers of the hexagrams selected determine
grid size and placement, interior grid size, image pattern, and
the hardness of the pencils used to draw them. Also the title
for the drawing is selected by chance. Dissertation contains no
drawings.

Reifler, Sam. *I Ching: A New Interpretation For Modern Times.* New York:
Bantam Books, 1974.

The sixteen-page introduction gives both the yarrow-
stalk and coin method. The translation is probably not original.
Both hexagram text and line text is given. There is no index or
bibliography.

Riseman, Tom. *Introduction to The I Ching: The History and Use of the World's
Most Ancient System of Divination.* New York: Samuel Weiser Inc., 1980.

A translation of the *I Ching;* hexagram and line text
are given. Coin method of divination is briefly explained. No
references, bibliography or index.

Sarton, George. *A History of Science: Ancient Science through the Golden Age
of Greece.* Cambridge: Harvard University Press, 1960.

Gives a brief explanation of the sexagenary (base 60)
cycle used in ancient China (pp. 11–13) and an impure sexagesimal system used in Mesopotamia (pp. 68–74).

Sarton writes:

The coexistence of sexagesimal ideas in
China and Mesopotamia is very striking (see
pp. 11–13). That is too slender a basis to con-
clude that one of these two cultures was influenced by the other; yet it is more convincing
to me than linguistic analogies. Sixty is a very
large number to agree upon. Its use as a number base or as a cycle implies a very high degree
of sophistication (p. 69, n. 23).

Schonberger, Martin. *The I Ching & the Genetic Code.* D. Q. Stephenson, trans. New York: ASI Publishers, Inc., 1979.

> Originally published in German as *Verborgener Schlussel zum Leben* [*The Hidden Key to Life*]. Munchen: O. W. Barth Berlag, 1973. One of the first to publish a highly speculative theory that there are significant similarities between the *I Ching* hexagrams and DNA.

Schoenholtz, Larry. *New Direction in the I Ching: The Yellow River Legacy.* Secaucus, New Jersey: University Books, 1975.

> Since it is more probable to obtain some hexagrams than others by the yarrow-stalk method, much of the book is devoted to exploring the significance of this. Also describes his invention, The Sixteen System, which is a fast, simple system of constructing the lines of a hexagram with the same probabilities as the yarrow-stalk method. Appendix A gives three methods of Divination: Yarrow-Stalk Method, Coin Method, and Six-Wands Method. Appendix B gives mathematical calculations for determining the probabilities of obtaining the lines by the yarrow-stalk method. Appendix C gives the schematic diagram for an electronic device, based on the Sixteen System, that will yield a hexagram.

Schulz, Larry James. "Lai Chih-Te (1525–1604) and the Phenomenology of the *Classic of Change (I Ching)*." Ph.D. diss. in Philosophy, Department of East Asian Studies: Princeton University, 1982.

> The author states that:

>> The present study is set in the sixteenth century, that time characterized by "reckless" ideas in classicism in general...It involves the *Classic of Change* exegesis of Lai Chih-te..., whose understanding of the *Change* was formed over thirty years of single-minded concentration upon it...he published in 1599 a commentary based on what he believed to have been discoveries of facts about the structure of the *Change* that had remained shrouded in mystery since the death of Confucius (p. 8). Like many other dissertations in the areas of East Asian studies, this scholarly dissertation contains material not found elsewhere in English.

Shaughnessy, Edward Louis. "The Composition of the *Zhouyi*." Ph.D. diss. in Chinese Studies: Stanford University, 1983.

The author writes:

> The present study... will use the methodology of context criticism to address the twin questions of how the *Zhouyi* came into being and what it meant to its original composers... The investigation is divided into two parts, the first being an attempt to describe the cultural milieu in which the *Zhouyi* was composed, while the second is strictly text critical.. Part One is further sub-divided into two separate studies: an attempt to date the text as precisely as possible, and a broad survey of the development of divination in ancient China together with a detailed study of *Zhouyi* divination (p. 13).

The author concludes that the evidence shows:

> the *Zhouyi* to be a product of the latter stage of the Western Zhou dynasty, and the historical context of this period suggests a composition date in the early years of King Xuan's reign: most probably, during the last two decades of the ninth century, B.C. (p. 49).

Also concluded is that the:

> tradition in *Zhouyi* of one hexagram "changing into" another has been shown to be anachronistic... and of a more literary nature, the 386 line statements of the *Zhouyi* do not owe their origin to specific divinations... On the other hand, we have seen that the *Zhouyi* line statements served as prognostications in these divinations... (pp. 102–03).

Also given is the sequence of the hexagrams in the Mawangdui manuscript, found in a tomb in 1973, and a study in intra-hexagrammatic relationships (pp. 168–74).

Shchutskii, Iulaim K. *Researches on the I Ching.* William L. MacDonald, Tsuyoshi Hasegawa, and Hellmut Wilhelm, trans. Princeton University Press, 1979.

> Written between 1928 and 1935 the work was published in Moscow in 1960. Shchutskii surveys and critically examines the literature dealing with the *I Ching* in Europe as well as in the Far East. Most interesting in this context is his description and appraisal of the translations of the *I Ching* by Legge and Richard Wilhelm. He then tries to understand the *I Ching* in terms of its own images and seeks to recapture the original meaning and structure of its language. It is excellent scholarship throughout. The forty-two page introduction to the English edition is written by Gerald W. Swanson—a former student of Hellmut Wilhelm—and is a masterful summary and evaluation of Shchutskii's accomplishments. The book is indexed and has an eleven-page bibliography to both Western and Eastern sources.

Sherrill, W. A. and W. K. Chu. *The Astrology of the I Ching.* New York: Samuel Weiser, Inc., 1976.

> Over four-hundred pages of divination procedures using astrology and the *I Ching.* The only reference given for the source of all this material is in the Preface, where the first author states: *"The Astrology of I Ching* is based on a manuscript in ancient classical Chinese, the title of which, translated literally, is 'Ho Map Lo Map Rational Number' " (p. ix). The book contains a short index, but no bibliography.

_____. *An Anthology of I Ching.* London, Boston, Melbourne and Henley: Routledge & Kegan Paul, Ltd., 1977.

> A handbook for those who wish to learn or practice divination in connection with the *I Ching.* The yarrow-stalk method is not covered. The contents are: Chapter 1. Basic Information; Chapter 2. Advanced Divination [Covered here is the Plum Blossom system. See Da Liu]; Chapter 3. Astrologies Related to the *I Ching;* Chapter 4. *Tai Shuan Ching* [a book written by Yang Hsiung. See Derek Walters]; Chapter 5. The *I Ching* and History; Chapter 6. The *I Ching* and Meditation; Chapter 7. The *I Ching* and Geomancy; and Chapter 8. Directionality. The three appendices consist of Table of Trigram Attributes, The Lunar Calendar, and Applicability of Advanced Divination, Tzu Pin and Astrology of the *I Ching* in the Southern Hemisphere. Few references are given. There is a short index, but no bibliography.
>
> Much information is given in this book: The Plum Blos-

som numerology system, a Chinese lunar calendar from 1910 to 1990, celestial stems and their related years, the horary branch hours, an extensive list of the attributes of the trigrams, and much more.

Simmons, Jayme F. *I Ching: A Philosophical Prophecy.* Ken White, ed. Anaheim, California: Dynamic Design Industries, 1972.

> This sixty-five page book, printed on two-holed stiff cardboard and bound with rings, comes in a box with three imitation Chinese coins. The coin method of divination is given and for each hexagram there are fortunes under the following categories: Money, Taking Risk, Business, Romance, and Traveling. No bibliography, index, or references.

Siu, R. G. H. *The Man of Many Qualities: A Legacy of the I Ching.* Cambridge, Massachusetts: The MIT Press, 1968.

> The meanings of the hexagrams are exemplified by "about 700 quotations by over 650 authors from nearly 60 countries over a period of 6000 years..." (p. vi). In my opinion, the examples do not help to clarify the meaning of the hexagrams.

Smith, G. E. Kidder. "Cheng Yi's (1033–1107) Commentary on the *Yijing.*" Ph.D. diss. in History: University of California, 1979.

> The author states that Cheng Yi's Commentary on the *Yijing* is:

> > the first reading of the *Yi* as a purely neo-Confucian document. With the commentary of Zhu Xi... it has dominated the last thousand years of *Yijing* study. Indeed the translations of James Legge and Richard Wilhelm are based largely on Cheng Yi's explanations of the text (p. iv).

> The author ends his work with the statement:

> > In Chapter One the author shows how *yili* and *xiangshu* schools develop from the ambiguous relationship of the hexagram configuration and its accompanying texts. This split remains the fundamental distinction between writings on the *Yi*. Even in modern America it is through these two aspects that people approach the book. Some build marvelous sys-

tems of its number; others elaborate its texts to their own fancies.

We are outside the world of classical China, but we need not trivialize the book. There is an alternative. This is to see the book, like so much of the classical belief system, as something aesthetic and historical. As literature and myth the *Yijing* still speaks to us directly. Under such a view the book must shed some of its universalistic claims. But something of its proper dignity is at least preserved (p. 125).

Stein, Diane. *The Kwan Yin Book of Changes*. St. Paul, Minnesota: Llewellyn Publications, 1985.

In the author's own words:

The Kwan Yin Book of Changes translates the male-dominated Chinese *I Ching* to women's values and into a Goddess system of religion... *The Kwan Yin Book of Changes* often totally diverges from traditional titles and hexagrams texts. (p. iii).

The author warns the reader that he may expect the unusual. Of the eight books listed in the bibliography the only translation of the *I Ching* listed is the Wilhelm/Baynes edition.

Sung, Z. D. *The Symbols of Yi King* or *The Symbols of the Chinese Logic of Changes*. New York: Paragon Book Reprint Corp., 1969a.

A reprint of the Shanghai 1934 edition. The contents of the book in the author's own words is:

the record of the writer's discoveries, after his life study on the fundamentals of this subject, namely, the perfect agreement of these symbols [hexagrams] with those of the algebraic terms of the expanded expression of a binomial sixth power, and the concord in the numerical value of the two technical terms, assigned in their elementary forms, to the length of day and night of the two solstices in China, or the explanation as to why those technical terms, 9 and 6, are used throughout the whole text in delineation of those symbols. (p. i).

Sung is one of the first to publish in English a book which advocates that the *I Ching* conceals numerous mathematical and scientific secrets. For example, Sung finds Aristotle's syllogistic, the theory of the parallelogram of forces, astronomical and geophysical data in the *I Ching* and much more. Sung's book is difficult to read. It is not always clear what he is trying to prove or how he is trying to prove it. However, it is—of its kind—an interesting and suggestive book.

————. *The Text of the I Ching (And Its Appendixes) Chinese Original with English Translation.* New York: Paragon Book Reprint Corp., 1969b.

A reprint of the Shanghai 1935 edition. One of the few English translations that give the Chinese text. Basically it is a more convenient arrangement of Legge's translation. Sung writes in the Preface:

> The conversion of Legge's work in the form of the Ancient Yi, into the present one of the Modern Yi, is the principal feature of this work... The difference between the two forms is that in the Ancient Yi, the Text and Confucian Appendices are each a separate book while in the Modern Yi, the pertinent portions of the Confucian Appendices are incorporated into the Text so that the works of the four sages are gathered in one place for the convenience of the students (p. vi).

Swanson, Gerald William. "The Great Treatise: Commentary Tradition to the *Book of Changes.*" Ph.D. diss.: University of Washington, 1974.

The only dissertation in English that I am aware of on the *Great Treatise.* Its topic is best described in Swanson's own words:

> This study represents the third English language translation of the *Great Treatise* in the last hundred years. It is the first translation directly from Chinese to English which provides commentary and analysis of the main ideas of the text (p. 1).

and

> ...the authors of the *Great Treatise* were concerned to place the older layers of the hexagram

and line texts into a metaphysical context consistent with and influenced by the **yin-yang**
and five elements theories. The present study is
primarily concerned with how this was brought
about (p. 12).

Tat, Wei. *An Exposition of the I Ching or Book of Changes.* Yang Ming Shan
Villa, Taipei, Taiwan, Republic of China: Institute of Cultural Studies,
Printed by the Printing Works of The College of Chinese Culture, 1970.
Distributed in the United States by Paragon Book Gallery, Ltd., New York.

Five hundred and sixty-five pages devoted to the first
two hexagrams of the *I Ching.* The Wen Yen, the 7th Wing, is
examined in detail. There is not much that is not mentioned
in this book. The Logos, the Egyptians, Hermes, Karma, King
Nebuchadnezzar, Krishna, Jesus, Cain, and so forth. However,
the book is suggestive and worthwhile reading. There are two
bibliographies: One to books in Chinese works and the other
to English works. Many of the books listed are not works on
the *I Ching.* Author is brother of Henry Wei, author of *The
Authentic I-Ching.* See below, Wei, Henry.

Tung, Gea. "Metaphore and Analogy in the *I CHING.*" Ph.D. diss. in Philosophy: Claremont Graduate School, Claremont, CA, 1975.

Dissertation contains six chapters. The first is enti-
tled "Introduction," the last "Conclusion." Chapter 2 is "The
Structuring of Experience as Dipolar in the *I Ching* and A.
N. Whitehead's *Process And Reality.*" Chapter 3 is "Historical
and Cultural Background of the *I Ching.*" Chapter 4 is "The
I Ching and its Appendices—The Systematic and Philosophical
Use of Metaphor and Analogy." Chapter 5 is "The *I Ching* in
the Tradition of Chinese Philosophy."
The author states: "In its ordering of metaphors and
analogies based on polar structures the *I Ching* puts forward a
method of expressing dynamically a process view of the cosmos
which it seems certain would reward further study" (p. 136).

Walker, Barbara G. *The I Ching of the Goddess.* San Francisco: Harper & Row,
1986.

A fanciful interpretation of the hexagrams. The lines
are not mentioned. Probably based on Blofeld and/or Legge's
translations, which are two of the five books listed in the bibliography.

Walters, Derek. *The T'ai Hsüan Ching: The Hidden Classic.* Wellingborough, Northamptonshire: The Aquarian Press, 1983.

> Worthwhile reading. The only translation and explanation of the method of divination invented by Yang Hsiung (53 B.C.–18 A.D.) in English. Like the *I Ching* it uses symbols composed of lines, but unlike the *I Ching* it uses tetragrams (4-lined symbols) not hexagrams (6-lined symbols). It also differs from the *I Ching* by using three kinds of lines: a whole line, a line divided into two parts, and one divided into three parts. Has an interesting appendix on nine magic squares of nine. These squares, when placed on top of one another, form a Cube of Nine, which has magical properties. Referenced with bibliography and index.

————. *The Alternative I Ching.* Published in 1987a. First published in 1983 as *The T'ai Hsüan Ching: The Hidden Classic.* Annotation given under this title.

————. *Chinese Astrology.* The Aquarian Press: Wellingborough, Northamptonshire, 1987b.

> Contains a forty-one-page chapter entitled "The Chinese Calendar" which contains material on the Chinese calendars not readily available elsewhere in English.

Waltham, Clae. *I Ching: The Chinese Book of Changes.* New York: Ace Publishing Corporation, 1969.

> As stated on the title page and in the table of contents, the information on the hexagrams is an arrangement of Legge's translation. A twenty-one page Alphabetical Reference is given, which is a glossary of terms and proper names.

Watson, Burton. *Early Chinese Literature.* New York: Columbia University Press, 1962.

> Gives a very good description of each of the five Confucian Classics of which one is the *I Ching.* All the major works of ancient China are covered: *Tso Chuang, Kuo Yu,* and so forth.

Wei, Henry. *The Authentic I-Ching.* A Newcastle Book, 1987. Obtainable from R. Reginald, The Borgo Press, San Bernardino, California.

> Introduction is by Professor Jay G. Williams, Chairman, Department of Religion, Hamilton College, who argues that the *I Ching* in its divinatory function "is a device for self-knowledge" (p. x). Also given is the justification for another translation, the one given in the book.

In the Preface the author points out the deficiencies of the Legge, Wilhelm/Baynes, and Blofeld translations. The Three-Coin method of divination is given in several pages entitled "Publisher's Note." The first seventy-four pages of the book gives the traditional account of the origin of the *I Ching* in some detail and describes the Ten Wings, which the author attributes to Confucius (some sections to Confucius' disciples). Covered also are the River Maps, the trigrams and their arrangements, Fu Hsi's and King Wen's arrangement of the hexagrams, the interpretation of a hexagram, the yarrow-stalk method of divination.

The translation covers "only the Text and the five Wings, (Appendices) directly related to it" (p. xxi). The *Great Treatise* is not translated. Sources used for translation are not made clear. No index, but two and a half pages of notes and references.

Author is graduate of Lingnan University, Canton, in Western and Chinese literature and holds a doctorate in International Relations from the University of Chicago. Author's brother is Wei Tat, author of *An Exposition of the I Ching or Book of Changes*. See above, Tat, Wei.

West, Patricia E. *The Aquarian Book of Change*. Wilmot, Wisconsin: Red Dragon Press, 1981.

A translation of the *I Ching*. On copyright page is statement "Adaptation from the I CHING WORKBOOK by R. L. Wing." Has a 24–page introduction which gives the coin method. No bibliography and no index.

Whincup, Greg. *Rediscovering the I Ching*. Garden City, New York: Doubleday & Company, Inc., 1986.

Whincup's translation of the *I Ching* differs significantly from the Legge and Wilhelm/Baynes in several places. Justification is given for all deviations from the standard interpretation. Whincup also presents the theory that the textual sequence of the sixty-four hexagrams can be interpreted as "a nobleman's rise from obscurity and weakness to a position of great power" (p. 5). The book also contains a short history of ancient China and a new explanation of the symbolism of the *I Ching*. Strongly recommended.

White, Douglass Alan. "Interpretations of the Central Concept of the *I-Ching* during the Han, Sung and Ming Dynasties." Ph.D. diss.: Harvard University, 1976.

> According to the author "The purpose of this study is to investigate how the major *I-ching* scholars interpreted the concept of centrality in the *I-ching*" (p. iii). Topics and Chinese scholars covered are: Meng Hsi, Ching Fang, The Han Apocrypha, Yang Hsiung's *The Canon of Great Subtlety,* The Kinship of the Three, Wang Pi, Buddhism and the *I Ching,* Chou Tun-I, Shao Yung, Ch'eng I, Chu Hsi, Yang Chien, Yu Yen, Liu Tsung-Chou, and Master Ou-I. The oracular aspects of the *I Ching* are not dealt with and the mathematical aspect is kept to a minimum (p. ii).

Wilhelm/Baynes. Wilhelm, Richard. *The I Ching or Book of Changes.*

Wilhelm, Hellmut. *Change: Eight Lecturers on the I Ching.* Cary F. Baynes, trans. New York & Evanston: Harper & Row Publishers, 1960.

> Required reading! The original was entitled *Die Wandlung; acht Vortäge zum 'I-Ging* and published in Peiping, 1944. Not a translation of the *I Ching,* but an introduction to the *I Ching.* Needham (vol. 2, pp. 307–8) writes "Much the best book in a Western language on the *I Ching* is, in my opinion, the small introduction by H. Wilhelm."
>
> The contents of the book are: Chapter 1. Origins; Chapter 2. The Concept of Change; Chapter 3. Two Fundamental Principles; Chapter 4. The Trigrams and the Hexagrams; Chapter 5. The Hexagrams Ch'ien and K'un; Chapter 6. The Ten Wings; Chapter 7. The Later History of the Book of Changes; Chapter 8. The Oracle Book.

_____. *Parerga: The Book of Changes in the Western Tradition: A Selective Bibliography.* Seattle: Institute for Comparative and Foreign Area Studies, University of Washington, 1975.

> A booklet of twenty-nine pages listing over 150 references (books and journal articles) concerning the *I Ching.* The majority of the references are annotated.

_____. *Heaven, Earth, and Man in the Book of Changes.* Seattle and London: University of Washington Press, 1977.

> Composed of seven lectures. They are entitled: 1. The Concept of Time; 2. The Creative Principle; 3. Human Events and Their Meaning; 4. The "Own City" as the Stage of Forma-

tion; 5. The Interaction of Heaven, Earth, and Man; 6. Wanderings of the Spirit; 7. The Interplay of Image and Concept. Required reading for all students of the *I Ching* as are all of Hellmut Wilhelm's books.

Wilhelm, Richard, trans. *The I Ching or Book of Changes.* 3rd edition. (Published in one volume.) Translated from German to English by C. F. Baynes. Princeton University Press, 1967.

> Richard Wilhelm (1873–1930), German theologian and sinologist, was a missionary in Tsing-tao (1899–1921). Started translating the *I Ching* into German in 1911. Published the translation in German in Jena in 1924, under the title *I Ging; Das Buch der Wandlungen.* Translated from German into English by Cary F. Baynes. First edition was published in two volumes for Bollingen Foundation Inc. by Pantheon Books Inc., 1950. In 1976 the book was in its third edition and thirteenth printing.

> The book is a scholarly and popular translation of the *I Ching* and the Ten Wings with explanatory annotations. Translation is based on an edition with the title *Chou I Che Chung,* arranged in 1662–1722 A.D. (p. lxi). Every serious student of the *I Ching* should have this book in his library. Needham says, speaking about Hellmut Wilhelm's book, "Probably the best translation [of the *I Ching*] is that by his father, R. Wilhelm though in many ways that of Legge is more useful." (*Science and Civilization in China,* vol. 2, p. 308). In a note on the same page Needham states that "The editions of R. Wilhelm, especially the English translation by Baynes (quite sound in itself), constitute unfortunately a sinological maze, and belong to the Department of Utter Confusion." For a sinologist of Needham's stature—who can read the *I Ching* in the original language—I have no doubt that his criticisms—made more specific in the rest of his note—should be heeded. However, for those who do not read Chinese, the Wilhelm/Baynes translation in conjunction with Legge's, Whincup's, Cleary's and others, is a valuable aid.

_____, trans. *The Secret of the Golden Flower.* Commentary by C. G. Jung. Translated into English by Cary F. Baynes. New York: Causeway Books, 1975.

> The *Thai I Chin Hua Tsung Chih (The Secret of the Golden Flower of Great Unity)* is a Taoist text of the 17th century A.D., author unknown.

At the end of the first introductory chapter Wilhelm states:

> As a supplement we must still add a few words about the use of the eight signs [the trigrams] of the *Book of Changes* (*I Ching*) in our text. The sign. . . [100, *Thunder*] is the beginning of all movement. The sign. . . [011, *Wind*] characterizes the streaming of the reality-forces into the form of the idea. . . The sign. . . [101, *Fire*] forms the protecting circle, and effects the rebirth. The sign. . . [000, *Earth*] as a tilled field, takes up the seed of Heaven and gives it form. The sign. . . [110, *Lake*] is an end condition on the *yin* side and therefore belongs to autumn. The sign . . . [111, *Heaven*] is the reality form of the *yang* principle which fertilizes. . . the receptive [000]. The sign. . . [010, *Water*] represents the region of *eros,* while. . . [101, *Fire*] stands for *logos.* The marriage of. . . [010, *Water* and 101, *Fire*] is the secret magical process which produces the child, the new man. The sign. . . [001, *Mountain*] represents meditation. . . Therefore. . . [001, *Mountain*] is the place where death and life meet. . . (p. 188–190).

————. *Lectures on the I Ching: Constancy and Change.* Irene Eber, trans. Princeton University Press: 1979.

> Published in German as *Wandlung und Dauer* in 1956. Consists of four lectures he gave between 1926 and 1929. They are entitled: Opposition and Fellowship, The Spirit of Art according to the *Book of Changes,* Constancy in Change, and Death and Renewal. References and index are given. All of Richard Wilhelm's books are worthwhile reading.

Wing, R. L. *The I Ching Work Book.* New York: Doubleday & Company, Inc., 1979.

> After a brief introduction to the *I Ching* and the coin method of divination, a translation is given. No source is mentioned. Alongside the textual material for each line are ruled columns and blank squares in which one may record how often the hexagram and line was obtained, and in response to what inquiries. No bibliography.

_____. *The Illustrated I Ching*. Garden City, New York: Dolphin/Doubleday & Company, Inc. 1982.

> A translation of the *I Ching* with each hexagram being accompanied by a Chinese painting. No color, all paintings are in black and white, but each painting is briefly explained. The Chinese text from which the translation was made is given, but its source is not indicated.

Yu, Titus. "The 'I Ching': An Etymological Perspective." Ph.D diss.: in Philosophy: California Institute of Integral Studies, San Francisco, 1983.

> A translation of the *I Ching*. Copy obtained through University Microfilms International has no page numbers, no table of contents, and no bibliography. Translation is modern as Hexagram 33 is named "The Pig" and Hexagram 36 the "Feigning Bird."

P

ANNOTATED BIBLIOGRAPHY B: JOURNAL ARTICLES

All references to journal articles in this work are listed in this bibliography. All articles listed here are in English, except for one. The annotations, which express my opinions, may prove useful in identifying articles of interest.

Anderson, Allan W. "Approaches to the Meaning of Ming, in the *I Ching* with Particular Reference to Self-Cultivation." *Journal of Chinese Philosophy* 9: (June 1982): 169–95.

> The author finds subjective and objective features to *ming* (will of Heaven).

> On the subjective side, *obedience, understanding,* and *effort* are the principal features. These three respectively when seen through "The Great Treatise": 1.4 (page 11 *supra*) reflect the virtues we commonly call faith, hope and love. Objectively, the principal features are a transcendent immanence, *ordaining, maintaining,* and *consummating* (p. 191).

--------. "On the Concept of Freedom in the *I Ching:* A Deconstructionist View of Self-Cultivation." *Journal of Chinese Philosophy* 17:3 (September 1990): 275–87.

> The author examines the concept of (spiritual) freedom by analyzing the text of certain hexagrams. The author states "Calculated thought bound to causalism, process and structure is blind to spirit yet in dread that it cannot control it. The authentic, concrete thought of spiritual freedom cannot be generated out of the dialectic" (p. 286).

Arguelles, Jose. "Compute and Evolve." *Main Currents in Modern Thought* 25 (Jan/Feb 1969): 663–67.

> The author's theme is that the *I Ching* can be viewed as a "psychic computer" (p. 66).

> The *I Ching* functions as a computer and its functioning is only according to the truth of the programming. The truth of the programming depends on how the person who consults the Book of Changes responds to its messages (p. 66).

Barde, Rene. "Recherches sur les origines arithmetiques du *Yi-king.*" *Archives internationales d'histoire des sciences* 5 (1952): 234–81.

> The only article in this bibliography that is not in English. Barde presents and develops an interesting theory; namely, that the hexagrams functioned as a device that did arithmetical calculations. He also postulates that the ancient Chinese might have used a number system based on five.

Brown, Chappell. "Inner Truth and the Origin of the Yarrow Stalk Oracle." *Journal of Chinese Philosophy* 9:2 (June 1982): 197–210.

> By a non-traditional assignment of numbers to the four images (emblems) and by forming ratios and equations using certain combinations of these numbers, Brown derives the Golden Ratio, which is $\frac{a}{b}$ as $\frac{b}{a+b}$.

————. "The Tetrahedron as an Archetype for the Concept of Change in the *I Ching.*" *Journal of Chinese Philosophy* 9:2 (June 1982): 159–68.

> Brown devises a system in which each trigram is a combination of two images (an image being a two-lined symbol). A tetrahedron is a four-sided three-dimensional figure, having triangles as sides, and four vertices. Brown assigns an image to each vertex. Each of the six edges is then represented by a trigram. Trigram 1 (all yang lines) and Trigram 2 (all yin lines) are formed, respectively, from the Great Yang Image (two yang lines) and the Great Yin Image (two yin lines). By using the magic square of 3 and by tracing certain paths on the edges of the tetrahedron Brown generates the Fu Hsi and King Wen sequence of the trigrams.

Cammann, Schuyler. "The Evolution of Magic Squares in China." *American Oriental Society Journal* LXXX (1960): 116–24.

> An interesting history on magic squares in China. Cammann states:
>
> > To sum up, we have seen that the Chinese probably did indeed invent the magic square of three, centuries before anyone else; but they were apparently so hypnotized by this early solution, and by all the cosmic and magical properties ascribed to it, that they continued to try to adapt the *Lo Shu* [square of three] principle to the solving of higher squares as well (p. 123).

———. "The Magic Square of Three in Old Chinese Philosophy and Religion." *History of Religion* I (1961): 37–80.

> Has seven parts, which are entitled: 1. Early Evidence for Chinese Knowledge of the "Lo Shu" Square; 2. The "Lo Shu" Square as an Expression of Centrality; 3. The Yin and Yang in the "Lo Shu" Square; 4. How the "Lo Shu" Square Represented the Five Elements; 5. The "Lo Shu" and the Cult of the T'ai-ti; 6. The Decline of the "Lo Shu" and the Fall of T'ai-ti; 7. Ultimate Fate of the "Lo Shu."

———. "Old Chinese Magic Squares." *Sinologica* 4 (1962): 14–53.

> Most of this paper is devoted to the magic squares in Yang Hui's book, the *Hsü-Ku Chai-chi Suan-fa* [Translated by Needham, vol. 2, p. 59 as, Continuation of Ancient Mathematical Methods for Elucidating the Strange (Properties of Numbers)]. Cammann's paper explains the construction of these magic squares with special emphasis on how some of them might have been obtained from the *Lo Shu* square of three. In this paper he gives Yang Hui's first magic square of eight, which Cammann said Yang Hui entitled *I-shu t'u* or "Plan of the I-(Ching) Numbers" (pp. 44–45).

Carroll, Thomas D. "The Hidden Significance of the I-Ching Diagrams." *Journal of the China Society* 2 (1962): 31–49.

> In the author's words:
>
>> This paper suggests that the *I-Ching* diagrams were invented to symbolize various stages in the annually recurring climatological cycle; and this symbolism is confirmed by arguments drawn from verisimilitude, from the supposed original order of the trigrams, from the supposed original order of the hexagrams, from the order of completion of the Late Heaven Sequence, and from striking parallels in Chinese astronomical history (p. 49).

Chang, Chi-Yun. "The *Book of Changes* (*I Ching*)—A Philosophical Masterpiece Mirroring the *Zeit-Geist* of the Western Chou Dynasty." *Chinese Culture* 6:4 (October 1965): 1–41.

> Part of the paper gives historical data that makes sense of some of the cryptic passages of the lines. For example, the author explains the expression "tapping the pitcher" (Hexagram

30, line 3) by pointing out that in ancient China people used their wine pitcher as a musical instrument by tapping it with their fingers. (p. 12). Parts of the paper are highly speculative. It is suggested that the concepts of space and time in the *I Ching* have much in common with the theory of relativity. The author also ascribes to the doctrine that Confucius wrote the Ten Wings to the *I Ching* and "cherished a strong love of the Philosophy of Changes." (p. 12).

Chen, Shih-Chuan. "How to Form a Hexagram and Consult the I Ching." *Journal of the American Oriental Society* 92:2 (1972): 237–49.

> The author states: "This paper is intended to deal with two basic and yet related problems: how a hexagram is acquired and how the *I Ching* is consulted." (p. 237). From the nineteen cases of consulting the *I Ching* described in the *Tso Chuan* and the four cases described in the *Kuo Yu* the author attempts to reconstruct the yarrow-stalk method used to obtain these hexagrams. This method is described in Chapter 10 of the present text and by [A] Whincup, pp. 228–29.

Cheng, Chung-Ying. "Li and Ch'i in the I Ching: Reconsideration of Being and Non-Being in Chinese Philosophy." *Journal of Chinese Philosophy* 14:1 (March 1987): 1–38.

> The author says:

> > we shall investigate here how the philosophical categories of *li* and *ch'i* might have been developed from the rich conceptual resources of the *I Ching*, and how difficulties involving this *li-ch'i* scheme in the Neo-Confucian philosophy of Chu Hsi can be overcome in light of a closer understanding of the metaphysical visions of the *I Ching*. (p. 2).

Cheng, Chung-Ying and Elton Johnson. "A Bibliography of the *I Ching* in Western Languages." *Journal of Chinese Philosophy* 14:1 (March 1987): 73–90.

> The bibliography has 235 entries, over half of them in English. It is one of the most complete bibliographies on *I Ching* literature printed in English.

Cheng, Yung-Hsiao. "*I Ching:* A Survey of Criticism in English." *Tamkang Review* 8:1 (April 1977): 207–25.

> The author states that a basic question concerning the *I Ching* is whether it should be treated as a philosophical text or simply as a manual of divination (p. 207). The views of James Legge, Homer Dubs, H. G. Creel, Hu Shih, Arthur Waley, Fung Yu-lan, Joseph Needham, David Mungello, Hellmut Wilhelm, C. G. Jung, Wayne McEvilly, and others are discussed.

Chou, Philip. "7,000 Years of Prognostication." *Free China Review* 14 (June 1964): 28–35.

> A somewhat sympathetic description of Chinese astrology.

Clarke, A. G. "Probability Theory Applied to the *I Ching.*" *Journal of Chinese Philosophy* 14:1 (March 1987): 65–72.

> Some of the data the author lists are the number of hexagrams of each type (e.g., the number of hexagrams with 5 yang lines and 1 yin line and having exactly two moving lines). He gives a table showing how probable it is to obtain hexagrams with different numbers of moving lines by the yarrow stalk and coin methods.

Cobb Jr., John B. "Post-Conference Reflections on Yin and Yang." *Journal of Chinese Philosophy* 6:4 (Dec. 1979): 421–26.

> The process philosophy of the *I Ching* is compared to Alfred North Whitehead's philosophy; differences and similarities are pointed out.

Dethlefsen, Edwin. "Computing the *I Ching* with a TRS-80." *Byte* 5:4 (April 1980): p. 96 and p. 102.

> A short, light discussion of the *I Ching.* A program for the TRS-80 is given, written in BASIC, that will cast a hexagram.

Doeringer, F. M. "Oracle and Symbol in the Redaction of the *I Ching.*" *Philosophy East and West* 30 (1980): 195–210.

> One of the major points of this article is that the commentaries of the *I Ching* "often seek to demonstrate how Confucian ethical values and relationships derive from the cosmic models displayed in the diagrams, making them the key link between ethics and cosmology" (p. 199).

De Saussure, Leopold. "On the Antiquity of the Yin-Yang Theory." *The New China Review* 4 (1922): 457–63.

> Title of article is somewhat misleading. The author's main point is that:

> > The *Yi King* treating precisely of astrology and of the changes which take place in the course of the cosmological revolution, it is clear one cannot grasp its sense if one ignores the existence of this cosmological system. Therefore the most eminent sinologists, for want of knowing this system, have hardly understood the general signification, both physical and metaphysical, of the trigrams (p. 459).

> According to the author the fundamental principle of the Chinese cosmology is "the Center surrounded by the four regions (or the eight half-regions)..." (p. 462).

Dubs, Homer H. "Did Confucius Study the 'Book of Changes'?" *T'ung Pao* 24 (1927): 82–90.

> An influential paper. For those interested in the subject it is required reading. In the *Analects,* Confucius is alleged to have said "If some years were added to my life, I would give fifty to the study of the *Book of Changes,* and then I might come to be free from great faults" (VII, xvi).

> Dubs states in the last paragraph:

> > We have thus found that study of the *Book of Changes* is plainly incompatible with the character of Confucius, and we have also found an adequate motive for the introduction of such a saying into the collection of genuine Confucian sayings. It seems highly improbable that he should ever have had anything to do with such a book (p. 90).

Edkins, Joseph. "The Yi King, With Notes On The 64 Kwa." *The China Review* 12 (1883-1884): 412–32.

> The author states:

> > The object of this inquiry was to learn whether there exist traces in this book of foreign origin, either in the text or in the names by which the sixty-four combinations of strokes are known, and also to find the general aim and

use of the book and the mode in which it originated.

The result of the inquiry is that the
structure of the work and the materials of which
it is made up all tend to show beyond doubt
that it is a diviner's guide book...not only a
diviner's manual with reserve and limitation,
but a diviner's manual with full intention and
adaptation...

...it is a book made up partly of earlier documents and partly of additions by Wen
Wang, and Cheu Kung" (pp. 424–25).

_____. "The Yi King of the Chinese, as a Book of Divination and Philosophy."
Journal of the Royal Asiatic Society 16 (1884): 360–80.

Takes the traditional view concerning the origin of the
I Ching, that "Wen wang, Chei kung, and Confucius, were all
editors, and Fu hi the original author" (p. 360).

In order to show that the *I Ching* is a "collection of
fragments added to, from time to time..." (p. 364), Edkins
analyzes Hexagrams 7, 15, 30, 31, 20, and 13.

_____. "The Yi King and its Appendices." *The China Review* 14 (1885–1886):
pp. 305–22.

The author states: "The result to which the preceding
investigations brings us is that the text of the Yi King belongs
to the Shang dynasty and the appendices to the Chow. The
chief part of the appendices was the work of court diviners and
others down to about the eighth century" (p. 322).

Passages in the *I Ching* which refer to a period of seven
days are cited and some space is devoted to seven day periods
in Chinese antiquity (pp. 303–307).

Eitel, E. J. "Chinese Philosophy before Confucius." *The China Review* 7 (1878–
1879): 388–92.

The author points out the postulates and axioms of
Chinese philosophy that make it difficult for those "tutored in
the logic of Aristotle" (p. 388) to judge it to be of any worth.
But the author points out:

It is indeed remarkable, that the most
recent discoveries of Western philosophy...
should have been the very postulates and axioms of Chinese philosophy thousands of years
ago (pp. 388–89).

"Philosophy in China before Confucius," the author states, "consisted of the *I Ching* literature, the 'Great Plan' (The Confucian Classics) and the *Tao Te Ching.*"

The article ends with a "(To be continued.)" but I have been unable to find its continuation.

Fang, Tung-mei. "The Creative Spirit of Confucius as Seen in the *Book of Changes:* A Criticism of the Accusations of Confucius by the Communist Party and Feng Yu-lan." *Chinese Studies in Philosophy* 7 (Spring 1976): 78–89.

Fang states that the "*Book of Changes,* a product of history that was transformed into a classic of philosophy...represents a kind of Confucian spirit..." (p. 79). Fang assumes that Confucius wrote the Ten Wings and defends Confucius against the Communist Party accusations that he was an antiquarian and a reactionary.

Feng, H. Y. and J. K. Shryock. "The Black Magic in China Known as *Ku.*" *Journal of the American Oriental Society* 55 (1935): 1–30.

The written word *ku* in Chinese is "formed by the radical meaning 'insects' or 'worms' placed above the radical meaning 'vessel' or 'dish' " (p. 2). The authors present the various meanings and practices referred to by the word *ku*. For example:

In the *Book of Changes,* a woman deluding a man, and wind throwing down [the trees of] a mountain, are *ku.* All these have the same signification (Feng, p. 2).

Also the authors state concerning Hexagram 18, which is named *Ku:*

The oracle bones show that the word *ku*, written as insects in a vessel, was in existence during the Shang period. The authors of this monograph advance the theory that if we had the Shang explanations of the hexagrams, the two trigrams which in the Chou period were held to represent mountains and wind, would be found to represent vessel and insects.

In using the eight symbols to represent many things, each symbol must do more than single duty. The written Chinese words for mountains and vessel are very similar. The theory advanced is that the trigram which in

the Chou period symbolized mountains, in the
Shang period symbolized vessel. This is merely
an hypothesis.

But in the case of the other trigram the authors give
very good evidence for the association of insects with wind (pp.
4–5).

Frawley, David. "The Cosmic Language of the *I Ching*." *Chinese Culture* 20:4
(December 1979): 45–51.

Frawley argues that:

The whole of Chinese culture arose essentially
through the images of contemplation of the *I
Ching,* the *Book of Changes.* The *I Ching* sets
forth the cosmic roots of Chinese language and
cosmic laws at the heart of Chinese culture.
The *I Ching* is a universal cultural basis out of
which many different cultures could arise. (p.
47).

Freeman, Michael. "From Adept to Worthy: The Philosophical Career of Shao
Young." *American Oriental Society Journal* 102 (1982): 477–91.

An interesting account of the life of Shao Yung (spelled
"Shao Young" in the title, but not in the text). However, very
little is said concerning the details of his theories of numerology,
although the general remarks concerning his cosmology are of
interest.

Fujino, Junko. "The *I Ching* and the Philosophy of Fortune." *The East* 8:8
(September, 1972): 19–28.

The author states that fortune tellers do a thriving business in large cities in Japan and that in Tokyo there are reported
to be some 5,000 professional diviners (p. 21).

The article gives a brief history of the *I Ching* and tells
how to divine by the yarrow-stalk method, which is *not* the
yarrow-stalk method given by Blofeld or Wilhelm/Baynes. Fujino describes a method in which after the forty-nine stalks have
been divided the diviner takes *eight* stalks at a time from the
left pile until eight or fewer stalks are left. Then the diviner con-
sults a table to see whether the number of stalks left signifies a
yin or yang line. This procedure is repeated until the six lines
of a hexagram have been formed. This method does not yield
moving or static lines as does the method described by Blofeld

and Wilhelm/Baynes. Also given is a six coin method. In this
method six coins are shaken in the hands then laid down on a
table one at a time. If heads the line is yang, if tails it is yin.
This method does not yield moving or static lines either.

Also given is the fortune associated with each of the
sixty-four hexagrams. The text associated with the lines is not
given.

Gardner, Martin. "Mathematical Games: The Combinatorial Basis of the 'I
Ching,' the Chinese Book of Divination and Wisdom." *Scientific American*
230:1 (January 1974): 109–13.

A concise introduction into the combinatory aspects of
the *I Ching*. Gardner states the problem of the textual sequences
very nicely: "Is there any kind of mathematical order that determines the sequence in which the hexagram pairs follow one
another? This is an unsolved problem" (p. 109).

Hacker, Edward A. "Brief Note on a Coin-Method Equivalent to the Yarrow
Stalk Method for Determining the Lines of a Hexagram in the *I Ching*."
Philosophy: East and West 30:4 (October 1980): pp. 535–36.

The author shows how by throwing one coin and then
three coins to establish each line of a hexagram, one can obtain
the same probabilities of getting a moving or static yin or yang
line as one can by the yarrow-stalk method.

_____. "Confusion Concerning the Linear Representation of the Four Images."
Journal of Chinese Philosophy 9: (1982a): pp. 349–52.

The author, quoting Wilhelm/Baynes, Legge, Blofeld,
and others, shows that there is no unanimity as to what symbol
is called the young yang or the young yin. Barring the possibility
of many typographical errors there is confusion on this issue.

_____. "A Note on Formal Properties of the Heaven Sequence." *Journal of
Chinese Philosophy* 10: (1983): pp. 169–72.

The author shows a way in which the Later Heaven Sequence (King Wen's arrangement of the trigrams) can be derived
from the *Lo shu* square (the Chinese magic square of three).
Other formal properties of the Later Heaven Sequence are given.

_____. "Order in the Textual Sequence of the Hexagrams of the *I Ching*."
Journal of Chinese Philosophy 14:1 (March 1987): pp. 59–64.

Based on a paper by Olsvanger. Author states, "The
purpose of this paper is to show that the textual sequence has

certain formal properties which make it unlikely that the sequence is a random one" (p. 59).

————. "Temperature and the Assignment of the Hexagrams of the *I-Ching* to the Calendar." *Journal of Chinese Philosophy* 9: (1982b): pp. 396–400.

In Fung Yu-lan's *A History of Chinese Philosophy* there is a table which assigns the 64 hexagrams to the days, months, and seasons of the year. The author seeks to prove that there is a positive correlation between the number of yang lines in a given season and temperature, that is to say, the warmer the month (or season) the greater the number of yang lines.

Jao, Tsung-I. "On the Divinatory Diagram (*I-kua*) in the Shang Dynasty." *Transactions of the International Congress of Orientalists In Japan* 25 (1980): 145-46.

The author's hypothesis is that the numbers on oracle bones from the Shang dynasty are "signs of hexagrams and based on this... hexagram names were commonly practiced in the late Shang Dynasty" (p. 146).

Journal of Chinese Philosophy 14:1 (March 1987).

This issue contains five articles on the *I Ching*. See: Chung-Ying Cheng, "*Li* and *Ch'i* in the *I Ching:* Reconsideration of Being and Non-Being in Chinese Philosophy"; Chung-Ying Cheng and Elton Johnson, "A Bibliography of the *I Ching* in Western Languages"; A. G. Clarke, "Probability Theory Applied to the *I Ching*;" Edward A. Hacker, "Order in the Textual Sequence of the Hexagrams of the *I Ching*"; and David Loy, "On the Meaning of the *I Ching*."

Journal of Chinese Philosophy 17:3 (September 1990).

This issue contains five articles on the *I Ching*. See: Allan W. Anderson, "On the Concept of Freedom in the *I Ching:* A Deconstructionist View of Self-Cultivation"; Shu-Hsien Liu, "On the Functional Unity of the Four Dimensions of Thought in the *Book of Changes*"; Larry J. Schulz, "Structural Motifs in the Arrangement of the 64 *Gua* in the *Zhouyi*"; Larry J. Schulz and Thomas J. Cunningham, "The Seasonal Structure Underlying the Arrangement of the Hexagrams in the *Yijing*"; Li Kuen Tong, "The Appropriation of Significance: The Concept of *Kang-Tung* in the *I Ching*."

Keightley, David. "The Religious Commitment: Shang Theology and the Genesis of Chinese Political Culture." *History of Religions:* 17 (1978): 211–25.

> Keightley tries to show that Chinese political culture had its roots in religious impulses: specifically Shang theology. And that contrary to general opinion "We misunderstand the new, more differentiated values, attitudes, and institutions of Chou and Han if we view them in purely secular terms" (p. 224).

Kiang, Kang-Hu. "The Yi Ching or 'Book of Changes.' " *The China Journal of Science and Arts* 3 (1925): 259–64.

> The author subscribes to the traditional view of the origin of the *I Ching,* and gives a brief introduction to the trigrams. No new ground is broken.

Kingsmill, Thomas. "The Construction of the Yih King." *The China Review* 21 (1894–1895): 272–75.

> Thesis is that the *I Ching* is a jumble of an archive ballad and an ancient commentary (p. 272). Five hexagrams are mentioned in support of this thesis: Hexagrams 3, 6, 7, 28, and 37. For example, the text of the lines of Hexagram 3 "describes a bridal chase" (p. 274).

Lach, Donald F. "Leibniz and China." *Journal of the History of Ideas* 14 (1945): 436–55.

> This paper describes and explains Leibniz's interest in the Chinese language, the *I Ching,* Confucius, and so forth.

Lai, Whalen. "The *I-Ching* and the Formation of the Hua-Yen Philosophy." *Journal of Chinese Philosophy* 7:1 (March 1980): 245–58.

> The author contends that "Fa-tsang [643–712 A.D.], the key patriarch of the Hua-yen school [a school of Chinese Buddhism], apparently drew on a mode of thought that is derived from the *I Ching,* the Book of Changes" (p. 246).

Lee, Jung Young. "Some Reflections on the Authorship of the I Ching." *Numen* 17 (December 1970): 200–10.

> The author attempts to "reconstruct somehow the authorship of the *I Ching* according to Chinese tradition" (p. 209).

_____. "The Yin-Yang Way of Thinking: A Possible Method for Ecumenical Theology." *International Review of Missions* 60 (July 1971): 363–70.

 The author's purpose is two-fold: "the limitation of the function of the either/or way of thinking in theology, and the search for the most inclusive category of thinking to complement it" (p. 365). This more inclusive category turns out to be *yin-yang* thinking: defined as both/and thinking. It includes either/or thinking.

_____. "Death is Birth and Birth is Death: The Parascientific Understanding of Death and Birth." *Journal of the Institute of Systematics* 9:4 (1972): 188–200.

 The author conclusion is that "from the parascientific point of view death is birth outwardly directed and birth is death inwardly directed. Death and birth are one and inseparable" (p. 199).
 The author claims that "What makes death really different from birth is none other than the movement of direction" (p. 193). This is illustrated by the changing number of yang and yin lines in a series of hexagrams.

_____. "Can God be Change Itself?" *Journal of Ecumenical Studies* 10:4 (1973): 752–70.

 It is claimed that "the *I Ching* is helpful in understanding the 'ultimate category of becoming'" (p. 752). The author concludes "that the concept of God as 'Change-itself' is...more in keeping with the Judeo-Christian tradition than the more dominant view derived from Greek philosophy" (p. 752).

_____. "The *I Ching* and Its Basic Philosophy of Inner Process." *Chinese Culture Research Institute* 16:2 (June 1975): 63–70.

 Author states that "While yin and yang are *ontic* units of inner process, the trigrams are the *functional* units of it. Because of this functional unit of three in all things, everything has a tendency toward procreation" (p. 70). He concludes, "Thus the *I* or Change is the essence of inner process, which patterns itself in the 64 germinal situations to disclose the secret of cosmic phenomena" (p. 70).

_____. "The *I Ching* as a Framework for Self-Therapy and a Practical Instrument for the Self-Healing Process." *Asian & Pacific Quarterly of Cultural and Social Affairs* 10:2 (1978): 13–21.

> The author claims that the *I Ching* is a book of healing as well as a book of divination. Indeed, "divination is none other than therapy" (p. 18). The *I Ching,* it is stated, presents a "holistic view of man and cosmos. This holistic approach to reality is fundamental to any therapeutic process" (p. 13).
> The author presents the theory that:

> > Yin and yang are the primary categories of all existence, because they are responsible for the formation of patterns in process... (p. 67).
> > ... The trigram is the complete unit of inner process. In every process of inner change there must be a threeness" (pp. 69).

_____. "The Origin and Significance of the Chongyok or Book of Correct Change." *Journal of Chinese Philosophy* 9:2 (June 1982): 211–42.

> The author discusses "the essential background for the origin and significances of this book [The Book of Correct Change] in relation to the Book of Change" (p. 211).
> The author explains that The Correct Book of Change (also known as The Book of Complete Change) was written in the 19th Century by Kim I-bu, a Korean whose given name was Kim Hang. Kim I-bu looked upon the two circular arrangements of the trigrams (Fu Hsi's and King Wen's Arrangement) as the first two stages of the *I Ching.* He considered King Wen's Arrangement to be incomplete, an intermediate stage. Kim I-bu offers a third—completed—arrangement of the trigrams.

Leung, Koon-Loon. "An Algebraic Truth in Divination." *Journal of Chinese Philosophy* 9:2 (June 1982): 243-58.

> It is pointed out that the ancient method of divination with yarrow stalks differs from the yarrow-stalk method described in most books (e.g., Wilhelm/Baynes, pp. 721–23). The two methods are equivalent, but in the ancient method the number of the line being determined (6, 7, 8, or 9) was reached by dividing by four the number of stalks in the remaining pile. In the modern method it is the number of stalks left in one's hand that determines the line. For example, $9 + 8 + 8 = 25$ stalks left in one's hand means a moving yin line. In the ancient

method this means $49 - 25 = 24$ stalks left in the pile, so $\frac{24}{4} = 6$ and 6 means a moving yin line.

By assigning 2 to the numbers 9 and 8, and 3 to the numbers 5 and 4, the number of stalks in one's hand can easily be converted to 6, 7, 8, or 9 (see Wilhelm/Baynes p. 722). For example, if one ends up with $9 + 8 + 8 = 25$ stalks in one hand then this is $2 + 2 + 2 = 6$, a moving yin line.

The paper shows that three other assignments of numbers to the numbers 9, 8, 5, and 4 work. Several hypotheses are offered as to why the numbers 2 and 3 were chosen.

Liang, Tao-wei. "A Comparative Study of the *I Ching* and Buddhism." *Transactions Of The International Congress Of Orientalists In Japan* 115 (1970): 111–14.

Points out that in the *I Ching* and Buddhism are found: 1, the belief that metaphysical study is based on mental laws; 2, indirect and direct teaching methods; 3, a common set of virtues; 4, a similar goal; and so forth.

Loewe, Michael A. N. "Manuscripts Found Recently in China: A Preliminary Survey." *T'oung Pao* 43:2–3 (1977): 99–186.

Gives a page and a quarter description of the *I Ching* silk manuscript found at the Mawangdui site in Changsha in 1973. The grave was made in 168 B.C. This is, by several centuries, the oldest known version of the *I Ching*.

The author writes that the finds include:

The *I-ching* together with three lost works that are appended. The text extends to 5200 characters, including the *Hsi-tz'u;* and while it is basically identical with that of the extant version, the order of the 64 hexagrams is completely different, retaining an original form of a more simple type. There is no separation into two sections...

The importance of this document lies in its relationship to the extant version of the *I-ching;* for whereas that version is derived from the *ku-wen* tradition, the copy on the silk manuscript derives from other traditions (p. 117).

Liu, Shu-Hsien. "On the Functional Unity of the Four Dimensions of Thought in the *Book of Changes*." *Journal of Chinese Philosophy* 17:3 (September 1990): 359–85.

> The author identifies and elaborates on four levels of meaning in the *I Ching*. These four levels are: 1, a system of mystical symbolism; 2, a system of rational-natural symbolism; 3, a system of cosmological symbolism; and 4, a system of ethical/metaphysical symbolism (p. 360).

Loy, David. "On the Meaning of the *I Ching*." *Journal of Chinese Philosophy* 14:1 (March 1987): 39–57.

> The author asks and attempts to answer two questions: First, what does *yin/yang* polarity *mean?* Second, can an understanding of that meaning give us insight into the sequence of hexagrams and/or trigrams? (p. 39).

MacGillivary, D. "A New Interpretation of the Book of Changes." *The Chinese Recorder* 49 (1918): 310–16.

> The author critically evaluates Wang Hsiang-Hsuang's book *The Uniting Bond of the I*. This book, MacGillivary says, is an attempt to demonstrate that the *I Ching* shows the "order of creation and events of history, and also to reconcile in one the great religions of the world" (p. 311). MacGillivary finds nothing of value in the book.

McClatchie, Thomas. "The Symbols of the Yih-King." *China Review* 1 (1872–1873): 151–63.

> The author claims that the three most ancient forms of Idolatry are: Sabianism (the worship of the heavenly host), Demonolatry (which includes the worship of the souls of deceased ancestors), and Materialism. The author contends that the *I Ching*:
>
> > ... not only gives us with great clearness the Material system set up at Babel, and which is found with more or less minuteness in all Heathen Philosophical writing throughout the world, but in it we find the most ancient form of Triplication, namely, that of **both** the Great Father and the Great Mother, thus making a family of Eight principal deities; the *Dii majorum gentium* of the Greeks and Romans (152).

McEvilly, Wayne. "Synchronicity and the I Ching." *Philosophy East and West* 18:3 (July 1968): 137–49.

> The author states that "Causality is a horizontal, temporal, empirical connective whereas synchronicity is a vertical, atemporal, ontological connective" (p. 139). Leibniz is claimed to have advocated an absolute synchronistic theory. Also mentioned are Schopenhauer and Kant. Synchronicity is claimed to presuppose that "reality is a psycho-physical structure" (p. 142). It seems that the author is claiming that the principle of causality is the principle of explanation for non-idealist philosophies and that synchronicity is the principle of explanation for idealist philosophies.

McKenna, Dennis J. and Victor H. Mair. "A Rendering of the Hexagrams of the I Ching." *Philosophy: East and West* 29 (October 1979): 421–41.

> Joseph Needham and Hellmut Wilhelm read this paper in manuscript and made a number of suggestions (p. 421 n.). The authors present a new order of the hexagrams based on the Gray Code. They argue that this order "follows a logical system of development, both in geometrical appearance and in the interpretations attached to the hexagrams" (p. 421).

Olsvanger, Immanuel. *Fu-Hsi: The Sage of Ancient China.* Jerusalem: Massadah Ltd. Printed by the Gesher Printing Press, 1948. Length 16 pages.

> An important paper for those interested in the textual sequence (King Wen's Arrangement) of the hexagrams. Olsvanger gives a number of mathematical properties of the textual sequence that results when the textual sequence is written in the form of a square such that the numbers in each cell of the square are decimal equivalents of the hexagrams regarded as binary numbers.

Riegel, Jeffrey K. "A Summary of Some Recent *Wenwu* and *Kaogu* Articles: Mawangdui Tombs Two and Three." *Early China* 1 (1975): 10–15.

> Fifteen references are given to articles on the Mawangdui tombs that were published in the second half of 1974 and the early part of 1975 in issues of *Wenwu* and *Kaogu*. Most of the article is a description of the objects found in Tomb Three.

_____. "A Textual Note on the *I Ching*." *Journal of the American Oriental Society* 103 (1983): 601–606.

The author states "This brief note offers at its conclusion a solution to a passage in the *K'un* (i.e., Hexagram 2) section of the *I Ching* which has long defied correct interpretation" (p. 601). The author concludes:

> I submit that the occurrence of what has been taken to be *pu huang* in each of the three stanzas of Mao 232 of the *Shih Ching* should in fact be read as *feng huang* "phoenix." The three lines containing the words have been misconstrued since the Han dynasty and should be rendered:
>
> . . .
>
> The Phoenix has attended the dawn levee!
>
> . . .
>
> The Phoenix has emerged!
>
> . . .
>
> The Phoenix is contented!

> To return to our *I Ching* passage. I would translate the opening of the :line statements, "Treading on frost. The Hard Ice will descend. Directed toward the (proper) quarter. The Great Wind will gust" (p. 606).

Schulz, Larry J. "Structural Motifs in the Arrangement of the 64 Hexagrams in the *Zhouyi*." *Journal of Chinese Philosophy* 17:3 (September 1990): 345–58.

> The author states, "The purpose of this paper is to discuss several consistent subpatterns in the overall *gua* [hexagram] sequence that imply the act of putting the 64 *gua* in their received order involved a range of calculated decisions" (p. 346).

Schulz, Larry J. and Thomas J. Cunningham. "The Seasonal Structure Underlying the Arrangement of Hexagrams in the *Yijing*." *Journal of Chinese Philosophy* 17:3 (September 1990): 289–313.

> The *Guaqi* system is the arrangement of the hexagrams assigned to the seasons by Meng Xi (ca. 138 B.C.). The author concludes:

>> Whatever principles of selection were employed, the *gua* [hexagrams] in the *Guaqi* arrangement appear to have been placed with reference to the cumulative sum, whether positive, *yang*, or negative, *yin*, of their component lines. Overall, the series reflects a statis-

tical summary based on some measurement of natural phenomena. The *Yijing* with its elegant but restrictive pairing requirement seems to adhere to a like structural strategy, and our tests suggest that a seasonal information set of close similarity may have formed the basis of the strategy in both cases (p. 299).

Sivin, Nathan. "Review of *The Book of Change* translated by John Blofeld." London: Allen and Unwin, 1965. Pg. 228. *Harvard Journal of Asiatic Studies* 26 (1966): 290–98.

Sivin says "Almost every sentence makes clear and engaging sense... Mr. Blofeld was realistic in his intentions and honest in his execution ..." (pp. 290–91). However Sivin adds:

...the text [of the *I Ching*] is archaic and corrupt enough to carry almost any message a moralist cares to read into it... Mr. Blofeld is, so far as one can tell from his writing, ignorant of these studies and even of the textual problems which make them so vital. He is, therefore, able to cherish the illusion that the text makes sense and the translator's greatest problem is the "terseness of the Chinese original" (p. 291).

The author concludes by saying that Blofeld's translation should "prove highly satisfactory for use in divination" (p. 295). Finally, to illustrate his point that the original text can be interpreted in a number of ways, Sivin gives his own interpretation of Hexagram 36, which he calls The Ming-I Bird. While Wilhelm/Baynes calls Hexagram 36, "Darkening of the Light," Blofeld calls it "Darkening of the Light. Injury."

Swetz, Frank. "The Evolution of Mathematics in Ancient China." *Mathematics Magazine* 52 (January 1979): 10–19.

The author shows how the *Lo shu* magic square can be used to construct magic squares of higher orders. Also presented are the Shang numerals from 1 to 9 and the mathematical notation of the Han dynasty.

The author concludes:

if comparisons must be made among the societies of the pre-Christian world, the quality of China's mathematical accomplishments stands in contention with those of Greece and Baby-

> lonia, and during the period designated in the
> West as pre-Renaissance, the sequence and scope
> of mathematical concepts and techniques orig-
> inating in China far exceeds that of any other
> contemporary society (pp. 17–18).

T'ang, Yung-T'ung. "Wang Pi's New Interpretation of the *I Ching* and *Lun-Yu*."
  Translation notes and foreword by Walter Liebenthal. *Harvard Journal of
  Asiatic Studies* 10 (1947): 124–61.

> Wang Pi (A.D. 226–249) was a Neo-Taoist. Liebenthal states:

> > The underlying conception which gave birth to
> > Wang's cosmology is that of the latent power
> > (*t'i*) which becomes manifest in application (*yung*).
> > The world is unfolding from the No-thing into
> > an extremely variegated Universe. We are in-
> > vited to participate in this Grand Manifestation
> > (p. 124).

Tong, Paul K. K. "The Concept of Time in Whitehead and the I Ching." *Journal
  of Chinese Philosophy* 3:1 (Dec. 1974): 373–93.

> The first of a projected series of papers on the relation
> between Whitehead's philosophy and Chinese philosophy. Cen-
> tral theme is that the meaning of time is the same in the philos-
> ophy of the *I Ching* as in Whitehead. Twenty points of "affinity
> between the Whiteheadean and the *I Ching* meta-physical sys-
> tems" are listed (pp. 386–88).

————. "A Cross-Cultural Study of the I-Ching." *Journal of Chinese Philosophy*
  3:1 (Dec. 1975): 73–84.

> Theme is that the *I Ching* does not advocate a dualistic
> outlook, such as: man vs. nature, conscious vs. subconscious,
> etc. Instead the outlook of the *I Ching* is in terms of "five
> continuum-events: (1) the cosmic continuum; (2) the continuum
> of good and evil; (3) the continuum of a psychological event and
> its cosmic horizon; (4) the continuum of cosmic and moral forces;
> and (5) the continuum of the conscious and the subconscious"
> (p. 75).

_____. "Whitehead and Chinese Philosophy: From the Vantage Point of the *I Ching.*" *Journal of Chinese Philosophy* 6:3 (September 1979): 297–321.

> The second of a projected series of papers on the relation between Whitehead's philosophy and Chinese philosophy. Author believes that there is more to the relationship between Whitehead and Chinese philosophy than theoretical similarities. There is, he believes, a "real historical dimension to this relation—and... a highly significant one" (p. 297).

Tong, Lik Kuen. "The Appropriation of Significance: The Concept of *Kang-T'ung* in the *I Ching.*" *Journal of Chinese Philosophy* 17:3 (September 1990): 315–44.

> The author claims that thinking, any kind of thinking, is basically a form of posturing, and that "Truth is what discloses itself in the rightness of posturing" (315).

> > What I propose to do in this paper is to reflect on the more general concept of *appropriation,* that is, the appropriation of significance, which is the postural basis of both truth and goodness. If truth is what shows itself in the rightness of posturing, then goodness is what realizes itself therein. The relation between truth and goodness is, in other words the relation between disclosure and realization conceived as two primary forms of appropriation. What is appropriated in goodness is the values of things, while what is appropriated in truth is their meanings, values and meanings being the two basic forms of appropriated significance. And this is where the concept of *kang-t'ung* enters. For *kang-t'ung* is the affective attunement and penetration of significance which constitutes the *experiential-spiritual* essence of appropriation. The rightness of posturing consists, indeed, in the rightness of *kang-t'ung* (315).

Tung, Gea. "A Conceptual Model for the Understanding of Opposites: Some Reflections on 'The I Ching.' " *Asian Thought and Society* 4:10 (April 1979): 83–86.

> Theme is that the "*I Ching* offers a simple model for the understanding of how opposites are interrelated" (p. 85).

Van der Bjif, F. "Combinational Aspects of the Hexagrams in the Chinese Book of Changes." *Scripta Mathematica* XXVIII:1 (1966): 37–49.

> In the author's words "One of the most interesting problems is to account for the various arrays of the 64 hexagrams" (p. 38). The author explains that the Fu Shi order can be interpreted as a binary order. The King Wen order, he admits, is still unsolved. The author gives a description of the order of the members of a Hexagram House, but does not relate this order to anything else. Some interesting relations are shown between the Yellow River diagram, the Lo River diagram, and Fu Hsi's Arrangement of the trigrams. Also given are the probabilities of obtaining a moving or static, yin or yang line, by the yarrow-stalk method.

Waley, Arthur. "The Book of Changes." *Bulletin of the Museum of Far Eastern Antiquities* 5 (1933): 121–42.

> The thesis is "that the *Book of Changes* is an arbitrary amalgam of two quite separate works: 1) An omen or 'peasant interpretation' text... 2) a divination text probably of later date and certainly of far more sophisticated nature" (p. 121). Waley distinguished three kinds of divining techniques: "1) Divination by plant-stalks..., 2) Divination by marks on the heated carapace of the tortoise..., 3) Divining-tablets, representing objects of omen" (p. 140).
>
> Waley makes sense out of many of the cryptic sayings assigned to the hexagrams by interpreting them as omens or magic rites.

————. Review of *Change: Eight Lecturers on the I Ching* by Hellmut Wilhelm. *The Listener* (March 1961): 579–80.

> This short review contains one paragraph worth noting. Waley points out that on page 103 (of *Change: Eight Lecturers on the I Ching*) Hellmut Wilhelm quotes the following from the Wilhelm/Baynes translation of line 4 of Hexagram 40, *Deliverance:*

> > Deliver yourself from your great toe.
> > Then the companion comes,
> > And him you can trust.

Hellmut Wilhelm then explains this passage by saying:

> > The work of deliverance must also be carried through on oneself; one must free one-

self from the ties dictated by custom, even if it means a radical severing, for otherwise one will not find the companions whose trust is needed in these times.

Concerning this interpretation, Waley says:

This interpretation, though traditional, seems to me quite crazy. As there is immediately afterwards a reference to shooting arrows and as 'thumb' not 'big-toe' is the explanation given to the word in question by the earliest commentary on the passage, we might venture to translate: 'Relax your thumb (on the bow-string). A friend (not an enemy) is coming.' This gives a good metaphorical instruction to relax unnecessary precautions (p. 580).

For more information on this passage see [A] Blofeld, p. 166 n. 5.

_____. "Leibniz and Fu-Shi." *Bulletin of the School of Oriental and African Studies* 1 (1921): 165–67.

Waley gives an account of Leibniz's discovery that the Fu Hsi arrangement of the trigrams and hexagrams can be interpreted as the natural number sequences written in binary notation. It is pointed out that although "this fact about the diagrams was known in the seventeenth century, no subsequent commentator, either Chinese or European, appears to have mentioned it" (p. 166).

Wen-Shan, Huang. "T'ai Chi Ch'uan and *I Ching,* or Book of Changes." *Chinese Culture* 10 (March 1969): 1–20.

The author contends that T'ai Chi Ch'uan derives its main principles from the *I Ching* (p. 15).

Wilhelm, Hellmut. "*I-Ching* Oracles in the *Tso-Chuan* and the *Kuo-Yu.*" *Journal of The American Oriental Society* 79 (1959): 275–80.

Author states:

In summary it can be said that all the cases where the wording of the *Tso-chuan* differs from our present version [of certain passages in the *I Ching*] are explained most readily if the *Tso-chuan* version is accepted as the earlier one... (p. 276).

> It thus appears that the material from which at least two, possibly three, of the ten wings were composed was already in use in Ch'un-ch'iu times [Spring and Autumn times: 722 to about 450 B.C.] and that in part the terminology even of the Ch'un-ch'iu period exactly coincides with our present version (p. 277).

————. "On the Oracle Recorded in Tso-chuan, Hsi 4 (656 B.C.)." *Journal of the American Oriental Society* 91 (1971): 504–05.

> This note points out that there are four places in the *Tso-chuan* in which the tortoise-shell method of divination is preferred to the yarrow-stalk method. A passage that "resembles in structure, diction, and imagery the texts contained in the older layers of the *Book of Changes...*" (p. 504) is discussed.

————. "Leibniz and the I-Ching." *Collectanea Commissionis Synodalis* 16:3/4 (March/April): 205–19.

> Paper presents a copy of the Former Heaven (Fu Hsi's) Arrangement of the hexagrams (both circular and square) that was sent to Leibniz by Bouvet. Wilhelm points out that the Former Heaven arrangement "is not of very high antiquity" (p. 210). It was invented, Wilhelm says, by Shao Yung (1011–1077) (p. 207). Leibniz's letter to Bouvet, giving his reactions to these diagrams is quoted at some length.

————. "The Interplay of Image and Concept." *Eranos Jahrbuch* 36 (1967): 31–57.

> In relation to the *I Ching* the yin yang polarity is discussed. Regarding the interplay between image and concept, Wilhelm concludes:

> > It can at least be said that this interplay works out differently in any given situation. No formula can be built to cover their functional relationship. It cannot even be said that the concept acts normatively and the image emotively. The intricate tensions within the human mind created by this polarity reflect, as they are reflected by, what the Great treatise calls 'the confused diversities under Heaven' (p. 56).

_____. "The Sacrifice, Idea and Attitude: Thoughts from the Book of Changes." *Harvest* 4 (1957): 14–29.

> Explores the role of sacrifice in the early Chou Dynasty. According to Wilhelm:

> > it is interesting to note that the conscious attitude of the performer of a sacrifice does not seem to have been a prerequisite for its effectiveness. A consciously realized readiness to sacrifice, a conscious submissiveness to the forces sacrificed to—piety, in other words—was a prerequisite attitude of later times only; it is never mentioned in the earlier texts (p. 18).

> > Timeliness, not piety, determines the validity of the sacrifice (p. 18).

> Wilhelm also states:

> > To the authors of the Book of changes, the meaning of sacrifice was... not to bring about human happiness or to ward off misfortune. To them, the purpose was to keep open the communication with the divine and with the spirits which inhabit the unconscious world (p. 21).

Wilhelm explains how a knowledge of God's manifestations—as evidenced by the cycle of the trigrams—gives an indication of the proper times to sacrifice. He concludes by explaining the different kinds of sacrifices alluded to by hexagrams 51, 20, 45, 42, 41, 47, 46, and 54, in this order.

Wong, S. Y. "The Book of Change: A New Interpretation." *Eastern Horizon* 2:3 (1962): 11–18.

> States that *Yi Ching* should be translated as *The Book of Change,* not *Book of Changes.* Purpose of paper is to "disperse the mystic fog that has shrouded *The Book of Change* for ages..." (p. 11). Author accepts traditional account of the *I Ching*'s origin, and gives as Fu Hsi's philosophy:

> > that change is the only reality, that motion is the underlying cause of change, and that permutation and combination is the over-riding rule of physical changes in a universe of unity... (p. 16).

Q

INDEX

Footnotes are not included in this index.